*f*P

LEBANON

GOLAN HEIGHTS

SYRIA

Safed

Sea of Galilee

Tiberias

Mash'had

Nazareth

Mediterranean Sea

Shaar Menashe

Nablus

West Bank

JORDAN

Tel Aviv

Bat Yam

Amman

Jerusalem

ISRAEL

Beit Jala
Bethlehem
Alon Shvut

Ashkelon

Hebron

Jabalya

Gaza City

Sderot

Kiryat Arba

Dead Sea

Nusseirat

Netivot

Gaza Strip

Rafah

EGYPT

20 miles
20 km

MAP DESIGNED BY JOE LERTOLA

Cain's

FAITH, FRATRICIDE, AND FEAR

FREE PRESS

Field

IN THE MIDDLE EAST

Matt Rees

NEW YORK · LONDON · TORONTO · SYDNEY

FREE PRESS
A Division of Simon & Schuster, Inc.
1230 Avenue of the Americas
New York, NY 10020

FREE PRESS and colophon are trademarks
of Simon & Schuster, Inc.

For information about special discounts for bulk purchases,
please contact Simon & Schuster Special Sales: 1-800-456-6798
or business@simonandschuster.com

DESIGNED BY PAUL DIPPOLITO

Manufactured in the United States of America

10   9   8   7   6   5   4   3   2   1

Library of Congress Cataloging-in-Publication Data
    Rees, Matt.
      Cain's Field: faith, fratricide, and fear in the Middle East /
    Matt Rees.
          p.   cm.
        1. Arab-Israeli conflict. 2. Arab-Israeli conflict—Religious
    aspects—Judaism. 3. Arab-Israeli conflict—Religious aspects—
    Islam. 4. Palestinian Arabs—Social conditions—20th century.
    5. Israel—Social conditions—20th century.
      I. Title.
      DS119.7 .R3655 2004
      2004056292

ISBN 0-7432-5047-8

To my Father and Mother,
David and Georgina

Contents

Cain's Field

Introduction: "Camels, Sand and Shit"

Your brother, your brother! He who has no brother is like one going to battle without a weapon.

—CHARTER OF THE ISLAMIC RESISTANCE MOVEMENT (HAMAS)

IN THE CLUTTERED DRAWER of a dark teak sideboard in her living room in a Welsh mining town, my grandmother kept a postcard her mother received in 1916. My great-great-uncle Dan sent it from the Imperial Camel Corps base camp at Abbasia, Egypt. The card bore a sepia photograph of a haughty camel tethered before a distant pyramid. On the yellowing reverse side, in a Victorian hand displaying surprisingly schoolmasterly penmanship for a man who dug coal during peacetime, was the message "Dear Sis, There's nothing here but camels, sand and shit. Your brother, Dan." When my grandmother showed me the card, I imagined her mother, a forbiddingly formal woman who called her own husband by his surname, waiting for news of her brother away at the war and receiving only this terse, black humor. My grandmother giggled at the naughtiness of the language. With a vocabulary more blithely scatological than hers, I was struck more powerfully by the contrast between the popular image of the Orient on the card's front and Dan's grimly authentic missive on the back.

I came to the Middle East eighty years after Dan and his brother Dai, who battled to Jerusalem as part of the World War I campaign that made a name for another Welsh-born soldier, Colonel T. E. Lawrence of Arabia. Fortunately, I came not as a combatant but as a journalist, aiming to understand why others continued to fight here

1

in a conflict that has halted for barely a single day since the Camel Corps crossed the Sinai. I soon saw that the dour bareness of Dan's note was not a great deal more simplistic than the framework through which many contemporary journalists and diplomats viewed the long struggle between Israelis and Palestinians. From Lawrence of Arabia to Bill Clinton, Westerners applied their apparently logical perceptions of the conflict to a potential resolution, colored by romantic notions of the noble desert Bedouin or an evangelical inspiration to succor the biblical Hebrews in their homeland. When I arrived in 1996, it soon became clear to me that these solutions failed because they missed something that, though intrinsic to the Middle East, never had become part of the picture-postcard myths of the mystical East or the biblical Holy Land. Westerners looked at it this way: there was a conflict between Palestinians and Israelis, and there was a need to keep both from violence. Seeking a solution, they came at it with preconceptions perhaps more susceptible to the arguments of one side or the other, but even the most impartial found that whatever they suggested met with the inevitable outrage of one of the parties.

I began to think of the understanding most outsiders bring to the Israeli-Palestinian conflict as neatly framed, yet incomplete, like Dan's postcard. I tried to look beyond the edge of the photograph, where diplomats and foreign correspondents and think-tank experts tended not to delve. I focused less on the contacts between Israelis and Palestinians and more on the relations within the two societies themselves. Those cracks in the structures of Palestinian and Israeli society were the places I looked—places that others largely ignored, because the complexity to be found there confused their theories and policy assessments or the tidy leads of their daily news stories, puncturing their unassailable definitiveness. For beyond the dualistic conventions of the Israeli-Palestinian conflict, which were as clichéd in the minds of Westerners as the image of a camel posed before a pyramid, there I believed I would learn the hopes of the man who rode the camel and the resentment of the peasant paid to shovel its shit for him, and the grudges of the two traders fighting over ownership of the same lone and level sands. The deeper I got, the further I went outside the frame of the photo, the more I found that it was the internal divisions of the two societies that provided a true reading of the conflict and a hope for its eventual resolution.

In both Israeli and Palestinian society, it is common to hear people admit that there are tremendous divisions—between, for example, religious and secular Israelis, or between Islamists and the Palestinian Authority. But in each case the typical assumption is that those internal divisions cannot be confronted unless the national conflict is resolved first. Over my years in Jerusalem, I realized that this was, in fact, at least halfway wrong. Without beginning to look for solutions to these divisions within their societies, neither Israelis nor Palestinians could feel secure enough in themselves to take the risk of a true peace deal. Without those internal solutions, Palestinians were always at the mercy of undemocratic elements committed to violence or narrow, local interests. Without those internal solutions, Israeli governments continued to undercut peace deals by building more West Bank outposts at the behest of a minority, the settlers. These, of course, were only some of the divisions that marred the chances of either side truly uniting behind a peace effort.

These two Middle Eastern nations battle over a land that was the field Cain farmed in the Book of Genesis. Cain's offering of "the fruit of the ground" pleased God less than the "firstlings of his flock" offered by his brother Abel, a shepherd. Cain felt wronged by a judgmental God and answered with a new wrong. As most Westerners do, I grew up believing Cain had been evil, the first murderer, without ever reading anything but a children's version of the story. As I traveled the hills of Palestine, I studied the original tale in Genesis and was struck with a sense of outrage on behalf of Cain. It seemed to me that God had been unfair. Cain, as a farmer, could hardly have offered anything but the grain he harvested. It was not the first time this notion of divine injustice occurred to me while living in and writing about the Middle East. Each of the stories I tell here delivered a visceral shock to me, a physical reaction to inequity and suffering and intolerance. The violence that followed Cain's offering mirrored the region's present horrors, where brothers who feel themselves wronged still contend with each other.

I began with a simple Westernized understanding of the biblical story of Cain. As I looked at it more deeply, I was able to empathize with Cain's simple humanity, no longer obscured by the symbolism with which the centuries weighted him. In the same way, as my understanding of Palestinian and Israeli societies deepened, I transcended the received Western interpretation of the conflict. If I could empathize with Cain, so too I could look upon the people who were the subject of this book not as they might appear in most Western media—as terrorists, oppressors, bullies, fanatics—but instead I could listen to their human voices as they told their stories.

Though many thoughtful Israelis and Palestinians acknowledge the veracity of my thesis, it runs counter to the received wisdom of their cultures. It's easier to blame the other side for all your problems. The point is that this leaks into their perceptions of their own societies until they live with such a deep personal sense of victimization that many develop a concomitant feeling that anything they might do, no matter how heedless of their compatriots or how unreasonable, is justified because of the forces arrayed against them. The Hamas charter delineates a series of shadowy "powers that support the enemy," including the Masons, the Rotary Club, and the Lions Club. A prominent Israeli academic, Dan Schueftan, told me, "The first thought that enters an Israeli's head when he wakes in the morning is, Fuck you. It's there before he even has an idea to whom he wants to say 'Fuck you.' "

For Israeli Jews, there is a historical sensitivity to any suggestion that Jew might battle Jew. It's rooted in the destructive fundamentalist fratricide of the Hasmoneans in 167 B.C., and the other bloody civil fighting that drew the Romans eventually to demolish the Temple in Jerusalem in A.D. 70 and, sixty-five years later, to expel the Jews from Judea. Even though a Jew killed Prime Minister Yitzhak Rabin in 1995 over his peace agreement with Arafat, Israelis play down the impact of their internal divisions and point to their supposed ability to pull together when Palestinian violence threatens them. The elements of their identity behind which they come together at those moments, however, are only superficially unifying. In fact, they are emblematic of the very divisions Israelis believe they override. There's a common bumper sticker in Israel that reads A Combat Soldier, That's the Best, My Brother. The daring, self-sacrificing Israeli reservist, taking up arms one month each year, is the symbol of the nation's unity and mission. But many Israelis don't serve in the army, let alone in combat roles: they are ultra-Orthodox, and are vilified by those Israelis that do fight. Few of Israel's Arab citizens, one-fifth of the population, enlist in the army, because they aren't trusted to fight other Arabs, and are shut out of both the kudos and the civic rights attached to military service. In no other country I have ever visited is it so common to hear someone call his countryman "Nazi," an epithet I heard used most often by demonstrators, secular and ultra-Orthodox, at various confrontations with police and army. Israelis' self-image is of a nation of Spartans—single-minded, selfless warriors. In fact, they're closer to the fickle, self-defeating, captious Athenians.

The least admirable among Israel's political class continue to promulgate the notion that Israel faces an existential threat to which the only answer is the combat soldier's long weeks of reserve duty and an uncompromising line against the Palestinians. It's easy to unite people behind such jingoism and it's also simple to illustrate it. Take a helicopter ride up Israel's coastal plain and you'll feel you could reach out and scrape your knuckles on the Judean hills inside the West Bank at the same time as the fingers of your other hand dabble in the Mediterranean. That sense of threat ought to be diminished by Israel's nuclear weapons capability, but it isn't, because of politicians for whom a little paranoia is a valuable excuse to hold on to occupied land. Again, the unity that comes with such reasoning is deceptive and soon falls away when tested by the pressures within Israeli society.

Palestinians, too, indulge in myths and clichés designed to prevent them from looking too harshly inward. When a Hamas bomb maker named Muhi ed-Din Sharif died in 1998, Yasser Arafat's Palestinian Authority suggested his comrades in the Islamic fundamentalist group had rubbed him out as part of an internal feud. In Ramallah, where Sharif died, Palestinians repeatedly told me it was inconceivable that a Palestinian would have killed another Palestinian. It was a parallel to the mantra of incomprehension heard everywhere after Rabin's death at the hands of a Jewish assassin. Yet it was evident to me that Jews killed Jews and Palestinians slew Palestinians, and when they didn't murder, they often abused and affronted their own. To ignore the impact of that civic violence and violation, to ascribe all ills to the national conflict seemed to me analogous to a paraplegic complaining that he'd walk fine if only someone would give him a new pair of sneakers.

When I came to Israel, it looked to some as though the national conflict might be near its end, because of the Oslo peace deal signed between Israel and the Palestinians in 1993. Since then, that great conflict between the two nations proved too big for the peace treaty. The commitment of both sides constantly eroded under the tension Oslo created within their societies and the unwillingness of various leaders to assuage that stress. Since then, too, my contemplation of the unity of purpose of my great-great-uncles led me to a personal understanding of the conflict that focuses on those battles *within* the two camps. Whereas Dai and Dan Beynon united through a mission and a faith, it seems that among Israelis and Palestinians such things divide more than they bind. Talmudic rabbis, who sought to expand upon the sparse details of the Book of Genesis, wrote that the argument between Cain and Abel was over the site where God's Holy Temple would be built: each wanted it constructed on his field. The eventual location of the Temple in Jerusalem is the source of dispute between Palestinians and Israelis, but just as powerfully between Israelis who would concede absolute control over the area and those who believe such an accommodation would signal the demise of their religion and their people.

I focused my reporting on the truly disturbing betrayals and hatreds within these two communities—between Islamic fundamentalists and Palestinian rulers, between Israeli settlers and peace campaigners, and other ruptures I would never have imagined. In my years of reporting on the supposedly bigger conflict between the two nations, it was these internecine stresses that provided me with the most unexpected, enlightening insights into just why the Holy Land remains at war. It even afforded me a glimpse of how that war might, just might, end. Only when Israelis and Palestinians no longer contend with their compatriots will they feel strong and secure enough to make a lasting peace with their national enemies.

Part I: The Palestinians

CHAPTER ONE

Kissing the Dead

Arafat and Hamas

ABEL: O earth, cover not the blood of Abel!
JEHOVAH: What vengeance dost thou require?
ABEL: Life for life!

—WILLIAM BLAKE, *THE GHOST OF ABEL*

WHEN HE KISSED ME, I felt death electric on his lips. I thought, The next time I see him will be after the violence that ends him. With the softness of bristles never shaved even in youth, his black beard brushed first my left cheek, then my right, and back again, until he had bestowed upon me the special recognition and warmth of five brotherly kisses. His right eye had a turn in it, skewing toward the low bridge of his thick nose, and I remembered how his other eyeball had aimed his specially modified M-16 assault rifle with its sniper sights. He held my shoulders between grubby fingers, slung the rifle across his chest so that it would be ready, and then he was gone, past the metal door and up the unfinished steps of poured concrete to the roof to make his escape. Even then, I focused on the face that had touched mine, so that I would remember it in this way—alive, with warm lips on my cheek, eyes open and friendly, fingers pressing my palm. I did this because I didn't want him to become like the other thousands, the blurred face of a dead "terrorist" made an ugly statistic in an Israeli newspaper, or a pallid mask at the end of a shattered body wrapped in a green Islamic flag and shouldered by sweating, crowding Hamas men, hoarsely chanting his corpse to its final rest with Allah and willing his soul to carry them, too, to paradise with the other martyrs. I felt the adrenaline of his inevitable death, as though it had seeped from his mouth through the flesh of my cheeks. There must have been similar thoughts cached within the minds of his two wives, or of his father who already had gazed upon the lethal gunshot wounds in the bodies of two of his sons: Soon we shall see you dead. Whether they wished him martyrdom and a seat close to the prophet Muhammed in *Jannah,* or whether they feared for what would happen to them once he was gone and that, without his strength to protect them, they would be persecuted, the imminence of his fate was the one certainty in the life of Imad Akel. That he would die was a question already answered, clean and clear; the unknown factor was a dirtier puzzle, whose answer could be read only if you were prepared to risk the touch of its sharply jagged edges. Would he die at the hands of the enemy Israeli army or of his compatriots in the Palestinian police?

For Imad Akel, a leader of the Hamas "military wing," was not just a fugitive from Israel, whose citizens he threatened and killed with the operations he planned from the Gaza City hideouts of the Izze-dine al-Qassam Brigades. The paramilitaries of Yasser Arafat's Palestinian Authority wanted him dead too.

I went to the sandy back alleys of Nusseirat refugee camp, because Akel's story told of the complex, dirty conspiracy that menaced all Palestinians. As I drove down the narrow dune road from Gaza above the tameless aquamarine Mediterranean breakers, I thought of the White House lawn and the deal Arafat signed there to police Hamas, regardless of human rights or of incarcerations without trial. In the fractious traffic of donkey carts and long yellow Mercedes taxis that manically jammed Nusseirat's main street that market day, I recalled how Arafat so often allowed Hamas to wreak its bloody work on Israelis in crowded marketplaces like this; how he used their violence to pressure Israel's peace negotiators; and how he sought, in contrast, to placate the Americans after the September 11 attacks by sending his riot police to block a pro-Osama bin Laden march of Hamas activists outside the Islamic University in Gaza. As Imad Akel's cousin directed me through the cinder-block labyrinth of the refugee camp to my meeting, I recollected the names of the three unarmed Palestinians gunned down by Arafat's police at the demonstration that day in October 2001: Franji, Abu Shamal, Akel. Yussef Akel.

I stared edgily at the frosted window of the claustrophobic reception room where I waited for Imad Akel, expecting an Israeli missile to smash through it at any moment as the army tried to nail the fugitive. It would be a message of deadly simplicity. But the missile didn't come, because it would be too facile and formulaic for the tale that I was reconstructing. Nothing in this story would have the clarity of Western news reports and the trite diplomatic pabulum of U.S. politicians. Every idea of right and wrong, of good guys and bad guys, would be more than turned on its head; it would be erased and replaced with shifting outlines like the waves off Gaza, a confusing clamor like the children hawking in the market, a maze of meanings less fathomable than the precise location of the metalwork shop deep in the convoluted heart of Nusseirat above which I now sat. Each important man—Arafat, Sharon, Bush, the Gaza police chief and his deputies—would bully his own truth out of the story's shadings, a truth vastly different from the one read there by average Palestinians. But Imad Akel would not let them get away with it. He fought back.

THE MOSQUE at the end of the street where Imad Akel grew up was a graffiti canvas of bulbous grenades and Hamas slogans. Muhammed Abdel-Hadi Akel Akel, named for the Prophet, then for his father, his grandfather and his clan, shuffled through the sandy gutter outside the house of prayer. It was October, but the air was heavy with the humidity of the sea and the reek of gasoline fumes from old delivery trucks that were never serviced. He kicked the sand with listless rancor. When he passed the daubings on the wall of the mosque, their fierce declarations turned his mind to his son Issam, the martyr. But the memory irritated him today, because he couldn't remember the exact date when Issam was killed. It was some time around the beginning of the Eid al-Adha in 1989. That holiday is always set for the time of the new moon that ends the period of the hajj in Mecca. The Eid of the Sacrifice, it starts on the tenth day of the Muslim month of Dhu'l-Hijjah, the month of the hajj, when the millions in Saudi Arabia who have made the pilgrimage sacrifice their animals. The lunar Muslim calendar means that like all other Islamic festivals, the Eid each year shifts its date eleven days earlier in the solar Western calendar. Muhammed couldn't remember if it had fallen that year during a particularly hot time. Or was it cold, wet? Israeli troops came to the camp. They opened fire. They killed twelve people. Yes, he remembered that. The day after, Issam went to visit relatives, and on the way, Israelis shot him. He had a bullet in the heart. Muhammed tried to reconstruct details about his son. Yes, it had been a bullet in the heart, when Issam was sixteen years old, he recalled. He remembered thinking that he lost Issam at the time of the Eid, the festival that marks the prophet Ibrahim's willingness to sacrifice the life of his firstborn son at Allah's command. Muhammed Akel had never questioned why Ibrahim's son should have been reprieved, but his own should have died. Allah inscribed the answer long ago, and Muhammed Akel was not privileged to read what the Master of the Universe wrote, only to believe and to submit. But when had it been? He would ask his wife, Aisha, when he got home. She would recall a fact like that as though it were constantly the foremost thought in her head, the detailed memory of the son she had lost.

Muhammed often asked Aisha to remind him of numbers and dates about one of his other sons, Imad Akel. People always wanted him to tell stories about the hero Imad, and Muhammed would do so with pride, sitting in the second-floor reception room of his rough concrete house, surrounded by Imad's children, who couldn't live with their fugitive father in his secret hideouts. Still, Muhammed would forget the details and he would call out to Aisha, as she sat just beyond the door, listening to the men's talk, ready to prepare another pot of mint tea. Someone would ask him how many children Imad had, and Muhammed would briefly count those chasing around him on the carpet and realize that he wasn't sure if this was all of them. Maybe there were a couple of others he was forgetting. "Ah, how many children does Imad have?" He would merely raise his voice. He wouldn't have to address Aisha by name. Her answer would come back sharply and immediately: "Six." Muhammed would turn to his guests: "Six, I think. He has six children."

In those moments when he was asked to tell the stories of Imad, there were other things, beyond the bare dates and numbers, that Muhammed never forgot: the sense of strength and decency that he knew in his son; the old tales of Imad the teenager who campaigned against Israel's soldiers as one of the stone-throwing kids of the first Palestinian intifada. "Since he was little, he was a very tough guy," Muhammed would tell people. "Of course, I raised him to hate the

Jews. He always gave them a very hard time with stones and they'd have to chase him from street to street." Muhammed brought up Imad to be just the kind of man he now was. To hate the Israelis but to value all Allah's other living creatures—that was why young Imad had bred birds to sell to children as pets. To remember that their family fled in 1948, at Israel's founding, from the village of Yibna that was now the Israeli town of Yavne.

Muhammed was born in 1949 and had never been to Yavne. I had. "There are groves of olives there that you couldn't imagine," Muhammed said, with the kind of nostalgic immediacy born of constant repetition that's so common among Palestinian refugees. He was right: I couldn't imagine them. South of Tel Aviv, Yavne is a neat, prosperous suburb that, unusually for Israel, is made up of individual houses, rather than apartment blocks. While Muhammed harked back to the pastoral Yavne his parents knew, I recalled sitting in the backyard of Meir Sheetrit, who was then Israel's treasury minister. His neighbor's boys kicked their football into his garden and Sheetrit threw it back. "Thanks, Finance Minister," they called mockingly. Despite the insolence of the boys next door, Sheetrit had earned some reverence in the community. He had been mayor of Yavne at twenty-one, and the force of his personality built the place out of the transit camp for new immigrants his family found there when they arrived from Morocco in 1956. The Sheetrits, like everyone else in the camp, lived then in a corrugated-iron shack of twenty square yards, where the lavish villas now stood. At the same time, he buried the Yibna of the Akel clan. But for Muhammed it remained real, and he made it live in Imad. It was in the stones the boy threw at Israelis in his teens, and, since the start of the Aqsa intifada in September 2000, it was in the bullets and the Qassam II rockets he fired at Israeli towns just across the Gaza Strip border.

That was how Muhammed raised his boy, and he had continued to instill the will to struggle for Yibna in Imad, even after the youngster went into hiding in 1991. The Israelis came for Imad back then at Muhammed's house. They asked the father where he was. "Imad's not here," he said. While the Israelis were distracted, Imad jumped out of the window. He cried, loudly, *"Allahu akbar." God is most great.* He shouted to surprise the soldiers, who did, indeed, stand and watch for a stunned moment, just long enough for Imad to jump the back wall and get away down the alleys. He returned to Muhammed's home from hiding many times, often enough to marry and to conceive his children, and to give bird-breeding advice to his younger brother Yussef, who had taken over the birdcages. The Israelis had no photograph of Imad, so it was hard for them to track him. He had been a fugitive and stayed alive longer than any other Hamas operative. His namesake, Imad Akel from the Jabalya refugee camp, was a colleague in the Izzedine al-Qassam Brigades and was better known than his friend Imad Akel of Nusseirat camp. But Israeli soldiers killed Akel of Jabalya in 1992. No one had gotten to Akel of Nusseirat—yet.

The reflected glory of Imad Akel was not enough for Muhammed. He liked to make sure his friends and visitors knew that it was he who molded his sons and handed down to them his own bravery. And that he suffered for it. Muhammed Akel used to earn a living as a laborer in Israel. But the Israelis denied him a work permit for six years and he was unemployed that whole time. Lighting a cheap Egyptian cigarette, Muhammed would tell how the Israelis tried to do a deal: they asked him to sell out the whereabouts of his son in return for a work permit. "They're so stupid," he'd say, exhaling smoke and shaking his head.

The Israelis offered Muhammed Akel the kind of nasty deal other Palestinians might have taken, faced with the alternative of desperate poverty for the eighteen Akels—wife, children, daughters-in-law, and grandchildren—living in his home. But the Palestinian Authority took a different approach to the problem of Imad Akel. In 1995 there was one of those intermittent periods when Yasser Arafat wanted to rein in Hamas. Arafat's police arrested many of the Islamist leaders in Gaza and the West Bank, including those who were known to be involved primarily in Hamas's political and charitable wings. As he did from time to time, Imad had returned to see his father, unannounced. He drove Muhammed through the camp in his car, talking about the crackdown. Suddenly a group of red-bereted Military Intelligence troops stepped out into the road. It was an impromptu roadblock, and one of the soldiers came to Imad's window. Knowing that he would be arrested if they asked for his papers, Imad opened the door quickly. He jumped out and grabbed the soldier in a headlock. With the other hand, he pulled a grenade from his vest, yanked the pin, and held the live bomb above his head. "If you want to take me, take me like this," he called. They stood that way for over an hour, the soldiers training their weapons on Imad and calling for him to surrender, and strong

Imad with his grip still tight around the soldier's neck and his thumb quivering with fatigue on the activating lever of the grenade.

A Palestinian officer came to the scene and made a deal with Imad. The soldiers wouldn't harm him if he would agree to go to the Sarraya, the police headquarters on Omar al-Mukhtar Street in the center of Gaza City. Imad went, but the Sarraya is also a jail and the police officer betrayed him. Imad sat in a cell in the Sarraya a few months. Muhammed believed Imad escaped from the Sarraya, but it was more likely that he was allowed to go free, as were many Hamas fighters when it served Arafat's purpose to halt his crackdown and unleash the bombers on Israel once more.

After that, Imad told his father he would never trust the Palestinian Authority again. "If they come to arrest me, I won't surrender," he said. Gradually, over the next seven years, Imad's friends in the Izzedine al-Qassam Brigades were arrested by the Palestinian Authority or by Israel, or killed by the Israelis. It became harder for him to find places to hide in Nusseirat. He moved to Gaza City, where the greater size of the place made it easier to disappear, and his visits to his father's home became fewer. In 1998 Imad spent nine months in a safe house and didn't go outside once.

Muhammed Akel turned down a dirty alley and through his front door. He went upstairs. He knew his wife would be somewhere about the house, so he flopped down on a foam mattress in the empty living room and, without introduction, called out the question that had been on his mind as he walked past the mosque. "When was Issam martyred?"

"May twenty-fifth, 1989," Aisha said immediately.

Muhammed sat in the hot living room, silent but for the chittering of the budgerigars bred by his youngest son. Yes, he thought, May 25, that was it. Issam was martyred on that day. The tiny birds swung in their cages on the balcony. He watched them fluttering, yellow and green, blue and black. Then he called to his wife again, "Where's Yussef?"

ABDULLAH FRANJI AWOKE at 3 A.M. The fourteen-year-old intended to fast, as it was a Thursday, when many religious Muslims refrain from food, so he wanted to eat a little of a bean-and-chickpea dish called *ful* before sunrise, just to have something that would keep him going through the day. It was hard to get up; he had been awake late, playing with his ten-year-old brother, Muhammed, in the courtyard outside the family's apartment. Abdullah pushed back the cheap, fluffy blanket. Outside on the balcony, his canaries and doves were quiet in the dark. It was chilly, but Abdullah had promised his mother they would practice the portion of the Koran he had been set to memorize by the sheikh. Abdullah's mother, Wafa, instructed girls and boys in the memorization of the Koran; her eldest son, Zuheir, had committed all 114 suras of the holy book to memory by the age of sixteen. Abdullah, who was deeply religious and intelligent, was more than halfway there, though he spent much of his time playing for the soccer teams at his mosque and school. Abdullah rubbed his short black hair forward, and rocking back and forth as a metronomical aid to memory, he closed his eyes and recited from sura 44, The Inner Apartments:

> If two parties of the believers contend with one another, do ye endeavor to compose the matter between them: and if the one of them offer an insult unto the other, fight against that party which offered the insult, until they return unto the judgment of God; and if they do return, make peace between them with equity: and act with justice; for God loveth those who act justly. Verily the true believers are brethren: wherefore reconcile your brethren; and fear God that ye may obtain mercy.

The boy stumbled here and there as Wafa listened. "This is still a little weak, Abdullah," she said quietly. Abdullah kissed her chubby cheeks and promised that he would have the entire chapter down by the time he returned from school. Wafa knew that her second son cared deeply about the meaning of what he learned from the Koran. He was unlike most of her pupils, who only wanted to chew their way through to the end of the task of memorization as though the holy book were a bad meal that must be endured for the sake of sustenance. "Try it again before you go," she said.

"If two parties of the believers contend with one another . . ."

Abdullah's school day began at 6:30 A.M. In Gaza, where money for education is short and the birthrate is high, children attend school in two shifts, one early and the other from 11 A.M. to 4 P.M. Abdullah arrived when the sky was still pink above Gaza. The

Mediterranean, two blocks from the school, was not yet lit to the translucent turquoise it has during the day. He pedaled his bicycle down dusty Talatin Street, one of Gaza's main thoroughfares. At the corner opposite the Islamic University, Abdullah turned into Mustafa Hafiz Street. Trash piled up against a white stucco wall down the western side of the road. On the wall hung a faded blue sign, painted with the globe of the United Nations: United Nations Relief and Works Agency. Zeitoun Prep School for Boys.

The last class of Abdullah's school day was physical training. Under his sweater that morning, he wore his best powder-blue soccer jersey. It was not the uniform of one of the teams he followed, but it was made of soft, silky polyester that seemed luxurious and fashionable to Abdullah. When school finished, it was almost midday and hot. He tied the sweater around his waist and wore the favorite soccer shirt for his ride home. He pushed his bicycle out of the gate by the UN sign.

At the corner, beneath the sand-colored dome and twin minarets of the Islamic University, a demonstration was beginning. The university students mostly followed the Islamic fundamentalist group Hamas. Many of the group's leaders worked there. Ismail Abu Shanab, who led Hamas's contacts with Arafat's Palestinian Authority, taught engineering at the Islamic University until his assassination in an Israeli rocket attack in August 2003. The demonstration that Abdullah Franji happened upon was against Israel, after just over a year of the Aqsa intifada, and against the United States, which clearly was preparing a forceful response against Muslims for the destruction of the World Trade Center in New York the month before. Though the students knew better than to proclaim it openly, the demonstration was also aimed at Arafat and his Authority. The Palestinian leader had recently called for a ceasefire in the battle against Israel; Arafat was embarrassed by the celebrations around Palestinian cities after the Trade Center attack—Palestinians shot rifles in the air and handed out candies in the streets of Bethlehem, Gaza, Tulkarem, and Nablus. Arafat had been forced to broach a halt in terrorism against Israelis for fear that the newly vengeful American administration would tar him with the same brush as Osama bin Laden. The Hamas activists from the university signaled their anger against Arafat, however; in the crowd, many students held banners with photographs of bin Laden. It was their way of insulting the Palestinian leader—something that is wisest done like this, tangentially, rather than through direct invective. Sometimes Arafat would choose not to decipher the code. This time he could not pretend to misunderstand the translation.

This was not all that would have drawn Abdullah Franji to the demonstration. For him, it would certainly have been a way to join with other believers in their protest, but it would also be simply an exciting opportunity to get involved in a demonstration at last. Since the intifada began, Abdullah had been frustrated that his parents and even his friends prevented him from heading north to the Israeli positions around the Erez Checkpoint or south to the Netzarim settlement overlooking the Sheikh Ijline sands below Gaza City. He tried to go to one of the demonstrations, but his school friends intercepted him on his way, and, telling him it was simply too dangerous, they dissuaded him. They were right to do so, for those were all lethal confrontations. Kids like Abdullah threw stones, harking back to the mythic exploits of the previous generation of Palestinian youth during the first intifada from 1987 to 1993. But the generation that fought Israel in the original intifada these days made life dangerous for its replacements. The graduates of that first set of battles, like Imad Akel, progressed from rocks to M-16s and AK-47s; the new stone throwers often provided cover, behind which the old hands would open fire on Israeli soldiers. Many youngsters like Abdullah died in the crossfire of those gunfights, while others perished just as pointlessly when Israelis fired their rubber-coated ball bearings—known by the deceptively anodyne label of "rubber bullets"—from lethally close range. But Abdullah Franji was born on December 6, 1987, the first day of the first intifada, and he grew up with a deep feeling that he wanted to be a part of the struggle that was born with him.

Abdullah began to push his bicycle along the fringe of the demonstration, glad finally to be part of this sweating, chanting mass. There were the green flags of Hamas, decorated with the elaborate script of the Fatiha, the introductory text of the Koran. The students from the university, though young, already wore dark beards. This was just like the funerals of the martyrs that Abdullah had attended in Gaza, but much better: it was the real thing. They walked fast along Talatin Street toward the headquarters of Arafat's police, a complex of buildings a couple of miles square. At the entrance, a stone plinth was decorated with a portrait of the *ra'is*, the "chief," as Arafat's people called him, smiling broadly to his right. It was the center of Arafat's Palestinian Authority, hidden behind the tall white walls. No demonstrator would be allowed to come close to this place. (A few months later, Israeli F-16s demolished the entire complex in a single massive raid. The only thing left standing was the portrait of Arafat, grinning like a lounge-lizard Ozymandias, unaware that a panorama of his destroyed power stretched behind him in a jumble of white and gray chunks.)

As the demonstration approached, the riot police moved in. Palestinian journalists covering the protest noticed a senior police officer handing out balaclava helmets to his men, so that their faces would be masked. They were about to do something bad, and they did not want to suffer the retribution that would follow if they were identified by any of the marchers. First the riot police struck out with clubs and shoved their victims with black shields. A few demonstrators raced out of the crowd and threw stones at the policemen, but at a distance of twenty yards or more, it was a harmless gesture. The riot police wore helmets and vests ribbed with padding across their chest and back that looked like a turtle's belly. Then the shooting began. The police would later say that Hamas activists in the crowd started the firing, or that it was initiated by collaborators with Israel who wanted to stir up internal divisions among the Palestinians. None of that was true. (They were the very same excuses the police used in 1994, when they killed fifteen Hamas supporters at the Palestine Mosque in Gaza.) All those who were there, including policemen who spoke privately, agreed that the police began the shooting. When the police opened fire, some of the students shot back. In the crowd, there were members of the Hamas military wing, Izzedine al-Qassam, and they were armed. But in the first volleys, Abdullah Franji's friends watched him drop his bicycle to the ground. Then his powder-blue shirt began to turn red with blood.

Wafa Franji heard that there was trouble near her son's school. Abdullah usually came home by 12:30, but he was not to be seen. She experienced a strange sense of nausea and began to feel a shortness of breath that grew from her anxiety. At 2 P.M. some of his friends came by. One of them wheeled Abdullah's bicycle. They shuffled uncomfortably; they knew their friend was dead, but they did not want to be the one to tell his mother.

"Where is Abdullah?" Wafa asked in a panic.

One of the boys spoke, though Wafa was so frantic she could not remember later which of them it was. "You haven't seen him?" the boy said.

"No. He hasn't been home."

There was a silence. "We saw him get hit in the head," one of the boys said slowly. "He's probably dead."

Wafa called her brother Ala, who lived near Shifa Hospital in Gaza. "Go and see if Abdullah's okay," she said. Then she hurried to the hospital.

Ala was in the big courtyard of the hospital when Wafa got there. The place was alive with crowds of youths, who had come from the demonstration, and with worried parents. They milled about among the pine trees. Wafa rushed to Ala. Abdullah's uncle had already seen the boy's body and identified him, but he refused to be the one to tell his sister that she had lost her son. He told her to go inside and see for herself.

As she went into the hospital, Wafa accepted that whatever she was about to learn had been willed by God—even if it was that her son had died. She was shown into a small room. There had been no time to take Abdullah's body across the courtyard to the morgue, where so many other martyrs of the intifada had been stored at three degrees Celsius in the stainless steel, Japanese-made refrigerated chests. Wafa leaned over her son. His soccer shirt had been removed, but there was blood all over his head and shoulders. She counted three stitches in a gash the bullet made above his left eye; she could see no exit wound. It had been a live round, and it killed Abdullah immediately. Someone had doused rose water on the boy's body, but Wafa believed it was the perfume of paradise, the scent that emanates from Islamic martyrs. Wafa reminded herself that a *shahid*—a martyr—of Palestine would be able to choose seventy of his relatives to sit with him in paradise; naturally, she would be one of the people Abdullah would elect to join him, and she remembered the kisses he gave her on her cheeks as they practiced his Koran homework that morning. But it did not comfort her that she would see Abdullah again in heaven. I have lost this child, she thought.

MUHAMMED AKEL didn't think about his son Yussef with the same pride he lavished on the boy's brother Imad. Muhammed glanced again at the birdcages on the balcony. Aisha told him Yussef cleaned the floors of the cages that morning, before midday prayers. Then he went to the mosque. Yussef Akel's face was cast like Imad's, with its bulky nose and wide cheeks. He cut his hair the same way—short, with a fringe chopped straight across the forehead an inch above the thick eyebrows. Yussef was like Imad, yes. He was even in Hamas, but not the way Imad was, Muhammed thought. Everyone in the Akel family was Hamas. But Imad was unique. Muhammed sometimes wondered what Yussef intended to do with himself. He couldn't sell twittering little budgerigars forever.

So Muhammed Akel sat and smoked and relaxed in his living room, while Yussef Akel went to Gaza City to take part in the demonstration at the Islamic University. He was deeper in Hamas than Muhammed recognized. For a time, he was deeper even than Imad knew. The Izzedine al-Qassam compartmentalized its operations so that if one of its cells was busted by the Shin Bet—Israel's domestic security agency—the damage shouldn't spread throughout the entire organization. The first Imad Akel knew of Yussef's involvement in the armed struggle against Israel was when the plan for a suicide-bomb operation against an Israeli settlement in the Gaza Strip was brought before the Qassam committee in Gaza. The man picked to sacrifice himself, to blow himself up, was Yussef Akel. Chairing the meeting, Imad was shocked. He went to his brother and dissuaded him from participating in the plan. Frankly, Imad told Yussef, suicide attacks within the Gaza Strip against heavily guarded settlements were hopeless; they could never kill as many Israelis as the bombers who sneaked out of the West Bank into Jerusalem or Tel Aviv and slaughtered dozens of Israelis in crowded cafés and on buses. Imad convinced Yussef that his life was worth more than that. Just as he, Imad, stayed alive through a decade on the run, despite his desire for martyrdom, Yussef must wait until he could honor Allah and the Palestinian people by striking a real blow against Israel through his sacrifice. Imad didn't tell their father of Yussef's intentions, but he knew he had to let his younger brother continue in the Hamas military organization. He had already heard how good Yussef was under pressure. One night, Yussef went out with a Hamas cell to lay an antitank mine in one of the dirt patrol tracks near the Israeli settlement of Netzarim. While he was planting the mine, a tank shuddered toward him. The rest of the Hamas crew fled as the terrifying, deafening bawl of the tank engine closed on Yussef. They assumed Yussef was dead and were on their way to tell Muhammed Akel that his son had been martyred, when Yussef returned, carrying the mine. "I just hid in a dip in the road," he told them. "The tank went right over me. I had to stay to bring back the mine. After all, I didn't get a chance to plant it and prime it correctly."

But Muhammed didn't know this. To cope with his long period of unemployment, he usually tried to empty his mind for much of the day. He didn't have many errands to run, because Aisha and his daughters-in-law took care of them. He played with the grandchildren a little, but he didn't enjoy it so much and, anyway, they were happier with their mothers. He prayed, as was his duty, and that took up some time. He used to watch Yussef talk to his birds and listen to them whistle back at him. He waited for Imad to come and see him.

While he was in this vacant state, Muhammed Akel's cellular phone trilled out the lambada. It was a friend of the family calling from Shifa Hospital. "Yussef had a serious wound, Abu Hussam," the friend said, using the familiar name by which Muhammed was known in the camp. "He's here at the hospital."

Muhammed stood and went to Aisha. "There was trouble at the university. Some kind of demonstration. Yussef went there," he said. "He's been injured." It was only when Aisha began crying and wailing that the vacuous calm left him and Muhammed, too, began to fear for his son.

Muhammed Akel took a cab. As the taxi bumped onto the coast road, Gaza City came into view with its tall, bright new towers. Beyond it, frosted by a blue haze, were the smokestacks and the long jetty of the deepwater port at Ashdod, inside Israel. Muhammed's cell phone rang again: "Abu Hussam, Yussef has been martyred." First, Muhammed told himself that Allah would protect his son's spirit and mumbled to himself the declaration of his faith in Allah and the Prophet. Muhammed wondered for a moment if he should turn back, but he figured he ought to be the one to bring his son's body home to Nusseirat for the funeral. There was something he didn't understand, something in that moment he couldn't put his finger on. The friend at the hospital told him that Yussef went to the demonstration because he thought some of his cousins might be there and he wanted to make sure they were safe. In reality, it was more likely that, as a member of Izzedine al-Qassam, Yussef went because he knew there would be a confrontation and felt it was his duty to be part of it. Muhammed didn't know that. He still doesn't.

It was 2 P.M. when Muhammed reached Shifa Hospital. It was crowded, but when they learned who he was, everyone around him panicked and shouted and hustled him along to the morgue. The body was gone. The police wanted to impound Yussef's corpse, so some young Hamas activists whisked it away from them to the Shati refugee camp.

Muhammed was confused. "The police want the body?"

"Of course," one of the doctors told him. "They don't want a proper medical examination."

"Why not?"

The doctor looked at Muhammed and paused. "Well, Abu Hussam, they killed him."

"Who did?"

"The police."

"Our police?"

The doctor held on to Muhammed's upper arm as though he thought the man would fall, and in fact Muhammed Akel did feel breathless and light-headed at that moment. He simply had assumed that the Israelis killed Yussef, somehow. The mysterious uneasiness he experienced when he took the phone call in the taxi returned. "There was a demonstration at the university and the riot police fired and killed three people," the doctor said. "One of them is a little boy, and there are two youths. One of the youths is your son."

Muhammed nodded. He was about to go. But wait, he didn't know where to collect the corpse. "Why did they take the body to Shati?"

"They thought he was from the Akel family up in Jabalya, so they went north from here, through the Shati camp. Someone called them and told them their mistake, so they're taking it south to Nusseirat now." The crowd was noisy around the doctor. Though they felt reverence and concern for Muhammed, they were angry, and beyond the immediate circle of onlookers, panicked parents and friends were trying to find other people injured in the riot. "Perhaps you'd better go home, Abu Hussam. To prepare for the mourning period."

Muhammed Akel didn't say anything to the doctor at that

moment. But in the taxi south to Nusseirat, he thought, How can I mourn for Yussef? How can I open up a mourning tent and hand out cups of bitter coffee and accept condolences? No, that happens when a man dies naturally or when he dies at the hands of a mortal enemy, like the Israelis. But when he is murdered by someone in the community, there is no mourning until vengeance is taken. When he got back to Nusseirat, there were thousands of neighbors gathered angrily around his house. They knew how Yussef died and they drew the same conclusion as Muhammed Akel. He went to Aisha and said, "There will be no mourning tent until someone has been called to account for Yussef's death."

Outside the house, the crowd swayed, surged as new people crushed into the street. They started to call out to Muhammed Akel that they were going to the police station to burn it down in protest. Muhammed didn't want that kind of vengeance. He wanted what was prescribed by Islam. A Muslim has the right to avenge himself on someone who harms his family, but is supposed to cede that right to the caliph, in effect allowing the government to punish offenders; but in a situation like this, when the forces of the government were the ones with blood on their hands, it's beholden upon a Muslim to act in his own name. Muhammed Akel called out to the street that he didn't want violence on this day, but no one could hear him above the angry crowd. From the second floor of his house, he saw some men on the edge of the crowd peeling away toward the camp's police station. He couldn't blame them. The way he saw it, the Palestinian Authority had held control of Nusseirat and much of the Gaza Strip since 1994, and in that time the weak got weaker and the big shots just became bigger.

When the funeral procession left the Akel house, the police station was already burning. The policemen ran away. Those who set fire to the building were back among the mourners as Yussef's body was lifted above the heads of the crowd and carried to Nusseirat's cemetery.

The cemetery had no name. The people of the camp called it "our cemetery." Nusseirat and the sands around it were almost flat, but the cemetery rose, impossibly steep, like the protuberance on the head of a cartoon cat struck with a massive mallet. It swelled above the main street and the market stalls at the center of the camp to a height of sixty feet, though it was barely twice that wide at its base. The grave-stones, placed at ninety degrees to the sloping earth, were silhouetted haphazardly against the clear sky. It was as though the earth stretched upward, above the stinking slum of the camp, to give the dead, laid to rest on their right side facing Mecca, a view of the holy city so far away from the impious tumult in which they lived.

The funeral procession reached the corner of the market near the cemetery. Under the shadow of the graveyard rise, Imad Akel stepped out of an alley. The mourners came to a halt and crowded the Hamas hero. They chanted his name and surrounded him, pressing against him. Muhammed Akel pushed through the crowd toward his son. When he reached him, Imad was kissing the face of his dead brother. Even when Imad had been in hiding, Muhammed recognized a spe-cial bond between the two boys, and now he saw tears of anger in Imad's eyes. He knew he did not have to tell Imad what was expected of him.

The people lifted Imad on their shoulders and, raising his gun in one hand, he called out to them, "I swear before you, I will avenge Yussef's death on whoever it was that killed him." Imad shouted over the cheers, "He was my brother and my best friend." The funeral con-tinued to the graveyard, and Imad Akel went back into the alleys.

When Muhammed Akel returned to his home with his relatives, Imad was waiting. The family sat in the room where Muhammed had been quiet and alone earlier. Their faces were distraught and shocked and bitter. All the gall that had been building in him beneath the grief at the funeral now poured out of Muhammed.

"It was a Palestinian who killed Yussef. These are our brothers," he said. He wanted everyone to hear, but it was to the silent, bowed head of Imad Akel that he addressed himself. "When you lose a son by the hand of the enemy, it's not so sore. But the Authority police were shooting to kill. They shot him in the heart." Muhammed called Imad by name, and the young man raised his head. "Imad, they shot him in the heart, exactly the same way the Israelis killed your brother Issam."

Three men came from the Fatah office, while Muhammed and Imad were still in the living room. The party of Yasser Arafat, Fatah had become an adjunct of the Palestinian Authority, though its local functionaries were often more attuned to the mood and needs of the people than the uniformed men, whose officers returned from exile in Tunis in 1994. One of them, a senior official in Nusseirat, promised he would try to bring justice for Yussef Akel through the legal system. It was then that Imad broke his silence and quieted the room with the understated venom of his words. "If you don't bring these policemen to justice, I'll blow them up myself with one of my own bombs," he said. He leaned forward, close to the Fatah man, and spoke in a deep, low voice. "You know my talents."

ABDULLAH FRANJI had been fasting still, when he died. As the daylight faded, Wafa cried in the arms of her husband, Muhammed Franji. He tried to console her by reminding her that Abdullah had abstained from food until the moment he was shot: "At the end of this day, Abdullah is breaking his fast now in paradise with the prophet Muhammed, peace be upon him."

Wafa remembered a hadith of the Prophet when he lost his son Ibrahim, and recited it to her husband: "The heart feels grief and the eye sheds a tear." Muhammed agreed and added that the Prophet had cried for his first wife, Khadijah, many years after her death. But there was anger after the sorrow, and Muhammed Franji knew whom to blame.

In the Sheikh Zeid Mosque, near the Islamic University, Yasser Arafat listened to recitations from the Koran a week after the fatal riot of the Hamas students. It was a festival to honor youngsters who memorized the entire Koran, as Abdullah Franji was trying to do on the morning of his death. At the end of the ceremony, Arafat straightened his checkered keffiyeh after his prostrations and began to make his way through the milling crowd, surrounded by his entourage. A man stepped out before him who Arafat did not know and held out his hand to the Palestinian leader. Arafat gripped it limply.

"I am Muhammed Franji, father of the martyr Abdullah Franji, who was killed in the incident at the university," the man said, "and I want you to give me my rights."

It took guts for Abdullah's father to approach Arafat like this. The Palestinian leader, after all, paid his wages as an agricultural engineer, inspecting the produce that came through the Karni Crossing between Israel and Gaza. But Muhammed Franji had made an appeal to tradition. As Imad Akel knew, relatives must avenge the victim even of a mistaken killing. Someone had to be punished. Arafat had to make amends to this man, or he knew it might lead to trouble.

"God willing," Arafat said, "we shall have an investigative committee that will discover the truth."

The Palestinian Authority set up an inquiry, but nothing happened. There were no hearings and certainly no findings. Muhammed Franji had been hopeful after he spoke to Arafat, but he soon realized that he had been brushed aside. With the families of the other victims of the riots, including the Akels, he launched a court case against the Palestinian police. He expected the case to take a long time, faced with the stonewalling of the Authority, which in any case was disintegrating under the pressure of the intifada and the Israeli army. But Muhammed refused to give up the memory of his son: it was written, literally, all over his home.

In a quiet dead-end street in Gaza's Sabra neighborhood, the Franji home was marked by graffiti of a masked man holding aloft an M-16. In the same puffy spray-can script used to scrawl rap handles across American subway walls, someone marked in red the name of the Islamic Resistance Movement, Hamas. When Muhammed Franji walked back from his encounter with Arafat at the mosque through his gate into the alley and to his front door, the bare cinder-block wall was gaudy with new Hamas artwork: the golden Dome of the Rock in Jerusalem with a bloody arm pointing toward the sky from the crescent at its pinnacle, representing the holiness, the sacrifice, and the strength of the Palestinian struggle. Wherever he sat in his living room, he saw Abdullah's face, squinting into the sun that no longer shone upon him. His portrait stood framed in the corner, clumsily drawn in bright colors. Next to it, two posters, at first apparently like all the martyrdom posters of the intifada, but these were not victims of Israeli arms. Abdullah and the two men killed in the same riot were inlaid on a background of the Aqsa Mosque in Jerusalem, designated holy martyrs by the group that printed the placards, Hamas.

When I went to the Franji house, I traced the graffiti on the alley wall into my notebook. A crowd of boys quit their soccer game to gather around me. In some ways, theirs was the usual performance when a foreigner comes to a poor neighborhood of Gaza. They watched me intently, nervously, wanting to make contact, but unsure how, jostling close to one another as though I might snatch at anyone who detached himself from the safety of the group like a seal hunting penguins. One ventured some English, rolling his *r* in the way of Arabic speech and slurring his words together: "Howerrryo. Byebye." It made a pleasant change from "Fuck you"—the single English phrase that every Palestinian youth appears to have picked up from Hollywood movies, which they blurt out sometimes with amusingly naive relish, sometimes with hatred for Westerners—so I smiled at the boys and said hello. I had come so far to read the ugly story that was written on the wall against which they kicked their football, but it was I—not the graffiti—that held *their* attention. I was glad to have given them some distraction from the darkness that was the backdrop to lives that should have been still innocent.

The story that I heard from the Franjis stripped another layer of my own innocence, as though the blood of Abdullah Franji and Yussef Akel were turned caustic by the manner of their unjust deaths at the hands of their compatriots. There was denial at work too. Like other Westerners, I wanted to see peace take hold, and I didn't want to acknowledge the force of the intra-communal wickedness that would uproot every shoot peace sent down. In spite of this, by the time I stood in the alley outside the Franji home, I felt my wishful repression giving way for the last time. After all, the blood of Abdullah and Yussef was not the first to corrode the smooth surface of Western preconceptions I brought with me when I came to cover the conflict between Israelis and Palestinians. It began the first time I ever went to the West Bank, in the summer of 1996.

I TOOK A SHARED TAXI from Damascus Gate, the grandest of the entrances through Suleiman the Magnificent's wall around the Old City of Jerusalem. For a few shekels, the long yellow Mercedes ferried me and six other cramped passengers along the passes of the Samarian hills to Nablus. When I flew into Tel Aviv from New York for the first time in June 1996, I was looking forward to my first trip to the infamous West Bank. I recall that I predicted that I would probably be writing about some Israeli violence done to a Palestinian, or interviewing the family of a Hamas terrorist who had spilled Israeli blood.

Instead, I was watching the barren, dusty hills around Jerusalem turn lush as we passed through Wadi Haramiyyeh, on my way to hear how Yasser Arafat's torturers killed Mahmoud Jumayel. Frankly, I didn't grasp the full significance of the story, even after I wrote an article about it. I suppose I figured Arafat must have had his reasons for employing a distastefully heavy hand against his own troublemakers. He was working to protect the peace process, wasn't he, and that could only be good for everyone in the end. Right?

The Jumayel family lived on a rise overlooking the mildewed domes of the old Casbah of Nablus. As I walked onto the wide balcony where the mourners gathered, there was a subdued anger about the men on the plastic chairs. It seemed to drain them of their will, like the afternoon heat, and make them listless. I passed under a broad black tarpaulin that flapped in the warm wind. The Islamic symbols of mourning—palm fronds and black flags tacked to broom handles—stood in two rusty oil drums. A neighbor guided me to Amin Jumayel, the dead man's eighteen-year-old brother. Thin and quiet, he seemed unable to lift himself from his chair. He held out his hand, and I shook it. It occurred to me that I had never before attended the funeral of someone whose family wouldn't have automatically expected me to be there. This was a hell of a way to start on this period in my career, in which I sometimes seemed to be qualifying as a professional mourner.

Taped to the wall behind Amin: a gruesome gallery, photos of Mahmoud Jumayel's corpse. It was still recognizably the body of a young man. Traces remained of what clearly had been beautiful. The skin was smooth and chestnut brown, the musculature lithe. Yet this handsome frame was so mutilated that it seemed as though even death might not have been enough to end Mahmoud Jumayel's unimaginable agony. It was burned and scarred and bruised all across the torso and face. Mahmoud's lower body was covered with a white sheet. Amin Jumayel pulled another selection of morbid snapshots from his pocket and flipped through them. I watched Amin's face: it was dull and fallen, so bereft that it seemed almost no longer to be living, as though it died with Mahmoud. "I place responsibility for the death of my brother on the Authority. They are Fascists. They are like Hitler. All the people know who killed my brother," he said. He gestured along the lines of silent, slightly embarrassed men beneath the black tarpaulin. None of them wanted to catch my eye when Amin spoke thus. "They are frightened, because there is no democracy here."

Mahmoud Jumayel was a leader of the Fatah Hawks, young men who, during the first intifada, were the muscle commanded by Arafat from his distant headquarters in Tunis. In the early years of the peace process, they were sometimes hotheaded and hard to control. Like many Palestinians who battled the Israelis in the alleys of the Casbah and endured almost six years in an Israeli jail while Arafat and his henchmen lived large in villas near the ruins of ancient Carthage, Jumayel felt he had some payback coming to him when the Palestinian Authority set up in Nablus. He wasn't expecting this. There was no clear reason for his arrest and the torture that led to his death. It seemed likely that his gang activities irritated a rival who either had better contacts in Arafat's security forces or who actually served in the police. In what was only the second year of Arafat's Authority, Jumayel was already the seventh man tortured to death in a Palestinian jail. The Israelis, who used widespread torture until 1997 and still use it in some cases today, only killed two prisoners by beating or shaking during interrogation. Perhaps the Israelis were just more practiced at the stinking art of almost killing. In the photos of Mahmoud Jumayel's corpse there were no signs of artfulness.

Thousands of Palestinians protested Jumayel's death. They feared that it was an important staging point for Arafat on the track to anarchy that his Authority later traveled right to the end of the line. Demonstrators tried to break down the doors of the jail in Tulkarem, another West Bank town, to free political prisoners held there. Police fired on the crowd and killed a man named Ibrahim Hadaydeh.

Up the road from the Jumayels' house, a few lazy Fatah cadres lingered inside the party's local office during the height of the afternoon sun, drinking coffee and smoking. They played down the anger that greeted Jumayel's death. Languidly Anis Sweydan explained that Arafat couldn't afford to allow democracy. "There is no democracy now," he said. "Maybe when we have our own state, there will be democracy. Until then, no."

"Even without democracy, how is it that a man is tortured to death in police custody?" I asked.

Sweydan gave me a little shrug, a puzzled downward turn at the corners of his mouth and a short, sniffing intake of breath. It was a gesture that I would see many times in the years that followed. I call it the "safeguard shrug," because it's a shield that averts the telling of a truth, without resorting to an actual lie. The gesture means many things, and perhaps I still miss some of its nuance, but in a moment it conveys a series of sometimes contradictory thoughts: Don't ask. What do you know? I agree, but what do you want me to do about it? If I told you what I thought, I'd regret it. Let's talk about something else.

The next day, with unseemly haste aimed at placating the public, Arafat convened a military court in Jericho, which, within a couple of hours, convicted three policemen of Jumayel's killing. The guilty men were committed to fifteen years' hard labor. I imagine that, when the judge brought down his gavel on the sentence, he must have looked at the convicts and given them the safeguard shrug.

The day of my visit to the Jumayel home, I saw a statement by Hamas's Izzedine al-Qassam Brigades. It said the Qassam would avenge the deaths of Jumayel and Hadaydeh, who died in the demonstration in Tulkarem, with attacks on "Zionist targets." Just as Hamas would later try to distance itself from Imad Akel's quarrel with the Authority, its leaders wanted to avoid a direct clash with Arafat. Instead, they would channel the people's anger at Arafat into support for violence against Israel. Thus, the internal battle caused by Arafat's gangsterism fueled the suicide bombs in Israel. When those suicide bombs came, however, foreign journalists would inevitably tie them to some event in the peace process calendar. Either the peace talks were going well and Hamas wanted to throw them off course, or the peace process was progressing badly and angry Palestinians were urging Hamas to take the offensive. Neither explanation made absolute sense, for all the thousands of citations you would find for each in newspapers all over the world. After all, Hamas constantly wanted to strike the peace process, to kill Israelis, because it was their way of attacking Arafat and the power he held over them.

Later, in Gaza, I stood outside Abdullah Franji's house. The boys heckled me jovially. I thought of how they ought to have been playing with their friend who, instead, had become a "martyr." I would not write Abdullah's tale as though it were a clichéd matter of politics or peace process. I knew that it propelled me along the stream of dreadful reality, the swell of internecine viciousness whose stirrings first eddied about me when I stepped between the palm fronds and black flags in Nablus in 1996. That tide of blood slowly changed my perceptions of my task as a journalist here, and of the greater importance of the fight between the Palestinian Authority and Hamas in relation to the more obvious battle between the Palestinians and Israel. If the struggle with Israel was a malady that was difficult to remedy, Arafat was an old-time quack doctor, leeching and bleeding his people closer to their demise, even as he professed himself to be the living cure. I would soon find out that Imad Akel would force Arafat to take some of his own medicine.

I WAITED OUTSIDE the Imam Shifai Mosque, peering from the unlit evening street into the blue-green fluorescent light glaring from the white plaster walls within. The sandy street was busy with donkey carts threading home through the evening from the market and with bearded, stocky men hurrying into the mosque to hear Dr. Abdel Aziz Rantisi's address. The most militant of Hamas's political leaders in Gaza stood somewhere beyond my sight in the crowd, under the sickly light, but his voice rattled out of the loudspeakers onto the street. The streams of men slipping off their shoes at the front step of the mosque watched me distrustfully. A crowd of sixth-grade boys amused themselves by trying to pinch my ass and occasionally tossing gravel at my back. I listened to Rantisi: "My beloved ones, you will continue your resistance until the day of victory. When Arabs speak about peace as a strategic option, it's because they can't be bothered to perform jihad. We feel pity in our very blood when they advocate negotiations. When Allah asks you, 'Why didn't you fight back?' I don't know what you'll answer." I wondered how that would sound to Imad Akel, who had been sitting in his hideout for months, pondering that very question. The sermon was certainly no message of understanding for Palestinians who took a different approach to the Hamas line, whether in regard to peace talks with Israel or to law and order within Palestinian society. Rantisi would not be able to give Imad Akel military orders, for he knew less than Akel about the mechanics of fighting and bomb making. But he was the guide of men like Imad Akel. His words were their guard against humiliation and defeat, and his phrases were to be followed without question.

Though Rantisi was careful and measured in his rhetoric when he spoke to foreigners like me, at the mosque he gave it to them straight: "Weapons are the only option. The only option is to shoot back."

A thousand men came pouring from the mosque. They began a chant: "I will never give up Islam. We are the soldiers of Hamas." I found Rantisi, sandwiched front and back by burly bodyguards holding M-16s at the ready, and as the march began, I took my position at his shoulder. He was fifty-five, with a beard of gray and white that looked as though it had been sketched in quickly with a soft-leaded pencil. He wore large-lensed glasses of a '70s vintage and dressed in a professorial checkered sport jacket. He greeted me, and it was as if his handshake carried me into the stir of energy within the march. The crowd started along the road toward the house where a man recently killed by the Israelis had lived. It glided fast through the dark and kicked up a cloud of dust from the unpaved street. I fell a few yards behind Rantisi. I didn't expect the march to move this fast, and because people stared at me with suspicion and surprise when I popped out of the dusty darkness next to them, I had to be careful not to bump into anyone as I tried to keep up, in case it started trouble. This was not the slow shuffle of demonstrators on the Washington Mall or Trafalgar Square. These men moved randomly and almost at a jog, like commuters dodging through a swarming station concourse, late for their trains. The swelling of the crowd jostled me, and green Islamic banners flapped into my face as the march went faster and the rhythm of the chant of *"Allahu akbar"* picked up pace. Except for Rantisi, eventually killed by the Israelis in April 2004, the crowd was made up of students and men younger than thirty. If they didn't already know that Hamas had the answers to their grievances, then they would feel it in the fervent torrent of youthful energy and brawn and belief that cascaded along the dirt street. These were muscles exercised by Islam and by tribalism and by hate, and Imad Akel, too, felt its power pushing him closer to his decisive moment.

This march was a tributary of a bigger procession that began not long after my great-great-uncles Dai and Dan Beynon left Palestine, leaving their British army colleagues to rule over the land for thirty years. The military wing of Hamas took its name from a Syrian-born, Egyptian-educated cleric, Sheikh Izzedine al-Qassam, who preached jihad in the lower Galilee for a decade until the British killed him in a gunfight in 1935. In a sermon in Haifa, Sheikh al-Qassam said, "You must know that nothing will save us but our arms." Rantisi was reading from the same text.

There was something more to Hamas, however, than defiance. The group built itself as a mirror image of the Palestine Liberation Organization. It often seemed to outsiders that Arafat's PLO was secular, modern, and therefore open to compromise, while Hamas was incorrigibly bloody-minded, living in another century and wanting to regress still further into history to when Islam was new and pure. But Hamas's history showed the contradictory feelings its leaders experienced in building their movement in the shadow of the PLO, unsure of whether to be an independent opposition, to make Israel their target, or to fight the corrupt nationalists of Fatah who seemed to have no place in the highly conservative society of Palestine. They were the same conflicting emotions experienced by Imad Akel, and as I looked closer, I saw into the historic heart of his confusion.

Hamas grew out of the Egyptian Muslim Brotherhood, which founded the Islamic Center, the Mujamma al-Islami, in Gaza in 1973. Its main role was not the fight against Israel, for, as the leaders of the Mujamma saw it, that would be only the second stage of their struggle. Israel's existence was the result of the neglect of true Islam, and only when Palestinians lived according to Islamic law would they be able to defeat Israel. The Islamists saw themselves as a political leadership merely because the PLO was militarily and politically bankrupt. In 1987 they formed the Harakat al-Makawama al-Islamiyyeh, whose acronym, Hamas, means "courage" and "enthusiasm" in Arabic.

The movement didn't set out to crash directly into the PLO. Like most Islamic movements in the Arab world, it started with reformist aims, domestically at least, and resorted to extreme violence only when it was forced underground. A Hamas leaflet released in 1988 described the PLO as its "father" organization: "Can the Muslim be alienated from his father, brother, relative, or friend?" Similarly, the Hamas charter argued against internal strife, but also characterized the extreme hurt that Imad Akel and others like him would experience later: "Oppression by one's next of kin is more painful to the soul than the assault of an Indian sword." By 1993, when its budget was as much as $50 million, Hamas was considering joining the political process as an Islamist party. Israeli agents saw the advantages of a group that would divert support from Arafat and secretly aided Hamas. With Israeli consent, the number of mosques in Gaza rose to more than 200. In 1967, under Egyptian rule, there were seventy-seven.

When Arafat signed the Oslo Accords, Hamas became a little more daring. Before the Palestinian Authority took control of Gaza and Jericho in 1994, Hamas increased its attacks against Israelis. Its leaders knew the Authority would eventually have to crack down; enhancing the status of Hamas now by striking Israel would make it politically tougher for Arafat to act against it later. Much of the time, Arafat had to walk a careful line in his handling of Hamas, trying to convince the sheikhs that his mass arrests were only a show to keep the United States off his back. The Authority also made gestures of solidarity with Hamas that prevented the Islamists from giving up on Arafat completely. In 1995, after Israel used an exploding cellular phone to assassinate Yihye Ayyash, the Hamas bomb maker known as the Engineer, Arafat paid a condolence call to a Hamas leader in Gaza and sent an honor guard of armed policemen to salute Ayyash at his graveside during the funeral. At a rally in the West Bank village of Dura, Arafat lauded "all the martyrs, with Ayyash at their head."

With such actions, Arafat whittled away the trust of Israelis, until his decision to launch the intifada in 2000 truly wiped it out for good. But such was Arafat's duplicity, that by then he had alienated the Islamists too. When the Aqsa intifada began, Hamas and Islamic Jihad stopped trying to pull Fatah away from the clutches of Israel; it was Fatah that ran to join the Islamists in the fight against Israel, for fear of losing out in the competition for battle honors and public support. This flight of his own men had been going on for a couple of years, but Arafat reacted only by alternating between oppression and conciliation. His strategy, in turn, made the situation worse. In Hebron in 1997, Khaled Amayreh, a columnist for the Hamas newspaper *al-Risala,* told me that Fatah people were drifting toward Hamas simply out of the need for a coherent strategy: "Fatah doesn't have an ideology." The town's Fatah chief, Muhammed Ali Takrouri, described the senseless, illogical game Arafat's tactics forced him to play. "If I forbid our people to fight the Israelis, they will go to Hamas," he said. "And if they go to Hamas, they will be against our national project, which is the peace process." Fatah gradually radicalized against the peace process to keep up with Hamas, until it was too late for Arafat to turn back. In early 2003, Ahmed Maher, Egypt's foreign minister, privately warned Arafat to "dissociate yourself from Hamas. We can't support you so long as you are besieged by Hamas." But by that time, Arafat had dealt from two decks for too long. The Israeli cabinet voted in December 2001 to declare Arafat "irrelevant" and, just over a year later, was instrumental in PLO secretary-general Mahmoud Abbas's installation as Palestinian prime minister, taking some of Arafat's powers from him. Though the prime ministerial maneuvers eventually failed, it was clear that no one would be too upset should Arafat pass from the scene.

In his Gaza home, a friend in the Palestinian leadership summed up for me Arafat's mistake. "Peace is a moral value, not a commodity to be traded," he said. "Peace cannot live beside all this corrupt bargaining. Arafat's rule has no stability. It's always crisis management."

Arafat relied on the leaders of Hamas not to turn the crisis into a catastrophe. Mostly they drew back when they sensed themselves on the verge of *fitna*, the civil conflicts that afflicted Muslim society during the reigns of the early caliphs and which were so often disastrous throughout Islamic history.

Imad Akel was a simple man. He hadn't read much history. But he listened to the speeches at the mosque, and he owned a gun.

DID THEY NOT KNOW that there was an intifada underway? These Palestinians who killed his brother, as though they were Israelis. These other Palestinians who urged him to exact immediate vengeance against his own kind, as though he were not preoccupied with the struggle against Israel. Quietly, in one of his hideouts, Imad Akel took a deep breath and held it, to concentrate. When he let the breath out, he said, "In the name of Allah the Merciful, I swear that I will see justice done, but help me that I should not be forced to raise my hand against a Palestinian." It was a promise to himself, to resist the pressure to hit the police. Instead, he would try to make the Authority resolve the mess it created.

Imad Akel was not given to complex thought. Still, he ran through the concepts that a religious Muslim must examine in a moment such as this. On its foundation, Islam continued the older tribal tradition of revenge that existed even before the Prophet's revelations. If harm was done on purpose, a Muslim should apply the ancient law of equal harm: an eye for an eye, known to Arabs as *il-qassas*. Imad Akel thought of the old phrase he had heard quoted by a sheikh in one of the mosques: "To whom shall I go for justice, if you are the judge *and* the criminal?" It seemed to argue in favor of action, to press the case of the old law. But Imad was confused. He recalled how the third caliph, Uthman, refused to fight for his life when other Muslims came to kill him, because he feared causing internal feuds among the first adherents of Islam. Oh, but neither was that conclusive guidance for Imad. After all, the prophet Muhammed, peace be upon him, told Uthman that he would perish one day at the hands of believers, and thus, of course, he had died. There had been no such prophetic message for Yussef Akel, and in any case what kind of Muslim was the man who attacked a crowd of his own people?

There was a name now, a name for the man Imad Akel wanted punished. Within a few days of the killings at the Islamic University, Colonel Rajah Abu Lihyeh went on Palestinian television and boasted that he gave the order to shoot that day. Abu Lihyeh, the head of the Palestinian Authority's riot police unit, was a big, ill-tempered man. He spent most of his days across the side street from his headquarters in Gaza's exclusive Rimal neighborhood, sitting on a chair with a couple of buddies in the shade of a tall sycamore tree. When he was called into action at the university, he had wanted to show the students that he was the boss and they were punks who couldn't mess with him. That was how the Palestinian Authority's police operated everywhere, after all. Policemen who were with Abu Lihyeh during the riot came to Imad Akel to tell him what happened. They knew Imad had announced his intention to avenge his brother, and they feared they would become targets. So they fingered Abu Lihyeh. One of them told Imad that Abu Lihyeh threatened to shoot a couple of policemen who didn't want to fire on the crowd. He jailed a handful of officers who still refused to take part. Abu Lihyeh himself used his pistol to shoot at the demonstrators.

Imad made some phone calls to politicians and contacts in the police force to push for a prosecution of the riot policeman. But, as a fugitive, Imad couldn't break cover to lobby for a trial, so he nominated his cousin, Iyad Akel, to lead the formal battle for legal redress. Iyad, an English teacher at a Nusseirat girls school, took the family's demands to members of the Palestinian Legislative Council. The legislators went to Abu Lihyeh's boss, Police Chief Ghazi Jabali. "Go home," Jabali told them. "It's a closed issue."

A sympathetic Fatah leader tried to calm Imad Akel. "Your brother wasn't the first one to die like this, and he won't be the last," the Fatah man said. "Just try to forget it. Why should it be different for your brother?" The Fatah man was scared of a full-scale war between the Palestinian police and Imad, with all the righteousness and resources of the Hamas military wing behind him. Yet he tried to dissuade Imad from pursuing the matter with the same corrupted fatalism he would have forced down the throats of an average, powerless Palestinian man.

Muhammed Akel pressed his son to act. "You vowed revenge, but you haven't done anything," he told Imad a couple of months after Yussef's death.

"I have to give them a chance to do the right thing," Imad said.

"You gave them a chance. They haven't done anything. It's time to react."

Imad paused. He didn't like to tell his father that there was any other consideration on his mind except the family vengeance they both craved. But he had to admit it. "Father, I'm a commander of Izzedine al-Qassam. I don't want it to be felt that I did this in the name of Hamas. That's why I'm hesitating. I don't want anyone to accuse the Izzedine al-Qassam Brigades of causing a civil war between the Palestinians."

"This family is Hamas. We've given everything to Hamas and we never expected anything back. Not even now," Muhammed Akel said. "But Yussef was not martyred because he was born an Akel. It was because he was Hamas. Let them think what they want. This is who we are. Imad, you are a leader of Hamas and you are qualified to avenge your brother Yussef."

Imad didn't like talking much, and he certainly didn't like to contradict his father. "*Insh'allah*," he said. God willing.

The reports from cousin Iyad were not good. Each political, bureaucratic, and legal avenue he pursued led nowhere. No one even bothered to make empty promises of a resolution. It was over. Forget about it. "It's as if a chicken had been slaughtered, not a man," Iyad told Imad. Iyad was an ally to Imad for the months in which the Hamas leader argued the family should give the judicial system a chance. Slight, cultured, and a little fey, Iyad seemed a sharp contrast to his cousin, the barrel-chested fighter. Imad trusted Iyad, though. Iyad had been tortured in a Palestinian jail for almost two months back when Arafat wanted to arrest Hamas militants. He never ratted on Imad.

It cost Imad dearly to restrain himself. The police should pay more respect to a man like me, he thought, who sacrificed his freedom of movement and ran the risk of death for a decade to fight the Israelis. One night, Imad was pacing his hideout. He felt that the Authority was ignoring his military skills, as though he would never follow through on his vow. It hurt his professional pride. He turned to Iyad. "Do they think I can't do this?" he said.

It was clear to Imad that Abu Lihyeh wasn't even trying to keep a low profile. When Imad drove through Rimal, Abu Lihyeh was still there, in the shade of the sycamore on Victor Hugo Street, next to the French Cultural Center. Imad thought that if time ran out for his legal campaign, it would be easy to hit Abu Lihyeh right here, a drive-by shooting. But even before his car made the end of the block, Imad decided such a quick strike would be wrong. He wanted to make Abu Lihyeh confess. If he wouldn't be forced to do so in a court of law, then Imad would make him admit what he had done in front of the people of Nusseirat. He would abduct him to the camp.

Abu Lihyeh must have known about Iyad's legal lobbying. To scare him off, he visited one of the Akels' relatives and said he would arrest the whole family after the intifada. Implicitly Abu Lihyeh made the link between Hamas and the Akels: he couldn't arrest Imad or his family now, not while Hamas had free rein to run its military operations out of Gaza, for the sake of the intifada. Abu Lihyeh knew that Police Chief Jabali, and undoubtedly Arafat too, would rather sacrifice the riot-police commander than go up against Hamas now. But when the intifada was over, there would be a reckoning with Hamas and the Akel family. "I'll bring the Akels one by one to prison," Abu Lihyeh said.

THE AGENT SAT nervously forward on the edge of the couch. His four-year-old son squirmed between his legs until he let him run outside to play in the stony yard. He stroked his thin mustache and brushed cigarette ash from his shirt as he lit another Marlboro. A polyester maze of topaz and navy, the shirt hung loose over his skinny frame. Suheil, whose second name I shan't disclose in order to protect his identity, was the top Hamas-catcher in the Palestinian Authority. But since the Aqsa intifada began, he had little to do, sitting idly as he did now, rumpling his son's hair each time the boy brought a brightly colored stone from the rubble in the yard to present to his father.

Early in the intifada, Suheil learned through his network of informers inside Hamas that a cell was planning an operation. The Hamas group intended to sneak through the fence that surrounds the Gaza Strip and attack Israeli soldiers at a bus stop. Suheil informed his boss in the Palestinian General Intelligence service. "Forget it," his boss told him.

"What do you mean?" Suheil asked.

"You heard what I said."

Suheil was outraged. He knew exactly what his boss meant. Before the intifada, his job was to arrest Hamas people because they threatened the peace process and, thus, could hit at the credibility of Arafat's Authority. Now there was no need to rein in the terrorists, because Arafat had made a decision to pressure the Israelis through violence. No matter that the intifada would soon run out of Arafat's control, or that Hamas would be the big winners in all this—that was the order, and officers like Suheil had to suck it up. Suheil had invested years of energy and diligence in his informer network and had committed himself to working for the peace process. He went out and arrested the Hamas cell anyway. Three months after the start of the intifada, Suheil brought in his suspects. He caught them in possession of belts and explosives to be used for suicide bombings. The Hamas men did not deny the accusation. But Suheil's boss was not going to let the evidence stand in the way of his orders. He released the Hamas men and suspended Suheil from duty.

The frustrated agent tried to get through to Amin al-Hindi, the head of the General Intelligence service in Gaza. But Suheil soon realized he had been frozen out. Only when he quieted down was he allowed back into a desk job with no connection to his old duties. Even so, it killed him to see the men he should have been arresting instead attaining hero status in the intifada.

One such man was Adnan al-Ghoul. Suheil watched al-Ghoul's operation grow; he even kept tabs on him during his suspension from work. Al-Ghoul began his career as a Hamas activist in Gaza. When Israeli prime minister Yitzhak Rabin misguidedly deported Hamas activists to Lebanon in 1992, al-Ghoul was one of many who took up with Hizballah operatives there. Hizballah and their Iranian Revolutionary Guard advisers trained him at bases in the Bekaa Valley. Within sight of the ancient Roman Temple of Jupiter in Baalbek, al-Ghoul plotted his role in the destruction of Israel, which he considered to have been implanted in the Middle East by European invaders, just as the columns and stylobate of the temple had been.

In 1996 al-Ghoul returned to Gaza on a false passport. At the start of the Aqsa intifada, he set up a bomb-making factory in Gaza City. His price list: $50 for a Mills bomb, the traditional pineapple-shaped hand grenade; $1,000 for a massive 50-kilogram bomb of TNT; and $3,000 for a special remote-controlled bomb that could be detonated as a roadside charge, technology specific to Hizballah. Al-Ghoul had no shortage of customers. His client list showed just how much the lines blurred between those who had signed on to the peace process and those who had always rejected and undermined it. Suheil watched as al-Ghoul sold his deadly merchandise to Hamas, to the Fatah Tanzim gunmen of the Aqsa Martyrs Brigades, and to the Preventive Security Service run by Arafat's Gaza sidekick Muhammed Dahlan and his deputy Rashid Abu Shoubak.

The Palestinian Authority vaporized as a force against violence. It entered into a competition with the terror groups, as soon as the intifada got out of Arafat's control. After about three months of intifada, the demonstrations at Israeli checkpoints more or less stopped. It became a shooting war and a suicide bomber's battle. When Israeli soldiers arrested the West Bank Fatah leader Marwan Barghouti, he told interrogators Israel should be grateful to him. He had saved the intifada from falling entirely under the control of Hamas by giving Fatah people a violent outlet. Arafat's men still thought they were moderates.

AT 1 A.M., Jabalya was haunted. Lit pale moon blue, its sandstone and cinder-block buildings were dark, as though the people had been extinguished with the supply of electricity. I went out into the eerie streets to find the ghosts, the men awaiting death, standing sentry over the sandy lanes where Israeli tanks would enter the refugee camp someday soon. At each corner, as I rolled slowly through the camp with Azmy Keshawi, a Gazan journalist, the gunmen emerged like ninja phantasms, darkly dressed, their faces obscured by stocking caps with eyeholes clipped out. On the edge of the camp that we first explored, the gunmen were dangerous and suspicious. Posted to stand alone, they were twitchy when we stopped, stiffening and still when our headlights caught them. They wore a green strip of cloth tied around their heads. Written in white along the headband: Izzedine al-Qassam Brigades. They were Hamas.

Abu Mujahid, as one of the Hamas men called himself, slurred his words to disguise his voice as we talked. He never lifted his finger from the trigger of his Karl Gustav submachine gun. "Our goal is jihad for the sake of Allah," he mumbled. It was as if Azmy were not there. Abu Mujahid kept his suspicious eyes firmly on me as they gleamed out of the holes cut in the black sack over his head. He moved them from this inquisitive foreigner with the notebook only to glance occasionally, nervously, toward the ridge 100 yards beyond the camp boundary. From there, the Israeli tanks and armored personnel carriers had come a month before. It was the second year of the intifada. Abu Mujahid's job was to be the sacrifice, to fire on the Israelis and alert the other fighters to the onset of invasion with the raucousness of his death. It could have come any moment as we stood there. I imagined him, after we left, isolated again, straining to hear the distant sound of a tank engine revving in the Israeli settlements a third of a mile from the camp. I couldn't but think of the medieval order of Assassins, the *hashashin* cult of the Ismailis that terrified Middle Eastern sultans and Crusaders alike with their eagerness for death and absolute obedience to their leader, the Old Man of the Mountain. Those men had been thought stoned on hashish, from which the word "assassin" is derived, because surely something must have skewed the mind of a man who would so readily surrender his life. For Abu Mujahid, his religion was the drug. Each night, before coming to his post, this thirty-three-year-old would perform an additional pair of *rakahs,* bowing, praying, and prostrating himself twice more than the customary three *rakahs* of Maghrib, the sunset prayer. It readied him, he said, for the end.

There were no officers of the Palestinian Authority here, no patrols watching for Israeli incursions. It was left to Abu Mujahid or, further along the camp perimeter, to gunmen of the Aqsa Martyrs Brigades to police what was effectively the front line in the intifada. Each of the gunmen I met that night spoke of defending their personal honor. They knew that they would die if they faced the Israelis, but they had reached a point of humiliation beyond which they would not let the Israelis push them—even if it was a Merkava tank doing the shoving. To resist was to preserve your sense of self, even if your body should be destroyed in that act. Arafat was not a party to that recapturing of pride. He had his chance to lead it, but he made shady deals and nasty compromises instead. In turn, that drove his people to hate what they and their society had become so much that they were ready to pull it down about them in a cataclysmic act of self-assertion. From under the rubble of Arafat's Palestine, these gunmen were climbing as new men, doomed but reborn.

The streets of Jabalya were carved into a slalom by massive sand-banks, to slow any car that drove through so the watching gunmen could hit them. Beneath the sand, there were bombs of up to 200 pounds, a trusted friend who holds a senior position in the Palestinian police told me. By day, I watched as little children slid and played in these explosive sandboxes. At night, the living dead rested on them until they saw Azmy and me approach in his little gold Daihatsu. Azmy cut the lights and leaned out the window as the three gunmen roused themselves stealthily from the sand. Two covered us with leveled Kalashnikovs as a third came to the window. "Greetings, lads," Azmy said chirpily, diving into his explanation of who we were. The important thing was to make it obvious that we weren't an undercover Israeli unit, come to arrest or assassinate someone in the camp. These three wore the same masks as Abu Mujahid, but the strip around their brows was white with black writing: *Kataib Shuhada' al-Aqsa*. The Aqsa Martyrs Brigades.

Abu al-Fahed, who came to the car to check us, took us to the cover of a storefront awning behind the fifteen-foot-high sandbank. Over his shoulder, the other two shifted their feet and their weapons nervously and stared into the dark, north toward the Israeli positions. The tension was so unbearably thick that I almost wished the Israelis would come now and have done with it, would give these men a release from this hopeless torment. "I'm prepared for martyrdom,"

Abu al-Fahed said. "The Israelis kill us Palestinians anyway, so I may as well resist. My dignity and honor is at stake."

A pair of headlights swung into the road out beyond the scrubland that led from the Israeli settlements. The three gunmen watched them come. It occurred to me that if this car carried an Israeli hit squad and if it were to be uncovered by the Martyrs Brigades men, the Israelis would surely kill these three and probably gun down Azmy and me, too, in the shadows where we stood. An old white Renault stopped where the gunmen waved it down. From the driver's accent, they heard that he was Palestinian, and they let him pass. The air was thick with dust from his tires and the pulsating adrenaline that came with the knowledge that, though this incident had passed easily, we remained still a ten-minute tank ride from certain death. That proximity to the end was instructive, and the lesson the gunmen drew— whether Islamists of Hamas or relatively secular Fatah activists who joined the Aqsa Martyrs Brigades—was the same: you will soon go to Allah, so ready yourself for him. "The lads who didn't used to pray found a connection to God now," Abu al-Fahed said. These men, who had been Arafat's soldiers and who still received payment from him through local Fatah chiefs, had become little different from the Hamas *hashashin* down the street, thanks to Arafat's inability to offer them an alternative path that was not also a crooked one.

As I drove slowly back to my hotel through the orange streetlights of the Zeitoun neighborhood, I glided past other ghostly groups of twitchy Hamas and Martyrs Brigades gunmen, masked, dressed in black, and seated on the edges of plastic garden chairs at the roadside. They wore their green or white headbands, but they were otherwise indistinguishable. The people who owed allegiance to Arafat and those who opposed him followed the same path of belligerence in their way of facing the Israelis. It struck me that the difference lay rather in the way they would respond to other Palestinians. The Palestinian Authority's only remaining function was the oppression of its own people.

IN NUSSEIRAT, the local Fatah leaders understood the precipitous decline in the Authority's power, as a result of its refusal to participate officially in the battle against Israel. Hamas fought hard against Israel in Gaza, attacking settlements and military positions, shooting its

Qassam II rockets over the fence into the Israeli town of Sderot. These local Fatah men knew they couldn't go up against Hamas, and as the months passed, they sensed that Imad Akel was running out of patience. One of them tried to persuade Police Chief Jabali to transfer Abu Lihyeh, the riot policeman, to the West Bank. "Just show that you did *something*. So the Akels will see that you didn't simply ignore the problem." Jabali did nothing.

A friend of Imad Akel who worked as a policeman came to him. He had been nearby as Abu Lihyeh held court on Victor Hugo Street beneath his sycamore. "Abu Lihyeh brags that he killed Yussef and that he's so tough even Imad Akel doesn't touch him," the friend said. Imad was enraged. It came at a time when Imad's father was pressing him harder than ever to end the waiting.

Imad started on his plan.

For three months, Imad Akel had Abu Lihyeh's home watched, while he remained in hiding in Gaza City. The Palestinian police were after Imad now, as well as the Israelis. His contacts in the police force told Imad that Chief Jabali had ordered his apprehension, dead or alive. The order made him angry, but Imad Akel noticed, too, that its severity didn't surprise him, as it would have done a year earlier. Imad sent people from his family to watch Abu Lihyeh's home in the Zahra Towers complex between Nusseirat and the Israeli settlement at Netzarim. Some of Abu Lihyeh's bodyguards were from Nusseirat. They recognized the Akel watchers and warned Abu Lihyeh. For a time, the riot-police chief was careful. He traveled with two escort cars full of bodyguards. Imad ruled out a roadside bomb, because he didn't want any more of his people's blood on his conscience than he felt absolutely forced to spill. If he had to take the life of this one Palestinian, he wouldn't do anything that would hurt the bodyguards, and certainly not bystanders. Then Imad learned from his surveillance team that Abu Lihyeh's white 1998 Hyundai van, with its blacked-out windows, had been used to ferry the policeman's daughters to school. Imad thanked Allah for restraining his hand or he would have bombed the van and killed the little girls by mistake.

The anniversary of Yussef Akel's death approached. Muhammed Akel asked his son if he was planning a hit on Abu Lihyeh for the same date as the demonstration in which Yussef died. "Just wait," Imad told his father. "Soon you will see something that will make you happy."

Abu Lihyeh noticed the anniversary approaching too. With his guards still spotting members of the Akel clan near the Zahra Towers, Abu Lihyeh suspected Imad Akel might be planning a fatal symmetry—an attack on the date of Yussef Akel's death. He moved his family home farther from Nusseirat, thinking he was leaving the Akels behind. Abu Lihyeh took an apartment in Gaza's Karameh neighborhood, but Imad Akel's hideout was in Gaza City, not Nusseirat. By fleeing, Abu Lihyeh had walked right toward the danger.

The watchers brought the news of Abu Lihyeh's move to Imad Akel. "Thanks be to Allah, Master of the Universe. He came to my playground," Imad said. Now Imad Akel sent the amateur watchers home. The surveillance became his personal task. Abu Lihyeh felt safer, because he had no more reports from his bodyguards of Nusseirat people tailing him. In fact, the danger had risen: the man watching his movements now was an expert operational commander. Abu Lihyeh canceled the extra contingent of guards. He settled into a routine. A driver took his daughters to school at 7.30 A.M. Two hours later Abu Lihyeh would come out of his building, walk five yards to his car, and get in. There were now only four bodyguards.

It was time to train the team. Imad Akel stood at the center of a group of eight of his relatives in a warehouse in Gaza City. He looked them over. None had ever participated in military activity. Imad didn't know how they would stand up to the hasty training or how they would react in the moments of danger they were sure to face. But that had been his choice. He hadn't asked his Izzedine al-Qassam colleagues to join him because, despite what his father said, Imad still wanted to keep Hamas out of this. Perhaps it was better this way, anyhow, he thought. All of these men desired desperately to act with honor for the sake of their family, and to make their notorious cousin Imad proud of them. Two of them had sold their wives' gold jewelry to buy Kalashnikovs.

Imad told the men that they would be disguised as Palestinian soldiers during the operation. He began by teaching them how to stand up straight, how to look like soldiers. He taught them to breathe deeply to reduce the stress and adrenaline that would hit them right before the action. He could see their nerves, even in the dark warehouse. "Relax. It'll only take a couple of minutes to finish the job," Imad said, smiling. "So don't worry."

In the center of the warehouse, there was a white Hyundai van, like Abu Lihyeh's. They rehearsed the kidnap with it. Imad watched the clumsy, nervous movements of his cousins. An army special unit would take weeks to hone an operation like this. Well, they were going to do it in two days. "When do we go?" they began to ask. Imad brought in a few other relatives and made the team rehearse with the new men acting the roles of Abu Lihyeh and his bodyguards. They hesitated when the men playing the guards pretended to struggle. "If we get to zero hour and the bodyguards react, shoot them in the legs if you have to," Imad said. They drilled again. It was smooth. "We go tomorrow morning."

Just after 9:30 A.M. on October 7, 2002, one day short of the first anniversary of the Islamic University demonstration, Imad Akel and his team jumped out of their cars on the road that led from Karameh toward central Gaza. They wore the light-brown camouflage fatigues and red berets of the Military Intelligence, which was not really an intelligence service but simply acted as another of Arafat's dueling militias. Two of the group waited in the cars as the rest fanned out, as if setting up an impromptu checkpoint. No one would have found it unusual. The Palestinian police set up their roadblocks all over town, sometimes seeking Hamas fugitives, or undercover Israelis, or just for the sake of something to do. The Akel team made a show of checking passing cars for two minutes. Imad noticed Abu Lihyeh's Hyundai van coming. He signaled the driver of his own car, who pulled up to the checkpoint. Imad leaned in to the driver, as if he were checking identity cards. The Hyundai stopped right behind. As they planned, the other Akel car moved up and closed the Hyundai in.

Imad paced toward the Hyundai. Palestinian policemen don't hurry when they set up real checkpoints, so keep it smooth, even a bit lazy, he told himself. He looked around at his cousins. He wondered if they were too jumpy. He had told them not to shoot from a distance, even if it meant allowing Abu Lihyeh to escape. He didn't want a gun battle on the road here. Imad Akel slid open the big side door of the Hyundai. That was the signal for the others to take up their positions. There was Abu Lihyeh, just as Imad had seen him from his car, reclining under the sycamore on Victor Hugo Street. Close enough to touch.

"I'm Colonel Abu Lihyeh," he said.

Imad saw there was a bodyguard missing. Usually Abu Lihyeh had a guard on either side of him. Today there was only one guard in the back, on the near side, and two in the front. Imad sized up the interior of the van.

"Listen, it's okay," the officer said, impatiently this time. "I'm Colonel Abu Lihyeh."

Imad turned to face him. "I know. You're the one we're looking for."

As Imad jumped inside, the rest of his team yanked open the doors and pulled the bodyguards out. They bundled them into their other two cars. Imad trained his gun on Abu Lihyeh. He noticed that a couple of officers in the police compound down the road saw what was going on. But the Hyundai was unmarked and Abu Lihyeh wore civilian clothing, so the police must have assumed Palestinian Authority soldiers were arresting somebody. They didn't react. The van and the two cars sped off down Third Street through the Ebad al-Rahman housing project.

Imad wanted Abu Lihyeh to think he had been arrested. That way, the man might get nervous, but he wouldn't fear for his safety, yet. He wouldn't make trouble for them. Imad wanted to take him alive all the way back to Nusseirat, and with such a big man it would be easier to accomplish that without him fighting for his life. Sitting beside him, Imad noticed that Abu Lihyeh was over six feet tall.

"What are you doing?" Abu Lihyeh said. "Why are you arresting me? I'm Colonel Rajah Abu Lihyeh."

Then the cousin driving the van made a mistake. "You're the one that killed Yussef at the Islamic University. Yussef Akel."

Imad Akel met Abu Lihyeh's suddenly wide stare. Imad was furious. He saw shock and terror and cunning in this man's eyes and he began to calculate how the officer might try to escape. Because now Abu Lihyeh surely guessed that this man sitting on his right was Imad Akel and that he intended to kill his brother's murderer. As they approached the end of Third Street, Imad sized up the situation inside the van. He sat on Abu Lihyeh's right, between him and the door. He had two guys up front, and another on Abu Lihyeh's left. Then Imad saw it: there was a second sliding door on the other side. The van they practiced on had only one back door and Imad had taken it upon himself to cover it, as the most likely line of escape for Abu Lihyeh. This Hyundai had an extra door.

In that instant, the van turned the corner onto Jalaa Street. This end of Jalaa was a junction of four roads, feeding into the six-lane thoroughfare across Sheikh Radwan and toward the center of town. There was a police post here with armed officers on two corners, round the clock. Imad was about to tell the cousin on the other side of Abu Lihyeh to watch the second door, when the hostage made his move. As the van slowed to take the corner, Abu Lihyeh threw himself toward the door. Spinning, he shoved it open and slid it back with his right hand, grabbed the Akel cousin who sat on his left, and tumbled out into the dirty street.

Abu Lihyeh held on to the cousin for cover and yelled out, "Police, police." The men on the corners looked over. They saw only a Military Intelligence officer wrestling with a big man in civilian clothes. Again, policemen misinterpreted what they saw and didn't react. But Imad Akel did. He leaned out of the open door and aimed at the tall man struggling beneath his cousin. Imad shot five bullets into Abu Lihyeh, then paused. "Get in," he called. His cousin leaped past him into the van. Imad Akel put ten more rounds into Abu Lihyeh. The policemen on the corners started to move now. The van took three rounds from the police as it screamed off up Jalaa Street.

The police came after the Akels in a turquoise jeep. The Hyundai dodged through the traffic at high speed. Imad looked back at the jeep for a moment. When he turned to watch the road, he held his breath: a Caterpillar digger was pulling out from a side road and trundling across Jalaa Street. The Hyundai swerved, nearly tipped. Inside, the cousins called out in fear. They were past the Caterpillar. But the police jeep slammed into the digger. Later Imad Akel found out that six policemen had been hurt in the collision. The police arrested the driver of the digger and beat him, believing he must have been part of the hit. But Imad Akel knew that Allah was protecting him.

Now the driving was calmer. The mood in the van, though, was quiet and dark. The cousins were glad they had killed Abu Lihyeh, but they sensed Imad was angry, sad. This hadn't been the way he planned it. The previous night he had again pictured himself standing on top of Abu Lihyeh's Hyundai in the center of Nusseirat with the colonel on his knees before him and two cousins at his side holding portraits of Yussef. He had fantasized that he would put a bullet through Abu Lihyeh's head in front of all the residents of the camp. Bouncing in the backseat of the van, he calmed himself and whispered a prayer, thanking Allah that it had ended the way it had, anyway.

At the junction of Jalaa and Third Streets, where Abu Lihyeh met his end, there is a chronicle written in the dust and concrete and heat about the different ways for Palestinians to die. As I stood in the simmering afternoon sun on the spot where Imad Akel killed Abu Lihyeh, a middle-aged woman in a long blue robe, with a white *mendil* covering her head, came out of a terrace of rough homes to tell me about her son. He was a suicide bomber who was sent on his mission by Islamic Jihad. Imad Kulab blew himself up on a bus at the French Hill Junction in northern Jerusalem; I remembered hearing the sirens of the ambulances racing to that one while I was drinking lemonade on a day of blazing heat in the courtyard of an old hotel in East Jerusalem. A romanticized portrait of the bearded youth backed by the golden Dome of the Rock and staring heroically into the distance stood thirty feet tall at the edge of the junction. Up Jalaa only twice the length of the martyr's picture, in late 2002, an Israeli missile hit the car of Muhammed Deif, the head of Izzedine al-Qassam, killing his bodyguards and seriously wounding Deif.

There were four Palestinian policemen at the junction. Two, slim and inattentive, stood over by Kulab's home, smoking cigarettes. The other two sat in the shade of a pile of cinder blocks that someone had dumped there until they had enough money to complete another scraggy story on their rotten home.

In a place where there is national conflict, quietus will concentrate in one spot like this: Abu Lihyeh, Deif's bodyguards, the martyr Kulab's poster. There is so much death and Gaza is too small for it to be spread out. But I knew that if I waited around too long, the lazy policemen would feel compelled to question me. They understood that I was surely here to examine the end of Abu Lihyeh, because the other victims of this intersection died in ways by now too horribly commonplace to attract a foreigner's attention. Deif's men or Kulab, these were one thing—a matter of Israeli aggression, of us versus them. But Abu Lihyeh, his extinction was off limits, because it touched upon the weakness at the heart of Palestinian political and social life. After a while, one of the policemen stood up, slung his

Kalashnikov over his shoulder, and shambled toward me. I gave a friendly wave and got into my car. I drove back to Nusseirat.

IMAD AKEL leaned out the window of Abu Lihyeh's Hyundai as his hit squad reached the edge of Nusseirat. The driver sounded the horn elatedly, and in between the blasts, Imad called to the people at the roadside, "Everybody, go to the center of the camp. I killed the guy that got Yussef." Young men and children began to stream after the van. At first, Imad Akel felt the release he had sought and believed the chasing youths were filled almost with a party atmosphere. He didn't yet recognize the darkness in the chants of *"Allahu akbar"* audible to him between the honking horn of the Hyundai and his own shouts.

When the van reached the marketplace, Imad Akel gave one brief look at the looming graveyard hillock where Yussef lay. Then he lifted himself up on top of the Hyundai, and just as he had called out to the camp at Yussef's funeral, he declared the fulfillment of the oath he made before them at that time. "I am Imad Akel. I took revenge, me and all the Akel family, on Abu Lihyeh. He killed our brother and we killed him."

Imad saw his parents coming through the crowd and jumped down from the Hyundai. The crowd swelled and pressed around him. He looked back at Abu Lihyeh's van and thanked Allah that he had not carried out his plan to bring the policeman alive to Nusseirat. The people smashed the vehicle and, almost in an instant, set it alight. If Abu Lihyeh had been in his hands, it would have been all Imad Akel could have done to carry out the execution in a dignified way. Certainly, he thought, once it was finished, the people would have mutilated and burned the body. He understood then that, though he acted in the name of his family to avenge the shooting of Yussef, the people felt he had operated somehow in the name of all Palestinians like them who suffered under the corruption and injustice of the Palestinian Authority. The flames licked the Hyundai even as Imad Akel reached his parents. He kissed his mother. "I got the guy responsible for Yussef's killing," he told her. Aisha began to cry.

Muhammed Akel kissed his son. "Allah will bless your hands," he told Imad. "I'm pleased by this. It will teach a lesson to the Authority." Imad saw that his father was proud of the justice he had achieved.

The Akels were carried to their house on a rolling press of bodies. Everywhere the people threw their fists in the air in unison as they chanted the name of Imad. When they reached the house, Muhammed told Aisha that now they could open a mourning tent for Yussef, because his death had been avenged. "Justice has been done," he said to her. Now their lament could be for their lost son, rather than for a wrong that remained to be righted.

Thousands of people crowded the street outside. Imad knew the Authority would send its policemen into the camp, either to arrest him or simply to clear the crowds that celebrated the death of one of their officers. Before he slipped away, Imad asked Muhammed Akel to send the people home to avoid trouble. It took some time, but once Imad was gone and the Hyundai stopped burning, people dispersed.

The police did come, but not in great numbers, initially. They found the Akels in their mourning tent, a black tarpaulin in front of Muhammed's house with lines of white and purple plastic garden chairs to accept mourners on that first evening. As Imad predicted, the police could not allow this affront to their authority to go unpunished. They had come for him. Several officers sat with thimbles of bitter cardamom-flavored coffee passed around by one of Imad's nephews. The senior policemen knew that there would be trouble in Nusseirat if they acted with force, so they tried a soft approach.

"What would you think if we gave Imad a fair trial for killing Abu Lihyeh?" one of them offered.

Imad's cousin Iyad, who led the family's fruitless negotiations with the Authority throughout the year, was amused by the suggestion. It had been proposed in a rising tone, as though the policeman were improvising some kind of novel new idea: a fair trial, hmmm, we hadn't thought of that? Iyad spoke up. "We appealed to you to apply justice. If you had applied the law from the very beginning, nothing would have happened this way."

"Well, then what do you want?"

Iyad held his arms out wide. "Start from the beginning. When you tell us who killed Yussef, Imad will come in for the killing of Abu Lihyeh. Yussef was killed a year ago. Where have you been since then?"

Iyad used the identical argument that same evening when the police asked some local members of the Palestinian Legislative Council to mediate for them. The councilors pressed Iyad: he was asking too much, and it would be better just to see that Imad had a fair trial. "Do you want to change the whole country?" one of them asked Iyad.

"Just apply the law," Iyad said. "Why is it that powerful people get away with everything, but you come to the weakest people to apply the law to them?" The councilors had no answer. Iyad laughed scornfully as they tried to excuse themselves. "You have no authority. You're a kind of decorative democracy."

As they left, one of the councilors turned to Iyad. "You understand that the Hamas leadership distanced itself from this killing. If this was simply an Akel family vendetta, the Authority will come after all of you, unless Imad turns himself in."

Iyad went to Imad Akel that night. Imad had kept the operation in the family, because he didn't want Hamas dragged into a major civil war with the Authority. But Iyad understood that Hamas was the family's only protection. If Imad were merely Imad, one tough man with none of the backing he had from the Izzedine al-Qassam Brigades, the Palestinian Authority could wipe out the Akels. It was Hamas that protected them and Imad at least ought to have shaded the distinction between the family and the Islamic Resistance Movement. "Why, Imad? You could have hit Abu Lihyeh without using all these family members," Iyad said.

Imad nodded. Now he understood how the family might be made to pay the price of his revenge attack. "I wanted all the people to know why this man was killed. I wanted it to be clear that it's me, Imad Akel, who killed him, for the death of Yussef. Not the Hamas military wing responding to the attack on the Hamas student protest."

It was clear to the two cousins that in Arafat's Palestine, it was somehow a mistake to act with clarity and righteousness. But Imad Akel couldn't help himself. He called Police Chief Ghazi Jabali. "We took our rights," Imad said. "I have no objection to turning myself in, but first apply the law and justice to those who killed before I did."

Jabali hung up on him.

The police chief's answer came that night in Nusseirat. His officers opened fire on the edge of the camp. Thousands of Palestinian Authority security personnel arrived in Nusseirat at 1 A.M., heading for the Akel home. The people of the camp came into the street and the Authority troops found themselves on the end of a riot more severe than anything the Israelis ever faced in Nusseirat. Imad's father, Muhammed, and all his male relatives had gone into hiding deep inside the camp six hours before. In the end, they would stay there until the conclusion of the holy month of Ramadan, when the heat appeared to be off. But that night anger burned hard against the Authority. The police fought in Nusseirat, and in the nearby Bureij camp, and in Gaza City's poor neighborhoods. The people torched the police stations in the refugee camps, but the Authority killed another three Nusseirat residents. Two more died in Gaza and another in Bureij. The Authority tried to enforce a curfew on Nusseirat. The soldiers drove around the camp with a loudspeaker telling people to stay in their homes, training their weapons on anyone who stuck his head out a window, just as the Israelis used to do before Arafat came. Imad Akel knew that it was not out of love for Abu Lihyeh that the police continued this killing. Unlike the men of Hamas, who formed a brotherhood whose bond was the belief in Allah and in the holiness of their cause and of their deaths, the Authority's military men trusted each other little. There had been too many small wars and assassinations between them over the decades of Arafat's duplicitous leadership for it to be otherwise. But they knew that when one of them died at the hands of an outsider, they must all draw together. They could unite against nothing, except a threat to their ability to frighten and coerce others for their own gain. They put on a show at Abu Lihyeh's funeral intended to intimidate the Akels, Hamas, and the rioters. On October 10, 2002, a procession of 20,000 Palestinian policemen marched Abu Lihyeh to his final rest. Fatah blamed Hamas for the attack, despite Imad Akel's claim that it was family vengeance. The policemen carried a banner that said All Factions Must Respect the Palestinian Authority, the Only Legitimate Authority. Arafat's chief plainclothes cop, Muhammed Dahlan, said Imad Akel "openly challenged the Palestinian Authority." Dahlan called the need to punish Imad Akel a "life-and-death question for us."

The violence lasted a few days, before the police began to back off. They saw that the entire population of Nusseirat protected the Akels. Imad Akel called Samir Mashrawi, a senior member of Preventive

Security, Arafat's detective force. He warned him not to come after the Akels. "Next time, I won't wait a whole year like I did this time," he said. "Any attempt to arrest or hurt my people will be answered the way I answered Abu Lihyeh." Soon Imad heard from his contacts in the security forces that Jabali received word from Authority political leaders not to cause any more riots through big operations in the camps. But there were orders, too, to arrest or kill Imad Akel at the first opportunity.

It was not over. Imad Akel saw that much. In his hideout, just as he had brooded about the timing of his hit on Abu Lihyeh, now he considered that after all these years of fighting Israelis, he had pulled the trigger on a Palestinian. He didn't feel good about it. "But what could I do?" he told himself again and again as he paced his room. "If I hadn't reacted, they'd be able to attack the weak people, those who have no influence over the Authority, whenever they wanted. I didn't do it without warning. If only they applied the law. They have to know that there are limits to their abuses. They have to know when to stop." But whatever he told himself, he had broken something deep within him. Now it was as if the men of the Authority were drawn from a different race, not from among his Palestinian brothers. If they pushed him, he would strike them, just as readily as if they had been Israelis. He sent a message to Jabali and to a political leader he heard wanted him brought in: "You're next, if you don't watch out." For Imad Akel, that was the fretful price of the revenge he wreaked.

Imad's cousin Iyad Akel paid too. While Imad planned the operation and pulled the trigger, the wrath of the Authority now fell on the schoolteacher who had been the family's main public voice of protest. Iyad was teaching an English class in Nusseirat's girls school, when plainclothes detectives came into the schoolyard. A young female teacher asked them their business, though she had already guessed it.

"We're looking for Iyad Akel."

"I don't think he's here, but I'll get the principal for you," the teacher said. She sent the principal to deal with the officers and then found Iyad, who ran to the third floor.

The principal came out to the detectives, who loitered near the entrance of the building and in the yard. She wanted to buy time for

Iyad to escape, maybe even turn the detectives away. "Have you got a warrant for Iyad?"

One of the policemen said, "No, but we know he's here."

"If there's no warrant, then please go away until you have something official."

Iyad looked out of the third-floor window. The principal impressed him, a woman standing alone before these thugs. But the police noticed him in the window above them and raced up the stairs. Iyad dodged into a classroom. He knew what would happen if they arrested him. The Palestinian Authority had jailed him for fifty days in 1998. For much of the time, he was held in solitary confinement. No one ever told him the accusations against him. He spent the twenty days before Ramadan and all of the holy month in a cell. Even after his release, he was refused a permit to travel to Australia to study for a master's degree, as he had planned.

Iyad thought of the wasted years in Nusseirat that should have been spent in the free, intellectual environment of an Australian university campus. He thought of the desperate, damaged future that lay ahead of him, whether he was arrested or not. But he knew, as he lifted himself onto the window ledge, that he wouldn't let them take him. He still held two English textbooks in his hands and his notebook with preparatory work for his lessons. He hesitated to drop them, because he loved books and books were rare in the camp. Down below, there was no clear spot on which he could land. A wall ran along the middle of the alley, and there were piles of trash on either side of it. He was no Imad Akel, no tough guy. But when the detectives came into the room behind him, Iyad Akel threw his books onto a desk and jumped out the window. He landed on top of the wall and fell off it. He felt a sharp pain as his ankle twisted and a rough blow to his back from something hard in the garbage on the floor. He ran away down the alley, crying out with each footfall of the injured leg.

Iyad Akel felt he had crossed a point that a man like him, a student of English who loves literature and his family, should never have had to pass. He knew that the detectives chasing him were Palestinian, not Israeli. But he couldn't quite let himself believe it. As he ran away from them down the alley, they shouted from the third-floor window. Their Arabic had the accent of Gaza, just like his—a hard *g* sound where West Bankers made a soft *j*. How can those voices be pursuing me? Iyad thought. He recalled how Imad first fled the Israelis ten years ago, jumping into an alley just like this one behind his father's house. But Imad Akel ran from the Israelis with defiance and the cry *"Allahu akbar."* Now, Iyad ran, too, but the pain in his leg and his back and the shouts of the Palestinian detectives and the tears of humiliation became one agonizing utterance that rolled like a death chant through his spinning head. "I am running through hell," he said to himself. "I am running through hell."

HELL HAS MANY CIRCLES. They all vector through the rotten slums still known by the misnomer "refugee camp." Palestinians like Iyad Akel, fleeing the Preventive Security detectives down the garbage-strewn alley, felt the heat of the inferno immediately surrounding them. Hamas warmed itself at the fire and piped the blaze into a violence that immolated hundreds of Israelis. Arafat controlled the flames even as he stoked them, until in the end a backdraft scalded him too. Nusseirat, Balata, Dehaisha: these are the camps where Palestinians lived in the greatest extremity, the places where they soon saw the hopeful incandescence of the Oslo peace process flare out. The fire blazing in the vacuum that replaced it consumed the Israeli peace movement, Washington's doves, and the corrupt centralism of Arafat's regime. The ashes that remained belonged to Hamas.

In Jabalya, one of the most broken-down of those "refugee camp" slums in the Gaza Strip, Shadi Sakaneh ran a barbershop and a craft workshop in the ground-floor garage of his family's narrow, four-story rowhouse. It was a satisfactory business for an eighteen-year-old, but in any case Sakaneh spent much of his time across the unpaved street in the local mosque. In his workshop he used to turn his hand to the kinds of *objets d'art* that appealed to his religious fervor and concomitant politics. Shadi carved a replica of the Dome of the Rock out of a hunk of cherrywood. He whittled rifles from old planks for the neighborhood boys. One day in January 2001, a customer in the barbershop noticed the kind of belt used by suicide bombers to strap ten to fifteen kilograms of explosives around their torsos, and a pile of guns. The Sakaneh family maintained later that the belt was another of Shadi's toys, like the carvings. The Palestinian Authority disagreed. In a sense, it did not matter, because Shadi Sakaneh became caught in a breakdown in law and order in Jabalya that had been prompted by the intifada and that would soon settle into a Wild West relationship between the police and Hamas. If Arafat had understood the breakdown in police authority in Jabalya at the beginning of the intifada, he would have instructed Colonel Rajah Abu Lihyeh to act differently one year later at the Islamic University demonstration. He would have seen the raging discontent of the people and the increasing kudos the intifada brought Hamas. If so, Yussef Akel and Abdullah Franji and Rajah Abu Lihyeh would not have died. Imad Akel would not have become the killer of one of his own. And Arafat would not have been Arafat.

"People were frustrated with the police," a senior Palestinian policeman told me. "The police do not get respect. On the other hand, we have no budget, and the political leadership is after *their* acceptance—the people in the camps. Arafat's real army is not us; it's them, these fucking child generals. So in the end, we policemen can always use our heads and we back off. Sometimes we forget that, and that's when there's trouble."

When Shadi Sakaneh's barbershop client reported the belt he had seen, the local police forgot that sordid equation and went after the child generals. Officers from the Jabalya branch of the Preventive Security turned up in a Mitsubishi Pajero and demanded the suicide bomber's belt, and the guns too.

Shadi lost his temper with these arrogant men in their ill-cut black leather jackets and fancy unmarked car. "You want my guns?" he yelled. "You can't have them. Get out of here."

The next day at noon, the security agents came back. Shadi was at the mosque across the street. The Preventive Security men happened to find Shadi's sixteen-year-old brother, Hamdi, outside the house. Hamdi was known in the family for his explosive temper, and when the Preventive Security agents tried to give him a subpoena for Shadi to appear in court over the disputed bomb belt, Hamdi blew up.

"We have experience with you guys around here," Hamdi shouted. "You're not here because he did anything wrong. You're here because he's Hamas. Leave him alone. Don't you get it? There's an intifada going on, you know."

Hamdi grabbed the subpoena and ripped it up. He threw it in the face of one of the Preventive Security men. He had gone too far. The agents shoved him into the back of their Pajero.

Hamdi's mother, Oqaila, came down the stairs and into the street. She grabbed her son through the car door and pushed the Preventive Security agents. "Leave him alone. He's a child," she said.

At that moment, prayers finished at the mosque across the street. Worshippers spilled out, lighting up smokes and chatting. Suddenly they noticed Hamdi struggling in the back of the jeep, and the crowd moved toward it. The Preventive Security men panicked. One of them fired a shot with his pistol into the ground at Oqaila's feet. She shrieked and jumped back. The crowd moved faster. Another shot in the air and the car sped away toward the police station. The crowd followed all the way, a distance of almost a mile, multiplying as it picked up angry locals along the route.

Oqaila followed the mob to the police station. She listened to what people were saying in the crowd as they filled in curious newcomers on the origins of the riot.

"Why are they doing this to us?" one man said. "We're Palestinians too."

The rumors were working their way through the crowd, making everything still more volatile. Some said an Israeli undercover unit had been arrested and taken to the Preventive Security offices; the crowd was trying to get to the Israelis to lynch them. Others shouted that Hamdi was arrested inside the mosque, a terrible violation of the sanctity of Islam.

Faced by a crowd of over 1,000 people, the Preventive Security released Hamdi within a few minutes.

But the story was not over. Three days later, the Sakanehs awoke at 1:30 A.M. to a terrific crash below their second-floor living quarters. The Preventive Security was back with almost 300 policemen. They drove a jeep through the metal shutters of the workshop; then they rushed up the stairs, arrested Hamdi and Shadi, and disappeared. It was the spark for three days of rioting in Jabalya. The police station was stoned and fifteen people were arrested. The Palestinian Authority's dismal brand of justice was not to be deterred, even when a judge ordered Hamdi released. He was rearrested one day later and held without trial. Shadi confessed—under torture, according to his family—that he had stoned the police station.

In his office up the road from Jabalya in the town of Beit Lihyeh, Fayez Abu Ayeta called community leaders around the teak conference table in his office. Abu Ayeta, the slick, thirty-three-year-old

Fatah chief of Beit Lihyeh, told the men from all the political factions, including Hamas, that the trouble had to stop. He didn't promise to free the Sakaneh boys. The local leaders bought his line, because
they didn't want Abu Ayeta to call in more troops. Still, the conclusions drawn by the people of Jabalya after their riots—conclusions
shared by ordinary people across Gaza—surely laid the foundation for
the violence that consumed Nusseirat and Bureij and Gaza City after
Imad Akel killed Abu Lihyeh.

Once the community leaders backed off, Fayez Abu Ayeta started
the damage control. When the disturbances stopped, he kicked back
in the tall black leather desk chair in his office and blithely told me
the riots "had nothing to do with anything else. There was no background and no consequences." Unless you happened to be Hamdi
Sakaneh or Imad Akel.

FOR EVERY ACTION a Palestinian takes, the history of his land is
such that there, indeed, must be background and consequences. Two
weeks after the killing of Abu Lihyeh, Imad Akel's wife gave birth to a
son. Imad named him Yussef, after the brother who died at the
policeman's hands. Imad held the boy and said, "I thank Allah that
when a martyr falls, we bring dozens more into the world to replace
him." It was for this reason that, after Yussef's death, Imad Akel took
a second wife. When she bears him a son, Imad Akel will name him
Yussef too.

At first, family members criticized Imad for taking another wife so
soon after Yussef died. His father Muhammed Akel lost his temper
one day, while he was urging Imad to take revenge on the police.
"You forgot your brother's blood and got married again," he yelled.
"And your wife will be the widow of a jihadi before she knows it."

Imad Akel was not angry with his father. "You forget that I want to
have more children, and with a second wife I can have *many* more. If
Allah gives me a long life, I will continue my jihad. If not, I wish to be
a martyr. I expect to be killed any minute, that's true, Father. But
Allah is merciful to me and didn't bless me with martyrdom. So
meanwhile I must get more children."

Muhammed smiled and apologized to his son. Neither man
thought about who would be the instrument of martyrdom for these

new young Akels: Israelis or Palestinians. Once, it would have been a certainty, but the story of Imad Akel and Colonel Abu Lihyeh showed that it was another unfathomable known only to Allah.

Imad Akel retained the glow of new fatherhood at the meeting when he bestowed the five kisses on me. The story I heard from him, and from the relatives and policemen who also spoke to me, was filled with complexity and cruelty. But Imad Akel didn't see any of that. That was his strength, just as it was the strength of other Hamas men, and of Islamic fighters I met elsewhere in the Arab world. Imad Akel faced a dilemma, and once he resolved it, he lived with the new reality as an absolute. The fight between Hamas political leaders and the Palestinian Authority is one of shadings and subtle shifts in emphasis, as both sides dance around the civil war that neither wants and that Imad Akel seemed to threaten to bring on. But the guerrillas of Hamas must see a sharp division between right and wrong or they cannot act. They would be immobilized by cavils if they, for example, were to see their enemy as a human being and, therefore, deserving of pity. So their minds run independently on two trajectories. They can live with conflicting facts, but not with irreconcilable realities of the kind that were the foundation of Arafat's state.

As I prepared to leave him, Imad Akel said that if I wrote truthfully about him, he and I would be in paradise together one day. He chose me to be among those he, as a martyr, would nominate to accompany him to *Jannah,* though as a non-Muslim I should not do so. I thought then that he surely would arrive before me, in any case. For he sought it and there were many who wished to send him to the world beyond life, whether he found paradise there or not. In October 2003 an Israeli missile attack struck a group of Palestinians in a jeep in Nusseirat. At first, the Israelis believed they had killed Imad Akel. Expecting immediate reprisals and riots in Palestinian towns for the death of a Hamas hero, the Israeli army woke its regional commanders with late-night phone calls and put them on alert. The Web site of the Israeli newspaper *Ha'aretz* reported Imad Akel dead, as did the next morning's edition of *The Jerusalem Post.* In fact, he survived. The hunt by the Israeli army and the Palestinian police continued. Imad Akel's bloody transport to paradise would have to wait.

CHAPTER TWO

Saladin's Gate

Gunmen Rulers of Palestinian Towns

Pray for the welfare of the state, since but for the fear thereof men would swallow each other alive whole.

—RABBI HANINA SGAN HA-KOHANIM,
IN *THE CHAPTERS OF THE FATHERS*

TWO ISRAELI FLAGS and the red, white, and black of Egypt's banner flashed above Bab Salah ed-Din, Saladin's Gate. To the south, an Egyptian woman hung laundry in the garden behind her single-story house. The long white djellabas on the washing line flew bright against the deep green of the olive orchard behind her and the black robe that swathed her. The normality of her domestic chores seemed almost monstrous in their juxtaposition with the devastation nearby, beyond Saladin's Gate, as though she hung the wet clothes with a quotidian languor designed to torment the residents on the other side of the border with their own horribly circumscribed existence. If the Egyptian woman had looked north beyond the gate a few months earlier, she would have seen a dense wall of cheap cinder-block dwellings, homes for the people of Shabourah, the refugee camp of Rafah, which is the southernmost town in the Gaza Strip. Two years into the Aqsa intifada, the homes were gone, crushed by Israeli bulldozers into a jagged thigh-high field of gray rubble, swelling higher here and there like the troubled surface of the sea on an overcast day.

From this concrete coastline began the part of Rafah that remained standing, though only as a tottering, dazed boxer awaiting the final blow that will crumple him to the canvas can be described as still on his feet. The main street, where merchants used to compete for the plots closest to Egypt and the rich cross-border trade, stretched away, quiet and eerie for hundreds of yards. The shop fronts, metal-shuttered and smeared with Hamas graffiti, were everywhere pocked and ripped by bullets from the tall Israeli border position, Termite. The bulky fortress loomed like an ogre clad in brown, desert camouflage netting, though nothing could disguise its massive outline. No one showed their face on the street until they were far enough away from Saladin's gate to be out of the direct line of fire of Termite. To walk down the road from the gate was to reenact the silent march through town of a movie cowboy pacing toward a gunfight: the empty main street, the punctuating crunch of dirt underfoot, the sweat beading down your back, and everywhere the silence and the sense of suspicious or hostile watchers.

Salah ed-Din ibn Ayyub, known in the West as Saladin, defeated the Crusaders in Palestine in the twelfth century. A Kurdish Muslim, he founded the Ayyubid dynasty, which ruled in the Levant more than sixty years after his death in 1193. In Palestinian towns, his name is everywhere, for he liberated Jerusalem, as Arafat and his people now dream of doing. Rafah was the first Palestinian town through which Arafat passed on his return to take control of Gaza in 1994, traveling by convoy from Egypt. Yet this gate still waits for a true liberator to enter it. Arafat's regime brought the people of Rafah a decade of lawlessness that sucked many of them into crime and propelled the rest into poverty. The men of Arafat's Fatah faction of the PLO fought the Israelis in Rafah so that they would have a cover for their criminal activities, smuggling goods and weapons and drugs under the Egyptian border in suffocating tunnels. Without the apparently nationalist violence, they would have been forced to halt their gangster brutality. The Palestinian Authority ignored Rafah, so distant from its ministries and residences in Gaza City, until it seemed that to live in the abject, ancient town was to drown in the pitching sea of concrete that lapped against Saladin's Gate, with no hope of rescue.

The inhabitants of Rafah adapted in the way of border communities throughout the world to the line Israel and Egypt agreed to draw through the middle of their hometown after their 1981 peace deal—Rafah turned to smuggling. Palestinian Rafah dug the tunnels, Egyptian Rafah supplied the cheap cigarettes, and a good trade went on under the sand and under the eyes of the troops Israel shipped to the isolated Termite post.

When Arafat's regime arrived, the smuggling took on a more sinister tone, as Fatah people tunneled under the Israelis to ship weapons into Gaza. The Israelis turned a blind eye, because they figured the Palestinian Authority's weapons were only going to be used against Hamas, after all. But small-time criminals in Rafah complain that during those years, the subterranean trade was taken out of the hands of cigarette smugglers like themselves and planted firmly in the realm of weapons traders, most with links to Arafat's Authority or to Fatah. Once the Aqsa intifada began, it was clear to the Israelis that the tunneling had to be stopped. What had been a matter for conveniently averting their gaze was suddenly a deadly military imperative.

Yet there was another face to the tunnel trade that few noticed. It amounted to one of the clearest demonstrations in any Palestinian town of the corrupt layers of Arafat's regime. It was obvious to locals that the gunmen running smuggling rings, trading weapons, and extorting protection money were criminals. Before Arafat came, that's all they were. But their connection to Arafat's Palestinian Authority and to Fatah gave them protection. By strutting around town with their guns and boasting of their attacks against the Israelis in Termite, their other activities as criminals were off limits for scrutiny by the law. They *became* the law. Though their attacks against Termite and other Israeli positions along the edge of Rafah were usually little more than gestures, they were histrionic enough that the townspeople got the message. If you tried to expose the heroic swagger of the Fatah fighters for the gangster chicanery that it truly was, you risked death as an Israeli collaborator. It became impossible to identify which came first, the resistance or the racket, for they were codependent. Yet if Arafat had wanted to do so, he could have robbed the gunmen of their shady deals and, with that, the incentive for the violence against Israel would have been reduced massively.

Rafah appealed to me immediately. It was distant, even from Gaza City, let alone from West Bank towns like Ramallah, where a foreign correspondent could get the one-dimensional analysis needed for a simple news story easily with a twenty-minute drive from Jerusalem to one of Arafat's sometimes capable—though never quite truthful—spokesmen. In Rafah, reality was quite literally underground, in the smugglers' tunnels and within the houses of townsfolk too scared of snipers to step outside. Rafah people were less jaded about journalists than their cousins in the West Bank. The place looked dustier than the rest of Palestine, more like Egypt, like another country. From my first visit, I started to sense that here, at the fringe of the conflict, the participants—whether Israeli or Palestinian, Arafat's men or Hamas—would feel less constrained than in the more frequented parts of the West Bank. They would display more of their true selves here, because they wouldn't think anyone was watching. But I watched as the villainous verities of battle and crime and deceit destroyed the town. As I observed, I felt something more than the disgust of someone who knows that the suffering he sees is pointless or that sacrifices inevitably are sold out. Rather, I experienced the thrill of understanding that comes when you see beyond the formulas of journalism. In Rafah, I felt the stimulation of witnessing something that had been ulterior gradually made clear.

As with so many aspects of the battles in Palestinian towns during the Aqsa intifada, the fighting in Rafah was more layered than the simple Israeli versus Palestinian equation. In Rafah, the Israeli campaign against the tunnels became, on the Palestinian side, a fight over control of criminal profits between the Akhras family, which mined Block J of the town's refugee camp, and the Sha'ir family, which claimed Block O. It also turned into a struggle between the Islamists and Arafat's henchmen for the political capital that was to be had by striking at the Israeli soldiers who sat at the edge of the town's crowded refugee camps. The residents, who stood to gain nothing from any of this, naturally paid the price.

Block O. Shabourah Refugee Camp, Rafah. 02:00, Jan.14, 2002. Ahmed Muhammed heard the churning of the mechanical diggers, distantly and with a hint of unearthly power, as though the Caterpillar D-9 were a passing jetliner or heavy clouds clashing above. At first, he thought it was just another of the converted Centurion tanks the Israeli army ran to ferry its guards in and out of the Termite post overlooking the ramshackle dwellings of Block O. The aged Centurions, which the army favored because of the sixteen inches of steel in the floor to guard against mines, stirred a huge racket into the silent darkness as their old engines struggled through the deep winter mud. They rolled loudly each night through the heavy morass of the border track known to the soldiers as Philadelphia Road. They brought soldiers to Termite, which looked menacing when viewed from the camp but which was in fact a hopelessly underfortified position. Termite was originally a three-story home among many others, but when the border was cut through the Bab Salah ed-Din neighborhood, Israel left this one house standing to serve as a guard post. Now that it was under nightly attack, the Israeli military knew that its patchwork of defenses was weak. To people like Muhammed, who lived in Termite's shadow, however, it appeared impregnably massive, spiny with MAG .50-caliber machine guns and billowing with its sheets of khaki and brown camouflage net. Each night, as the tunnelers set to work, Palestinians from the Fatah Tanzim militia commanded by Jamal Abu Samouhadana or local gunmen from Hamas would open up with Kalashnikovs at the post. Or they would tie homemade pipe bombs to lengths of rope, swinging them like a lariat for momentum so that they could be thrown from a greater distance. The Israelis would fire back into the dark and sometimes they would kill. But the distraction would keep the Israeli soldiers inside their post, instead of outside looking for the sounds of tunneling and plunging depth charges to destroy the shafts. The contraband rolled through the darkness, including weapons and, one senior Palestinian intelligence officer told me, hard drugs like heroin.

To the residents of Block O, the rattle and thud of these senseless skirmishes was their lullaby. It was strangely appropriate that those who made their homes on the utmost fringe of Palestinian territory— in rough dwellings that ceased truly to be a "camp" decades ago but that for just as long constituted a desperate slum—should feel themselves utterly marginalized by Arafat's regime while also living their lives in the very epicenter of the intifada's violence. There was an immediate explanation for their place in the debased regime Arafat built, as the occasional journalist who found his way to Rafah might see it: there was a conflict between the Israelis and the Palestinians, and here it was simply at its most raw. Yet there was a complexity latent beyond this easily apparent duality. Jamal Abu Samouhadana, who shrouded his criminal activity in the violence of nationalist struggle, would have been arrested or crushed or otherwise silenced were it not for his family relation to cousin Sami Abu Samouhadana, an extremely close friend of Muhammed Dahlan and Rashid Abu

Shoubak. Dahlan and Abu Shoubak were head and deputy chief of Preventive Security in Gaza, the very organ of Arafat's regime that was supposed to track down criminals whose activities menaced the peace process. For a time, Dahlan even became head of security and de facto interior minister under Prime Minister Mahmoud Abbas, when the United States forced Arafat to give up some of his powers in spring 2003. The Americans wanted a new leadership that would eschew Arafat's close ties to the groups that violated the peace process. Dahlan, the Americans' candidate, took over, as Abbas secured a ceasefire agreement from all the Palestinian groups, including Hamas and the Fatah Tanzim. Jamal Abu Samouhadana's men were the first to violate the truce by shooting at Israeli soldiers in Rafah. The skirmish was the earliest portent of the ultimate doom of the U.S. maneuver, though it was as if it hadn't happened: Dahlan didn't send his agents to halt the violation, the Israelis didn't protest the attack, and the United States didn't note it in any of the multitude of diplomatic contacts buzzing between Jerusalem, Ramallah, and Washington at the time. Of course not: it happened in Rafah.

That night in January 2002, Ahmed Muhammed sensed that the noisy engines cutting through the silence had moved beyond Termite, which stood only a few hundred yards along the border from his home. His house, two stories of wafer-light poured concrete and cinder block, was fifty yards from the frontier. Israeli diggers had destroyed some of the other houses along the border over the previous few months. Muhammed sat up; tonight they were coming for him.

"Get the kids," he said, shaking his wife's shoulder. She looked at him drowsily. Then she heard the engines. The couple had already spoken of the possibility that the Israelis would come to demolish their home. There was no need for Muhammed to explain what he meant. With his five children, he ran out into the darkness and fled along the narrow alley into the camp, away from the border, away from the engines, away from the noise of falling masonry that now began behind him. Away from his home.

When he came back soon after daylight, Muhammed paused on the same alley down which he had fled. At its end, he could see a palm tree on its side. It had stood in his neighbor's yard. Where houses had darkened the alley, now there was a winter sky, white and blank with flat cloud. He lit a cheap, Israeli-made Time cigarette and walked to the corner. His house had been to the right. He made the turn. His mother-in-law, whose home was across the passage from his, stood on her doorstep. The wind was stronger, now that he had rounded the corner. It blew straight across from the dunes on the Egyptian side of the border. His home was in the last row of houses demolished. The freezing wind rustled the fronds of the flattened palm tree. In the ruins of his home, Muhammed's eye picked out the pots and pans from his kitchen, battered by the falling masonry, but bright amid the gray rubble. A few weeks before, after some other homes nearby were crushed, he had cleared out most of what he owned—which was little, in any case—because he knew that this might happen. In front of his mother-in-law, he fought with all the emotions that came upon him. He felt the desperation of a man who had lost his home after spending the entire intifada unemployed—he used to travel to work daily in Israel as a tiler, and like two-thirds of Rafah men, he was now out of a job. He felt the humiliation of his mother-in-law's pity, as she wailed beside him and flapped her arms metronomically heavenward in lamentation. He felt anger, because he knew that no one from the Palestinian Authority was going to help him. They got me into this position, he thought, and now I'll be left to face this alone. Rafah is forgotten, and so am I.

After they lost their homes, the men of Block O moved into a huddle of white tents pitched along the muddy main street of Rafah. They would not come right out and say it, but their presence there was a reminder to the Palestinian Authority that there were people in Rafah who needed help. After all, the men could have moved in with their wives and children, who had been found rented accommodation by local Islamic Jihad and Hamas activists.

Soon after the first big round of demolitions in the camp, Muhammed Najjar worked with a rake to gather the cigarette butts and chocolate wrappers swept into his tent by the torrential downpour of the night hours. "It's cold in here, isn't it," the twenty-seven-year-old ambulance driver said. The other men in the tent—Najjar's two brothers and three other men from Block O—were silent. They waited for Najjar to finish cleaning; then they watched as he lit a fire in a cheap barbecue grill of thin metal and sat an old black teapot in the flames. As Najjar shifted the pot to test its warmth, the others complained that Arafat had abandoned them. "This blanket, which is all I sleep under, was brought here by Hamas," said Rafiq Arafat, who lost his home the same night Ahmed Muhammed's house was destroyed. "The Authority made promises to us, but we didn't get a thing." The others joined in with their own complaints, loud, all at once, resentment bursting forth. Then Najjar spoke up: "The Authority is our government and we should support it." There was suddenly silence in the tent; nobody wanted to tell him in public that he should cut the crap, but it was written sulkily on the faces that they averted from him.

In the battle for the support of the 135,000 people of Rafah, Hamas was the big winner during the intifada. Its charitable work with refugees from the onslaught of the Israeli diggers showed Hamas to be more concerned, in the eyes of the town, with the welfare of ordinary people than the Authority was. In the fighting on the border, too, Hamas's violence appeared cleaner, more clearly aimed at hitting the Israelis than the skirmishes by Fatah smugglers, who used the violence as cover to make a buck. The Fatah gunmen only sniped at the Israelis in Termite or along the Philadelphia Road to divert the soldiers from the smuggling tunnels. Hamas was really out to get them.

On November 23, 2001, Hamas fighters detonated 400 pounds of TNT cached in a tunnel beneath Termite. It blew a hole in the wall and forced the panicked Israelis to evacuate for a week. When they returned, the Israelis sent only a token force. The soldiers inside knew their numbers had been reduced because their commanders feared the next Hamas assault might be successful and wanted to limit the scope of that potential disaster.

Hamas activists were twice winners in fights like the battle for Termite. They built their domestic power by showing that they could take on the Israelis, and as the Israelis tried to protect the post, Hamas drew an Israeli response that gave the Islamists another chance to gain support by helping the victims of the retaliation. To the people of Rafah, it made a heroic contrast with the exploitation and callousness of Arafat's Fatah people.

A month before the Hamas mine blew up under Termite, Khalil Abu Labdeh had been expecting trouble. There were gunfights each night in Block O of the refugee camp, where he lived. The residents elected a few young men to stay up and call out warnings when the Israelis moved in. In the middle of the night, the cries came from the lookouts. Abu Labdeh jumped out of bed and ran. He was with a small group of neighbors sprinting down a narrow alley away from the Israeli post. He was sleepy, but waking up fast with the surge of fear. A shell exploded in the wall just ahead of the group. It was so bright that, for a moment, Abu Labdeh could not see. He looked around, dazed. Oh, I'm sitting on the ground, he thought drowsily. There were three of his neighbors dead on the floor of the same damp alley. He took in the scene absentmindedly, as though he were not close enough to touch the bodies. Abu Labdeh saw two children bleeding on the ground too—the shrapnel had blinded them both. Then Abu Labdeh saw the lower half of a leg, clad in gray sweatpants, severed by a piece of metal that had sprayed jaggedly out of the tank shell when it detonated against the wall. He looked hard at the leg. It was his. He passed out.

The thirty-seven-year-old spent the next three months limping along on his crutches down the same narrow alleys. His leg was a stump, its end rounded and smooth, more like plastic than skin. He understood that he would never be able to work as a laborer again. He told himself it wasn't so bad and joked sourly with his friends, "There are plenty of people here with two legs that also are unemployed, eh?"

In January of 2002, Abu Labdeh found himself once more rushing, stumbling, searching for a footing for his new metal crutch in the uneven surface of the same alley where he lost his leg, fleeing again from the Israelis in the middle of the night. After the Hamas attack that blew the wall off Termite, after more nights of increasing shooting at the army position, after informers in the town reported new hauls of weapons smuggled beneath the border, the Israelis came to demolish a huge section of Block O. In a sense, they came with Arafat's approval. Under the peace deal Arafat struck with Israel, the army was permitted to take responsibility for security in a 200-yard strip running inside the border; on the maps appended to the peace treaty, this narrow "pink zone" looked like nothing, but on the ground it stretched deep into Rafah and left the people without even the slightest hope of official protection. Abu Labdeh's home was within this pink zone, though he had never heard of it. So was the bulldozed house of Ahmed Muhammed. Homeless, Abu Labdeh moved into one of the tents on the main street. He consoled himself that he had no family to support, but otherwise it was clear to him that he had lost everything. The only people who tried to help him were from Islamic Jihad and Hamas.

Around the brazier one night, Abu Labdeh swilled some bitter coffee. It was freezing in the tent, and the cold caused his stump to ache, though he put a second thick sock over it to protect it from the damp chill. One of the other men in the tent was talking about the possibility of work with the Palestinian Authority. The man had visited someone in the governor's office and been mildly encouraged. Abu Labdeh knew it was dangerous to say what was on his mind, but he could not help himself. He wiped the coffee from his ragged black mustache. "You have to have connections just to get the lousiest job with the Authority," he spat. "Rafah is the worst place there is. We're forgotten since the intifada began. We always will be." The other men looked at him in silence. He could tell some of them viewed him with pity, as though he were just a washed-up, bitter cripple. But he could see from the way most of them avoided his gaze that he spoke what was on their minds. That was the night a burly fellow named Salah from Islamic Jihad brought them some blankets.

IF THE PALESTINIAN AUTHORITY showed little concern for people like Abu Labdeh, it didn't do much more for its own employees. Abdel Nasser Odwan, who was born in Rafah, had gone into exile as a fighter with Fatah. Living in Cairo, he married an Egyptian woman and fathered three children. In 1993 he took his chance to return to his homeland with the first detachment of Palestinian police that came to Jericho with Arafat, under the peace agreement with Israel. Relatives and Palestinian police officials say Israel denied Odwan's repeated requests to bring his family with him. To a man from Rafah, there seemed to be only one way to be reunited with his wife and children. A smuggler in the town agreed to get Odwan through the border to visit his family. As soon as he was beyond the fence, however, he was arrested by an Egyptian patrol and sent back. The Palestinian police tried him for desertion and he spent six years in the Sarraya, the central military prison in Gaza where Imad Akel was held briefly. By the time he was released at the start of the Aqsa intifada, Odwan's wife and children had been smuggled into Gaza by his immediate family. It should have been a good time, but the police refused to reinstate him in his old job and there was no other employment to be had in Rafah now that the uprising was underway. Again he drifted toward the only option open to a man from Rafah.

Odwan went a year without work before his old smuggling contact recruited him. Back when he had first been arrested, it was still possible to sneak through the border fence. By this time, the smuggler dealt only with tunnels. They were two feet square, airless and long, lit merely by the flashlight a man might carry. The tunneling was mostly done by hand, clawing through the sand. But the money was good, if you were a desperate man, and Abdel Nasser Odwan was desperate. The thirty-five-year-old made his first subterranean trip in late 2001. He bought cheap cigarettes in Egypt and sold them in Rafah. The town was awash with such contraband. Unlike the legal cigarettes sold elsewhere, which came through Israel and were marked in Hebrew, the smuggled Egyptian packs were recognizable because the health warnings were written in Arabic. Odwan made $300 profit, a huge amount in Rafah. His nephew Muhammed warned him that he was flirting with another disaster. "You're acting like this is a big adventure," Muhammed said. "You're like a big kid." Abdel Nasser laughed and flipped a packet of the smuggled cigarettes at Muhammed. It was the large gesture of a man who believed he was finally on his way to something good.

On Odwan's second trip, in December 2001, Egyptian police caught him and jailed him for a year. Once more his wife and children, who were in Gaza illegally, found themselves on the wrong side of the border and unable to visit the luckless father. Palestinian police officials said Israeli soldiers would probably arrest Odwan if he ever tried to get back across the border through the official Rafah crossing. Though there was never anything evil about the man, except the circumstances of life in his hometown, Abdel Nasser Odwan crossed the border illegally and had to pay the price for it the rest of his life: these are the rules of Rafah.

The Rafah tunnels are like the relationship between Arafat, his militias, and the Islamists—hidden from all but the most prying of eyes, dangerous and dirty, sometimes a matter of cooperation and other times of hateful conflict. This gateway to Gaza was a perfect illustration of the tactics employed in the struggle between the Palestinian Authority and Hamas and their counterpoint to the criminal activity that overcame normal life in many Palestinian towns, sucking the Israelis into the fringes of what might otherwise have been local gang wars. In his spacious office, Sofian al-Agha, the governor appointed by Arafat for the Rafah district, sat in a low wooden armchair designed back in the 1970s when the PLO's brand of pseudo-socialist, revolutionary chic had some hepcat cachet. Al-Agha smoked Marlboros and mumbled defiantly into space, as though he were practicing a public address rather than talking to me in the chair next to him. Of course, if he had a speech to make, he would only dream of preaching to the converted. Al-Agha's rhetoric was full of the politics of victimization, venturing only halfway to the truth of what had gone sour in his society. The Palestinians were "oppressed by occupation and that is what brings out the hatefulness in us, though we still trust in the wisdom and leadership of Yasser Arafat." He got up and ambled across his office. Behind his mahogany desk, the dark, varnished door was scarred by shrapnel, which seared through the wood a few days previously when he was at his desk. The shrapnel was from an Israeli helicopter attack on the Palestinian Authority's military offices across the courtyard. "The Palestinians don't have anything more to lose," said al-Agha. "We in the Authority can control the situation to a certain point, but if a political solution does not come, nobody can control the people." As though the people were not highly controlled by Arafat's dictatorship; as though ceding control wouldn't leave a vacuum, to be filled by Hamas; as though the supposed failure of control were not intended to be a weapon against Israel in negotiations. For officials like al-Agha, the solution was not to be found within the Palestinian community, by reforming its government or providing greater services to the people of Rafah, for example. "What we need is for the international community to produce a plan and to bring economic aid for the Palestinian people," al-Agha said.

It was that lack of ideas and responsibility, that dearth of answers, which crippled the Palestinian Authority—particularly when average Palestinians compared it to Hamas, which proclaimed its absolute conviction that it had the solution at every opportunity. Authority people never quite knew to which side of the peace-or-violence equation their leaders wanted them to hew; and those that decided of their own accord for peace never knew when their apparently encouraging leaders were going to sell them out as enemy agents working against the brave resistance fighters. The Palestinian Authority and its vast staff waited for answers, and yet no one can afford to wait too long. Al-Agha sang a line of a song by the classical Egyptian diva, Um Kulthoum, called "Patience Has Its Limits." "If you stay in Rafah a week, you'll be singing this song like me," he said. I wrote down his quip; then I looked at him, bored and slumped in his charcoal business suit, surrounded by gray aides and blue tobacco smoke, and I thought, It is people like him who wrote the tune.

It is typically little more than rhetoric when Palestinian politicians talk about "unity." The Palestinians are divided, politically and socially. Just as the Israelis divide the Palestinians physically by isolating communities within the West Bank and the Gaza Strip, so the battle between the Palestinian gangs sets up figurative checkpoints, creating an atmosphere in certain towns where the people feel Arafat has closed them out. In Rafah, that perception leaves the field all too open to local leaders. The problem for Arafat is that the local leaders nominally loyal to him are gunmen like Jamal Abu Samouhadana, bent only on expanding their own power to control crime, a purpose served by their supporting role in the fight against Israel. Islamist leaders, on the other hand, take advantage of that vacuum to build support—with the blankets to the homeless men in the tents, for example. At a secret meeting of the Rafah leadership of Islamic Jihad seventeen months into the Aqsa intifada, the blanket delivery man, Salah, whose thick lips made it hard for his mouth to keep up with the speed of his speech, cracked a joke: "We ought to declare the Independent Republic of Rafah." The men around the table laughed loudly at a jest that held for them many resonances. For one, it mocked Arafat's constant delaying of the declaration of an independent Palestinian state. It also turned their laughter self-deprecatingly on their own war-torn, poverty-stricken town, because, after all, who would want a state like this? Most of all, it was a measure of the reality that Rafah was on its own and that the Islamists were the honest ones who did the most to help the people there, while Arafat's crew swaggered and profiteered.

In the Brazil neighborhood of Rafah's refugee camp, I entered the

National Institute for Development and Services. Usually Palestinian businesses take names that tell you exactly what they do. My favorite is the less-than-snappy Gaza Company for the Importation of Egyptian Consumer Goods. In the case of this National Institute, the name was, to say the least, misleading: it was the den of one of the town's leading smugglers. Fayez showed me into his office. I sat on one of the black leather sofas, of which there were at least two more than necessary in a room of this size, cramped around Fayez's big horseshoe-shaped ebony desk. Red plush carpet covered the walls. There were boxes of electronic equipment piled in the corners and in the corridor. The room reminded me of the lounges of seedy recording studios I had known in New York City, male and unkempt and decorated with more money than sense or taste. A deaf-mute teenager held up a teacup. Fayez, who was in his mid-thirties, nodded and wiggled his hand, signaling the youth to prepare the tea with a medium amount of sugar.

Fayez spent eighteen months in an Egyptian jail for smuggling before the intifada. Back then, Palestinian police tried to intercept smugglers, because the Authority wanted to collect taxes on goods. The intifada changed that. The government ceased to function, so the police needed to cull their cut directly, as partners with criminals like Fayez. His new partners also dictated that he should expand beyond the baby formula and Marlboros that formed the bulk of his original business. Instead of a few Kalashnikovs on demand, Fayez noticed, smugglers were moving more and more weapons. As long as no one traded in drugs, which could harm the community, Fayez didn't see any problem; he was just giving the customers what they wanted. "Services and goods that people can get here legally in Rafah are at a lower level than anywhere in the world, except maybe Afghanistan," he said.

The gunmen and the smugglers brought disaster down upon the heads of their fellow townspeople, because they needed the cover of war against the Israeli soldiers of Termite for their criminal operations. They were demonstrably awful men—violent, coercive, and ruthless. Yet, with his stated reluctance to trade in drugs, Fayez wanted at least to appear as though he respected moral boundaries. When I left him, I walked again along the bullet-ripped strip of shop fronts near Saladin's Gate. Around a corner, safe from the Israeli guns, four traders sat in the afternoon shade drinking tea. A middle-aged man named Abu Maher offered me a glass considerably sweeter than the one I drank with Fayez. From chewing betel, his teeth were stained to the color of the tea he proffered. His skin was dark from the sun and scored deeply at every fold. There was another man leaning, bored, on a trolley of green peppers, and nearby, someone had lined five watermelons along the curb. This empty street was the town's market. "No, it's not that this is a particularly bad day for business," Abu Maher said. "Every day is shit here." I asked him if he would work in the tunnels. "I'm ready to smuggle heroin if it brings food for my kids. But it's not easy anymore. It's dangerous." He tipped out the tea dregs from his glass and looked around the corner toward Termite. Nothing moved in the hot afternoon. The Israeli and Egyptian flags at the border hung limp. Abu Maher groaned and slouched across to the other side of the street.

I went northward from Rafah along the Saladin Road, which travels the length of the Gaza Strip. I knew the route well: the sycamore-lined avenue through Khan Yunis near the UN Relief and Works Agency school, where it always seemed to be time for the kids to flood home, teetering forward beneath their enormous, colorful back-packs and laughing at me, the tall foreigner, when I stopped to buy a Coke; Deir el-Balah, where the road was shaded by wondrously soaring date palms; the rolling final stage into Gaza City with the watch-tower of the Israeli settlement at Netzarim rising like a sinister fairground helter-skelter away across the dunes. Each of the towns I passed through along the length of the Gaza Strip had its own character, but somehow the same predicaments pertained. Sometimes people would say that certain towns had a particular political bent: that Khan Yunis, for example, tended to support the Popular Front for the Liberation of Palestine (PFLP) more than other places. It struck me that the intifada broke down those assumptions. If Khan Yunis aligned with the PFLP before 2000, then the onset of the intifada saw some of the PFLP hardmen soon ally themselves with Fatah and Democratic Front gunmen, and others who never before had been involved in politics, and yet others who had always been nothing more than criminals. Ideology broke down beneath the onslaught of the Israeli army and the toll it took on the thinkers and experienced activists among the Palestinians, arresting or assassinating them, leav-

ing their foot soldiers filled with fear and anger, burning for any kind
of revenge for its own sake rather than as part of a political or religious program, and heavily armed. Those who were left might gen-
uinely have taken to their political groupings out of a desire to carry
on the struggle against Israel, but plenty of the new men saw their
chance to use the established local factions as personal power bases. It
was a phenomenon Arafat and his sidekicks had used to their advantage for decades. In his autobiography, Salah Khalaf—one of Arafat's
most prominent PLO rivals, who was known as Abu Iyad—wrote that
young Fatah men had long been frustrated by the inability of the
Palestinians to wage full-scale war against Israel and so had determined to embark on terrorist attacks. Abu Iyad wrote that the PLO
leadership faced no choice but "to channel the wave of anger, to
structure it and give it political content." It wasn't a foolproof channel, as Abu Iyad found to his cost in 1991, when one such young
man, his bodyguard, came up with some unorthodox "political content" of his own and killed Abu Iyad. In a broader way, the same
thing happened to Arafat in the Aqsa intifada. His West Bank Fatah
chief Hussein e-Sheikh told me when the intifada was less than two
weeks old that Arafat's regime decided to wage "the battle for final
status," meaning that the Palestinian Authority wanted to use the
violent demonstrations and the alarming death toll among its own
people to pressure Israel into negotiating concessions at peace talks
on a "final status" agreement, but the strategy went out of control,
and the flimsy ideological framework Arafat tried to impose on the
violence was overwhelmed by what, with foresight, the long-dead
Abu Iyad had called "an individualistic and anarchistic" direction.

Even the Fatah offshoot, the Aqsa Martyrs Brigades—which frequently rejected the decisions of its paymaster Arafat or darkly
warned Mahmoud Abbas, during his brief tenure as prime minister, of
the consequences of treading softly with Israel—recognized the need
to tame those anarchistic tendencies. On the road north from Rafah,
I made a stop in the town of Jabalya, whose borders over the years
had melted into the refugee camp of the same name and the expanding northern edge of Gaza City to form a single, slovenly conurbation. As traffic crept along the main street, a mustard Volkswagen van
came in the opposite direction with loudspeakers howling, at a volume that seemed to site the bass drum directly inside my spine,

"Arafat is the leader. We will never accept another." Young men leaned out of both sides of the VW handing leaflets to drivers traveling in the other lane or to pedestrians dodging between the traffic with their fingers in their ears. It was a communiqué from the Martyrs Brigades: "If anyone tries to get money from you and says it's for the Aqsa Martyrs Brigades, report him and we will deal with him." I noticed the contradiction at once, even as I began to move out of Jabalya toward the crossing point into Israel. The gunmen of the Martyrs Brigades saw themselves as an established organization whose reputation was besmirched by the thieves who forced money out of ordinary people at the end of a rifle, knowing that anyone who refused could be accused of hampering the struggle against Israel; yet even as the Brigades tried to show that its hands were clean, its chiefs couldn't resist the threat to "deal with" transgressors. The police, the Authority, was not an option. Only the gunmen would decide.

CARVED IN A SQUARE of slashy Kufic script above the entrance to the Abdel Hadi Palace, the year of its construction: 1250 by the Muslim reckoning of time gauged from the Prophet's hegira, his journey between Mecca and Medina. It was barely legible through a 170-year patina of lichen and accumulated dirt. It seemed appropriate to me that time should be measured by the calculation of Islamic tradition here as I stepped from a vaulted walkway through the arch, which seemed unchanged by the centuries, and savored the scent of cardamom from the sacks outside the spice store on the corner. Then I swallowed a gulp of the cloud of gnats and the stench of urine and damp earth in the courtyard, and it came to me that tradition might mean something entirely less fragrant to those who lived in this decrepit place. The Casbah of Nablus, built on the ruins of Roman Neapolis, dense with the heavy stonework and narrow alleys of Saladin's Ayyubid dynasty and of the Ottomans who followed, once was home to rich families like the Abdel Hadis and the Toukans, but was now populated by refugees who could afford no better than to live as though it were still 1250 hegira.

A little girl with a plump, dirt-smeared face shuffled barefoot in the muddy yard. The women of the Zakari family leaned out of their window, a pitted Ottoman arch. I called up to them to make certain this was the palace of the Abdel Hadis, as I had wandered the Casbah a long time already to find it. "Yes, but it's not a palace anymore," said Najah Zakari, the mother of one of the six large families that squeezed into quarters once meant for a single wealthy household. "Do you think they'd let people like us live in a real palace?" Najah beckoned to the spiral stone staircase, past the reeking squatting toilet, to her apartment, where she gave me mint tea. Her seventy-year-old husband, Yussef, was out, pushing a delivery trolley for $2 a day, too proud to let his unemployed sons do the heavy work for him.

A week before my visit, the Casbah was the center of the bloodiest battle of the intifada. More than 500 Palestinian gunmen adopted the dubious military tactic of hiding out in the confined area of the old neighborhood. Easily surrounded, they put up a fight, but ultimately the Israelis only had to go house to house to apprehend or kill them. In the process, they destroyed many buildings in the ancient district to make a route wide enough for their armor and took all the young men, including Najah Zakari's twenty-one-year-old son, Khalil. I walked around the Casbah with Khalil, touring the Ottoman palaces where his relatives and friends now strung their laundry and penned their goats. Standing in the shade of a pomegranate tree in another dilapidated courtyard, Khalil told how he was detained two days in an Israeli camp outside Nablus with all the other young men of the Casbah, huddling without shelter. He was beaten when he refused to recite a crude rhyme:

> Wahad hummus, wahad ful,
> Ana bahib mishmar ha-gvul,
> Wahad hummus, wahad tahini,
> Kus im il-falastiniyyeh.

He finally parroted it for the soldiers to avoid being struck again. Even when I saw him days later, he took my notebook and wrote the words, too ashamed to speak them aloud:

> One [order of] hummus, one [order of] ful,
> I love the Border Police,
> One hummus, one tahini,
> [Fuck] the cunt of the Palestinian mother.

It struck me that Khalil Zakari's life was one of constant such humiliations. Refugees from Haifa, the Zakaris were consigned to a dismal life in this rotten, ancient core of Nablus, literally and figuratively at the bottom of the city. Anyone with money lived up on the slopes of Mount Gerizim, where the air was fresher, overlooking the Casbah and the refugee camps. On the mountain's peak, a leading member of the powerful Masri family had constructed a monumental domed mansion. Designed apparently to form a montage of Thomas Jefferson's Monticello and the Taj Mahal, it was visible from every point in Nablus, including the rooftop garden where Khalil Zakari stood below the pomegranate tree. Yet those who resided in the clear air could surely smell the resentment that eddied in the swells of heat rising from the valley floor. Refugees, who make up about two-thirds of the total Palestinian population of five million, are mostly poor, particularly the 17 percent that still live in the crowded slums they built over the sites of their initial tent camps.

In every Palestinian town, the poor refugees battled against the more established families, but in Nablus it was a conflict of particularly drastic proportions. In 2001 a man from the Balata Refugee Camp, which seals the head of the valley southeast of Nablus, raced his stolen Volkswagen truck along the crowded, chaotic main street through the city. Kamel Salameh weaved at full speed through the traffic, until he slammed into Islam Attallah, a nine-year-old schoolgirl, who spun off his hood like a doll. Salameh turned his truck and roared toward Balata. Atallah lay dead in the road as Palestinian policemen chased Salameh to the narrow alleys of Balata. In the camp, the graffiti covering the walls marked the territories of clan-based gangs like the Dan-Dan or personal militias that owed their allegiance to local leaders with nicknames like Baz-Baz. Here this was the law, not the apprehensive policemen who entered the camp on the heels of Islam Attallah's killer. They found no trace of Salameh, who knew he could disappear in Balata, a fifth of a square mile that was home to 30,000 people. However, the police found his truck in the camp and a dozen other stolen vehicles, which they impounded.

That afternoon there was gunfire, the accompaniment to a street protest. But it was not the sudden, needless death of the little girl Islam Atallah that outraged the demonstrators. The people of Balata responded to the invasion of their territory by the policemen. Forty stolen cars, each without license plates, rolled slowly out of the camp, past the mile-long strip of chop shops where cars stolen inside Israel were gutted for parts, on through the center of Nablus. Each one was loaded with car thieves firing rifles in the air. Behind them walked hundreds of Balata residents. The air around the police station and the municipality filled with the deafening rattle of M-16s. The towns-people fled in fear, and the mayor got the message. He told the police chief not to go to Balata again. Mayor Ghassan Shaka'a also put two guards with Kalashnikovs at the door to his office. At the end of 2003, Balata gunmen went so far as to shoot dead the mayor's brother. There's an Arabic proverb: "People follow the religion of their king." Arafat, his mayor, his police force, adhered to a creed of corruption, so the poorest lived by the same doctrine. The refugees of Balata and the other camps around Nablus came under the control of criminals, car thieves, and gunmen. Everyone knew they weren't the best of men, but they stood up for the camps and their clans, so they were unassailable and, in fact, rather admirable to those around them. The gunmen showed themselves to be ineffective whenever the Israelis sent a large force into the camp, but they seemed a worthwhile form of protection for the refugees against Arafat's people.

Hussam Khader, the most prominent political figure in Balata, was extremely critical of Arafat. Khader was a camp leader during the first intifada, when an organizing committee made up of refugees safe-guarded the structure of the community. There were only ten people from the camp accused of car theft and petty crimes during that upris-ing. By the time of the Aqsa intifada the people of Balata learned their lessons from Arafat's Authority. Crime by Balata residents against Nablus people had increased dramatically; nonpolitical murders, a pre-viously unheard-of phenomenon, were on the rise. In February 2001 four men from Balata killed a Palestinian from a nearby village in a conflict over money and women. Balata used to be a symbol of dedi-cation to the resistance, but under Arafat its better impulses were cor-rupted until it was simply a byword for lawlessness. On one of my visits to his office on the edge of the camp, Khader showed me a fax a friend sent him from Arafat's office. It was one of Khader's own bul-letins, accusing Arafat's henchmen of profiting from the monopolies in trade with Israel that they received as part of the Oslo peace bar-gain, at the expense of ordinary people and less well-connected businessmen. In Arafat's jagged handwriting, scribbled at an angle across the top corner of the page, a dark statement: "Shut this guy up."

THE SHAHINES ate the *iftar* meal to break their fast at the end of another day of Ramadan. The Aqsa intifada was less than three months old. In December 2000 it was still possible to believe that the uprising was just like its predecessor, a popular battle against occupation fought by kids with stones at Israeli roadblocks. Just possible—if, unlike me, you were a journalist who hadn't spoken to Arafat's West Bank Fatah chief Hussein e-Sheikh about the true, strategic nature of the fighting or if, as some observers did, you wrote off the increasing number of shooting attacks as the somehow inevitable outgrowth of stones and Molotov cocktails. In Bethlehem, the violence already showed signs of drawing the Israeli army right into the Palestinian towns. Almost nightly, local gunmen went to the edge of the city, to a village of mostly middle-class Palestinian Christians called Beit Jala, and fired across the deep wadi at the Israeli apartment blocks in the Jerusalem suburb of Gilo. In turn, the Israelis would dispatch their helicopters overhead and, as their rotors churned, the reverberations would rumble through the cloudy winter nights like thunder to the very opposite end of Bethlehem, to the Saff neighborhood in the southwest of town where the Shahines shared their evening meal.

Jalila Shahine handed her thirty-eight-year-old son, Adnan, a flat yellow pancake to mop up the gravy on his plate. She was proud of her son, a housepainter who had spent years in Israeli jails for his membership in Fatah. Slight and black-bearded, he sat beside his two wives. The first had given him two boys and two girls. He married a second, Haifa, who was twenty-four, a month ago, and already she was pregnant. It was news of this grandchild that made Jalila Shahine feel the greatness of this breakfast, even more so than usual.

There was a knock at the door. "Adnan, go and see who it is," Jalila said. The meal continued. There was no sound, no voice loud enough for Jalila to hear, though the front door was only a couple of yards across the hall from the dining room. When Adnan didn't return, Jalila went to look. She noticed that the door was open, but Adnan was not there. Then she saw him on the steps outside. There were two men with him, and she felt a strange stab of shock. They wore black balaclava helmets, stocking masks with eyes and mouth cut out, and they were armed. The town was full of rumors of Israeli undercover units. Maybe Adnan was involved in operations against the Israelis and one of the undercover squads had come for him. "What's going on?" Jalila said.

"He's wanted by General Intelligence," one of the men said. He wore the turquoise-and-black camouflage pants of the Palestinian police's Rapid Reaction Force and carried a pistol. His accent was authentic—he was no Israeli. The other man, who wore a pair of jeans, carried a Kalashnikov.

"Why? Why's he wanted?" Jalila said.

"Look, the jeep is down the hill, waiting," the man said to Jalila, gesturing impatiently along the empty street. He nudged Adnan: "Let's go."

Adnan slipped on his shoes, which he had left on the top step outside the front door. The man with the pistol gripped Adnan's left arm. They got to the bottom of the steps. Jalila looked around; she didn't see the jeep they mentioned. Now the gunmen each grasped one of Adnan's arms, marching him down the hill, his hands bound in plastic cuffs that she hadn't noticed at first. Jalila followed with Adnan's new wife, Haifa. "Why did you handcuff him?" They walked faster. Jalila thought of asking a neighbor for help, but the street was deserted. Everyone was breaking their fast or praying at the mosque.

Jalila caught up again. She saw panic on Adnan's face now. She sensed that he knew the identity of these two men in the masks and that the situation had become more serious than he evidently first thought. "Don't leave me, Mother," he said.

"Shut up," said the man with the pistol. He turned on Jalila, who was tall for a Palestinian woman and strongly built. "And you, go home," he said to the mother and the wife.

"I'm not going to leave him. You can shoot me, but I won't leave," Jalila said.

The man with the pistol halted for a second, as though coming to a decision, then he moved. He pulled Adnan to the middle of the narrow street and pushed him to his knees. Adnan began to sob. "I'm warning you, go back to your house," the man shouted at Jalila.

"I'm not going," she said.

The two gunmen walked seven yards away from Jalila's quivering son. Quickly the first raised his pistol and fired. The bullet hit Adnan in the left shoulder. When it struck, he was looking at his wife and mother, and despite the impact, his pleading eyes stayed on them. The gunmen stepped a few yards farther away, and the pistol fired again. This time it blasted into Adnan Shahine's neck, and he fell dead. By the time Jalila reached Adnan, the gunmen were away down an alley.

Jalila Shahine fell to her knees. She reached her hands to heaven and called out to God. She dipped her hands in the blood that ran from Adnan's neck and smeared it across her cheeks and forehead. "God is most great, God is most great. Come out, all of you," she cried to her neighbors. None paid attention. No door opened.

The gunmen who killed Adnan Shahine published their version of why he died, spreading it through the networks of activists in Bethlehem. Shahine was slain because he worked as a collaborator with Israel, according to the gunmen's account. He and another collaborator, who fled to the nearest Israeli command post at Kfar Etzion after Shahine's death, guided an Israeli assassination squad on an operation a few days before Adnan's death. They went to the home of Yussef Abu Sway in a glade of pines in the valley of Artas. Abu Sway knew he was wanted by Israel, for smuggling weapons. As he crept home through the trees in the afternoon to eat a Ramadan *iftar,* Israeli snipers shot him from the road above. His mother, Na'ima, recognized the body lying outside the family house in a radish patch; she knew the denim jacket and trousers she had bought for Yussef. Na'ima Abu Sway ran and lamented over her son, whose corpse bore the marks of nineteen bullets, as Jalila Shahine had done over the body of Adnan. Yussef and Adnan were both members of Fatah.

The story that Shahine was a collaborator, which in itself was hard enough for a foreign reporter to uncover, was not the real explanation. For months it seemed to me the most likely reason, until I finally met a man who knew the secrets of Fatah in Bethlehem and whose integrity I did not doubt. I asked him about Shahine. He remembered the case.

"Was he a collaborator with Israel?" I said.

"No," the Fatah man said.

"So why did they kill him?"

The man smiled bitterly and breathed a long stream of cigarette smoke. "Because they wanted to show they could kill a collaborator."

It only made sense if you knew how utterly appalling was the under-world of the Palestinian cities during the intifada. A few months into the uprising, the gunmen saw that Israel's hit squads were starting to strike at them effectively. Some of that success was based on informa-tion gathered from the Shin Bet's network of Palestinian collabora-tors. The gunmen had to kill one of those collaborators so that other informers would think twice before helping the Israelis. But the gun-men didn't know the identity of any collaborators. That meant they had to kill someone who wasn't really a collaborator and put it about that he had been an informant. In the absence of law that was born under the Palestinian Authority and that grew with the onset of the intifada, the gunmen couldn't pick a victim from a prominent, pow-erful family, because the relatives would demand tribal retribution. So they chose Adnan Shahine, whose clan was small and weak. And they killed him.

That was it. I found it so astonishing that I asked my Fatah contact to reprise the reasoning three times. Then I stopped, because I feared that if I heard it once more, it might start to make sense.

The gunmen came to their conclusion because they were cruel and criminal, but also because they understood the political culture Arafat created. Palestinian military courts issued death sentences to collaborators after precipitate trials and executed them in public, before audiences of officials far more numerous than the two screaming women who watched Shahine die. The gunmen took over as the law in Bethlehem even at that early stage of the intifada, just as they became the criminals and the enforcers all over the West Bank and Gaza. Most Palestinians believed collaborators, who were typically paid less than $200 a month by their Israeli Shin Bet opera-tors, ought to die. When the gunmen killed someone like Adnan Shahine, it looked as though they were upholding the morals of the struggle against Israel. But there was something stronger at work: the lack of democracy and due process that eventually turned everyone against the Authority, from Imad Akel to Arafat's own ministers. The collaborators often led the Israelis to members of the Fatah Tanzim militia, which mixed its anti-Israel violence with protection rackets. In Bethlehem, the Tanzim was drawn from members of the Ta'amra tribe, which lived in outlying villages, primarily the Abayat family. Only fifty years of settled village life separated the Abayat Ta'amra from their nomadic desert history, and they still followed tribal law. One night soon after Adnan Shahine died, a crowd of Abayats showed up outside Bethlehem's jail, where five accused collaborators were held. One of the collaborators, Muhammed Nawawra, confessed to helping the Israelis assassinate Hussein Abayat, a leading gunman. Though there was no doubt that Arafat's courts would deliver a merciless sentence upon Nawawra, the Abayats repeatedly tried to break into the jail to lynch him.

The swagger of the gunmen was that of the bully, boastful and violent when supported by numbers of his own, but fearful when confronted by a greater power. Abdullah Abu Hadid, one of the leading Ta'amra gunmen, used to work as a housepainter in the Israeli settlements near Bethlehem. In the early 1990s, he would buy weapons and bring them to a settler friend of mine to get his assessment of them. Usually they were old Jordanian army revolvers and carbines that would be most dangerous to the one pulling the trigger. These guns were no threat to the Israeli army, but they commanded alarm and obedience in Bethlehem. When the Ta'amra began to shoot at the Israeli suburb of Gilo, Abu Hadid fed off the fear. He sauntered around Bethlehem extorting cash from businessmen and even wandered into the mayor's office, slammed his Kalashnikov on the desk, and demanded a government salary. But to live from the dread he instilled in others, he also had to understand fear sufficiently to feel it himself. Abu Hadid repeatedly called Israeli intelligence agents who he knew from the days of cooperation before the intifada. "You're aware I'm not the one shooting at Gilo, aren't you?" he begged. "Don't blame me. Don't come and kill me."

The most dreadful aspect of the intifada's effect on the people of Palestinian towns was the hypocritical profiteering of men like Abu Hadid. The Ta'amra and the Tanzim eventually melted into the equally uncontrollable Aqsa Martyrs Brigades. One of that group's local leaders in Bethlehem was Ahmed al-Mughrabi, who sent Muhammed Daraghmeh to blow himself up at the age of eighteen. Daraghmeh died in Jerusalem's religious Jewish neighborhood of Beit Yisrael in April 2002, killing nine Israelis, including an entire family.

Muhammed was a carpenter. He installed cherrywood kitchen cabinets for my partner's cousin. There was little work, because of the intifada, so he took a job in a butcher's shop. No one in his family understood that it was not only in that position that he would be reduced to slaughter.

On the day Muhammed Daraghmeh died, his mother, Ibtisam, was watching the television news on the second floor of the family's roughly built home on a narrow hilltop street in the Dehaisha refugee camp near Bethlehem. It was 9:30 P.M. She had not seen Muhammed since that morning, when he had been playing with his sisters as Ibtisam washed dishes. The news flashed a report about a bombing in Jerusalem. Then a group of Fatah gunmen started shooting into the air outside the family's house. Ibtisam's husband, Ahmed, went outside to find out why they were firing. He came back, his face white. Ibtisam fainted and was taken to the hospital. She was injected with a sedative and received an insulin shot for her diabetes. Four hours later, when she came home, she was speechless, weeping uncontrollably and silently. Muhammed's brother Amr approached her and tried to kiss her cheeks. "Is Muhammed martyred?" she managed to ask him. Amr nodded. Ibtisam fainted again.

Two weeks later, a neighbor named Um Sabri came around in the evening to pay a condolence call on Ibtisam. Um Sabri said, "I wish I was Muhammed's mother, so that I could say that my son is a martyr." Ibtisam began to cry. She could not stop. Amr was angry at Um Sabri, angry at this bullshit rhetoric. He wanted to tell the woman that his mother had been in shock ever since Muhammed's death and that there was no pleasure in having a martyr in the family. He kicked Um Sabri out of the house.

Before Muhammed Daraghmeh went to Jerusalem, he shaved his head to look like a hip young Israeli. Then he put on a black-and-white keffiyeh, tied like a bandanna around his forehead, and posed with a Kalashnikov while Ahmed al-Mughrabi recorded his "martyrdom message" on videotape. As he read his final statement, Muhammed lifted the assault rifle, resting the butt on his hip. He looked down at the text of his message as he read it. His face was soft and a light bronze color. Ibtisam didn't recognize him when she saw the footage. She noticed that Muhammed wore a ring on his left hand. When the girl who gave it to him turned up at the mourning tent, it turned out Muhammed had had a secret girlfriend as well as a secret mission. The bomb maker, al-Mughrabi, sold the rights to broadcast Muhammed's martyrdom message to an Arab satellite news station for $10,000. He split the cash with an officer in Arafat's General Intelligence who helped prepare Muhammed's mission.

As I watched the tears of Ibtisam Daraghmeh, I wondered about her son, about al-Mughrabi, and about Adnan Shahine, the man tarred as a collaborator. I wondered which was worse: to sell out your people to the enemy for money, or to send someone to his death for money? The answer, of course, is that the two are distinct only in that people fear the collaborator until they know his identity, whereas men like al-Mughrabi rely on the widespread association of their name with fear to protect them and to further their profit. After all, al-Mughrabi was just like Shahine, a man who was not backed by a big clan like the Abayats and, therefore, could fall victim to powerful gangsters if he were not also feared. He came to Dehaisha from Libya, where his family was in exile, when Arafat founded the Palestinian Authority.

There was no consciousness among the gunmen of the suffering they might cause to the people of Bethlehem. In May 2003, Palestinian police arrested a ring of bank robbers who also happened to be members of the Popular Front for the Liberation of Palestine. The police held the robbers at their Bethlehem lockup. The night after the arrests, PFLP gunmen went to Beit Jala and fired shots across the wadi toward Gilo. It was a year since anyone had opened fire on the Jerusalem suburb, because it became clear there was no military or political gain to doing so. But the PFLP found a rationale. They wanted to draw the Israelis into an invasion of the whole of Bethlehem, knowing that the Palestinian police always emptied their jails on those occasions so that the Israelis wouldn't be able to take all the prisoners away for interrogation. To secure the freedom of their partners in crime, the gunmen were ready to see an entire town cowering behind closed doors as enemy tanks patrolled the streets. It was another illustration of terrorist action apparently aimed at Israel that, in fact, was driven by an internal Palestinian dispute.

The Aqsa Martyrs Brigades gunmen sent boys like Muhammed Daraghmeh to die among Israelis, while they strutted around Bethlehem. They possessed guns and money. The only element of gangster chic they lacked was women. They found that in a tiny stone house above an olive grove on the steep hill of Sidr, a neighborhood at the edge of Beit Jala. Even by the repulsive standards of the Martyrs Brigades, what they did there was appalling.

Rada Amaro lived in that house. She was twenty-four, beautiful, tall, with stylishly bobbed black hair. Her eyes made the exotic, long-lashed ovals that Westerners find so alluring and mysterious in Oriental women when they are framed, coyly, by a veil. But Rada wore no veil. As a Christian, she was free to dress more daringly and she took that license to the limit, even a little beyond. At Peter's, a hair salon where she worked in Beit Jala, she would wear tops that by conservative Palestinian standards exposed a good deal of her smooth ochre shoulders and cleavage. There were other things that she exposed at the salon: a client once gave her money for her family, when Rada told her times were hard for the Amaros. Rada and her eighteen-year-old sister, Dunya, lived with their aging parents. Moussa Amaro, their father, was seventy-two and had been without a job for years. His other four daughters were married, as was one of his sons. His second boy, Jeriez, made a scant wage as a glazier and lived with his parents in the old blockhouse, the poorest dwelling in an otherwise middle-class area. Moussa's wife brought home a small wage from her cleaning job at the Talitha Kumi School, which was run by German Protestants.

It was a dull existence for a beautiful young girl who knew about the excitement the world could offer from television but who had no opportunity to escape her dead-end life through further education. The way she dressed and her girlish flirtatiousness was sufficient to bring Rada Amaro a reputation as a woman of loose morals in the puritan world of the Palestinians. Even though she was from the Christian minority and not bound by the strictures of Muslim society, neighbors judged her negatively simply because she stood out. Stood out enough to attract the attention of the Abayats.

Atef Abayat and Issa Abayat led the Martyrs Brigades in the Bethlehem area. They began to have sex with Rada Amaro, according to people close to the Martyrs Brigades in Bethlehem. However it began, the girl undoubtedly was scared to say no to men feared by the whole town. She could turn to no one. She was a Christian and therefore lacked the tight social backing that might have protected a Muslim woman in the refugee camps. Her family was poor, so she didn't have even the moderate clout that a wealthy Christian clan might have been able to muster. Some other Martyrs Brigades gunmen tried to rape a Christian woman in Beit Sahour, a suburb on the other side of

Bethlehem from Beit Jala. The woman's father was wealthy enough to send her to safety in Jordan. Moussa Amaro was powerless and penniless. Once it started, there was no way out for Rada. If Rada had tried to stop sleeping with the Abayats, she would have feared they might hurt her. Even if they let her go, they could ruin her chances of ever finding a husband by letting it be known what she had done. Her reputation was already bad enough, when she had done nothing more than to wear sexy clothing.

In the end, the decision was not Rada Amaro's to make. Just as the Martyrs Brigades gunmen used Adnan Shahine to show that they would be merciless on collaborators, they decided Rada could serve to boost their moral standing among the public. On August 28, 2001, Martyrs Brigades gunmen went to the Sidr blockhouse. It was the time of the afternoon when the heat was slow on the dusty hill and the grasshoppers susurrated in the olive grove below the Amaros' home. The gunmen found Rada there alone. They put her on the bed and covered her face with a pillow. They shot her through the pillow. Before they left, her sister Dunya came home unexpectedly. They forced her onto the bed next to her sister and shot her through another pillow. At 4 P.M. Moussa Amaro found his two daughters with bullets in their heads.

The Martyrs Brigades issued a statement. They asserted their responsibility for the killing of the two Amaro girls. "We wanted to clean the Palestinian house of prostitutes," the statement said. The Martyrs Brigades thugs sexually degraded Rada Amaro, punished her for it, and then claimed the position of moral champions from a society that they more than anyone were responsible for sullying.

Within a few months, the two Abayats were dead, slain by an Israeli helicopter missile while driving a stolen jeep. Palestinian officials expressed outrage at Israel's killing of Atef and Issa Abayat, though the same political leaders never had anything to say about the death of Rada Amaro at the hands of gangsters on Arafat's payroll. Foreign correspondents scrutinized the morality of Israel's assassination policy, as so often before. But when I talked to the people of Bethlehem, I found they saw a pitiless justice in the end of the Abayats. Unlike Rada Amaro, those who tormented her merited their violent demise.

CHAPTER THREE

The Heroic Scum

Arafat's Fractious Henchmen

[We] turn midgets into heroes
And heroes into scum.

—NIZAR QABBANI, "FOOTNOTES TO
THE BOOK OF SETBACK"

ZAKARIA BALOUSH WANTED to get out of the dirty game. In 1986 he moved to Cairo, married a second time, and started a new family. For two decades he had fought the Israelis and been consumed by the hostilities within the Palestine Liberation Organization. He no longer wanted to battle Abu Jihad, nor to infight for Arafat, nor to attack Abu Iyad. He had done it all and worse, tarnished his record and his soul for the sake of these assholes. From his base in Egypt, he could stay in the contest, but keep clear enough of all the muck and danger that he also might raise a family. He could manage the PLO's contacts with worldwide intelligence agencies, which was his job, and use the vital knowledge he gathered to secure himself against the jealousy and violence of his colleagues at headquarters in Tunis. Most of all, he could protect himself from Yasser Arafat.

When Arafat decided to send a forward-planning detachment of his top men to Gaza in 1994 as part of the implementation of the Oslo Accords, Zakaria Baloush could have remained in Cairo. There were other senior Arafat people, including Farouk Kaddoumi, head of the PLO's Political Department, who refused to have anything to do with the new agreement and stayed in Tunis. But Baloush returned to Gaza as part of Arafat's advance guard. The dirty game, he thought, was over, now that a peace deal was signed. The soldiers of the PLO would become the overseers of peace in the Palestinian territories. He had joined Fatah in 1964 and the following year became a member of its military wing. The marks of that long struggle through Egypt and Jordan and Lebanon, and of the secret missions to European governments and weapons dealers, and of the times he was jailed or hunted were evident in his face. His thick brown cheeks and broad nose were swaddled by a graying mustache and short hair streaked with white. A hearty eater, he carried before him a belly like a basketball. The mission wouldn't be easy for the men Arafat would send ahead to Gaza. Zakaria Baloush understood that there would be a tough job ahead dealing with Hamas, and who knew how trustworthy the Israelis would be?

In fact, it was to be even harder than he foresaw. The Israelis refused permission for him to enter Gaza. They knew his career and his contacts in the arms business. They knew he wasn't one of those most easily controlled by Arafat, and the Israelis wanted everyone to do just as Arafat ordered, because they still believed they could manipulate him through a corrupt network of monopolies and mutual dependency. But Zakaria Baloush sneaked into the Gaza Strip anyway. As the Palestinians were preparing to leave for Gaza, he approached Ghazi Jabali, whom Israel had accepted as Arafat's police chief, and told him he wanted to masquerade as Jabali's driver to get through the border. "Will you carry my luggage?" Jabali asked.

"Fine, I'll carry your bags," Zakaria said.

At the Rafah border crossing, an Israeli soldier opened the wire gate and looked through the window of the car. "I'm Ghazi Jabali and this is my driver." The soldier didn't ask for identity papers. Zakaria Baloush was through to Gaza for the first time in a quarter century.

Baloush went to the military building on the edge of Rafah's refugee camp where PLO officers were gathered with Israeli soldiers and Shin Bet agents. This meeting was held to figure out the details of the handover of power when Arafat would return in a few months. Baloush pushed out his chest and held up his head confidently. Israelis weren't used to Palestinians behaving with assurance around them. They let Baloush go inside and up the stairs. A woman in the uniform of an Israeli lieutenant colonel saw him in the corridor. In Arabic she asked, "Who are you?"

"I am Brigadier General Zakaria Baloush. Where is the conference room?" he said. "I am carrying a message to the Israelis from Yasser Arafat."

The Israeli officer showed him to a door and opened it. Inside, Israelis and Palestinians sat across from each other around a long table. Zakaria's old comrade Ziad al-Atrash was running the meeting for the Palestinians. He turned to see who had entered. Al-Atrash didn't give anything away, but Zakaria saw his lip curl beneath his heavy mustache and his eyebrows rise as if he were thinking, You old bastard, you made it through after all. Al-Atrash asked for a break in the meeting while he consulted with Zakaria.

When the talks restarted, one of the Israelis stared across the table at Zakaria. He was young, pale, stocky, and shaven-headed, and he wore civilian clothes. Zakaria could tell he was Shin Bet. "Who are you?" the Israeli asked.

"Zakaria Brahim Brahim Baloush. I was born in 1944 and I'm from Majdal." Zakaria saw that the Israeli recognized the Arab name for the town of Ashkelon, just up the Israeli coast from the northern end of the Gaza Strip. "And who are you?"

"I'm Yuval. You'll shake hands with me?"

"What's your job?"

"I'm *mukhabarat*," the Israeli said, using the Arabic word for intelligence service. "And you?"

"I'm also *mukhabarat*."

"Welcome," said Yuval.

"I shall be bringing arms and weapons to Gaza," Zakaria told him when they had been talking for a while.

"Do you have the agreement of Yasser Arafat about this?"

Curious, Zakaria thought. These Israelis ought to have understood better how Arafat worked before they signed a peace deal with him. If Zakaria had waited for Arafat's approval, he would still be loitering in Cairo instead of negotiating with the Israelis in Gaza. "Don't worry," he said. "After it's done, I'll have Yasser Arafat's agreement. That's his way."

It was also Arafat's way to be the one man in the PLO allowed to hand out cash. He carried a briefcase with him wherever he traveled. He kept it filled with dollars. When he wanted to buy someone, he would produce anywhere up to $50,000 from the case and slide it across his desk, along with smiling thanks "for your loyalty." Arafat also made sure to spend his money only where he thought it would be useful. Just in case things didn't work out with the peace agreement, he gave the advance guard in Gaza no funds. The generals and colonels negotiating with the Israelis lacked means to pay even for their lodgings. The owner of the Adam Hotel on the seafront was so happy at the imminent institution of Palestinian rule that he let them stay on the promise of future payment. For three months, they took laundry, food, and accommodation from the hotel. It was a long time before Arafat paid the Adam.

In the new Palestinian Authority, Zakaria Baloush was named deputy chief of General Intelligence in the Gaza Strip. He saw that it was a ploy by Arafat to preoccupy him with watching his back. Arafat wanted Zakaria focused on the machinations of his own boss, Amin al-Hindi, rather than building a power base with which he might challenge Arafat. Arafat did the same thing almost throughout the unnecessarily complex array of twelve different security services he formed on his arrival in Gaza. The old soldiers of the PLO, who commanded respect among the ranks, received low-paid, second-tier jobs designed to keep them dependent on Arafat's personal favor and anxious about relations with their immediate commander, who was always, of course, an Arafat crony.

In his new job, Baloush worked to control Hamas, to convince its leaders not to attack Israel and wreck the peace process, and to keep track of its operational cells. He also built contacts among the Israelis. With one Israeli officer, Baloush crossed the Erez Checkpoint into Israel and drove up to the edge of Ashkelon. The two men stood in a field and Zakaria pointed to the spot where his father's house, the home where he was born, had stood.

"How can you be so sure it was right there?" the Israeli asked, gazing at the long grass and small piles of old stone blocks.

"Because the last time I stood there, I was so scared that it's imprinted on my memory exactly." Zakaria refused to go nearer than fifty yards from the site of the house. He shook just to be that close. He recalled an Israeli plane flying overhead, so low to the ground that the four-year-old Zakaria could see the face of the gunner, and his mother screaming and Zakaria clutching his little brother to his body to protect him. It was his first memory.

The peace agreement that Zakaria Baloush worked to defend was, for him, the remedy to all the lost years of the village of Majdal. In the moment that he stood with the Israeli officer in the emptiness where his family once lived, Baloush remembered what had been in that place. There was a typical village house built in stone around a courtyard, split into two since Zakaria's grandfather died and shared his property between Zakaria's father and his uncle. His was a family of fellahin—peasant farmers—who also ran a carpentry workshop. The women embroidered robes and underwear in a style particular to Ashkelon with silk imported from Aleppo and cotton from India, rather than the Egyptian cotton used by other Palestinians. There were 12,000 people in the village. Baloush was one of the oldest clans, alongside the Satoums and Salouls, and they believed they had lived on the shores of the Mediterranean since even before the Assyrian king Sennacherib forced Ashkelon's surrender in 701 B.C. Zakaria Baloush didn't expect to return to the field and rebuild the house. That wasn't what he foresaw from the peace process. He worked so hard to enforce the Oslo Accords because he wanted to end the vacuum that suffocated his people for fifty years, to let in the oxygen that was burned up by the Arab world's manipulation of the Palestinian issue and its rhetoric about returning people like him to his home. That only served to keep them in the penurious limbo of the "refugee," generation after generation.

The people of Majdal scattered when the Israelis came. Some went to Lydda and Ramla where they became Israelis and eventually lived with the noise of the flights taking off from Ben-Gurion International Airport next door. Others ran to Zarqa, a Jordanian backwater. The rest, the unluckiest, were cast into the Egyptian-ruled Gaza Strip. The Egyptians gave them tents and told them to stay in Beit Hanoun, a flat area right at the northernmost inland tip of Gaza. The Gazans didn't like the Majdalawis. It was very difficult for a man from Majdal to find a bride from a Gazan clan. Even when Baloush and his comrades returned in 1994, they discovered that the Palestinian Authority registered their families as "refugees," as opposed to "citizens" of Gaza. Since boyhood, Zakaria Baloush, who was forced to flee from his home by the Israeli enemy, had found his compatriots unwelcoming. It bestowed upon him a cynical view of Palestinian nationhood and the emptiness of its impassioned oratory of unity that, in turn, gave him the healthy sense of suspicion that kept him alive later.

Even that long history of cynicism was not enough to protect Zakaria Baloush during the Oslo years from a growing disgust at the double game Arafat and the Israelis played. He identified a number of Hamas activists in Gaza who he believed might be prepared to "retire." They started out as reckless youths, but by the time Zakaria came to them, they had families and wanted to come in from the cold, to lead normal lives. With two of them, Osama Abu Taha and Muhammed Milahi, Baloush was about to close the deal and get them to quit the Hamas military wing, when Israel assassinated Yihye Ayyash, the Engineer, with a booby-trapped cellular phone. Though it was Israel that destroyed those negotiations, Arafat worked against him too. Baloush was in charge of the PLO's information-gathering about Israeli MIAs, and he began to talk to the head of the Shin Bet about helping to recover the bodies of at least three soldiers missing since the battle of Sultan Yakoub in Lebanon in 1982. The Israelis would have given a good deal in return for the information Baloush possessed, which included intelligence that the three men were buried just outside Damascus. After all, in earlier deals Israel swapped live Arab prisoners of war for the bodies of slain Israeli soldiers, just so they could bring them home and give the parents a grave over which to grieve. But when Baloush brought the Shin Bet men to Arafat, he found the Palestinian leader politely uncooperative.

"Zakaria is sick and I want him to look after his health," Arafat said. "So, no, he can't help you on this."

"We'll give him the best treatment for his illness in our hospitals," one of the senior Israelis offered.

Zakaria and Arafat both knew that his health was fine. "No, I prefer that he should stay at home," Arafat said. Baloush saw that Arafat didn't want him to earn the gratitude of the top Shin Bet officials or to be an alternative Palestinian conduit for them. Arafat wouldn't let any of his men gain that kind of strength, in case they might use it to threaten him or to screw something out of him. It was the same way Arafat dealt with his senior appointments in the security services. He tried to ensure that the top men were indebted exclusively to him. People like Zakaria, who had their own networks of support, didn't receive the top jobs, because they were able, at least to some degree, to resist the corruption of the *ra'is*. One mid-ranking officer in Arafat's Force 17 guard unit with decades of experience in the personal service of the *ra'is* complained to me that Faisal Abu Sharaq, who Arafat made the commander of the unit, was a talentless yes-man who used to be his driver. Arafat's head of National Security Forces, General Nasser Yussef, refused attempts to make him part of the corrupt money-making schemes that were the reward of Arafat's top officers. At a meeting of senior Palestinian Authority military men in 1996, Arafat turned to General Yussef: "Why don't you find yourself a project?" he said. He meant one of the business monopolies other senior officers and ministers cornered, like the importing of computer parts or the distribution of gasoline.

"No, thanks," Yussef said.

After the meeting, Zakaria Baloush approached Yussef. "*Ya basha,*" he said, using the Arabic term of respect for a commander, "if you don't let him corrupt you, you'll never be at the top for long." Nasser Yussef, who commanded considerable respect even among Israeli officers, was soon sidelined. He kept his job, but for years he was able to accomplish little, as power shifted to the hands of men who hadn't said no to Arafat's Mephistophelian deal. Yussef and Baloush were among the Palestinian guerrillas who had fought for years with conviction and now brought that same sincerity to bear on their work to uphold the peace agreement. The gangsters Arafat named as their commanders and comrades undermined that project until Zakaria Baloush felt there was nothing left of it.

Sometimes Baloush wondered why it should surprise him. There had been times when he, too, did Arafat's dirty work for him. In 1988 Arafat summoned Baloush to his office at Hammam al-Shat in Tunis. "I want you to do me a favor," Arafat said. "I want you to shake up Abu Iyad and Abu al-Hawl." These were two men on the Fatah Central Committee who were working behind the scenes to expel Arafat from the organization. Abu Iyad, whose name was Salah Khalaf, was the more powerful of the two, with a strong personal following. He supervised the Black September terrorist group that attacked Israeli athletes at the Munich Olympics in 1972. His bodyguard killed him in 1991, probably on the orders of Abu Nidal, another Palestinian faction leader. Abd al-Hamid Ha'il, known as Abu al-Hawl, was a weaker figure, though he took over the running of terrorist operations inside

Israel after Abu Jihad's assassination in 1988. A supporter of Abu Nidal killed Abu al-Hawl in 1991. But while they were alive, they remained a threat to Arafat.

Arafat told Zakaria Baloush that he would set up a fake committee of inquiry. The subject of the inquiry would be a bogus accusation that Zakaria had stolen $2 million from PLO funds. When Zakaria came before the committee, he would turn the tables by revealing that Abu Iyad had received $10 million from Libya to assassinate Egyptian president Anwar Sadat. Zakaria knew from his sources in Arab intelligence agencies that Abu Iyad truly did take the money, though Islamic fundamentalists beat him to the punch and killed Sadat in 1981. Abu Iyad kept the cash and, in any case, probably never actually intended to do the job. Zakaria had informed Arafat about the Libyan money sometime before, and it was now that the PLO leader decided to use the information. Abu Iyad would be unable to deny the accusation with any credibility, because everyone on the committee would understand that Zakaria, whose job was to liaise with the Arab intelligence services, spoke from a position of knowledge.

The next morning the Fatah Central Committee convened, and Zakaria made his startling revelation. Abu Iyad and Abu al-Hawl were floored. Arafat turned on them, faked surprise and outrage widening his eyes to melodramatic balloons. "I won't sit at the table with spies," he yelled. The two men slunk out of the room, their challenge to Arafat's leadership sidelined for the moment.

Not long before his assassination, Abu Iyad met *Time*'s Palestinian correspondent Jamil Hamad for a drink in a hotel in Amman, Jordan. Jamil asked him about the chances that the intifada then underway in the West Bank and Gaza would lead to a Palestinian state. "Jamil, there'll be a Palestinian state with Jerusalem as its capital only when Yasser Arafat has disposed of all his friends," Abu Iyad said. Only when Arafat could be certain of absolute, dictatorial control would he truly want to become head of state. For that reason, there are many senior PLO officials who believe the Fatah Revolutionary Council, whose leader Abu Nidal broke away from the PLO in 1974, was not as independent of Arafat's influence as the *ra'is* made out. All the while Abu Nidal was busy assassinating those around Arafat.

Zakaria Baloush began his political work before the PLO existed.

Borrowing slogans from the Muslim Brotherhood and the Communists, he distributed leaflets around Gaza while he was in high school in the late 1950s. The leaflets condemned the regime of President Gamal Abdel Nasser, the Egyptian leader who ruled Gaza. Zakaria posted a few of them cheekily in the complaints box outside the Egyptian governor's office in Gaza City, and he organized student strikes. The Egyptians jailed him for twenty days with some of his fellow students and beat them. They brought a vicious dog to the cell and set it on one of Zakaria's friends. When the Egyptians called the dog off, Zakaria noticed bloody chunks of his comrade's forearm hanging from its teeth. Even so, Baloush's talent as a soccer player attracted the attention of one of the Egyptian commanders, who sent him to the Military College in Cairo. There were only a few places at the college open to Gazans, and powerful clans usually had them sewn up. Zakaria took his chance, but he hated the stinking, cramped quarters for the cadets, and he left the college to study at Asyut University, farther south in Egypt.

At Asyut, Zakaria Baloush channeled his political work specifically toward the Palestinian cause for the first time. A number of other future PLO chiefs, including Abu Iyad, attended the university during that period. Zakaria headed the Palestinian Students' Union and built a strong bond with Hail Abdel Hamid, the secret Fatah representative in Cairo. In 1964 Baloush joined Fatah, but quit after a year because the Gazans who ran the group looked down on the boy from Majdal. In any case, Fatah wasn't the biggest party among the Palestinians at Asyut. Already they were demonstrating their talent for factionalism, with Fatah students angrily debating their compatriots from the Heroes of the Return group and the Palestine Liberation Army, among others. The PLO, which was founded in 1964, was thought by the students to be funded by the United States, and its first leader was written off as a stooge of the Egyptians. Baloush was more direct and not built for political debates. He joined al-Asifa (the Storm), Fatah's military wing, and started an arms-smuggling route from Gaza to the West Bank, using a donkey.

Zakaria Baloush first met Yasser Arafat in mid-1968, less than a year before the Fatah chief took control of the PLO. Even then, Arafat was a dubious figure to young comrades like Baloush. The *ra'is* was in Cairo on a visit to Nasser. He came to the Fatah office, and instinctively, Zakaria kept his mouth shut. "What do you do here?" Arafat asked him.

"I work in the media center," Zakaria said. It was untrue. He was, in fact, beginning to move his base to Jordan where, under cover of a job in an engineering office, he took command of al-Asifa's operations in the West Bank. He knew Egyptian police accompanied Arafat and that they were not to be trusted.

The next encounter with Arafat was a dangerous one. The PLO moved its base to Jordan, and began to threaten the stability of the Hashemite regime there, attacking Israel in the Jordan Valley, drawing Israeli reprisal raids, and behaving as though outside the law in Jordan itself. The lawlessness of the PLO fighters forced King Hussein to take them on. In 1970 the king's army defeated them in what became known as Black September. The PLO men fled. Baloush first went to Syria with another officer. They knew Arafat blamed ranking field officers like them for the defeat in Jordan. Someone, probably sent by the political leadership of Fatah, shot Baloush's colleague in the back. Zakaria moved on to Lebanon, where he lived as an outlaw from Fatah until Arafat, needing men for a new mission, decided to forgive him.

The years the PLO spent in Lebanon coincided with the times of greatest left-wing sympathy for its cause in Europe. Arafat put Zakaria Baloush in charge of European operations and contacts. He built a fine relationship with Italian antiterrorist intelligence. His biggest coup, however, was a secret mission to West Germany. Through Libyan intelligence, West Germany asked the PLO for a deal. In 1980 Zakaria went to West Germany with a delegation of PLO officials. They agreed not to carry out any attacks on West German territory. In return they were allowed to operate in West Germany and exchange information with the West Germans. Other PLO leaders accused Zakaria Baloush of working for West German intelligence, but Arafat accepted the deal. Baloush believed that the Europeans wanted to help the PLO just enough to create a balance, a mutual threat between the Palestinians and the Israelis. It was a dangerous game for Zakaria. He went to Belgium in October 1981 with cash from Libyan leader Moammar Ghaddafi, intending to buy FROG-7 missiles, Soviet short-range rockets. The Israelis attempted to assassinate him there. At other times, they tried to shoot him in

Rome and Paris, and they blew up his car in Beirut too. At least, he believed it was the Israelis.

Zakaria Baloush could never be sure who was working against him, threatening him. In Beirut he learned of an unnerving episode that highlighted the uncertainty and suspicion constantly washing through the lives of PLO officers like himself. In 1979 Abu Iyad approached Arafat's personal secretary, a suave man with a small mustache who was known as Abu Reja'i. "I want you to assassinate Ali Hassan Salameh," Abu Iyad said. Salameh was the playboy mastermind of the Munich Olympics attack on Israeli athletes. Arafat frequently spoke of his fatherly feelings toward Salameh. He defended Salameh's patronage of a casino in Lebanon, though it was run by the PLO's Syrian enemies. When Zakaria complained about Salameh's visits to the gaming tables, Arafat brushed him off and said, "This is high policy." Abu Reja'i made no immediate reply to Abu Iyad. Instead he went to Arafat and told him what Abu Iyad requested of him.

"What was your reaction?" Arafat said, looking hard at Abu Reja'i. It was a chilling moment. Arafat gave nothing away. He wanted to test his underling. It was impossible for Abu Reja'i to guess the right answer. Could Arafat really desire the death of the man who was like a son to him? Or would he think Abu Reja'i was working for Abu Iyad?

Quietly, taking care not to let his discomfort show on his face, Abu Reja'i said, "Nothing. I had no reaction."

"Did you make an agreement with Abu Iyad?"

Abu Reja'i made no reply. Arafat paced his office.

Four days later, Salameh was dead. His car blew up in Beirut in an operation widely credited to the Mossad, Israel's international espionage agency. The quiet scene that passed between Abu Reja'i and the PLO chief in Arafat's office was dreadful and mafia-like. Arafat knew that Abu Reja'i had a personal connection to Salameh, because his wife was related to Salameh's wife. Arafat's message was clear: no matter how close you are to me, I may allow you to die. This was how Arafat lived throughout his years as a terrorist chief, and despite what Westerners believed, he didn't change. During the Oslo years, Israelis looked upon Arafat as an almost comical figure, made benign by the peace process, stuttering his way through the satirical television puppet show *Hatzufim,* where he was depicted passionately diving beneath the covers with Prime Minister Netanyahu. But even at those times, Arafat didn't halt his contacts in the terrorist underworld. Arafat kept closer relations with Abu Nidal than was thought, even after the breakaway PLO faction leader assassinated many of Arafat's supposed comrades over the years. Senior Palestinian security figures told me Arafat paid some of Abu Nidal's medical bills.

It was Arafat's same tactic of keeping his commanders in a state of constant doubt that caused so many problems for the Oslo peace process. Just after the start of the Aqsa intifada in 2000, Arafat held a meeting of his Security Council. The ministers and officers tried hard to pin down their leader. Should they escalate the violence or use their forces to control the rioting, to keep the youths away from Israeli checkpoints and put a stop to the rising death toll. Arafat was vague, as he likes to be. Eventually cabinet secretary Tayyeb Abdel Rahim called out to him in exasperation, "Mr. Arafat, what do you want? Peace? Or War? You have to tell us." Arafat didn't reply. A year later I went into Arafat's Ramallah compound to see one of his top officers, though Israeli tanks surrounded the gates. The officer told me the besieged Arafat rode his exercise bicycle every morning, paced his office for an hour each afternoon for exercise, and talked constantly of how the Palestinians would continue to defy the Israelis. The *ra'is* was in his element. "In his mind, it's 1982 and he's in his bunker in Beirut again," the officer said, shaking his head in disbelief. "This is when he's at his happiest."

Arafat's preference for winks and nods rather than definite orders was the result of decades of avoiding accountability. If anything went wrong, his officers knew the trail of blame would never lead from them to Arafat. It was a trait of shiftiness written in the differing versions of his very birth. Arafat variously claimed to have been born in Jerusalem and Cairo (the more likely of the two). His name at birth was Muhammed Abder Rauf Arafat al-Kudwa al-Husseini, but he adapted his name to that of a follower of the prophet Muhammed, Amar ibn Yasser. He thus became Yasser Arafat, and took the nom de guerre Abu Amar, which is how he is known in the daily speech of most Palestinians. His divisive style of leadership was not out of place in the recent history of the Palestinian battle against Zionism. The years of British rule in Palestine saw fighting between Arabs and Zionist colonists, but it was also a time of vicious rivalry between the two most powerful Jerusalem clans, the Nashishibis and the Husseinis, to whom Arafat claims a family relationship. In 1929 the Husseinis won control of the Palestinian Arab Executive, effectively the government of the Arabs in Palestine, so their Nashishibi rivals began to work with the British. Eight years later, the Husseinis tried to assassinate one of the leading members of the Nashishibi clan in a mini civil war. Some of the victims of that fighting died by being dropped into pits with scorpions and snakes. The Arab Revolt of 1936-1939 claimed the lives of many Jews, but it degenerated into foraging attacks on Palestinian villages by roving bands of Arab gunmen. More Palestinians died at the hands of their own compatriots than were killed by Jews or the British military. When the Arab armies gathered to invade the new State of Israel in 1948, the Iraqi general designated to lead the force was unseated as a result of political infighting among his subordinates. He later wrote that Arab officers were more interested in jockeying for good jobs than defeating Israel.

In contrast to these forces of competing Arab nations and Palestinian clans, Fatah, the Arabic acronym for the Palestinian National Liberation Movement, held a promise of victory ("al-Fatah," or the victory, is also the title of sura 48 of the Koran) and unity. To many, that promise seemed fulfilled on July 1, 1994, when Arafat's motorcade made its way across the Egyptian border into Gaza, marking his return to head the Palestinian Authority. Arafat held elections in January 1996 that gave him an approval rating akin to those attained in bogus shows of democracy by the presidents of Egypt and Syria. The reality was that, elected or not, Arafat dealt with opposition groups such as Hamas and supporters within the Palestinian Authority in the same manner: as a dictator. Barely answerable to his own people, Arafat needed to maintain Israel as an enemy, no matter his dependence on the peace process nor his vulnerability to Israeli attack. On a visit to South Africa in 1994, Arafat compared his peace deal to a temporary, tactical truce made by the Prophet in 628. In a speech in a mosque, he also called for a jihad to liberate Jerusalem. Palestinians often tried to explain such language and the apparent contradiction of Arafat's signature on the Oslo peace agreement by pointing out the general emptiness of Arabic rhetoric. The impact of public Arabic speech is not in its logic but in its tone and use of repeated, emotive phrases. It is intended to stir the emotions, rather than to convince through rational argument. The late Palestinian intellectual Edward Said described it as "an enthusiasm for distant generality that covers up particular experiences and, with them, immediate failure." When I first met Arafat in person in 1998, I thought of his words, of his speech in South Africa, and of the nature of Arabic rhetoric, and I thought perhaps he had to get himself fired up so that he, too, wouldn't feel like a failure for accepting the compromise of the Oslo deal. He seemed tiny, not just short, but slight as a prepubescent boy. If he could keep the peace process going, albeit in a corrupt and shaky manner, I thought maybe that was how things had to be done in the Middle East, and I just about felt inclined to pardon the disturbing things I was learning about his regime.

Many Palestinians were less forgiving. I went to Gaza in May 2000. It happened that I was there two days after a big riot against the Israelis to commemorate the anniversary of the *naqba,* the catastrophe, which is how Palestinians refer to the foundation of the State of Israel. I ate fried fish at the Salaam restaurant on the seashore, where the stereo played a seemingly interminable Muzak album. Driven from my table prematurely by the awful alto saxophone meanderings of Kenny G, I left the Salaam without washing down my meal with mint tea, as I usually would have done. I walked through the warm night to the square outside the Palestinian Legislative Council. Beneath a statue of an unknown soldier, Palestinians strolled through this rare open green space and sat on the benches drinking tea from plastic cups. I looked around for the vendor, but, of course, he found me first. Fadi, a twelve-year-old, filled a cup from a thermos and charged me the premium price of five shekels. When he learned I was a journalist, he showed me the pink welt on his buttocks where an Israeli rubber bullet struck him during the riots. The wheal was about the size of the five-shekel coin I had just given him. Then he asked me why I was still in Gaza, now that the riots were over. "I'm writing a story about Hamas and the Authority," I said.

Fadi nodded. "Hamas is good, because Sheikh Ahmed Yassin is clean," he said. "The Authority is corrupt and dirty. But Abu Amar is the shit on my shoe." For emphasis, he lifted his foot and tapped the heel of his shabby sandal with the thermos. Before too long, many of Arafat's closest advisers and military staff would think the same way.

HE WORE A RUSSET check sport coat and a raffish mustache. On entering the hut at the Erez Checkpoint between Israel and Gaza, he interrupted my conversation with an Israeli officer, slapping a hand-shake and loudly greeting the captain, as though he were running for Congress and canvassing for votes at a shopping mall. I informed him that I was approaching an urgent deadline and asked him to wait until my business was completed before continuing his chat with the officer. He smiled conspiratorially at the Israeli and jabbed a finger into my chest. "I am a VIP," he said in Hebrew. "You are no V-I-P." With each syllable, a jab of the finger: *You-are-no-V-I-P.* The VIP pass issued by the Israeli Civil Administration in the territories—its posses-sion was the greatest accomplishment of the peace process for many leading Palestinians, and yet it was no benefit at all to most residents of Gaza and the West Bank that men like this should have been able to travel freely with their VIP cards through checkpoints often barred to ordinary Palestinians. This man was Yasser Arafat's justice minister Freih Abu Medein.

The day after I encountered Abu Medein, I went to the office of Riad Khoudery, the head of al-Azhar University in Gaza. I came to dis-cuss one of his professors, Fathi Suboh, jailed for assigning students an essay titled "What does democracy mean to you?" (Evidently, the cor-rect answer was: More than it meant to Arafat's regime, which kept Professor Suboh in prison without charge several months for seem-ingly inviting criticism of the administration of law and government in Gaza.) Khoudery, who approved of the academic's disgraceful incar-ceration, tried to deflect the heat of bad publicity by diverting my sympathy from the poor professor to a character much more deeply wronged: Khoudery himself. "The Israelis will not give me a VIP card," he said. "I, a member of the PLO Executive Committee, must line up with all the ordinary workers at the Erez Checkpoint like so much cat-tle." Palestinian laborers arose daily at 2 A.M. and headed for the lines at Erez, where they shuffled through long pens to an Israeli identity check. If they were lucky, they made it to their jobs thirty miles away in Tel Aviv by 8 A.M. Khoudery wrinkled his nose, as though he could smell the sweaty bodies of the workers even as we sat in his breezy office. Then he smiled and lifted the lapel of his suit jacket, rubbing it between his thumb and middle finger like a tailor asking a client to feel the quality: "But one of the Israeli soldiers noticed my clothes and asked me who I was. When I told him, he pushed everyone aside to allow me through." Laughing proudly, Khoudery mimed the action of the soldier. He chopped with an imaginary rifle to clear a path in imitation of the Israeli clubbing a gangway through Khoudery's own people as they struggled, tired and hot, to their ill-paid jobs. He seemed aware of nothing unseemly about his delectation at the further humiliation of the men whose interests he was supposed to represent in the PLO. I began to think perhaps the Israelis had understood the venality of the Palestinian leadership better than anyone else. Ariel Sharon, the Israeli politician who best manipulated the traditions of power and personal status and pride among Middle Easterners, broke into a 1997 cabinet discussion about whether to impose a "closure" on Palestinian towns that would bar workers from crossing into Israel: "Don't punish the ordinary workers with a closure. Take away the VIP cards, so the PLO chiefs can't go to Tel Aviv to see their whores. That's the way to get them to do what we want," he said.

The leadership Arafat imposed on the Palestinians was largely a VIP-card-carrying mafia devoted to privilege, corruption, and threat. But, unlike the Cosa Nostra, there was no such thing as a made man, no one who could not be sacrificed. In the empty dining room of the Beach Hotel in Gaza, the owner, Abu Amr, sat at the central table by the window on a quiet morning in spring 2001, smoking a nargileh with Hisham Mikki, the director of Arafat's Palestinian Broadcasting Corporation. Mikki told Abu Amr that he had to leave for an appointment with his sister, but Abu Amr persuaded him to stay to smoke another waterpipe. Mikki chose an apple-flavored Bahraini tobacco for his nargileh. The two men chatted and stared out at the azure Mediterranean, breaking below the terrace. Hisham Mikki had returned to Gaza with Arafat. Top Palestinian Authority people believed that, as head of the television station, he had amassed a millionaire's fortune, but he also became a focus of the accusations of corruption against the regime when his wife was stopped at the border crossing with a suitcase full of cash.

As the apple-scented cloud drifted in the air, a man walked quickly through the dining-room door. He strode purposefully toward Mikki. Mikki turned to look at him. Abu Amr slipped silently beneath the table. The man reached Mikki and lifted a handgun. He shot him in a pattern hit men call "Mozambique style": a bullet in the forehead and one in each breast.

Someone killed Mikki to set an example against corruption. But it was not one of the opposition groups, such as Hamas—the "Mozambique style" technique was far too professional. Palestinian military insiders told me someone from the Preventive Security Service had carried out the shooting. Arafat's plainclothes detectives learned those forms of killing techniques from the CIA. Senior Palestinian security people told me the Mikki hit was intended merely to relieve community pressure about sleaze in the Palestinian Authority without changing the fundamentally corrupt structure of the economy, and also so that Arafat could dispose of a man whose cupidity had become a public embarrassment.

I wrote a story in *Newsweek* on Palestinian Authority corruption in spring 2000. It detailed the stories of a series of businessmen cheated of land or contracts by Arafat's sidekicks. There was Mahmoud Hamdouni, a Jericho landowner jailed and forced to sign over his gas station to a couple of top Palestinian Authority officials for $1. "Who can help me when my land is taken by the forty thieves?" Hamdouni said. "Arafat is Ali Baba." Then there was Muhammed Masrouji, owner of the Jerusalem Pharmaceuticals Company, whose requests for import licenses on new drugs were delayed for over a year while an Arafat minister named Jamil Tarifi set up a firm that was miraculously able to register fifty new drugs in one day. "I lived all my life dreaming of a Palestinian state as something beautiful and disciplined," Masrouji said. "I am sad and disappointed." And the Arafat-appointed mayor of Ramallah, Ayoub Rabbah, who owned a flour mill and managed to get 60 percent tariffs added to his competitors' imported flour. "People will be paying more than they pay now for flour," Rabbah told me after the tariffs were introduced. Without apparent irony, he added, "The only way we can improve our economy is to protect local businesses, like my flour mill." When my story appeared, it became the focus of talk shows and dinner tables throughout the Arab world. Everyone knew about the Palestinian Authority's corruption, but here for the first time was a respected Western publication detailing the dishonesty, and giving an opportunity to discuss it openly. Arafat responded in typical fashion. Some Authority thugs went to Muhammed Masrouji's office on the edge of Ramallah and trashed it. In one of his security meetings, Arafat furiously demanded that I be arrested or barred from Gaza. He was dissuaded by one of his generals.

The private response to Arafat's corrupt regime among Palestinians was, disappointingly but perhaps logically, one of greater outrage than was shown by the international community, whose representatives were far better placed than ordinary Palestinians to confront Arafat about the matter. In his large office at the magnificent old U.S. consulate on Agron Street in Jerusalem, Consul John Herbst, the senior American diplomatic envoy to the Palestinians, met all the examples of Palestinian Authority corruption I threw at him with the same bored expression and languid posture. "I'm not sure corruption here is greater than elsewhere in the Middle East," Herbst drawled. It was the kind of pragmatic, complacent American support for a dishonest regime that was exposed by the attacks of September 11 as such a failure throughout the Arab world. U.S. policy focused on stability, on Arab leaders who could be bought, maintained, and perhaps restrained. The Aqsa intifada proved Arafat didn't fit that category, no matter how hard State Department diplomats clung to him, just as Osama bin Laden later demonstrated that the Saudis weren't quite what Foggy Bottom took them for, either. Wealthy Palestinians who lived in the West and, therefore, weren't so open to Arafat's intimidation saw their first, hopeful investments in the new Palestine run afoul of the corrupt Authority. Abdel Muhsen Qattan, a rich Palestinian based in London, told me he limited his endowments strictly to charitable donations, because any business venture was corrupted instantly. It was the result of Arafat's authoritarianism: "A dictator can't be surrounded by honest people. They must be the flies around the honey." A 1997 report by the Palestinian Authority comptroller found 40 percent of its budget was wasted or skimmed off through corruption. Arafat ordered immediate action: he told the comptroller to keep his future reports secret. The world's richest Palestinian, Hassib Sabbagh, billionaire owner of an Athens construction conglomerate, eagerly sank his money into a new $70 million power plant in Gaza. He told me, with a combination of resignation and disgust, that it would have cost $20 million less if it weren't for the price of Palestinian corruption and Israeli taxes. A few days before I met Sabbagh, Arafat invited him to his office. Ingratiatingly, the *ra'is* offered a comparison between the situation of the Palestinians and the early Zionists, who benefited from the largesse of Baron Edmond de Rothschild. "We need a Palestinian Rothschild," Arafat said, smiling.

Sabbagh's cutting reply checked Arafat's grin: "When there is a Palestinian Ben-Gurion, maybe then there will be a Rothschild."

To the outsider, the eventual breakdown of the system Arafat set up was linked entirely to the collapse of the peace process. Peace talks failed in summer 2000; violence began, and grew so bad that Israel sent its soldiers into the Palestinian towns. But that received wisdom misses a key element—the speed with which the violence flared, and the extent to which it spun out of Arafat's hands and into the sphere of people who never gained from his fraudulent regime. From the moment Arafat sent his advance guard to Gaza in spring 1994, the Palestinian leadership was divided. The "Outside" leadership, known as such because it returned from decades in Lebanon and Europe, soon sewed up all the best jobs in the ministries and the security establishment. Palestinians called them "the Tunisians," after their last place of exile. The "Inside" leadership, in turn, felt cheated. They had lived through the occupation and many had been jailed during the tough years of the intifada, which they, after all, had headed and which had been the point of pressure that led to Israel's willingness to make a peace deal at all. Furthermore, they had greater support among the people, who knew and in some cases respected them, as opposed to the unknown or, at best, distant figures of the Outside leadership. The Insiders found their only seat of power in the Palestinian parliament, the Legislative Council, but were stymied even there, because Arafat simply neglected to give final, presidential approval to most of their democratic and bureaucratic reforms. In the end, the Inside leadership became so disenchanted with the regime that when Arafat decided to start a new, limited intifada in September 2000, the Insiders quickly took hold of the uprising and used it to bring the entire Oslo edifice crashing down on top of Arafat's government. If they crushed themselves along with it, no matter, because, after all, they believed they had gained little from the years of peace and had nothing to lose.

The man who led that Inside takeover of the Aqsa intifada was Marwan Barghouti, the West Bank chief of Arafat's Fatah faction but also a prominent Legislative Council critic of the way the spoils of Oslo were divided among the Palestinian leadership. Outside the council chamber in November 1997, Barghouti made some remarks to me that, at the time, I simply scribbled in my notebook and attributed to a combination of bluster, bluff, and sour grapes from a man who figured he needed to make a public stink before his boss would give him a promotion. "The Inside leadership still feels they don't have what's coming to them," Barghouti said in his rapid English. "Former intifada leaders, who were very important, are nothing now. Not one of them is in the leadership of the Authority. The people who lived through the intifada will insist on freedom. As a result, maybe the intifada will be renewed, but maybe this time with more violence."

Arafat tried to squash Barghouti by pushing his own candidate, Hussein e-Sheikh, to take over the job of West Bank Fatah chief. Hussein e-Sheikh won election to the job, but Barghouti didn't step down. Arafat allowed both men to hold the same title, thinking that at least the rivalry would make Barghouti feel a little more insecure and dissuade him from angering Arafat. But when the Aqsa intifada began, over three years after Marwan Barghouti and I spoke at the Legislative Council, Barghouti could be found every day at the roadblocks and barricades and addressing the funerals of martyrs in a hoarse tenor. It became clear to me that he foresaw what would happen if Arafat didn't placate leaders like him. When forced to eat dirt, as he perceived it, Barghouti eventually lost patience, grabbed Arafat by his checkered keffiyeh, and rubbed the old man's nose in it instead.

The hardships of the intifada only made the hatred of ordinary people for the Outsiders more pronounced. Alexis de Tocqueville wrote in *L'Ancien Régime et la Révolution* that the French people detested the aristocrats much more strongly in the period immediately before the revolution, when the aristocrats had been stripped of their power but retained their fortunes: it was not simply oppression by the aristocrats that drove the masses to destroy them, but rather the nobility's eventual lack of any function, without the surrender of its privileges. In the same way, once the Aqsa intifada got underway, Palestinians saw the hollowness of the Outside leadership's promise to protect them from the Israeli army. The Authority's status dropped so low that it became the kind of object on which people either would step or spit, but certainly wouldn't touch. Once the balance provided by the pretense of its role as a barricade against the Israelis was destroyed, the corruption and inequality became unbearable.

At the UN Food Distribution Center in Gaza's Tuffah neighborhood, I watched Palestinians crowd toward a chicken-wire window in a booth by the entrance. They waved small pink squares of paper, the ration slip for UN food handouts to Palestinian refugees who were unable to travel to their jobs in Israel because of the intifada. There was utter confusion in the crush around the booth. Everyone shouted at once. A man shoving to get to the clerk in the steamy kiosk threw a punch and was held back by others in the crowd. Abu Amira came past with his donkey cart loaded with the meager rations for his family. He was sweaty, dirty, and angry. He came early, but it had been hot even at 8 A.M. First he pressed through the crowd to hand his ticket, to the clerk. The clerk stamped the ticket, and Abu Amira jockeyed at another window for the second stamp required by the officials who actually handed out the food. On the battered cart, he showed me what he received. It was loaded with enough irradiated milk, olive oil, sugar, and rice to last his family of five for a week, at most—but it was the ration for the month. The yard around us was dusty and stank of the dung of pack animals. Boys maneuvered their donkeys through the crush with heavy blows from sticks and loud curses. Every few minutes a bottleneck formed and the shouting grew louder. The place made Abu Amira boil with rage, but his real anger was for the "Tunisians" like Abu Mazen and Um Jihad, the two top Palestinian Authority officials with the showiest mansions in Gaza. Their palatial, red-roofed dwellings were surrounded incongruously by rubble-strewn sandlots where their bodyguards lounged in the shade. "I spit on the day they came from Tunis," Abu Amira said. "I'd like to see them all shot in the street." Typically, U.S. policymakers chose Abu Mazen, PLO secretary-general Mahmoud Abbas, the definitive Outside leader with absolutely no support among ordinary Palestinians, as the man they would use to edge aside Arafat in 2003. Of course, he failed.

The Palestinian people viewed the "Tunisians" as a unified group, systematically milking them dry. The "Tunisians" didn't see it that way. They learned, as Zakaria Baloush did, from their years around Arafat that their first duty was to look out for their own personal interests. Sometimes the conflict of the intifada, nominally a battle against the Israelis, afforded the Tunisians fine opportunities to dispose of a rival. When the Israelis advanced into Ramallah at the end of April

2002, Jibril Rajoub, head of Preventive Security in the West Bank, received a phone call from one of Arafat's diplomatic advisers, Saeb Erakat. According to Rajoub, Erakat informed him that, although there were wanted Hamas men in the jail at Rajoub's compound, an American mediator assured him the Israelis didn't intend to take the building by force. Rajoub's Gaza counterpart, Muhammed Dahlan, also called to say a senior White House official had told him the Israelis wouldn't enter Rajoub's compound. So Rajoub left the wanted men in the jailhouse across the yard from his elaborate three-story offices.

Then the Israelis attacked.

Rajoub and I pulled into the compound in his armored black Mercedes sedan a few days after the end of the Israeli assault. He climbed out of the car and shoved his thick hands into the pockets of his blue suit. Bulky and powerful, he crunched across the gravel past some of his plainclothes agents, who stood at attention. "Hello, lads," Rajoub said in his rasping voice. He seemed a little cowed by the destruction of his empire and, perhaps, by the awareness that he had fallen into a trap. Despite his reputation for roughness, his burly physique, and massive, bony cranium, Rajoub had remarkably pretty blue eyes, long-lashed and sad. He kept them on the ground as he approached the jail. Tank shells had blackened the walls, and the barred cell doors dangled at crazy angles. He couldn't bear to look inside the main building, so he hung around in the parking lot next to some of his burned-out staff cars while I went into his office.

Rajoub's Preventive Security Service embodied the enigma of the Oslo peace process. Cooperating in training and operations with the CIA, it was the most effective of Arafat's militias. During the periods when Arafat wanted to placate the Israelis and Americans by arresting Hamas activists, it was Rajoub's men who did so. He could stand up to Arafat when he wanted to. Back during the Tunis exile, he once refused Arafat's request to drive Suha Tawil, who would later become the wife of the *ra'is*, to the airport, saying he wouldn't "chauffeur a whore." But Rajoub, who was born near Hebron and whose brother Nayif was a hard-line Hamas sheikh, entered into the dark side of the Oslo years just as forcefully. He held the lucrative monopoly on gasoline distribution in the West Bank. He also arrested a number of Hebron-area businessmen suspected of being collaborators with Israel and forced them to pay tens of thousands of dollars to secure their release. In April 2000 his men entered the office of the Palestinian environment minister and pistol-whipped him, because he tried to fire the ministry's director-general, a Rajoub supporter.

Before the Israelis attacked, I had sat on several occasions with Rajoub in his office. It radiated power from its crystal ashtrays, deep leather armchairs, and souvenir presentation shields from visiting international law enforcement delegations. His young aides rushed about him, and his many cellular phones shrouded the entire coffee table. After the destruction, I walked up through the silent, burned-out building. Rajoub's office door was stuck, obstructed by a shattered jamb, so I kicked it in and shoved it aside with my shoulder. The walls of the private office were scorched by fire, the paint puffed brown and yellow like the toasted top of a lemon meringue pie. The tan curtains billowed in the gusts through the smashed windows. Bullet holes had torn the leather seats. I leaned out the window. Down below, outside the fence ten yards away, there was an Israeli tank. The attack on Rajoub's compound lasted eighteen hours, before he turned over the half-dozen Hamas prisoners in exchange for his men's safe-conduct. The Israelis stayed close by, in any case. When I emerged, Rajoub was still in the parking lot, stooping to read advertisements on the page of a newspaper fluttering by in the breeze that caught under the heel of his wing tips. "This scene of destruction"—he gestured to his wrecked headquarters—"isn't merited by the arrest of six people. It's unbeliev-able, eh?" He had stopped wanting to talk about Erakat and Dahlan and the trap they laid for him, but it was clear he felt outmaneuvered and duped by his rivals. At one point, he rounded on me and growled, "I *was* powerful and I *am* powerful." To admit weakness was to invite the deathblow.

BRIGADIER GENERAL Zakaria Baloush, the deputy head of General Intelligence in the Gaza Strip, assessed the force under his command as the end of the second year of the intifada approached. He gave it a failing grade. There were perhaps seventy agents who were both honest and active, still trying to operate despite the intifada. The other 2,930 on the payroll were either dishonest or sitting out the uprising, or both. Spread those three score and ten over the entire Gaza Strip among a population of more than 1.5 million and their ability to keep law and order was negligible. It was not unusual for a Palestinian security force to fall apart during the intifada as the General Intelligence had, even in Gaza where the Israeli army's profile was lower than in the West Bank. But the job of General Intelligence was to combat the very groups that fought the intifada, like Hamas or the Aqsa Martyrs Brigades: it was General Intelligence that dropped off the map, while the militias became more and more popular.

In a fainthearted, misguided way, Baloush's boss tried to turn things around. In April 2002 Amin al-Hindi, the commander of General Intelligence in the Gaza Strip, went to a meeting of the directors of all Arafat's militias, the Security Council, with a message from the CIA: "We, the CIA, are coming to the field," al-Hindi recited. "We will be choosing new directors, and we will be running their work according to our expectations."

The CIA had always been deeply involved in measuring the performance of the Palestinian security services, but as the discontent of the Israelis and the disquiet of the White House grew throughout the Oslo years, Langley came to the same conclusion as Zakaria Baloush about Arafat's duplicitous game and took a gradually bigger role. Yet the CIA also seemed to back the wrong bullies. For what they wanted to accomplish against determined terrorist groups, they needed to wager on a truly unshakeable bastard. Al-Hindi was not that man.

Rashid Abu Shoubak, the deputy head of Preventive Security in Gaza, listened to al-Hindi's comment at the Security Council meeting. Abu Shoubak looked sinister. His face was thin, with black hair flopping limply over his baggy eyes. He smoked incessantly, which made him susceptible to illness. In one hand there was always a Marlboro, while the other gathered the phlegm he coughed into a tissue and wiped his jet mustache. He slouched and swiveled his chair habitually, but when al-Hindi delivered his CIA threat, he sat upright and yelled across the table at him, "This is total surrender."

Al-Hindi lost his nerve. His face was no match for the malign visage of Abu Shoubak, and it allowed his rivals to read the weakness within. His eyes were always nervous and insecure, and the skin along his jaw was slack and soft. Though his hair was short and gray, colleagues remarked that there was something feminine and distasteful in his manner. At the Security Council, he answered mockingly, but it was clear the menace in Abu Shoubak's voice shocked him.

"Forget what I said," he replied. "We will dress like suicide bombers and we will fight the Israeli sons of bitches to the bitter end."

Zakaria Baloush appreciated what al-Hindi was trying to do. The General Intelligence chief even attempted to arrest the Hamas hardliner Abdel Aziz al-Rantisi a few days before the Security Council meeting, but al-Rantisi's men fired a volley of shots from the doorway of his house in the Sheikh Radwan neighborhood, so al-Hindi turned his squad cars around and ran. Though the CIA was trying to use him as a conduit, he didn't have the full backing of Arafat, and that was a very insecure position from which to go up against ruthless opponents like al-Rantisi or even Machiavellian allies like Abu Shoubak.

In June 2002 Zakaria Baloush went with a fellow officer to General Abdel Razak al-Majaideh, the Gaza commander of the National Security Forces. The Palestinian economy was a mess and Arafat's regime was under greater Israeli pressure than ever before. Baloush and his fellow officers had received no salary for two months. At the same time as they went without pay, they learned from contacts in the Fatah militias that Arafat sent $2 million to the Aqsa Martyrs Brigades in Gaza. Al-Majaideh didn't know about the cash for the Martyrs Brigades. When Zakaria told him, al-Majaideh was amazed. "I really don't have any money," al-Majaideh said. "Arafat gave me only thirty thousand dollars to pay the salaries of everyone in the Gaza Strip." The officers sat angrily and silent. The math was easy to figure: $2 million versus $30,000. It was the equation of Arafat's interests. To Zakaria Baloush, it seemed Arafat was working against his own people, ignoring them while he shoveled wads of cash to the gunmen.

Baloush composed a letter to Yasser Arafat. In the summer of 2002 the Americans were pressing for democratic and economic reform of the Palestinian Authority. It seemed Arafat would have to call presidential elections for early 2003, though the devious ra'is had his procrastinatory excuses ready, of course. After he announced his intention to hold the elections, he waited a few days and then said that obviously it would be impractical to set a date for the poll until Israeli soldiers ended their occupation of the Palestinian towns. Zakaria Baloush wanted things changed, and unlike the yes-men who surrounded Arafat, he didn't believe in self-serving speeches; he was a man who got things done, and this time he would try for a job that would truly enable him to improve the lives of ordinary Palestinians. He wrote to Arafat telling him that he, Zakaria Baloush, would run against him in the presidential election. He requested that Arafat endorse his campaign. As a civil servant, he believed he needed Arafat's approval to stand in any election. Arafat didn't write back, so Zakaria took that to mean the president wouldn't block his candidacy at that time. Arafat could be a sore in your mouth or a kiss on your feet, but in either case the attention he paid you connoted the potential for him to betray you. When Arafat ignored you, those with long experience of his behavior knew to be thankful for a small mercy.

The Palestinians, in Zakaria's opinion, required a realistic program from their president. They needed neither the delusional dream of returning to their orchards in Jaffa, long plowed over for Israeli condominiums, nor the heated rhetoric of absolutist preconditions for a peace settlement, which in the end kept them exactly where they were and without peace. They should be served by someone who would tell them honestly about the kind of deal that could be won for them. Baloush believed that, in the tribal way of Palestine, he would have the support at the very least of the 120,000 people descended from the refugees of Majdal now living in the Gaza Strip. He began signing his letters on behalf of this population to show the support—and the protection—he could claim. He halted his intelligence work, but kept the title of security adviser to the National Security Forces in Gaza. Then he watched as the global pressure for a presidential election faded. It didn't surprise him, in some ways. Arafat wriggled out of it, as he previously shirked ceasefires and international treaties and private pledges. The Americans and Israelis came to realize that, no matter how unpopular Arafat might be, Palestinians always would reelect him by a landslide so long as there was a conflict with Israel and interfering pressure from Washington for a new leader. The last thing the Americans wanted was for Arafat to win what he surely would claim as a renewed mandate, so they switched their focus to sidelining Arafat in the role of president with merely ceremonial powers. U.S. diplomats fixed on Mahmoud Abbas as their chosen prime minister who would truly run the government and the security forces. Known as Abu Mazen, Abbas made his rather half-hearted stab at the new role before quitting, because Arafat stymied his every move.

Zakaria Baloush still thought of himself as a presidential candidate. He spent his time in the company of other officers—old comrades who, like him, lapsed largely into unemployment during the intifada, though they kept their positions and some even visited their offices. He made himself somewhat independent of Arafat's purse strings by selling shampoo he manufactured in a small factory behind his house, down a sandy lane east of Jabalya. Just as with Inside leaders like Marwan Barghouti, the complaints of Baloush's fellow Outside officers were part principle, part financial. They hated that Arafat promoted corrupt mediocrities, but they also couldn't stand that their salaries—when they eventually received them—were all spent by the twentieth of each month these days. After the death in early 2003 of Ziad al-Atrash, the senior officer who good-naturedly held up the meeting with the Israelis when Zakaria suddenly appeared back in 1994, the plight of Arafat's old guard was clear. Al-Atrash never was corrupt, surviving instead on Arafat's meager handouts. He bequeathed considerable debts to his wife. His adult children he left with scant, resentful memories of a father who was usually absent training or running missions for Arafat in distant corners of the Arab world.

PLO soldiers like al-Atrash lived complex lives, watching their backs for traitors or rivals who would climb over them to secure Arafat's favor, or fearing Israeli hit squads. Yet at heart they were simple men who, in the manner of soldiers everywhere, preferred clear orders and pre-planned procedures. No matter how accustomed they became over the decades to espionage and to reading the tea leaves of Arafat's hints and silences, the confusion of the intifada was too much for many of them. In July 2003 Major General al-Majaideh stopped in at Zakaria Baloush's home after a visit to his men at the nearby Erez Checkpoint. The officer was desperately puzzled and frustrated. Hamas and Islamic Jihad had recently announced a ceasefire, but al-Majaideh couldn't get a clear answer from Arafat about how he ought to proceed. Should he try to impound illegal weapons, as Prime Minister Abu Mazen promised in accepting President Bush's Road Map peace plan, or ought he to try not to disturb the ceasefire by keeping his distance from the Islamists? "Arafat talks nonsense," al-Majaideh said. "This is all insane." It was just as bad with the European diplomats and CIA officials who sometimes met al-Majaideh. They made elliptical suggestions or expressed preferences, but they left the interpretation to al-Majaideh, whose own leader made him doubt exactly where he stood. None of them understood that the major general just wanted someone to give him an order and to be allowed to carry it out.

The Bush Road Map put Arafat under pressure. He worked against Abu Mazen behind the scenes, because he believed that if the prime minister failed, the Americans would turn once more to him. He retained command of most of the Palestinian security forces, including General Intelligence. That left Abu Mazen hamstrung in his ability to threaten Hamas. But Arafat needed more than nominal control over those security services. He also wanted to regain the support of the malcontents in the senior ranks like Zakaria Baloush. These were the men who always had done his dirty work for him, not the corrupt, ineffectual wheeler-dealers he promoted above them. He had to ensure they wouldn't go over to Abu Mazen's side and that, if he did engineer a return to credibility with the Americans and Israelis by promising to rein in the terrorists who eluded Abu Mazen, he would be able to use Zakaria and his comrades to get the job done.

At 1 A.M. in late July 2003, Zakaria Baloush sat in his study reading summaries of newspapers, magazines, and radio broadcasts. Senior officers in the security forces received daily briefs on media from all over the region, from Kuwait, Jordan, Israel. Baloush kept up with the reports and translations. As he read, his phone rang. It was Arafat. It was his first call since Zakaria wrote the letter announcing he would run against Arafat for president. "Now you remember me?" Zakaria said.

"*Habibi,* don't be hard on me," Arafat pleaded, using the Arabic word for a dear friend. Arafat tried to be exaggeratedly polite and friendly. "We spent so many years together, you and I. We must advance together to Jerusalem."

Zakaria believed Arafat wanted to send a message to the Israelis, who tapped every call from his compound in Ramallah, that he was mending his relations with supporters of the peace process like Baloush. "You lost everyone," he said.

"I need you," Arafat said. "Allah will be with us. Please come to see me in Ramallah. I would like to appoint you as a deputy minister."

"Of what?"

"That's not important."

"Deputy minister of whatever I want, eh?" Zakaria sneered.

"Will you work for the General Intelligence?"

"I can't work with Amin al-Hindi as my boss," Zakaria said. "He's a good man, but I don't think he has always been straight with me."

"So kick him out," Arafat said exuberantly. "Throw him into the sea!"

"Why don't you write that down?" Zakaria said. "Just put that in writing." He knew Arafat never would—that was not his way.

The next day, Zakaria went to Amin al-Hindi's office and recounted his conversation with Arafat. Al-Hindi looked surprised. "Beware," he said. "Yasser Arafat wants to make trouble between us. But we're friends."

Baloush told al-Hindi that he would take his old job back, but he wouldn't be going to the office. He tired of al-Hindi's attempts to ingratiate himself with his returning deputy. He lost his temper. "Fuck Abu Amar and fuck you too," he said. Then he walked out.

Zakaria Baloush went home and waited, watching to see how the *ra'is* would play out his strategy. He had expected the telephone call from Arafat. Even so, it brought back to him the oppressively unnerving sensation of all those years in the PLO. He hadn't lost hope that the dirty game could be over one day, just as he had wanted to put it behind him when he went to live in Cairo with his new family or when he came to Gaza in 1994 to police the peace process. But with Arafat around, it was hard to imagine honesty and straightforwardness prevailing. It was also hard to see how you could retire from that life and settle down to making shampoo. Arafat would come and pull you back into the addictive circle of conflict.

I drove with Zakaria through Jabalya en route to his home. As we sped through the narrow streets, he pointed out a small storefront at the roadside. Its iron shutters were folded back. Inside, the walls were of bare concrete and the space was empty. A few workmen shoveled sand into a cement mixer on the front step. It was clear no one paid much attention to the store, which was apparently like thousands of others in Gaza. This was where al-Asifa, the Fatah military wing, was founded in an underground meeting in the late 1950s. It struck me that it was a place where something momentous happened and that it would have been a candidate for some kind of memorial. I asked Zakaria Baloush why there was no commemorative plaque on the wall. "A memorial, there?" He laughed until it became a choking cough. "We should knock it down and grind it up." It was his bitterness speaking, but it wasn't an entirely inappropriate suggestion. That, after all, was what Arafat did to the men who served him.

CHAPTER FOUR

Nizar's Resistance

Citizens of an Occupied Homeland

"But we aren't your enemies."
"You're not on my side, either."

—EMILE HABIBY, *THE SECRET LIFE OF SAEED*

NIZAR HASSAN'S MOTHER closed the living-room door carefully behind her so that she could tell him a secret. Furtively she addressed herself to her four-year-old eldest boy: "My dear, I will tell you a story that you will never, never tell anyone, because the Israelis will fire me from my job at the school. This place is not called Israel. This place is called Palestine. It's our homeland." Proudly little Nizar understood that his mother had treated him as a man, as one capable of bearing the responsibility of something that could have serious consequences for her. He didn't know quite how consequential it would come to be for him too. It was 1964. Those Palestinians who did not flee their homeland upon the foundation of Israel became citizens of the new state and lived under martial law. Any display of Palestinian national-ism, either in public speech or by the flying of a flag, was repressed. For a state employee, an elementary-school teacher like Nizar's mother, these daring words would surely have meant the loss of her job if her little boy blurted them out at the wrong moment, as chil-dren often do. Nizar's younger brother and sister watched uncompre-hending as his mother went on: "This is what happened in '48: they came and they occupied our homeland." She explained to Nizar how it was that the Hassans didn't flee to Lebanon in 1948 as so many neighbors in the Nazareth area did. Nizar burned with pride that his beloved mother, so beautiful and chic in her modern clothing, entrusted him with the responsibility of the secret story of his family and of his homeland. Then she gave him a great charge that would remain with him always. "Do not forget," she said, "that you have to get back your homeland." The child gazed upon the woman's serious face and thought, I won't disappoint my mother.

That was the beginning, the unveiling of the future for Nizar Hassan, the time when he understood what would be the ultimate task of his life. Frivolous things and easy choices and simple thoughts were shut out forever by the door his mother was forced to close behind her when she came to him with the secrets of his people. Before this, there was only the recollection of his birth, remolded later into the suspicion that the first thing he saw when he came from the womb was not his mother but the face of a Jewish nurse. That was a bad memory, once he learned the story between Israelis and Palestinians. It would be years before he found the path by which he might contribute to the liberation of his people, but his mother had instilled in him the desire to resist.

The resistance that shaped Nizar Hassan's life was always at odds with the behavior Israeli Jews expected from the one-fifth of the country's citizenry that was Palestinian. To live in peace with the Israelis, to be allowed by the dominant political culture to call himself a peace-lover, Hassan saw he would be expected to accept Israel the way it was, with all the inequality and harshness of its rule over the Palestinian population. If he wanted to change it, to accommodate his own society or national aspirations in some way, Israel would accuse him of rejecting the very idea of peace. How could he be a lover of peace and yet refuse to accept that he was an inferior who deserved less than full possession of his homeland? Or that he happened to live in the Galilee by mistake and that he was present in his homeland on the sufferance of another people that took possession of that territory?

Nizar Hassan's father gave him the first clue. The elder Hassan built a role in local politics in Mash'had. He encouraged Nizar to focus on his own community. Once that was organized and won over, the power of the Israelis could be challenged. "The Jews aren't the problem," he told Nizar. "Think about yourself first, not them. You and your own society." Nizar's father stood in Mash'had's municipal elections when his son was a toddler. The politics of Israel's Palestinian citizens, such as they were at that time, were dominated by clan leaders focused entirely on local issues. The clan chiefs were placated easily by Israeli government money, because their only concern was to maintain control over their town, a task easier to accomplish when the distribution of state funds and contracts was at their disposal. But the Hassan slate brought together young people from many different clans. It was a threat to the hegemony of the two biggest families in the city, which united to push Hassan out of the race. Years later, Nizar learned from one of the senior members of the powerful Suleiman clan that the Shin Bet ordered them to defeat Nizar's father. Nizar passed that information along, but his father already knew of the old plot.

So the political life of Israel's Palestinian population continued to be dominated by fights for government cash, education funds, roads, and infrastructure budgets, all of which were dealt out at a fraction of the amount given to Jewish municipalities. The liberation of the homeland of which Nizar's mother spoke was not on the agenda of "Israeli Arab" political leaders; no one would stick their neck out, for they knew that with no national political mobilization their only support was from their clan. The Palestinian population of Israel was cut off from the Arab world, which regarded those who refused to flee in 1948 as suspect, even as collaborators with Israel and traitors to the Arab people. In response, the Arabs of the Galilee and of the towns on the coastal plain near Tel Aviv adhered to the concept of *sumoud*. The word means "steadfastness" and, in Arabic, bears a connotation of confrontation as well as endurance. It was a way in which the "Palestinians of '48," as those who remained in Israel were known to other Arabs, could think of themselves as noble, suffering, and persistent. Nizar Hassan always knew that *sumoud* was a ridiculous concept, because he understood from the story of his own parents how much it was due to chance and accident that one family may have fled or been forced out while its neighbors remained.

Nizar Hassan's father and uncles began to flee in 1948. They went only two miles before they turned back. Nizar's grandfather firmly declined to leave. He was a trader who made regular trips to Lebanon and simply refused to quit his homeland to live there. His sons couldn't leave their father, so they cut short their flight and stayed.

The story was similar to the other side of Nizar's family. His maternal grandmother adamantly dismissed any flight from her home, and so the entire family remained in the Nazareth area as the Israelis took over.

Even if his grandparents could truly have foreseen the future, their choice would still have been difficult. In Lebanon, 400,000 Palestinians who fled the Galilee continue to live in the worst conditions of any of their compatriots. Unlike Syria and Jordan, Lebanon bars the refugees from jobs outside the camps. They are mistrusted deeply by the contentious religious sects of Lebanon, who fear the Palestinians' numbers could tilt the demographic balance toward the Sunni Muslims, and they are blamed for the Israeli invasion of 1982 and much of the two-decade civil war. In Israel, life also was difficult and, in a different way, isolated for the Palestinians who stayed behind. In 1948 the majority of Palestinians, 940,000 of them, lived in what became Israel. By the end of the war that accompanied Israel's foundation, only 150,000 remained, under Israeli control. Many villagers didn't have the option of staying, as Nizar's grandparents did, because Israeli soldiers ran them out of their homes. Three-quarters of all Arab-owned land was expropriated over the years, so day-laboring peasants became dependent on the Israeli Jewish economy. Emergency regulations introduced by the British in 1945 remained in place for Israel's Arab citizens. Travel from one town to another required a permit from the military governor. Most newspapers were closed; one, *al-Ittihad,* was permitted to distribute in some locations and banned in other towns. After military law was lifted in 1966, Shmuel Toledano, who was for ten years the prime minister's adviser on Arab affairs, admitted that its contribution to Israel's security was "a total zero."

Though military law was lifted when Nizar Hassan was still a small boy, it colored the injunction his mother laid upon him at the age of four. As he grew up, the "emergency regulations" continued to bar association with any group that called itself Palestinian. So Nizar, in the absolutist and romantic way of an intelligent youth, began to believe that resistance lay in the path of the fedayin, the guerrillas based in Lebanon and Jordan. At seventeen, Nizar Hassan started plotting to become a fighter with the Popular Front for the Liberation of Palestine. Without telling his family, he obtained his first passport and started trying to figure out how to make contact with the Marxist PFLP in Europe. It was a moment of decision. Perhaps he felt too cowardly, or just not desperate enough to give up a relatively comfortable life. Maybe he saw his own fears reflected in his mother's face, read there what was in fact written in his own heart and made it his excuse. In the living room of his parents' house, Nizar saw his mother watching him from the corner of her eye. He sensed she knew he was plotting something; she didn't know what. She would have been proud if she had known that he wanted to confront the Israelis, but she simply didn't want her boy to leave home. In her expression, there was fear of losing him to prison or to exile, and fear of his death. The apprehension he detected in those eyes convinced Nizar not to take up arms. I can't do this to my mother, he thought. This was not, he believed, the kind of resistance she wanted to instill in him when he was four.

The next year, Nizar Hassan went to college. He became a leader of the Ibnaa il-Balad at Haifa University. It was a Marxist-nationalist group, whose members translated its name as Sons of the Homeland. (Israeli media and academics translated the group's name as Sons of the Village, which Hassan believed was intended to make it seem primitive and to deny that Palestinians were an indigenous people.) It aimed to end clan control over the politics of the Palestinians inside Israel. The mainstream Israeli political parties had little sway in the Palestinian towns. The Sons of the Homeland demonstrated as Palestinians, demanding recognition as Palestinians for the people the state called "Israeli Arabs." Hassan's role in the Sons of the Homeland, which later split over a dispute about whether to run a slate in Knesset elections, earned him a year of house arrest under the old British "emergency regulations."

For most of the first year of Hassan's university studies, he was confined to Mash'had, his small village on a bend in the descending road north of Nazareth. Each morning he was compelled to show up at the Nazareth police station to register. For the rest of the daylight hours, he had to stay in Mash'had. When darkness fell, he was ordered to remain inside his parents' home.

Still, it was a good year. During the period when he was considering joining the PFLP, Nizar had been distant from his parents, preoccupied with his fears and secrets and dreams. Even beyond his guerrilla plans, his teenage concerns had separated him from his parents in the way of all rebellious seventeen-year-olds. He grew a Frank Zappa mustache, and his hair dangled down his back to his waist. That year, confined in his parents' house, he became close once more with his father and mother. Nizar read many books and discussed them with his father, who always kept a library of volumes on the Arab world. His mother taught him to cook eggplant and zucchini and vine leaves stuffed with rice, though he could never make them taste quite as delicious as hers.

The house arrest brought prestige too. Nizar's brother and the people of the village regarded him as someone who stood up to the Israelis. He knew it would not last: he understood from his failure to join the fedayin that the physical, rough side of politics and the violence of its enforcement were not for him. His resistance would take a different form. It would be something more intellectual, but no less significant.

After a year, Nizar Hassan's lawyer won an appeal that transferred his house arrest from the confines of Mash'had to the city of Haifa. Though still restricted to his apartment by night, he was allowed during the day to move anywhere in Haifa, the biggest city in northern Israel. He studied anthropology and found in it the roots of his future career. As he saw it, anthropology began as an offshoot of colonial thinking, studying exotic tribes or black neighborhoods of Washington. By the time Hassan came to the field, the trend in anthropology was to examine one's own experience *within* that tribe or neighborhood. He wanted to express that through art, rather than the dryness of a Ph.D. in anthropology. So, at the age of thirty, Nizar Hassan produced his first documentary film.

Hassan wanted to make his films without Israeli production money. He traveled to Switzerland and Germany to meet potential backers. He knew they had links to the PLO, but he figured there ought to be no strings attached. The PLO would be content just to have intelligent documentaries produced about the Palestinians, simply to promote awareness of the cause, and in return Nizar would get to make his movie. In Berlin, the man he courted as a financier for his film took him to a bar near the railway station. It was 3 A.M. and they had drunk plenty when he asked Hassan, "Tell me something. Can you help us to photograph some military sites or sensitive locations in Israel?"

Hassan was shocked. "Listen," he said, "I want to be a filmmaker. If I wanted to be an agent for the PLO, I wouldn't do it this way. And another thing, if you really are an agent for the PLO, I want you to know that it's the stupidest political and national movement, and I've always thought so. Thank you for your hospitality, but I don't think we shall meet again." After he left the bar, it seemed almost comical to Hassan. If this is how intelligence is gathered, he thought as he walked to the station to catch his train, oh, boy!

Nizar Hassan persisted with his fund-raising efforts from Arabs in London and elsewhere. But he soon discovered that few would trust him, because of his Israeli passport. It was clear no Palestinian would fund a movie made by an Israeli, even if that Israeli were Nizar Hassan and considered himself to be just as Palestinian as anybody else. Hassan made a forty-minute film for the Arab Women's Association about a children's home the group ran in Acre, the ancient walled port in northern Israel where much of the population was poor and Palestinian. It was good training, but to finance the significant, artistic films he really wanted to make, Hassan saw he would have to go to Israeli television. It would make his work questionable to many in the Arab world, and international festivals would sometimes present his movies as Israeli rather than Palestinian productions. Hassan decided to take the funding and get on with his work: They got my homeland, so I'll get some rent money from them, he thought. There were constant reminders, however, of the compromise forced upon him. His work took him frequently to Tel Aviv, where he felt more alienated than in any other Israeli city by what he saw as the escapist provincialism of the residents. They tried so hard to divorce themselves from the things that were an inescapable reality to Palestinians or even to Jews living in Jerusalem that Hassan felt contempt for the place.

Though Nizar Hassan was compelled to take Israeli production money, his revenge would be to use it to liberate the people of Palestine. He began to think that the reason Palestinians and Israelis shared no meaningful dialogue was the absence of an internal Palestinian discourse. He saw this as the role that could be fulfilled by an artist, a moviemaker: not to liberate the piece of land called Palestine, which he acknowledged was by no means the most beautiful or most desirable territory he ever saw, but to liberate its people by bringing them self-respect. Once Palestinians could face themselves, he believed, there would follow an ability to confront and perhaps accept the other, the Israeli. In any case, he would challenge himself in his films, bravely, and in doing so he would force Israelis to see what they had done to their Arab citizens, the Palestinians in their midst. When Hassan began his career, Western and Israeli documentaries typically portrayed a common film image of the Palestinians: it was largely one of fatalistic, passive victims. That was not how Nizar Hassan saw himself, and he set out to document the things he felt. He remembered what his father told him: to concern himself with his own community. First, he would connect the Palestinians to each other; then he would link them to the Arab world that for so long rejected them.

In 1996 Hassan released one of his most successful movies, *Yasmin*. A Palestinian woman from Ramla, in central Israel, Yasmin was jailed as an accomplice in the killing of her sister. In her interview with Hassan, Yasmin described the subservience of women and the almost casual way in which she herself accepted a beating from her brother. Her younger sister, Amal, ran away with an older man whom she didn't intend to marry. Yasmin tried to keep the news from their brother, but when he found out, it incensed him. Torn between her desire to protect her sister and her sense of female obedience to her brother, Yasmin went along with his plan to beat Amal. Yasmin told Hassan she never expected that her brother would bring the punishment to the deadly conclusion known as an honor killing. Hassan surrounded the Yasmin interview sequences with conversations he conducted with Palestinian men and women: an Islamic sheikh, a liberal journalist and his wife, a fashion model and her mother. He revealed the depth of traditional values about relations between men and women, and the frustrations they bring. Hassan also showed his own complicity in that male-dominated structure. He included a sequence in which he tried to persuade his fashionable, intelligent sister, who was studying for a Ph.D. in Jerusalem and enjoying the freedom of the big city, to return to live in the narrowly traditional world of Mash'had. "Listen to yourself," his sister told him as they sat in one of West Jerusalem's trendiest cafés. "You benefit from all this too. Because you're a man." Near the end of the film, Hassan asked Yasmin, "Did you kill Amal?" When I saw the film, I realized he might not be addressing that question only to Yasmin. It could just as easily be asked of the sheikh, of Hassan himself, of any Palestinian, or of any Arab who accepts life in a society with this long-established, unchallenged structure.

With *Yasmin*, Hassan found his style. The movie, which took two years to make, placed the director within the story and structured the narrative in such a way that it was poised on the border of factual documentary and fiction. It was a pitiless counter to the colorful quaintness and easy compassion of Western documentaries about Palestinians. It also sidestepped the chauvinistic nativism of some other Palestinian filmmakers, who prefer to reveal nothing critical of their own people or culture. Hassan wanted those who saw the film, which won the documentary prize at the Jerusalem Film Festival, to understand that, like Yasmin, no one was simply a victim or a perpetrator, whether they were Israeli or Palestinian. He wanted to force both sides to look more critically at themselves.

The stylistic stroke that made *Yasmin* so compelling was that Nizar Hassan sited himself at the center of the story. He wore a mustache, common among Arab men (which he shaved immediately after the end of the production) as though he wanted even his facial hair to symbolize his Arabness and his role in the documentary as another representative of his society's male values. In contrast to what Israelis would describe as his minority status within their state, Hassan portrayed himself as part of the Middle East's dominant Arab culture. That made the Israelis the minority and Hassan part of the majority. Being at the center means even the apparently powerless can take control of the narrative. An artist, a framer of narratives, is uniquely positioned to do just that.

NIZAR HASSAN came down the main road of Nazareth that curves below the Basilica of the Annunciation to Mary's Well. Tall and thin with a pile of curly black hair trimmed tight at the sides and back, he smiled when he came close enough to recognize me. I told him I was in Nazareth to report a story on the Shihab ed-Din Mosque, which hit the news that month, April 1999. The Christian mayor of the city, Ramiz Jeraisi, had demolished a school building at the foot of the hill beneath the basilica to make a pedestrian plaza. Jeraisi figured there would be large numbers of Christian tourists in the town where Jesus grew up during the pope's visit later that year and even more for a celebration of the two millennia since Christ's birth. The Islamic Movement's political leader on the city council, Salman Abu Ahmed, took advantage of the issue. He sent a group of Muslims to move into the demolished area. Right behind the plaza was a small medieval cupola that marked a tomb. The Muslims claimed it was the burial place of Shihab ed-Din, the nephew of Salah ed-Din and a hero in the fight against the Crusaders. Abu Ahmed demanded that a mosque be built on the site, which he said belonged to Islamic religious authorities in any case. Jeraisi refused. A senior Likud Party aide stirred things up, believing he might win some political support from the Muslims by promising to build the mosque. It was a return to the clannish bargaining for votes and local influence, always with the pot stirred by the Israeli government, that Nizar Hassan's father had tried to oppose years before. The town's Christians, who were predominantly Communist voters, felt threatened by the local Islamists and by the Jewish right wing in the central government. The week before I visited, some Christian youths on the way down the slope of Casa Nova Street from the basilica started a fight with the Muslims staging a sit-in at Shihab ed-Din's tomb. A riot followed that lasted two days. When I arrived, the main street was filled with flak-jacketed police, checking cars and identity cards within sight of the basilica's massive conical roof.

"This whole thing with the mosque of Shihab ed-Din is something that the Israelis will be very happy to see happening," Nizar said. The Muslims and Christians of Nazareth didn't share the kind of extreme differences that affected the comparable groups in the Palestinian towns of the West Bank, like Beit Jala, he believed. The Muslims had become the majority in the traditionally Christian city over the last couple of decades, accounting for about 60 percent of the population, but there was never such trouble before. Nizar, a Muslim, was on his way to a studio to edit a television advertisement he directed for Azmi Bishara, a Palestinian nationalist and Christian politician who ran for the job of Israeli prime minister in the 1999 election.

At the Shihab ed-Din mosque, which was not quite a protest tent nor even a building that could be called a place of worship, a group of men sat listlessly in the afternoon sun beneath a black tarpaulin. Behind the 134 square yards designated as the visitors plaza, there was a tiny green-domed building, its white walls roughly plastered. As bright and brittle as plastic grocery bags, cheap prayer mats were spread next to the rectangular block beneath the dome that was the tomb of the hero. A young man named Hathem Abdou showed me around the site, then promised me that if workmen came to build the piazza for the pope, "I will fight them and kill them. Shihab ed-Din was a saint who fought for Allah and we gain strength from him."

The political map of Israel's Palestinian population changed in the last decade as the Islamic Movement grew. Earlier the battle for public support was always between nationalist parties, who focused on opposition to Israel's expropriation of land, and the Communists, who worked for a broader equality. Salman Abu Ahmed initially gained from the Shihab ed-Din controversy, winning control over the city council. But the Christian mayor held on to his position, and the mosque dispute angered the Roman Catholic Church so much that far fewer pilgrims went to Nazareth during the millennium than the city's businesspeople and political leaders banked on. It seemed as though there was something self-destructive for the Palestinians in Israel about the very debate over whether to enter Israeli political life or not. Even the Islamic Movement split over the decision to run candidates in the 1996 election. By 2003 the two branches of the Movement were very different. Sheikh Ibrahim Nimr Darwish, who began the Movement in the 1970s as an advocate of violent struggle, told me he believed Palestinians should give up the pseudo-sacred notion of a "right of return" for refugees. Soon after, his rival, Sheikh Raed Salah, the head of the more radical wing of the Islamic Movement, described to me his interrogation by Shin Bet agents and, a few days later, was indicted for supporting Hamas. I thought of a Palestinian filmmaker from Ramallah, Rashid Mashrawi, who captured this constant duality of compromise and principle, firmness and realism in the eponymous hero of his film *Haifa*. "Haifa always has one eye laughing and one eye crying," Mashrawi told me. "We have here this conflict, each one within himself."

There was a feeling among the people of Nazareth that competing interests closed about them, exacerbating that conflict within their selves but never helping resolve it. They had no truly independent political leaders. The two most prominent representatives of Israel's Palestinians in the Knesset were Azmi Bishara, who many thought was too close to the line of the Syrian government, and Ahmed Tibi, a former adviser to Yasser Arafat who by no means severed his ties with his old boss. The political isolation of Israel's Palestinian citizens couldn't be better illustrated than the night I spent with the Lawabdeh family watching the returns from the prime ministerial election in February 2001.

The first time I visited, Subhi Lawabdeh welcomed me at the entrance to his home on a dirt alley. He wore green tartan slippers, a gray woolen hat, and a blue anorak. There were deep black circles about his old eyes as we shook hands. On the doorpost, the same hand that clasped mine had made two prints, signs of sacrifice marked on the whitewashed wall with the blood of his son Iyad.

On October 2, 2000, the first weekend of the intifada, Subhi Lawabdeh sat with his grown sons listening to the Arabic radio reports of deadly clashes around the West Bank and in Jerusalem between Palestinian demonstrators and Israeli soldiers. The lethal litany, delivered by the broadcaster in a tone of deep seriousness and urgency, fired up the whole house. Others, listening as the Lawabdehs did, spilled out onto the streets of Arab towns in the Galilee, raging against the police in sympathy with their fellow Palestinians a few miles away in the West Bank. Radio 2000 reported Israeli tanks entering Um al-Fakhm, a town inside Israel populated by Palestinians with Israeli citizenship like the Lawabdehs. (There were no tanks in the town, though an investigative committee almost three years later condemned the police for using lethal sniper fire.) Iyad, Subhi's twenty-seven-year-old son and one of his thirteen children, decided to go down to Nazareth's main street to protest.

"Don't go," Subhi said. "The police are firing live bullets. Stay here until the evening."

"Don't worry," Iyad said.

Iyad's mother chased him to the door. "Come back," she called. Iyad turned and kissed her, asked her to wish him well. He wound along the steep, narrow lanes, whose shabbiness never appears in the pilgrimage guidebooks of Nazareth, and down to a side street near the basilica. There were thirty young men there in a small square. Israeli police fired tear gas at them. Iyad and his friends believed the Israelis wanted to enter an old people's home behind the square. Some of them told me later they had visions of some horrible massacre of the elderly. The frightened old people had begun to scream as the sounds of rioting and gunfire approached, and that was what sparked the fatal series of events. In fact, something just as unconscionable was to occur. "Over our dead bodies will they get through here," the small crowd chanted. Iyad picked up a tear-gas canister to throw it back at the police, covering his nose and mouth with a handkerchief. He returned three before a policeman shot him through the heart.

Subhi Lawabdeh received a call from the English Hospital just before 3 P.M. His son was dead. A retired high-school lab technician, Subhi wished then that he owned a gun so that he might kill in return. He stumbled down the same sheer alleyways that took his son to his death. His old legs couldn't carry him fast enough to match the frenzy and rage in his heart. For decades, he paid his taxes and kept his nose clean, politically, so that the police should reward him now with the killing of his boy, as though he were less than fully human. When he reached the little square by the old people's home, he picked up stones and threw them at the cops. Hundreds of people came to join him, as word spread of Iyad's death. Subhi wanted revenge. He carried a butcher's knife from his kitchen. He pulled it from under his coat and he advanced on the Israelis. The people held him back. "You will follow your son. You will die," one of them warned him.

"I don't care," Subhi cried.

"Allah will punish them," said one of the men who restrained him.

That weekend, Israeli police killed thirteen Palestinians in Israeli towns, including twelve citizens of the state. It was clear the police had no idea how to handle riots without causing death and that their antagonistic way of thinking about Arabs—citizens of Israel, or not— contributed to a devastatingly brutal use of force. In the end, they treated their fellow citizens no differently than the army handled the Palestinians of Gaza and Ramallah. For years, Palestinian Israelis felt a growing identification with their compatriots in the West Bank, while Israel's Jewish leadership argued that "our Arabs" were perfectly happy and, in fact, a lot better off than most citizens of the twenty-two repressive, inequitable Arab countries of the Middle East and North Africa. The first weekend of the intifada, the Israelis were proved wrong by the bullets of their own policemen.

The prime minister who oversaw the fatal shooting of twelve Palestinian Israelis was Ehud Barak, whose Labor Party had come to count on Arab voters for it to have any hope of leading the government. In February 2001 he faced Ariel Sharon in a runoff for his job. The deaths in Nazareth and Um al-Fakhm prompted a broad boycott of the election by Israel's Palestinians. That surely hurt Barak, whose inept handling of the early months of the intifada ensured that a majority of Jewish voters would reject him. To Arab voters, it seemed time to register their protest, to show that a leftist candidate couldn't simply view their ballots as in his pocket even before the campaign began. The boycott was almost total. At a polling station in Nazareth, I watched Jamila Akawi, whose middle-aged brother Omar was killed by the Israeli police, plead with the handful of people who came to vote that they should not do so. Most left without voting, rather than experience the guilt of bypassing her. The boycott represented a moment of self-assertion. The generation of Palestinians who remained in their homes in 1948 and lived as adults through the years of the military government had learned to keep their heads down. Subhi Lawabdeh told me that on each of his three pilgrimages to Mecca for the *hajj*, he used to recount to other Arabs just how well the Palestinian citizens of Israel were treated. "I explained to them about our free health care and the social welfare system. We were governed by Jews, I used to say, but we enjoyed many good things." The next generation, the contemporaries of Nizar Hassan and then of Iyad Lawabdeh, didn't reach maturity until after the cowing experience of military government ended. They were more assertive and identified more strongly with the cause of the Palestinians of the West Bank and Gaza. One of that new generation's leaders, a Galilee politician named Jamal Zahalka, told me he and his supporters wanted to "force the Israelis to see the contradiction between Zionism and democracy," between a Jewish state and a state in which all its citizens share equal rights. Even before the intifada and the bloodshed that claimed the life of Iyad Lawabdeh, 15 percent of Palestinian citizens rejected Israel's right to exist, and 46 percent believed it ought not to be a Jewish-Zionist state but a "state of all its citizens." There was a strong current in early Zionism led by the philosopher Martin Buber that argued for a state in Palestine that would be shared by Jews and Arabs, but the separatist current within the Zionist movement won out and Israel classified itself as a Jewish state, rather than a state defined by its citizenry. Almost a century after Buber's campaign, his ideas were buried beneath so much propaganda and conventional wisdom that Israel's ruling politicians and its police chiefs were unable to register the change in the mood of their Palestinian citizens. Until it was too late.

The night of the runoff election between Ehud Barak and Ariel Sharon, Subhi Lawabdeh came to his door to greet me once more. The gory handprints remained, though the red had faded to an emerald green, as though the blood were rotting like Iyad's body, four months in the tomb. He said Shimon Peres, the former Labor prime minister, called him the week before the elections. Peres said, "There's no difference between Arabs and Jews. I feel sorry for what happened." Subhi told Peres he was a liar and hung up the phone. The family settled in for the poll results, Subhi and his wife, Raoufa, and five of their sons and the absence of another son. There was expectation that Barak would truly be hammered and that a lesson would be taught to the Israeli left not to take for granted the votes of the Palestinian citizens. Raoufa began to cry shortly before the first exit polls at 10 P.M. Her tears dampened the bitter sense of triumph that circulated among the brothers. The results: a massive victory for Sharon, and silence in the Lawabdeh home. Was this what they wanted? This man who Palestinians saw as the Israeli politician most responsible for hurting them and most set against their achievement of freedom? "We fired Barak," said one of the sons, breaking the stillness. Subhi responded, "And the madman took over."

The election provided no resolution to the Lawabdehs' grief. The revenge against Barak was empty, because it brought to power a prime minister whose hand would be even heavier against the Palestinians in the West Bank and Gaza and who would certainly do little to improve life in Nazareth. The television stations rolled out a string of politicians for their reactions and assessments. Shlomo Ben-Ami, the police minister who fancied himself a liberal intellectual but ended up carrying the can for the brutal killings in October, came on-screen. "Fuck your sister's cunt," Subhi said, addressing the prissy, gabbling face of the politician. "Turn it off. I've had enough of him. Let's watch the funeral." One of his sons flipped a cassette into the VCR and ran the tape. There was the face of Iyad, a close-up, mouth open in death, pink rose petals sprayed across his corpse when it was laid out before the funeral. As the crowd took him through Nazareth, they chanted, "With spirit and blood, we'll sacrifice for the martyr." The chant came again and again from the television, enveloping the silent family in their living room. As a soft, midnight breeze drew through the open front door, the Lawabdehs watched in a silence punctuated only by Raoufa's sobs.

It was at this moment that I understood what Nizar Hassan meant a few weeks before, as we sat drinking cardamom-flavored coffee in front of the Gustav Klimt print in his salon: "I need to stop thinking about what the Israelis say. I need to think about myself. Give me a break! Power will shift when we know what we want." The Lawab-dehs wanted the boycott of Barak, but they didn't want Sharon. They wanted revenge, but the election results bit back. When they tried to think about themselves, they could think only of their dead boy. Nothing changed.

THE ISRAELI TANKS ground past on long, flatbed transporters, convoys of them heading south past the Israeli town of Afula toward Jenin. Each morning in early April 2002, as Nizar Hassan skirted the West Bank to drive on to meetings in Tel Aviv, their monstrous, terri-fying bulks passed him. He imagined the horror of being at the other end of the assault those mammoth war machines would launch. At night, he watched from the heights where Nazareth stands, looking down across the Jezreel Valley, which Arabs call the Plain of Ibn Amr, gazing toward the northernmost Palestinian town in the West Bank. For twelve days that month, the fatal fireworks of battle in Jenin refugee camp shocked the darkness, as though the 14,000 people who lived there had stuck their fingers simultaneously into a giant electri-cal outlet.

The battle was the most controversial of the Israeli invasion of Palestinian towns codenamed Operation Defensive Shield. It followed a month of almost daily Palestinian suicide bombings that led the Israelis to reverse the final vestiges of the Oslo peace agreements. Their troops took over every Palestinian town, pinning Yasser Arafat inside his compound in Ramallah and skirmishing in the ancient alleys of the Nablus Casbah. Jenin's refugee camp was the center of the most deadly Islamic Jihad cell and the target the Israelis most wanted to subdue. The fighting went on there almost two weeks. Journalists were prevented from entering. Israel suffered its worst day of combat losses since the Lebanon war, and Palestinian officials began to talk emotively of a massacre of hundreds of women and children. By the time the fighting was over, the myths were too pungent for some to accept that they never had been true. A British journalist wrote of "the stench of death" in the air as proof that the rumored masses of bodies did, indeed, lie beneath the wreckage, though it could just as easily have been the reek of smashed sewage pipes one smelled on the devastated streets and among the detritus of 110 demolished buildings in the Hawashine Quarter of the camp. When I first went there, it was clear to me that the awful reality— inscribed across an entire hillside in chunks of colorless concrete and random, bright dabs from the clothing of dazed residents sitting in their lost homes—needed no overwrought journalistic embroidery. There had been a long battle in which a few dozen Palestinian fighters and a slightly smaller number of civilians perished. Eventually responsible Palestinian leaders quietly ditched the accusation of a massacre of 500 people, but they still talked of the camp residents as victims. On the day after the fighting stopped, Nizar Hassan entered the camp to find out exactly what the people of Jenin camp thought of their ordeal.

As Nizar Hassan approached Jenin, he was skeptical about the massacre claim. If the Israelis wanted to kill all the people of Jenin camp, he thought, why did they fight so long to secure it? Why not simply kill everyone on day two or three with a couple of massive bombs delivered from an airplane? In the end, he discovered there were fifty-six Palestinian dead, including twenty-six civilians. But it was the manner of their death that kept him filming for twenty-eight consecutive days in the camp—not their deaths as victims of Israel, but as those who resisted Israel. The people he interviewed told Hassan that they wanted the propaganda of massacre and victimhood to stop. They wanted him to show how they stood up to the Israelis. What he learned from them was this: when they heard the Israelis coming, they knew what they *wanted* and that was to resist; they were not passive; they didn't wait for Arafat's Palestinian Authority to protect them, which, of course, would have been an interminable wait; and they didn't expect to liberate all Palestine, or even to win.

Hassan made his film *Egteyah* (Invasion) about Jenin refugee camp. It was not Israeli money that funded the movie this time. At a film festival in Qatar in 2001, Hassan met some Lebanese filmmakers who introduced him to a producer from Beirut, from whom he obtained some of the funding. Hassan's friend Raed Andoni, a Palestinian from Bethlehem confined by an Israeli curfew throughout the production, filled much of the producer's role. Hassan began filming with only $9,000 from Swedish TV. But between the two producers and Hassan, they were able to raise a real budget from the Sundance Institute and a Finnish television station. The greatest value for Hassan of working with Raed Andoni was in not having to explain himself, as he did with Israeli or foreign producers. There was no gap of understanding, no compromises because his ideas weren't clear to them, no extra layer. The connection was instant, like the reflection in a mirror.

Hassan celebrated the all-Arab production team by premiering the movie on February 22, 2003, with a simultaneous screening in Nazareth and Beirut. The two audiences, linked by an open phone line, heard the film introduced by Dmitri Khoudour, a Lebanese filmmaker. "Hello, Nazareth," he said. "We met Nizar Hassan two years ago, and I apologize that we used to think about the Palestinians of '48 in a very negative way. I apologize for that. Through Nizar, we discovered that this is not the case. I promise personally to do everything I can to remedy that way of thinking." There were more speeches before Khoudour came back on the line. "Now, in Beirut and Nazareth we both push the button at the same time to see the movie and to end it at exactly the same minute."

Egteyah showed the story of several residents of Jenin refugee camp who were injured, who fought the Israelis, or who lost loved ones in the fighting. It delivered no simplistic condemnation of the Israelis, in the way that another documentary about Jenin by a Palestinian citizen of Israel did. The one Israeli soldier interviewed at length was also shown laughing and joking with his girlfriend at the seashore, like any other normal human being. Hassan's movie tried to show that the Israeli soldier internalized evil. For Hassan, Israel is a racist state that discriminates against its Palestinian citizens and oppresses their compatriots in the West Bank. In doing so, inevitably, it forces the souls of its sons into evil.

Hassan felt a sense of triumph. When I asked him how those days in Jenin changed him, he said that it gave him "the absolute conviction that we will win. We *will* win." For Nizar Hassan, there was pride and sadness in this conviction, but no hate. From the people of Jenin camp, he learned no longer to feel that it was "us or them."

In August 2003 Nizar Hassan took his film to the place the refugees called Ground Zero, the slope of the Hawashine Quarter where the fighting was fiercest and Israeli D-9 Caterpillar bulldozers demolished all but one of the buildings. Since the fighting ended, the hillside had been cleared of thousands of tons of debris, so that on the night of the screening it was a bare incline of dust. The people of the camp sat on the hill and looked up toward the one building remaining. Hassan set up a screen on the side of the house with a sophisticated projector. As night fell, he saw that people covered the entire hill—there were at least 10,000 there from the camp. He looked at his watch and noted the time: 8:35 P.M. A Palestinian who worked as a correspondent for al-Jazeera, the Qatari satellite news channel, introduced the evening's speakers. At the Nazareth premiere, there had been remarks from the mayor of the town and a famous Lebanese actress. The addresses in the Jenin camp were somewhat grittier. The local leader of Islamic Jihad was followed by the top Hamas activist in the camp and by Zakaria Zubeideh, the head of the Aqsa Martyrs Brigades. After his speech, Zubeideh came down from the stage and brought Nizar Hassan to the microphone, surrounding him with an armed escort of Martyrs Brigades gunmen. Nizar looked down over the masses on the hill. It was the first screening of a film ever in the camp, the first major gathering which men and women attended together.

"There's one thing I learned from Jenin," Nizar Hassan told them. "People usually want to think of resistance as being only a military matter. But I learned that resistance comes from people who love life, have a passion for life." He ended by thanking his wife, who came with him that night to Jenin. The Martyrs Brigades fired a volley of shots into the air in his honor. The movie began.

After twenty minutes, the camp mosque broadcast the call to prayer from the loudspeaker on its minaret. Nobody left the film to pray, not even the Islamist leaders. The Hamas chief in the camp leaned over to Nizar Hassan, smiling, and joked, "Allah will send you to hell, because it's the first time that many of these people missed a prayer."

At the end of the film, the crowd rose and applauded and cheered. Afloat on the swell of adulation that resounded through the ruins of Jenin camp, Nizar Hassan thought perhaps this was not really happening to him. After all, it was always his dream as a filmmaker to connect his own people through his art, to create a film that was entirely a part of the people. He, a Palestinian of '48, had touched the universe of these refugees. Weeks later, he still felt the adrenaline of that night. In the Egyptian town of Ismailia, *Egteyah* became the first of his films to win a prize at an Arab film festival. As an artist, he had accomplished the mission his mother assigned him when she closed the living-room door and knelt by her four-year-old son. He had opened that door, and now all Palestinians could step through it together.

Part II: The Israelis

CHAPTER FIVE

The Dark Refuge

Holocaust Survivors and Native Israelis

Here, in this carload
I, Eve,
With Abel, my son.
If you see my older son
Cain son of Adam
Tell him that I

—DAN PAGIS, *"WRITTEN IN PENCIL*
IN THE SEALED FREIGHT CAR"

ON HIS FIRST DAY as head of psychogeriatrics at Abarbanel Mental Health Center in Bat Yam, a slum suburb south of Tel Aviv, Dr. Yoram Barak yanked open the heavy metal door of the old British barracks that housed the hospital's elderly people. He knew the ward well enough, after a few years as a resident at the state-run facility, mostly on night shifts when he might be called suddenly to all parts of the hospital. Before entering, he surveyed the scene outside the ward. Bougainvillea splashed purple across the tan pebble-dash walls of the single-story building; dazed patients wandered the leafy central lane of the hospital in pajamas and slippers, smoking in the intense late-summer light of September 1994. Then Barak stepped out of the sunshine and into his new empire. Unlike the scattered patients in the shade of the trees beyond, his charges were locked in. Most were too far gone even to be allowed to stroll the hospital's small garden.

Barak turned the lock behind him. There was his office, by the entrance, and another room for his head nurse, Hannah. He noted

143

the heat, thicker than outside, and the astringent hospital odor, competing with the ripe smell of decaying humanity, the moldering scent of people simply heedless of themselves. He stepped into the small, central courtyard. A few patients sat beneath the broad shade of a plane tree in their sky-blue pajamas. Their hands jerked uncontrollably and their jaws projected in grotesque, exaggerated chewing motions, side effects of the antipsychotic drugs administered to them in the 1960s and 1970s. Barak turned along the corridor that skirted the courtyard. He stepped over an old woman spread motionless along the floor with her smock hitched up and her bony, pale, veinous legs exposed. There was no air-conditioning on the ward, and Barak knew that the best many patients could do to keep cool was to hug the stone floor tiles like this, yet it always disturbed him to see a patient lying prone and motionless. In the first dormitory there were a few shaky, masticating patients in their iron bedsteads. The beds were shunted close to each other. There were no closets, no room for the patients to keep personal belongings. A tiny man shuffled past Barak clutching a plastic bag stuffed with the few papers and trinkets that he owned. He was a patient Barak recognized from his night shifts. The man turned his skinny, wrinkled neck to look briefly at Barak, to take him in—Barak's shaven head exposing the fleshy rolls in the neck at the back, his gold stud earring, his sybaritic lips a deep red. The patient dropped his cigarette butt on the floor and struggled past the doctor to the bathroom.

Yoram Barak went to his office, sat down at his desk, and put away the few papers he had brought with him. The chief nurse entered. "Hi. Congratulations," she said. Hannah had not seen Barak since his appointment to head the department.

"Oh, thanks," Barak said.

"Why did you leave your door open?" she asked.

"Maybe one or two of the patients will want to come in and talk," he said. "They're probably aware there's been a change of doctor."

Hannah clicked her tongue and lifted her chin, which in Israel signifies the negative, like a shake of the head. "Nobody ever talks here."

"What do you mean? This is a psychiatric ward. All we do is talk," Barak said. He laughed. "Maybe we talk too much, but that's practically all we do."

Hannah had been on the ward fourteen years. She paused; then she repeated, "Nobody ever talks here."

Barak stopped laughing. Now he was confused. "So how do you do the rounds?"

"Here, in this room."

"With the door closed? You must be joking. The patients don't come here, and you don't go to see them?" Barak stood up from behind his desk and leaned across it toward Hannah.

"Well, once a week, but, you know . . ." Hannah didn't look at the doctor straight. "Nobody will talk to you."

Barak had his first sense that something was terribly wrong in the psychogeriatrics department. He had thought his biggest problem was the decrepit old building, constructed to house shell-shocked British soldiers during World War II. But this conversation disturbed him. He felt a touch of anger toward his predecessor, who apparently accepted the silence of his patients, but mostly he was deeply surprised. In a psychiatric hospital patients always clamor for attention, desperate for the doctor's time, knocking on his office door and reeling off breathless requests for help while he tries to persuade them that he's busy right now and they ought to come back later. Here nobody came. Barak left his door open all day; not a single patient stopped by to glance at the new head of department, who ought to have been the most important person in their lives. It was an extremely eerie feeling.

Barak could not know it then, but this ghostly quiet was a mirror of the silence that greeted these people in Israel when they came from Europe. It was not only Barak's predecessor who was complicit. An entire society refused to listen to these patients, until they eventually stopped talking.

Yoram Barak wanted to listen. First he set about making them talk. The next morning, he told Hannah that no one had come to him, as she predicted. "So, okay, let's go and meet the patients," he said.

This was new to Hannah, but she agreed. She loaded up a cart with the patients' records and wheeled it from room to room behind Barak. When he sat at their bedside, many of them ignored him. In any case, some had become mute. Slowly their vocal cords had atrophied from lack of stimulus over their decades in the hospital. But as weeks passed, some responded. A few began to come to the doctor's open door, even after the rounds were done. But something still puzzled Barak. In the hospital records, the birthplace of many of his patients was vague—"Poland," or simply, "Europe." As he talked to them, he noted that practically everyone on the ward seemed to be a Holocaust survivor. There were plenty of elderly people in Israel who had not been through the Holocaust. Why should this ward be so disproportionately filled with Hitler's victims?

Barak walked along Abarbanel's central lane and turned through the staff parking lot to the outpatients clinic. During his years as a resident, he had come to value the advice and mentoring of the clinic's chief, Dr. Henry Szor. He came to him now. In his office, Szor smiled at Barak and straightened his thick-rimmed glasses. His hair, curly and rising frenziedly from his head, was beginning to gray and recede. He was born in Poland after the war and raised in Germany, and he spoke with the Central European accent of the stereotypical shrink. But there was a softness and sensitivity in his voice and manner that Barak, who was much more brusque, more Israeli, cherished.

Barak began with an Israeli idiom. Long after it was banned in the United States, Israelis still used DDT to kill the cockroaches that swarm the country in hot weather, but if you didn't hit them with sufficient spray, the roaches would race around madly, hitting the walls until eventually they dropped dead, giving Hebrew the phrase Barak now employed. "Listen, my patients are all Holocaust survivors and they're all crazy like cockroaches," he said. "They won't speak to me, and everything is very strange."

"They're *all* survivors of the Holocaust?" Szor said.

"Well, about seventy percent of them." Barak told Szor of the disproportionate number of survivors in the ward. In Israeli society, Holocaust survivors made up only a third of the elderly population. That more than two-thirds of the 120 patients on Barak's ward should have lived through a concentration camp or spent the war hiding from the Nazis was something that ought to have been picked up years before.

"And they've got every condition under the sun," Barak said. "When I saw their records, it was like the history of psychiatry." Most of the patients on Barak's ward had been there since soon after they arrived in Israel, in the early 1950s for the most part. They were treated first with insulin shocks and cold-water showers. Then their doctors, who diagnosed almost all of them as schizophrenic, moved on to new French antipsychotic drugs. By the 1960s, they were administering Haloperidol and electroconvulsive treatments. When

lithium came along in the 1970s, the psychogeriatric ward at Abarbanel dosed it out, without any success or even much apparent hope
on the part of the doctors.

"Nothing worked, Henry," Barak told Szor. He felt a sudden burst
of the disappointment and exasperation that had built in him during
his first weeks in his new job. "Fuck, what's wrong here? This is not
psychiatry. In psychiatry, you treat people; you do the best you can;
some of them get better. These people are going nowhere."

The Holocaust connection was the tip Szor needed. It was the one
true note sounding clearly through the pandemonium of tuning
instruments in the orchestra pit of Barak's confusion. Szor's Polish
parents survived Hitler's murderous campaign. After he immigrated
to Israel, Szor worked under another doctor who encouraged him to
use his own sensitivity to the Holocaust in his treatment of survivors.
Szor and Barak talked about post-traumatic stress disorder, a condition that doctors periodically touched upon but which was often dis-
credited or ignored throughout the twentieth century. Essentially
psychiatrists around the world failed to identify fully the problems of
trauma until the years after World War II, and even then it was only
the rare doctor who took it seriously. In Israel, some psychiatrists
worked during the 1980s with traumatized survivors of the 1973 Yom
Kippur War. But in government hospitals like Abarbanel, it had never
been on the agenda. Szor thought it might be at work, in a very
extreme form, in the elderly Holocaust survivors in Barak's ward.
Some of the most chronic symptoms of trauma can easily be mistaken for schizophrenia, particularly in former captives who may
experience themselves as being controlled by another personality or
by disembodied voices, just as the Nazi camp guards once held
absolute power over them.

With Szor's insights in mind, Barak changed the routine in his
ward. He told Hannah he wanted to convene a group therapy session
each Sunday from 11 A.M. for ninety minutes with every patient on
the ward in attendance. "We'll all talk about the week that passed and
the one that's coming," he said.

"People will come into the room because we call them," the chief
nurse said. "But don't expect too much." It took months for most of
the patients to begin to speak freely there, and some began only years
later. But they did speak.

Lunch was at 12:30. At 2 P.M. a nurse went around the ward with a tray of cake. So soon after lunch, no one was hungry. But no patient dared say so, for fear the cake would be taken away for good. Barak had the cake left out for them to take when they were hungry.

At 8 P.M. a nurse distributed sleep medication. Barak stopped her. "I don't go to sleep at eight," he said. "Neither do my old parents. Why should the patients?"

The nurse protested. "But they'll sit up watching television until one a.m."

"What's wrong with that? The last patient that goes to bed turns off the television. What do you care?"

The staff didn't like the changes to their old, accustomed procedures, but Barak's reforms angered the patients too. Barak stopped the practice of all the patients wearing hospital pajamas. He kept a few in the sky-blue suits, because he thought they might use regular clothing to kill themselves or that they would try to escape from the hospital if they were given ordinary garments that would allow them to go unnoticed in the outside world. The rest received cheap tartan shirts, polyester pants, or loose smocks printed with floral patterns for the women. It was poor clothing, but normal clothing. One of the patients came to Barak, angry: "Listen, you're not right in the head."

"That has been said before," Barak said, "but why do you mention it?"

"It's these clothes. Why do we have to wear them?"

"I'm not going to walk around in hospital pajamas for fifty years, and neither should you," Barak said. "It's ridiculous."

The patient raised his voice. "If we wear civilian clothes, and *we* decide what we eat and when we have our cake here, and *we* decide when we go to sleep and what programs to watch on television, eventually you'll throw us out of here because you will have decided that we've become . . ."

"Yes?"

"Happy."

Barak was glad. The dialogue had begun.

Yoram Barak's own dialogue with the Holocaust, with Jewish history, was older. In a sense, it was why he came to Abarbanel in the first place. Later the young psychiatrist would come to understand that it was his family history, his perception of a world of anti-

Semitism snapping hungrily at the borders of Israel, that enabled him to change the way mentally ill Holocaust survivors were treated in Israel. But it was also because he was Israeli to his core. Barak identified a cultural paranoia within himself. He believed that the Arabs wanted to exterminate the Jews. He never traveled to Germany or Austria, the centers of Nazism. He joked macabrely with his father, who served in the pre-state Haganah militia and later in the Israeli army, about his reasons for picking psychiatry as a career: "It's almost the only specialty where medicine hasn't been overwhelmed by technology," he said. "If anyone ever destroys this country, wipes out Israel, and we survive in some refugee camp in Cyprus, I'll be able to set up my clinic within a day. I just need two chairs, and people will pay me to talk to them. I'll survive. They won't kill me. That's it."

Barak chose psychogeriatrics because of the strong bond he built with his grandparents, all of whom lived until he was well into his thirties. For him, they represented a connection to the Jewish history of their native Eastern Europe and to the early days of Zionism, when they came to what was then Palestine. It was that link that convinced Yoram Barak of the importance of Israel's very existence. Barak's paternal grandmother, Rachel Silber, a niece of the early Zionist propagandist Berl Katznelson, fled a pogrom in Belarus as a child in 1892 and later founded one of the first kibbutz communes. In Tel Aviv, she met his grandfather, Zalman Basin, a Russian dandy who cut a dashing figure as a mounted officer in the British police force. By the time Hitler started to murder the helpless Jews of Europe, the Basin family was established as the new kind of "strong Jew" cherished by Katznelson and other Zionist leaders. Yoram Barak's parents matched that image, and more. Both served in the Haganah. His father, Levi, was a career army officer who adopted the name Barak in 1951, when he took a posting in Philadelphia. Prime Minister David Ben-Gurion's order was that any Israeli official traveling abroad had first to change his European name to a Hebrew one. Perhaps Levi Barak chose the Hebrew word for "lightning" because he was an army electrician; Yoram Barak doesn't believe his father put much thought into it. That, too, was typical of Sabras—native-born Israelis—so casual when dealing with matters of appearances and protocol, things that were not concrete, conventions that were considered important in the staid European societies they left behind.

Yoram Barak studied medicine at Tel Aviv University and worked for his specialty at the Institute of Psychiatry in London, the world's foremost center for old-age psychiatric training. His close ties to his grandparents gave him a fascination with the inner world of the elderly. But he also decided to work with old people because he knew that most doctors didn't want to do so. He had a sense of service, an idea of Zionist noblesse oblige that he, as the scion of an establishment family, probably romanticized. An outstanding student, he could have chosen any specialty, an area of medicine much more lucrative than psychiatry, with its patients shunned by a society ashamed and repulsed and guilty, its hospitals consigned to the slums and outskirts where few have to face them. "Who needs another plastic surgeon?" he told friends who doubted his choice. It put him at odds with the Americanized consumer culture developing in Israel, overtaking the old values of service and sacrifice nominally at the ideological heart of Zionism.

It was with this advanced training that Barak came to his dilapidated ward at Abarbanel. But most of all, it was a sense of empathy that he brought to the survivors, quivering and gurgling on their beds as he talked to them. Barak found that most of the patients had no more familial history of psychological disorder than patients who didn't go through the Holocaust. In some sense, he realized, they must have been mentally strong to survive Auschwitz. A schizophrenic or a depressive probably wouldn't have lived through that ordeal. So they weren't sick before the Holocaust, he figured. Yet they came out of the death camps with a psychotic illness that had resisted treatment for fifty years. Barak and Szor decided it was not schizophrenia that afflicted their patients. They developed a new diagnosis that they called "lifelong post-traumatic psychosis." They posited the notion that their patients were post-traumatic *and* psychotic. It was a revolutionary concept. Usually a psychosis isn't related to a real event; a psychotic might *believe* that imaginary Germans wanted to kill him, but the psychosis of the patients at Abarbanel was rooted deeply in the reality that a massive state apparatus indeed tried to destroy them. The Nazi campaign of genocide was so unconscionable, so beyond the scope of normal reality, that it somehow had the same effect on these patients as the fictions of a psychotic. Barak and Szor felt they had found the key to treating the devastated residents of the old British barracks.

Behind the bougainvillea, a group of tortured people had been consigned to little more than a steamy dungeon for half a century by the State of Israel, the country that was supposed to be a haven for people just like this. The young psychiatrists began to figure out how to make the nation hear their story.

HENRY SZOR LISTENED with a horror that crept cold across him like an advancing shadow as Yoram Barak recounted the case of Naomi. The excited younger doctor had found a case that he felt proved at least one patient was held in Abarbanel specifically because of the Holocaust. Her case tested and verified their theory, and their reading of Israel's attitude to the survivors over the years. Naomi lived through a concentration camp, where she was tortured horribly. She came to Israel. She married, and bore two daughters and a son. She developed paranoia and was hospitalized. Her greatest pride was her son. She wanted him to become a doctor, as her father was before the Nazis killed him. The boy's career would make some partial restoration for her of the world that Hitler destroyed. There was a dreadful complication to her story, though. While she was hospitalized, her nineteen-year-old son shot himself in the head during his compulsory army service. This was twenty years before Barak came to Abarbanel. The family approached Naomi's doctor at Abarbanel back then and asked him to agree not to tell her of her son's death. They were certain that if she knew, it would kill her. As Barak told the story that he gleaned from Naomi's file, Szor realized what that pact meant. Naomi could never be released from the closed ward of the hospital, for outside she would immediately discover that her son was gone. The family came to visit her almost every day, but never spoke about the son. Yet Naomi created an imaginary life for him.

"You ask her how many children she has, she says three: two daughters and a son," Barak told Szor. "She says her son is a physician in Paris, of all places. He's so busy saving people as a famous surgeon that he doesn't have time to come and visit her. He marries, he has children, opens a new clinic. Now look, her daughters and her husband didn't supply this information. *She* created it. All because of this pact."

"You don't agree with the pact her doctor made with the family?" Szor asked.

"I'm very much opposed to it," Barak said. "I think she knows that her son is dead. She chooses not to express that, not to know. She's not a stupid woman, and she chooses not to know."

Henry Szor nodded. "You must understand that the Holocaust is like radioactive material. Once you experience it, it's inside you and it keeps giving out lethal radiation—lethal to your body and your mind. But people can survive for a time with this deadly thing inside them. They survive because of their psychosis, which allows them to keep it somehow repressed. For them, the Holocaust never really finished." Szor breathed deeply as he considered how best to explain this idea to Barak. "This radioactive nature of the Holocaust is true for the patients, and it's also true for their doctors."

Szor thought of how he reacted when Barak first brought him the news of the disproportionate population of Holocaust survivors in his ward. For ten years he had come each day to his outpatients clinic, a few hundred yards from the psychogeriatrics ward. He had been so close to the center of a terrible, cruel oversight, yet he had not seen. He recalled saying to Barak, "I didn't know. Nobody told me." Then he remembered thinking, My God, I sound like a German, excusing himself for not stopping the Holocaust. The radiation inside him, he felt it.

Henry Szor was born in Poland in 1949. His father survived the war in the Russian army, and his mother lived through a concentration camp. Everyone else, the whole extended family, died there. In 1956 the Szors—parents, daughter, and little Henry—went to Germany, where Henry stayed until 1977, when he came to Israel. At Shalvata Hospital he worked under Dr. Shammai Davidson, a Polish-born psychiatrist who escaped the Holocaust in London but lost his entire family back in Europe. Szor told Davidson that, though there were Holocaust survivors in the hospital, he wasn't interested in working with them; he believed it would mix his personal history and his professional life in a way that would be detrimental. But, in a sensitive and subtle way, Davidson gradually forced Szor to help the Holocaust survivors.

The patients at Shalvata were the lucky ones. They had a hospital director who understood their problems and a brilliant young doctor who eventually committed himself to helping them. Moreover, they suffered only from acute psychosis, unlike the chronic cases of Abarbanel. It was here that the ugly side of Israel's treatment of Holocaust survivors became problematic. It was a story tied to the horrible inequities of patronage and the corruption inherent in the system founded by the ruling Labor Zionists. One of the most powerful institutions in Jewish Palestine and, after the foundation of the state, in Israel was the Histadrut, the main labor federation. The Histadrut worked hand in glove with Ben-Gurion's pre-state Jewish Agency and, after 1948, with his government to ensure that the jobs and money stayed with their supporters. Political opponents were frozen out of everything from clerical jobs to farm equipment. And medical services. Until 1994 the Histadrut ran the Kupat Holim Klalit, the General Sick Fund, the most important and best-financed medical organization in the country. Established in 1911, it soon became one of the primary channels of recruiting Histadrut members and, thus, promoting the power of Ben-Gurion's doctrinaire regime. Mental health became perhaps the most divided of all the areas of this already unfair distribution of medical funding. The Kupat Holim ran Shalvata, where Szor first worked. The Histadrut directives were that only acute cases should be treated there; chronic patients should be referred to government-funded hospitals. So patients lucky enough to be in a sufficiently mild condition to benefit from Shalvata's care might be returned to the community, but those with more serious psychoses would be shipped along to Abarbanel, because the Histadrut didn't want to be stuck with the cost of people who might never rehabilitate as productive strivers for the Zionist cause. Those unconnected to the Histadrut never even got a shot at Shalvata and went directly to the government hospital. At Abarbanel, resources were scarce. No decent doctor wanted to work there in the early decades of the state, if they could possibly find a job at the better-funded Histadrut hospitals. When Barak brought the Holocaust survivors to his attention, Szor realized they must have been consigned to this darkened corner of the system years ago. Someone like him, working only on less severe cases, would have affirmed that they were chronic cases and needed to go to the government hospital, because they didn't meet the Kupat Holim's guidelines for patients to be treated at Shalvata. And so they fell into a black hole.

The funding truly did make a difference in the hospitals. Bright young doctors at Shalvata had been treating Holocaust survivors with lesser symptoms successfully for years. One of these psychiatrists was Dr. Avner Elizur, who became director of Abarbanel when the inequitable division of health funds began to change in 1985, and who subsequently appointed Yoram Barak to the psychogeriatrics ward. Elizur and other doctors at Shalvata in the 1960s identified the symptoms of concentration camp syndrome. They called it *"Ka-Tset* syndrome," after the German acronym for a concentration camp. It was a severe version of post-traumatic stress disorder characterized by terrible dreams. But Elizur and his colleagues treated only the neuroses of their patients, the anxieties and depression, and ignored the psychoses. Psychotics got nothing more than a free ride to Abarbanel.

Henry Szor knew where to place responsibility for the black hole of the psychotics in Israeli history. He thought later that there had been "a conspiracy of silence, a moral problem with the whole country." It was rooted in the shameful way Ben-Gurion's Zionists behaved toward Holocaust victims even before they arrived in Palestine and certainly how they were scarred once they came. In turn, this treatment was the result of the Zionist desire to see themselves as somehow different, as people who would have gone down fighting rather than be shunted into cattle cars on the railroad to the gas chamber. In 1942 Ben-Gurion addressed a Zionist assembly about evidence that the Nazis were exterminating helpless Jews in Europe. "Give us our right to fight and die as Jews," he said. The rightist Zionist leader Ze'ev Jabotinsky called upon Israel to breed "a new psychological race of Jew," as though it had been the weak mental state of European Jewry that allowed Hitler to round them up at the end of a machine-gun barrel. In 1959 Israel instituted Holocaust Martyrs' and Heroes' Remembrance Day. The relatively small number of Jews who did hit back, the Warsaw Ghetto fighters, for example, are the ones Israel's leaders wanted to memorialize, not the pitiful millions who couldn't defend themselves.

Here was the foremost context for all Israel's militarism. After Israeli troops won a dramatic victory in the Six-Day War against combined Arab armies, the Jewish philosopher Emil Fackenheim wrote that it was the "commanding voice of Auschwitz" that Israeli soldiers heard in June 1967 "when they refused to lie down and be slaughtered." In other words, this was a new breed of Jews, more forceful and powerful, simply better than the weak-willed ones who died in the camps.

This was the attitude that colored the arrival of Holocaust survivors in Israel. Their absorption was rough and heedless of their sufferings. Many of them, like the novelist Aharon Appelfeld, later reported feeling defiled and violated a second time by the Jews who received them in Israel, even before they recovered from their earlier mistreatment at the hands of the Nazis. Ben-Gurion displayed perhaps the lowest opinion of the Holocaust survivors when he suggested that somehow, in order to survive, they must have been worse than those who died: "Among the survivors of the German concentration camps are people who would not have prevailed had they not been what they are—hard, bad and egoistical. And everything that happened to them excised all that is good from their souls."

The national disrespect grew partially out of the boorishness cultivated by the socialist Zionist leaders as a reaction to the manners of the cultured Europe they left behind. But mostly it was a result of a sense of shame among native Israelis or settlers from earlier waves of aliyah—Jewish immigration to Palestine—that their people in Europe should have behaved so contemptibly. The new Israel lauded the ancient Zealots who committed suicide on Masada rather than surrender to the Romans, although if all Jews had taken the same course, there would never have been survivors to live through two millennia in the Diaspora and to refound Israel. The Zionist leaders didn't want to acknowledge that had the Germans beaten the British in North Africa, the Jews of Palestine would have gone to their fate just as easily and inevitably as their cousins in Hungary and Poland and Germany.

Dr. Davidson taught Henry Szor that it was heroic to have survived. When he drew the stories of their time in the camps from his patients, Szor remembered the positive, supportive nature of Davidson. He made it clear to his patients that their histories spoke to him not of humiliation and destruction but of their own resilience. That was what Szor, with his Polish birth and Holocaust-survivor parents, was able to pass on to Barak, whose own contact with the Holocaust had been largely intellectual.

Szor and Barak discussed at great length the relation of their new theory of long-term trauma with the history of trauma treatment. A British textbook on shell shock written in 1919 condemned those soldiers paralyzed by the psychological agonies of trench warfare as "moral invalids." After World War II, British psychiatrists began to formulate a more thorough idea of trauma and its effects that led to studies of different kinds of trauma: those affecting abused children, rape victims, and people who had been kidnapped or imprisoned. Captives, such as those in Nazi camps, typically shut down their feelings and surrendered their initiative to their guards. Prisoners came to see themselves as robots or nonhuman life forms. The feeling of abandonment experienced in the camps led to alienation from society, from family, from God—the victim of trauma believed himself more dead than alive. A prominent American psychiatrist named Judith Herman described traumatized people as carrying the mark of Cain. Yet it was only in 1980 that the American Psychiatric Association included posttraumatic stress disorder in its manual of mental conditions.

When Barak and Szor began to treat the patients in the psychogeriatrics ward for trauma, the results were startling. Psychological trauma was, they decided, an affliction of the powerless in the face of an overwhelming force, like that of the highly institutionalized Nazi death machine. Barak and Szor used a technique developed for the treatment of former political prisoners in Chile called "testimony therapy." The psychiatrists took verbatim transcripts of their patients' stories over a period of weeks. By telling their stories, the patients were able to see themselves as survivors, rather than simply hopeless victims. In this process, I became an eyewitness, Barak thought later. The story of the death camps couldn't be erased, but it could be partially neutralized; the patient, when he became a narrator, could see himself as dignified and strong again. A second form of treatment, "pet enhancement therapy," helped recover the years of a patient's life *before* the Holocaust. For many, those years had ceased to exist; the horror of the Holocaust was everything, an encompassing maw that consumed all trust or enjoyment of life. Working with animals in the ward allowed some patients to rebuild memories of happy childhoods spent with their pet dogs and cats. Others, who could not take responsibility for themselves in matters of hygiene, learned to do so by realizing how satisfied it made them feel to look after otherwise helpless animals. Barak and Szor were the first doctors to validate this method of therapy in practice. They did something similar with music therapy, re-creating good childhood associations with old lullabies. The therapies worked: in the first years after Barak and Szor started their new programs, 26 of their 120 patients improved enough that they could be transferred out of the closed ward of the hospital to specialized hostels.

The hardest thing for Barak, however, was to withhold help. As with Naomi, Barak's impulse was to cure, to move his patients along through the mental health system and back into the world. Szor helped him to see that this wasn't always the best thing, certainly not for people who had lived decades in the Abarbanel black hole. "How far are we allowed to go with treatment of a psychosis that, in a sense, protects patients from the Holocaust radiation sickness that they carry within them?" Barak asked Szor once.

Szor looked out his office window at the pines and honeysuckle in the sunny garden. "They must have some protection, otherwise they can't survive," he said. "Most people who went through the Holocaust re-created a life and a family afterward. But for those who didn't and became extremely ill, their fantasy world, their hallucinations and voices are their only protection. Is it our duty to treat them until we take that away from them? What will we leave them with?" He looked at Barak and shrugged. "There is no right and wrong answer."

Barak grew to understand Szor's wisdom as the years passed in the psychogeriatrics ward. The new therapies brought some successes, but there were cases that even Barak refused to confront. The Treblinka cannibal was one such dilemma. Now a manic depressive patient in Barak's ward, this man had been trapped in the cellar of an outbuilding at the Treblinka concentration camp with other inmates when it collapsed around them during a bombing raid. In the weeks before they were dug out, the patient and some of his comrades survived by eating the bodies of others who died in the bombing. When depressed, the patient recalled the cannibalism as a horrifying reality, as though he were experiencing it still; when euphoric, he had no memory of it. Barak knew that many doctors would urge that he force the man to confront what he had done. Instead, he medicated him with antidepressants so that he would never descend into the depths that brought back the taste of human flesh as though it were rolling across his palate at that very moment.

When Szor and Barak were certain of their results, they took their findings to top Holocaust experts in Israel. At a symposium, Szor told Yehuda Bauer, a leading professor of Holocaust studies, that there was an additional horror beyond the abandonment of the mentally ill

survivors in Abarbanel: the payments due these survivors from the
Israeli state were not getting to them, because of obstructive bureaucrats. When Szor, for example, wanted to buy air-conditioning units
for the psychogeriatrics ward, he tried to fund them with money held
by the government on behalf of some of the patients who had no
other guardian or trustee to authorize payments. But the bureaucrats
refused to release the money because it would go to benefit many
patients, rather than only the few individuals whose cash allocations
were to be used. Bauer was shocked and helped get the case into a
leading Israeli newspaper.

It was situations like this that truly disgusted Henry Szor. He knew
that the psychiatrists and conditions at Abarbanel had been substan-
dard for decades. He grew reconciled to that past injustice, because
finally he and Barak had begun to make changes. Yet that the Israeli
state, which founded so much of its national mythmaking on its role
as a refuge for Holocaust victims, should have played a part not just
in the neglect but also in the active cheating of survivors dismayed
him. He and Barak decided it was not enough for them to improve
only their own psychogeriatrics ward at Abarbanel. They had to
ensure that the same changes were made throughout Israel.

MOTI MARK helped Szor and Barak because of the goose bumps he
felt when he thought of his mother and the time she mistook him for
an SS officer. The chief psychiatrist at Israel's Health Ministry joined
the crusade of the young doctors from Abarbanel and forced through
the kind of broad changes only someone with national authority
could effect. Mark was a self-assured former army man, who had been
chief psychiatrist first of the air force and then of the entire Israeli
military. He was garrulous and well connected, a little conceited, and
demonstratively chummy. Married to another senior army officer, he
had the sort of life and character Israelis would envy. But when he
thought of his mother, there was a blank, a silence filled with the
awful memories of her decades of depression and psychosis. He
would sit in his characteristic manner, chatting with his hands
behind his head and his legs crossed expansively. But then he would
think of her sufferings. It would chill him and he would sit upright
and hug himself with a shiver.

One day in 1986, Mark drove out of the army base at Tel Hashomer to visit his mother at nearby Geha Psychiatric Hospital, in central Israel. Colonel Mark was head of mental health services for the entire army at that time. As he strode into the hospital, he wore the informal olive drab of the Israeli military: a shirt with sleeves rolled up above the elbow, baggy trousers, and lace-up boots. His beret was tucked under the left epaulet with the three stars. Yocheved Mark lay in a private room. Doctors assessed that she was dangerous to herself and others, so they kept her alone. When her youngest son entered, she began to scream. She shrank from him, abject and terri-fied, and called out that he wanted to hurt her, to kill her. She called him SS. She called him Nazi. She screamed at him in German.

Mark stepped into the corridor. His heart raced. He had grown used to his mother's psychosis over the years, but it never had hit him like this. He couldn't understand what had set her off. When the doc-tor came to calm Yocheved, Moti Mark left the hospital. He drove back to his base, fretting about her. He knew so little of her early years, because she never talked about the war. She was born in Bukov-ina, in Romania, but he didn't even know in which concentration camp she had been captive. He knew his father's story much more clearly. Mark's father, Moshe, escaped Romanian soldiers working for the Nazis by hiding with his brother in their village synagogue. A Romanian major discovered them and recognized them as the sons of the village rabbi. The major, a devout Christian, respected the rabbi's religious learning and decided to help the boys. He told them to stay where they were, hidden behind the ark in the hall of the synagogue. They stayed there three days, and when they came out, the street was carpeted with Jewish corpses.

Mark recalled Moshe's deep emotion on the day the army pro-moted his son to major. When Moti Mark reached that rank in the Israeli army, it gave a sense of closure to his father, because the "major" represented power to him, absolute protective power over life and death, as well as a remembrance of the mercy shown by the Romanian officer. But Moshe did not suffer quite the same terrible trauma that overwhelmed Yocheved. She had been hospitalized peri-odically since the age of twenty-three, when she gave birth to Mark's elder brother. At first doctors thought it was postpartum depression, then recurrent depression, schizophrenia, bipolar disorder. Like

Barak's patients in the forgotten ward at Abarbanel, Yocheved Mark's file was a catalog of the history of psychiatry. Only near the end did she get a diagnosis of concentration camp syndrome. There were flashbacks, nightmares, depressions. Mark also felt he recognized what psychiatrists call "double consciousness." He believed that, even as she yelled in German at the terrifying SS man, she also knew that she was in an Israeli hospital alone in a room with her son. She was the little child who smuggled food into the ghetto for her family, and she was a mother living in Israel, at the same moment.

The next day Mark returned to Geha Psychiatric Hospital. It was his day off work and he didn't wear his uniform. He realized that something about the visit was going better than the previous day, and as he sat with his mother, he understood it had been the uniform that set her off. He couldn't imagine any similarity between the casual scruffiness of an Israeli uniform and the threatening, stiff black of the SS. Yet that was what seemed to have sparked her terrible memories. Still she spoke to him in German. Weeks later, when she finally reverted to Hebrew, she did so with a German accent that took yet more weeks to wear off. Two years later, when Mark was at the end of his army service, he went to a symposium in northern Israel and took along his six-year-old son, Natan, so they could visit the beach at the Sea of Galilee afterward. One of the army psychiatrists at the conference was describing the symptoms of depression when Natan interrupted him: "You forgot to say that if you are depressed you speak German." It was the spontaneous, innocent observation of a child, and when Mark laughed it was with a deep, redemptive feeling of relief.

After he left the army, Mark took a sabbatical at a Veterans Administration hospital in Kansas, where he was first exposed in a thorough way to the study of post-traumatic stress disorder, largely through observing soldiers who had served in Vietnam. When he returned to Israel, Mark became commissioner of mental health at the Health Ministry and undertook a tour of the country's psychiatric hospitals. He noticed that patients, particularly in the small private hospitals that dotted Israel, lived in poor conditions. Many were crowded twelve to a room. Worse, a large number had been hospitalized long-term and seemed to have no prospect of improvement. Of 4,800 patients hospitalized for more than a year, 1,100 were Holocaust survivors—far out of proportion to their representation in society overall. Yet they were not treated systematically as Holocaust survivors:

each had his own diagnosis, as a schizophrenic or chronic depressive. One of the worst hospitals Mark identified was Abarbanel.

Then Mark met Szor and Barak. When he heard how they began to use new therapies for the trauma of the Holocaust, he realized that if he could improve conditions for the survivors, those therapies would work even better. Mark pushed for the Health Ministry to open new hostels for the Holocaust survivors in the grounds of existing hospitals. He wanted to clear out as many survivors as he could from the state hospitals and all of them from the private clinics—which received a fee per patient from the state and, therefore, had no incentive to return their patients to the outside world. He wanted to find them a place that would afford more cultural and social interaction and better facilities for the kinds of treatments Barak and Szor began at Abarbanel.

Mark viewed these hostels as some kind of amends the state might make to people like his mother. He knew from her case that most of the Holocaust survivors hiding in the dark corners of the mental health system were not beyond help. When Yocheved Mark finished her last hospital stay, she joined a support group called Amcha, at which survivors shared stories about the war and also about their current lives, their children, and their successes. Mark's father told him that she seemed to have become once more like the young woman he married, the happy woman Moti Mark never knew. In 1999 Yocheved died of pancreatic cancer. She left behind a journal she wrote for her Amcha group. Mark found it after her funeral. It told of how she had studied at a Romanian school where most children were not Jews. They bullied her because of her religion, but she helped them with their homework because she was the smartest. She traded her pencils with the other students for food to take back home. She was six years old. Mark read the journal and tried to imagine one of his children, studying and trading and carrying the responsibility for feeding the family and surviving, all while little more than an infant. He was proud of the work he did with Szor and Barak to build the hostels. It just seemed to Mark that it was so little and it had taken so long. It was a shame.

ALEXANDER KLEIN passed me a plate of pomegranate seeds in his thin hand, which was scarred by the IVs of his most recent hospital visit. Alexander used to have a strong build from the years in which he farmed a plot on Moshav Sde Yitzhak and sat up late watching for the Arabs who would sneak across the nearby border with the West Bank to steal his cows. Now that he was seventy-seven, age had shrunk him, so that he seemed tiny in the chair next to his son, a man of over six feet, my Israeli military affairs correspondent at *Time* magazine, Aharon Klein. I picked up the seed—white where it had been attached to the core and blood red in the thickest part of the bulb, like a pinched fingernail. When the Nazis imprisoned Alexander Klein at Melk, a seed like this would have been a luxurious meal. He ate a snail once, in the camp, talking to it gently before he devoured it, apologizing for consuming it alive. But that was past. He tried to make light of it, and he truly believed there was nothing for him to complain about now. Not for himself at least. Something upset him, though; something that made him feel the persecution of Europe's Jews was continuing, right here in Israel's fertile central plain.

Aharon Klein brought me to see his parents in their simple cottage, the standard shape and size for the moshav, or farm cooperative where he grew up, because I couldn't quite believe what he told me about the way Israeli bureaucrats treated Holocaust survivors. In my office one morning, Aharon told me that his parents volunteered at a hostel for mentally ill Holocaust survivors near their home. "They say it's terrible there," Aharon said. "The patients don't have money for false teeth, for tombstones."

"But this is Israel," I said. "How could they treat Holocaust survivors like that here, of all places?" Later I would feel almost ashamed of the naiveté in that statement. Like anyone who never studied the abuse and neglect of Holocaust survivors from the early days of the state until today, I assumed that Israel was founded primarily *because of* the Holocaust. I thought of the origins of the country as a sanctuary for Jews, mainly those victimized by Hitler. I never wondered exactly how dark that refuge had been.

I drove Alexander and Aharon's mother, Atara, to the hostel at Shaar Menashe Mental Health Center, where they did their voluntary work. In the car, Alexander recounted the story of a patient there who hadn't spoken for years. Alexander, who, like his wife, was born in eastern Hungary, and deported by the Nazis in 1944, approached the man and talked to him in Hungarian. The patient looked up and, struggling to use a voice so long unemployed, replied in the same language. Hungarian Jews didn't speak Yiddish, Russian, Hebrew, or even German, and no one else there in the hostel spoke any Hungarian. The result had been a long silence for the patient, but one that Alexander Klein felt was made deafening with all the bitterness of these lost lives. "There's something stinking about what happened to them," he said.

Alexander and Atara shared a history with these mentally ill people at the hostel. He was deported to the labor camp at Melk in Austria and, later in the war as the Nazis withdrew, to another camp at Ebensee, where he almost starved to death. The Nazis took Atara to Auschwitz, and after the war, she tried to make it to Palestine. The British rulers of Palestine intercepted her ship, the *Shaar Yishuv,* and imprisoned her on Cyprus with other refugees until Israel's foundation, when she joined her father, sister, and brother in the new state. Alexander arrived at Haifa and was pressed immediately into the artillery to fight Israel's War of Independence. Both retained their sanity, but they understood the torment in the minds of the inmates at Shaar Menashe.

We came to the door of the main hostel. Inside, a small stream of patients shuffled across the floor in their old carpet slippers and robes. "Who wants a cigarette?" a nurse called out. The faces were blank and staring as they shambled toward her. It was as though their walkers responded to the offer of the hourly smoke, not their bodies. They gathered around the counter, and the nurse proffered a light, one after the other kindling the cigarettes in their shaky hands. They dragged on the cheap tobacco with toothless mouths, scored around by deep wrinkles, then turned and padded to the door to finish smoking in the heat outside. I held the door for them, and they passed me as if in a trance. They breathed the nicotine deeply and long, as though they might not live to smoke another cigarette.

The 100 residents of Shaar Menashe's Holocaust survivors hostel were the beneficiaries of Dr. Moti Mark's work to find places for those mental patients whose conditions improved when they were treated for trauma, as Yoram Barak and Henry Szor suggested. Mark gathered these patients from government hospitals like Abarbanel and private institutions, most of which he had closed in his capacity as chief psychiatrist at the Health Ministry. The advantage of the hostel was that its clean new building allowed the survivors more privacy, and there was greater emphasis on social activities than in the hospitals. In the private hospitals, many patients had been physically abused and left in solitary confinement. A former nurse at one private hospital told me about staff who would tie patients to beds for hours at a time; others would beat incontinent patients when they soiled themselves. In the private hospitals, untrained nurses on low wages administered drugs and gave injections. The hostels Mark constructed at Shaar Menashe and in the grounds of two other mental institutions were the main signs that Israel was beginning to face up to its responsibility for these helpless people.

As I investigated the story of the mentally ill survivors, I found that it was not only these few thousand who were neglected by Israel. There were many more among the 300,000 Holocaust survivors living in Israel who had been cheated of compensation or property by the very state whose declared intention had been to provide a refuge from the ill-treatment suffered by Jews around the world. Like many of history's most shameful episodes, money was at the root of it.

In 1953 David Ben-Gurion accepted a deal with West Germany on reparations for Holocaust survivors. The West Germans offered Ben-Gurion $715 million in goods and services for Israel over twelve years, as well as $107 million to Jewish organizations. In return, Israel agreed to take over compensation payments to Holocaust survivors already in Israel at that time. There were riots outside the Knesset at the prospect of accepting German blood money. Still, it seemed like a good deal to the prime minister of a poor, new country. In fact, it turned out to be disastrous. Ben-Gurion underestimated the number of survivors in Israel, and yet the state had to keep paying them year after year. There are 40,000 survivors in Israel who don't get money from Germany and, therefore, are entitled to payments from the Israeli state. Of course, the cash Ben-Gurion received from West Germany went to building roads, buying weapons, developing drip irrigation systems, paying salaries for government bureaucrats. It wasn't used to set up institutions to help the Holocaust survivors.

The Israeli government soon realized it would run through the West German cash quickly if it paid survivors their due. So the Finance Ministry office set up to handle claims by Holocaust survivors aimed mainly to keep its payouts to a minimum. Until the 1980s, a survivor's first contact with the office was with a team of former police detectives whose job was to root out cheats, rather than process legitimate claims. When Rafi Pinto took over the department in 1994, his predecessor told him, "Your job is to save the state's money." Only in 1997 did Pinto's department publish details of Holocaust survivors' entitlements that had been on the books since the 1950s. "There was a problem," Pinto told me sheepishly, fumbling with a glass of milky Nescafé in his Tel Aviv office. "People really didn't know what they were due."

"When you finally published the guidelines, did the number of survivors claiming go up?" I asked.

Pinto looked at his hands and laughed nervously. "It increased four times over."

The Finance Ministry didn't change of its own accord. A few legislators forced it at least to pay the same compensation as Germany did: it had been paying 24 percent less than the Germans to people with the same Holocaust history. Many survivors hired lawyers to deal with the ministerial bureaucracy. Between 1995 and 2000, the lawyers took $25 million in fees from Holocaust survivors off the top of their government entitlements. Pinto believes the state will be paying out to survivors who were children in the Holocaust for another thirty years, although 1,200 die annually in Israel. Lawyers, no doubt, will be drawing the fees still.

Other Israeli ministries also were forced only recently to reform their mishandling of Holocaust survivors. In 2000 Justice Minister Yossi Beilin decided it looked bad for Israel to ignore the question of lost Holocaust funds and properties in its own institutions, at a time when banks in Switzerland and elsewhere were being pressured by Jewish organizations to hand over billions of dollars belonging to Hitler's victims. Beilin charged Aharon Shindler, a ministry official, with sifting through abandoned properties and bank accounts to find which owners probably died in the Holocaust. The list Shindler and a team of ten graduate students drew up was the starting point for a squad of investigators hired to track down heirs. After picking through 17,000 items, Shindler reckoned Israel held $35 million in assets belonging to people who died in the Holocaust.

Before Shindler began his work, claimants arriving at the office of the Justice Ministry's custodian-general received the bureaucratic equivalent of a closed door, and a shocking lack of understanding for the suffering of survivors and their descendants. Gabriel Weiss, a retired merchant seaman, spent more than five years trying to recover money belonging to a Romanian relative who deposited it in a bank in what was then Palestine and who later perished in Auschwitz. Weiss, a courtly, cultured man with a white goatee, showed me a file three inches thick of letters from ministry lawyers repeatedly demanding more proof of his claim, which they valued at $40,000. We sat an entire afternoon in Weiss's Caesarea home going through that file. Each time Weiss drew a new letter from the pile in his lap, he held his breath, shocked, just as he did when they came to him through the mail. "This one asks whether my relative was gassed before or after his wife. These people went up in smoke. Why does the government need more proof? How can they heap such degradation on our backs?" Eventually Weiss may get the money. Then he'll receive one last letter from the government—an invoice for a 5 percent "administration fee" levied for keeping hold of the property all these years.

At the root of the mistreatment of survivors was the disregard for individuals that tainted early Zionism. For Ben-Gurion, it was not so much the threat to Europe's Jews that was important about the Holocaust, but the role it might play in the Zionist project to found and build a state. A month after *Kristallnacht,* Ben-Gurion said that "if I knew it were possible to save all the Jewish children of Germany by their transfer to England and only half of them by transferring them to *Eretz-Yisrael* [the Land of Israel], I would chose the latter." In 1942 he said that "the catastrophe of European Jewry is not, in a direct manner, my business."

There was something horribly steely and inhumane about the pronouncements of Israel's first leaders on the subject of Holocaust survivors. It was this unforgiving environment that bred still more hatred. I began to think of this cycle as total psychosis, which may not be the most exact of psychiatric diagnoses but seemed to me a tool to sum up the origins and effects of a system of collective behavior that I witnessed all around me in Israel. The myths of Eden suggested to me that there was once a time of purity and innocence. This idyllic state was confused by Adam and Eve's fall from Eden and shattered by Cain's murder of Abel. Cain called out to God, "My punishment is greater than I can bear!" There was no Yoram Barak, no Henry Szor to come along and ask Cain how he felt, to help him resolve his guilt and depression, his isolation and paranoia. Human history since then has been a constant amassing of suffering on suffering, like the layers of a city that crushes its simple early settlements beneath the maze of tunnels and pipes and steel pilings of modernity. So, too, native Israelis heaped anguish upon those who came to make new lives in the country, from Holocaust survivors to Mizrahi Jews. The violence that surrounds Israelis added to the trauma of their arrival to create a society in which almost all individuals behave as though suffering from post-traumatic stress disorder. They display sudden rage, constant feelings of victimization, the sense that someone is trying to put one over on them, even in the line at the post office. It also makes them easily manipulated by politicians, who can punch the raw spots on the collective psyche and, thus, easily direct widespread and extreme hatred at opponents. That's a factor in mainstream Israeli politics, but the most serious manifestation of this violent, communal reaction is the vengeful ideology of Rabbi Meir Kahane. The racist founder of the Kach Party believed that the Holocaust and the centuries of pogroms that preceded it damaged the Jewish national psyche. The only way to recover, he posited, was to take revenge by physically humiliating Gentiles. But the power of this argument among Israelis is not born from persecution in the Diaspora alone. Most Israelis have no memory of that. Persecution, to most Israelis, is of their nation by the Arabs *and* of their group within Israeli society at the hands of some other faction or authority in the nation. Their ugliness to each other promulgated the sense that threat was everywhere; that preemptive attack at home, at the workplace, on the road, is the only way to prevent torment. In fact, as Yoram Barak and Henry Szor would tell them, that's how torment turns on oneself, to feed and nourish the terrors one would deny.

On December 25, 2002, I drove back to Moshav Sde Yitzhak through a cold, midday rainstorm. The lane outside the Klein home was crowded with cars. A group of women wept on the small porch. The night before, Alexander Klein died of complications from pneumonia. A man from the *hevra kadisha,* the burial society, cut a small diagonal slice into his son Aharon's shirt to symbolize the mourner's rending of his garments. We walked down to the moshav's small cemetery. At the graveside, Aharon eulogized his father as a man whose every day was heroic, because he survived the Holocaust and lived on. I thought of the lost souls a mile away at Shaar Menashe, on whose behalf Alexander had felt such outrage and whom he helped quietly to live on. Who would look upon them as heroes? It was a eulogy every Israeli ought to be made to hear.

AVNER ELIZUR watched the minister of health's white Volvo roll along the lane at the center of Abarbanel, past the low barracks where the psychogeriatrics ward had been and into the spur in front of the new Holocaust survivors unit. Abarbanel's director looked up thoughtfully for a moment at the modernistic white façade of the building that had taken such a struggle to erect. He turned back to the broad smile of Health Minister Roni Milo as he stepped out of the limousine and began glad-handing with the local dignitaries. Elizur had lost count of the number of health ministers who came and went in the fourteen years since he took over at Abarbanel in 1985. Next to him stood Moti Mark, Yoram Barak, Henry Szor. They smiled at the minister as he progressed along the receiving line, but they all thought the same thing: Here's another political hack briefly passing through. Milo had been mayor of Tel Aviv; a Likud Party "prince" disappointed with his advancement, he switched to the new Center Party and never built much expertise in health services during his short ministerial tenure. The Volvo, however, he would certainly have liked. That's how it was in Israel, where governments changed and cabinets shuffled almost before the new ministers had a chance to line up their family photos on their desks. Milo made his opening speech. It was dutiful and a little witty and then, when he came to the Holocaust, sententious and weighty. This was the national myth at work, after all. He didn't talk about the half-century in which the inmates of the new building languished in a shack where they lay prone on the floor tiles in lieu of air-conditioning. It was $1.5 million from the Claims Conference, an international Holocaust reparations body, and the Joint Distribution Committee that paid for the new wing, not the Israeli government. Another round of handshakes and Milo was back in the white Volvo and off, away from Bat Yam's dismal tenements. The dignitaries cleared gradually. The doctors remained.

The patients in the ward ground their jaws and shook and shuffled along the clean new corridors to their new accommodations. They would sleep only two to a room now, instead of packed closely. For Avner Elizur, it was small reparation for what Israel did to them. He thought of his first contact with the Holocaust back in high school in Tel Aviv, just after World War II. His best friend was a Holocaust survivor named Moshe. In the school people called survivors "soaps," because they felt contempt for those who allowed themselves to be slaughtered by the Nazis and made into soap. Elizur's family did not suffer in the Holocaust; he was born in Palestine. He noted something that was different about Moshe, a Polish Jew who hid in Russia throughout the war. He saw that his friend was less impulsive, not as judgmental and outspoken as the Sabras born in Tel Aviv. Elizur and Moshe went together through the army and their studies at the Haifa Technion, and they remained close in the decades after. In 1975 Elizur observed Moshe's gentleness as he tended his dying wife. He drew on Moshe's support during the years after Szor and Barak first alerted him to the scandal of the Holocaust survivors in the psychogeriatrics ward. Moshe, who became a successful engineer, gave money to the hospital, but also helped Elizur to keep going when he faced resistance to his plan for a new Holocaust survivors ward.

The people of Bat Yam didn't want Abarbanel in their midst. So long as the hospital was just a collection of old British army huts shaded by tall, straight plane trees, the townspeople figured there was a chance the mental patients might be moved away to another, better facility. The plan to put up a big, new center for the Holocaust victims made it clear that Abarbanel would stay. For several years, Elizur juggled objections at the municipality with finance meetings at the Health Ministry in Jerusalem. Furious locals alleged that the inmates raped a woman, that they stole from shops, and that their presence drove down the value of property. The town-planning committee came to him claiming to be all in favor of better facilities for people who had suffered at the hands of Hitler—but wouldn't it be much nicer for them, they said, down in the Negev somewhere, where they'd have fresh air and open spaces? Somewhere, anywhere—not here. Few communities anywhere in the world relish proximity to mental hospitals, but Bat Yam's reaction was tinged with a deeper repulsion, which Elizur sensed was tied to both the Holocaust and the project for the new wing. To the locals, as long as these patients continued to relive the Holocaust each day, it was as if a little corner of their town was Auschwitz.

The Holocaust survivors themselves felt a strong mistrust of the doctors' intentions. Just as Barak encountered opposition to the introduction of regular clothing and late-night television, Elizur had to persuade small groups of patients to visit the new building before everyone moved in. For many of them the idea of transfer was still loaded with the horror of the Nazi cattle cars. Finally, they made the move on the eve of Yom Kippur. The patients were in the new building weeks before most of them came to see it as a real, permanent place for them, not some kind of transit camp.

Moti Mark, whose contact with the minister as a senior official in his office was more regular, also felt the anticlimax of the ceremony at Abarbanel's new wing. Minister Milo, the dignitaries, the doctors—everyone shared their good feelings, hugged, shook hands. Mark had worked hard to get the ministry to assist Elizur on the project. But now he felt bitterness. For the best psychiatric care, these broken people waited fifty years. So now they had it. Big deal. There could be no compensation. He thought of the next wave of Holocaust survivors who would be coming through the gates of the hospital. They were arriving already, people who were young during the Holocaust and who had buried their trauma under a cloak of workaholism until the time came for them to retire. When they left their jobs, huge expanses of time suddenly opened up before them that were filled by the dread memories of the death camps, nightmares that could be ended only by suicide. Mark heard from Barak and Szor that they found a suicide rate among aged Holocaust survivors 40 percent higher than that of other elderly Israelis. *Arbeit macht frei,* work makes you free: bitterly Mark remembered the words cast above the gate of Auschwitz. For the people who once walked through those gates, immersion in work kept them functional, but as soon as employment stopped and retirement began, they became once more enslaved by the horrors of that camp. Soon they would pass through the gates of Abarbanel. At least now there would be doctors waiting for them who understood and would help.

Those new survivors, finally breaking down after years of repressing their memories, would not walk straight down the avenue to Abarbanel's Holocaust wing. They would turn right, past the doctors parking lot to Henry Szor's outpatients clinic. After the ceremony to open the new wing, Szor wondered if some of those consigned to live out their lives in the new building could have taken a different path if only the hospital's doctors had uncovered their secrets twenty years earlier. Some of the patients were only at that time turning into chronic cases. It would never have occurred to Szor to work at Abarbanel back then. It was a lousy hospital, he thought. Yet Szor's character was deeply constructive. He didn't sink into bitterness about those wasted years and the psyches whose health drowned in the inequity of the Israeli health system and in rejection by its society. Even if it was late, Szor knew that he and Barak and Mark had done a job that needed doing. They didn't leave things as they found them. Later he would think of the changes they made as a cause for happiness: "If we hadn't discovered them, it would never have occurred to Israeli society or to others around the world that people can break down and be forgotten, even in a society that was, in a way, established for them and to prevent such a thing ever happening."

Szor knew that it was too late for most of the patients in the psychogeriatrics ward at Abarbanel, but he wanted to ensure that they would be the last generation whose traumatic suffering was overlooked by Israel. In 1998 with a psychiatrist from Bar-Ilan University, Szor helped found Natal, a center in Tel Aviv for the treatment of people suffering from trauma caused by national conflicts. Its therapists and telephone help line aided soldiers suffering from shell shock due to Israel's long wars; they worked with people injured in terrorist bombings, or even people who watched too much of the endless terror coverage on Israeli television news broadcasts. Although Natal was underfunded and received very little money from the Israeli government, Szor believed something had changed in the country's attitude toward survivors and their suffering. For a long time, Israelis were trained to view Holocaust victims as somehow complicit in their own deaths or incarceration: they should have fought back. But it's not so easy to think in such a dismissive way when you know that at any moment, in your favorite café or on the bus you take to work every day, you could fall victim to a suicide bomber. Would it be wrong then to enter the café or ride the bus? Would it be weakness, or complicity with the terrorists? Some Israelis began to internalize the message Szor saw in all this: simply to survive, to live on, can be heroic.

YORAM BARAK lived at the touching point of these two worlds, of the brash native-born Israelis who believed they would have beaten

the Nazis or died trying, and of the European victims who could not
free themselves from the presence of the horror into which they had
been herded. Barak locked himself into the Psychogeriatrics ward six
days a week, where the furies of the Holocaust were not abstract; they
took him in their grip and inhabited him as they did perhaps no
other Israeli who was never physically in the camps and the ghettoes.
As Barak saw it, it took generations for Israelis to understand that
they, too, have no immunity from extinction. Whether he was in the
foyer of the Holocaust survivors block at Abarbanel, surrounded by
the sudden inarticulate cries of the patients, or out for the evening at
a Tel Aviv café in the babble of the throng, Barak knew that he was
among the same people, united by their shared vulnerability. Because
they were Jews. Someone had wanted to obliterate his patients and,
so, the café-goers in turn erased the presence of these victims from
their society. If they did not, they would live all the time with the
knowledge that in a decade or two, perhaps in a century, someone
else might inflict genocide upon them. This was what Yoram Barak
learned from his years in the psychogeriatrics department: he drew
closer and closer to the survivors on his ward, because he saw deeper
into their vulnerability and realized that, as a Jew, he shared it. It
overwhelmed the Zionist "new Jew" that Israel tried to breed him to
be. Most Israelis wanted to believe it couldn't happen here and to
them. But they were driven, in fact, by the latent perception that it
not only *could* happen, but one day it *would*. It was this that made
Israelis spin so quickly from a willingness to accept broad concessions
for a peace deal with the Palestinians at Camp David in the summer
of 2000 to a furious pugilism as soon as the bullets of the Aqsa
intifada began to rack up their victims. The nation responded like a
traumatized person—trapped, fearful, striking out with absolute and
sometimes disproportionate force.

Barak's colleagues, particularly Henry Szor, noticed a seductiveness
in his relationships with patients, a closeness that they thought inad-
visable for his own sake. Psychiatrists who work with post-traumatic
patients are known to be in danger of being pulled into the trauma's
psychological effects. But Szor rarely spoke about this observation to
Barak, because it was Yoram Barak, after all, who knew the patients
best and who had to decide how to handle them. Barak encountered
the most damaged of Holocaust patients in his ward. For Szor, his out-

patients were mostly able at least to describe for him what happened to them in the death camps; there was a personal narrative, something to which he could address his treatment. Barak's engagement was with something unnamable for his patients, something dark and terrifying and overwhelming, where a doctor's logic was needed less than his intuition and his heart. That was at the root of the collaboration between Henry Szor and Yoram Barak. Barak could go to Szor for the words to fill the perplexing silence; Szor learned from Barak about the barren land beyond language.

Barak's commitment to his patients sometimes baffled his staff. He took patients on outings to places where the nurses feared the survivors might draw stares or embarrass people. The nurses thought that way because they lived outside the hospital; they connected with the patients largely as people just doing their jobs, cleaning them and administering drugs and guarding the keys to the staff toilet. Barak lived with the patients and entered their heads, and he didn't give a damn about the outside world or anyone else's feelings.

The Tel Aviv Yiddish Theater contacted Barak in late 2002. The director of a new stage version of S. Y. Agnon's *A Simple Story* wanted Barak's help. The theater planned an adaptation of the novel by Agnon, Israel's only Nobel literature laureate. Typically for that dense and allusive writer, it was, in fact, not a simple story at all. It's the tale of a young Jew in Galicia in the interwar years who's denied the chance to marry his true love by his parents. He acquiesces in an alternative, arranged marriage, but the strain of denial and passivity eventually makes him break down, and he's sent to a psychiatrist. The theater director wanted to come with his leading actor to study the behavior of the Eastern European patients in Barak's ward, who had, after all, been children in the very environment in which *A Simple Story* was set and still spoke the language in which the play would be produced. "You want to see what it is to be crazy in Yiddish and this is the place to get hold of Yiddish crazies," Barak said. "So come, but on one condition."

"What's that?" the director asked.

"When the production is on, you invite those patients who speak Yiddish to see the play."

"Of course, if you want."

Barak's nurses didn't like the idea. The head nurse worried that there would be an embarrassing scene in the Tel Aviv theater. Some of the patients Barak intended to take were severely regressed; almost all were heavy smokers accustomed to lighting up constantly; without awareness of boundaries, one of them might begin screaming at one of the actors in the midst of a psychotic conversation. Barak didn't care. "Not to worry," he said. "First of all, who cares? They're entitled. This is Israel, this is a Yiddish theater, so who's more entitled to see the show than them? Worse comes to worst, we take any patient who's agitated out into the lobby. Even if they have to stop the play for a few minutes while we take someone out, who cares? Let's go see the play."

The women on the ward, who had shuffled about in slippers for years, began to worry about finding high-heeled shoes for the theater. Men who hadn't wanted to discard their hospital pajamas when Barak revised the dress code looked in the communal laundry to find a nice shirt for their night out. Excitement buzzed around the white corridors of the ward and in the television room, where usually everyone stared at the screen in silence. The bus came for them at 7 P.M. They left their cigarettes behind and sat quietly in the lobby of the theater at the Zionist Organization of America House, off Ibn Gvirol Street in Tel Aviv, listening to the director describe the symbolism of the play in Yiddish. When the two dozen patients from Abarbanel entered the auditorium just before the curtain, the audience turned their heads, noted the walkers, the bad haircuts, and the cheap old dresses the women wore. Then, for the entire two hours of the play, no one on Barak's row uttered a sound. They laughed and cried, but only when laughter and tears came to the rest of the audience too. In spite of himself, Barak was amazed. Some of these patients hallucinated on the ward. Here they were enraptured.

Barak read the Hebrew translation as it flashed across a screen above the stage. He was transfixed by the symbolism and depth of Agnon's Hebrew, and by the great writer's insight. It was as if the novel, published in 1935, when Barak's patients had yet to be damaged, prefigured the fate they would suffer. Agnon wrote:

Of all life's misfortunes, madness may have been the only one to which the afflicted person was himself insensitive; to his family and his relations, however, the blow was doubly cruel, for not only were other troubles gotten over and forgotten while this one was passed down from one generation to the next, but, while other chronic patients could be put in special wards run by chronic idlers, nobody wanted to care for a madman: on the contrary, people either fled at the sight of him or else tormented him and turned him into a bogeyman to scare their children.

The Holocaust survivors who sat in the dark with Barak, absorbed by the play, had been discarded by a society ashamed of their flaws and fearful that somehow they might be communicable, genetic. They were living bogeymen, and Israelis had been ready to do almost anything that they should not consider themselves similarly weak. When they sent their children to the army for compulsory service and returned for reserve duty every year until the age of forty-eight, they did so because they didn't want to be like these survivors.

After the play, the theater director asked Barak's patients how they enjoyed it. One spoke up: "You know, I haven't been to the theater in fifty years. The first time I went to the theater was in my village, my *shtetl* in Poland, and then I was taken to Birkenau, and when I came to Israel, I went to the mental hospital. And the first time I go to the theater in all this time it's to see a play about a Jew from the *shtetl* and he goes crazy? Are you joking?" He wagged his finger playfully and laughed. "Was this some cynical joke, to invite us to this play?"

"To be a truly great actor," the director said, "you have to be a bit crazy."

"You're talking about the good kind of meshuggah," the patient replied. "Not the kind where you get locked up for fifty years."

The play did say something about such long incarceration. When the main character is taken to a sanatorium, the psychiatrist tells the youth's parents that the treatment he plans is aimed at avoiding committal to a mental hospital: "What is crucial . . . is to keep your son out of the lunatic asylum, because it could make even a sane man crazy." There was a hint of that in Yoram Barak, in the way his years with the psychogeriatric patients shaped him. He knew something of its effect from the insights of his partner Sarit. "You've become mute over the years," she told him. "You're the only psychiatrist I know who doesn't like to talk. You are becoming more and more like *them*. Sometimes it's a little frightening." By "them," she meant the silent survivors who consumed his days and his thoughts. What most people would call suffering meant little to Barak, the small pains of the world outside his agonized ward. His daughter Ella joked with him that he wouldn't allow her a sick day off school unless she could present him with her death certificate.

Some psychiatrists identify with their patients and become hopeless, as filled with rage as the victims they treat. Others find it difficult to enjoy the pleasures of ordinary life. Barak judged himself harshly, as did Moti Mark, for whom there remained the feeling that the new Holocaust wing at Abarbanel and all the new hostels like the one at Shaar Menashe were little recompense and late. But Barak did not replace the sufferings of a normal life with the horrible distress of his patients. He decided that this state of being was a part of the continuum of the Jewish people, of its destiny; something from which he believed Israelis ran in fear. To Barak, Ben-Gurion's new Jew had become frivolous and faddish, so keen were Israelis to convince themselves that Jewish suffering ended with the Holocaust. Live slowly and enjoy it, Barak told himself. Don't be in such a hurry to leave the Holocaust behind that you bypass all that's good and Jewish in yourself and your life by transforming yourself into a half-baked copy of an American.

The truth of all this came to Yoram Barak from Naomi, the patient whose family made the pact with her doctor to keep her in the hospital and protect her from the knowledge of her son's suicide. In 2000 Naomi began coughing and developed the symptoms of pneumonia. She was in her late seventies and a heavy smoker. She had lung cancer. Barak told her.

"Naomi, I have some bad news," he said. "We can do some radiation therapy, maybe surgery, but basically it's a terminal illness."

"Enough is enough," Naomi wheezed. "I don't want treatment. I've had enough."

Barak was quiet at her bedside, leaning forward with his elbows on his knees, as he did when he shared some intimacy on the ward.

"I would like to die here," Naomi said. "Don't send me to a hospice or anything. I've been here the last thirty years, so here's where I'll stay."

Barak gave her steroids, painkillers, morphine. As she died, Naomi talked to Barak with a new freedom. There were things that had been hidden from her, but she knew about them, she said. "I know my husband has had a lover for many years while I've been in here," she said. "I know that one of my daughters has a child, though she's unmarried." Then she said, "I know everything about the life of my family." Naomi didn't say she knew all along that her son was dead, that she was conscious of making up the proud stories of his successful practice as a Paris surgeon, but Barak sensed that this was the latent meaning of that sentence. Barak remembered how at first he had condemned the ethics of keeping these things from Naomi, of not forcing her to confront them. But he had learned that it was the essence of treating people who were "crazy in Yiddish."

In their last conversation, Naomi looked at Barak. "I'm not a Holocaust survivor," she said.

"What are you talking about?" Barak said. "You're the archetype of a Holocaust survivor."

"No, you are."

"What? What do you mean, *I* am?"

"You survived the Holocaust," Naomi said. "I didn't."

It was the greatest single insight Yoram Barak ever heard from a patient, and it stunned him. It was true. He survived, his parents who lived in Palestine and fought for Israel survived, Moti Mark and Henry Szor survived. But after the decades in which Israel kept them in the shadows of the psychogeriatrics ward, Barak's patients were not survivors; they were sufferers. They died in the camps.

CHAPTER SIX

Yudel's Candle

Ultrareligious and Secular Jews

*Let the sinners be consumed out of the earth,
and let the wicked be no more.*

—PSALM 104

WE PICKED UP THE ISRAELI WOMEN in midtown Manhattan.
When they slipped into the back of the taxi, I greeted them in
Hebrew. They giggled disbelievingly. It was May 1995, during what
my brother mockingly calls my "Hugh Grant period." I guess I didn't
look like the kind of guy who'd speak the language of the Torah. I
persisted with a few more phrases I had cribbed off a friend, until
Dalit and Dafna started to be convinced that I really did speak the
language. Then I ran out of Hebrew.

My friend Tom was engaged to an Israeli woman, whose two
friends he and I were taking to the Brooklyn Academy of Music auditorium that evening. The Cameri Theater Company of Tel Aviv had
brought its production of a play called *Fleischer* to New York, and
these two dark-haired, intelligent women, who spent their days
speaking a foreign language and listening to Americans babble about
the latest catastrophic violence in their homeland, were eager to
savor their native culture. Tom had made a few trips to Israel with his
fiancée, but he was little more aware of the country's hidden truths
than I, who wouldn't arrive in Jerusalem for another thirteen
months. Without knowing it, I was about to have my introduction to
the societal battles and fervent emotions at the heart of this book.

178

As the lights dimmed in the BAM auditorium, I noticed that Tom and I were among the few in the audience taking advantage of the black headsets that piped in the voices of the translators. New York was full of Israeli exiles, mostly diamond dealers and house movers living in Queens, but also high-tech businessmen and trendy hair-dressers in Manhattan. Like Dafna and Dalit, they all yearned for their home and for the sound of Hebrew, and they felt a guilt at their absence from the land of Israel encapsulated in the word for those countrymen who go to live abroad: *yordim,* which translates as "those who go down," who abandon the higher calling and spiritual value of life in the promised land. In the theater's darkness, the power of those emotions soon emerged. It was evident that I was missing something more than the original language of the play.

Igal Even-Or's drama tells the story of a butcher named Fleischer, who sells decidedly non-kosher meat and sausages in an old Israeli neighborhood. Even down to his short-sleeved, open-necked shirt, he fits the traditional image of the brusque, hearty, secular Zionist. He's the kind of man on whom Israel was built. But as the ageing Zionists of the neighborhood die out, ultra-Orthodox Jews encroach on the area. Fleischer and his wife, who survived Hitler's concentration camps, resist the appeals of a religious real-estate broker to sell their store and move out of the district. Instead, they sink their savings into a renovation to attract the newcomers. But even when Fleischer's store swaps its old, drab ceramic tiles for modern stainless steel, the religious customers don't come. One of them chats nicely with Berta, the butcher's wife, but buys no meat. "There's no kosher certificate in the shop," she advises. Fleischer pays a bribe to get a kosher certifi-cate. He displays it on the shop wall next to his commendation for bravery in the 1948 War of Independence, only to discover that it's the wrong piece of paper. The ultra-Orthodox don't trust the state rabbis who issued it; they shop where their own Rabbi Fuchs approves a *hechsher* and nowhere else.

Barely a third of the way through the play, I sensed a tension grow-ing in the darkness. Dalit bit her nails and Dafna fidgeted. There was the unmistakable, low slap of seats lifting as people stormed angrily from the hall. Onstage, Fleischer was agitated too: "I lived through the Germans and Poles and Arabs. I'll live through whatever the Jews do to me as well." But it only gets worse. More friends die off, or sell out to the religious. With their business disintegrating, Fleischer and Berta can no longer afford to keep their mentally handicapped son in a special home. They bring Shlomeleh to live in their apartment. The young man's behavior is erratic and violent. He plays with matches all the time. He's too much for his aged parents to handle.

One of Fleischer's old friends, Gershon, understands that the increase in ultra-Orthodox power is irresistible. To make his own life easier, he begins helping the newcomers. A municipal worker, he assists a relative of Rabbi Fuchs in obtaining a permit to open a kosher butcher's shop in the neighborhood. Betrayed, Fleischer castigates his friend. "Soon the whole country will be theirs," Gershon cries defensively.

As Fleischer's business collapses, Shlomeleh encounters Rabbi Fuchs's teenage daughter alone on the street. He's infatuated with her, but when her rules of modesty dictate that she should refuse the flower he offers her, Shlomeleh wrestles her to the ground. He rapes the girl.

Rabbi Fuchs and the Fleischers finally confront each other. At first, unaware of what Shlomeleh has done, Berta castigates the rabbi for his congregation's persecution of her and her husband. She shows the rabbi the blue tattoo on her forearm, the mark of Hitler's camps: "I never saw God there. But I got this kosher certificate from Hitler." The rabbi tries to persuade Berta and Fleischer to leave the neighborhood, but eventually breaks and tells them that Shlomeleh raped his daughter. "Every man has his portion of suffering," the rabbi says, crying. "You got yours at the hands of a Gentile. I got mine too. From a Jew." Of course, it's a long time since the German Gentiles harmed Fleischer. His more recent hardships are at the hands of Jews too: religious ones.

Fleischer breaks. Under the pressure of his business failure and his poor son's beastly act, his mind collapses. Drunk, he tells Shlomeleh to flee "to the forest," as though they were back in Poland, hunted by Nazis. "Make a big fire," he tells his son. "There's no God. Make a big fire."

Shlomeleh lights a match in the darkness. He burns down the store. Berta and Fleischer die in the blaze. The final scene shows their funeral. Rabbi Fuchs teaches Shlomeleh how to recite the Kaddish prayer over his dead parents. "We did all we did in the name of the traditions of the people of Israel," the rabbi says. From now on, he intends to raise the boy.

As people left the auditorium, there was almost total silence. Everyone's face bore a concentrated expression of anger. I looked with confusion at my friend Tom. We both understood that we had witnessed a powerful drama, but we couldn't figure out why everyone remained quite so upset after the final curtain. "It's hard to explain," said Dalit. "It's difficult to talk about." We went to a jazz club in Greenwich Village and spoke no more about *Fleischer*, but when I came to Israel a year later, I often had cause to remember the stern silence of the audience that night in Brooklyn.

Fleischer was extremely controversial in Israel. The Knesset discussed the play angrily, and the newspaper of the National Religious Party condemned it. It was apiece with the radical history of the Cameri, which was founded in 1944 as an alternative to the more conservative repertoire of Ha-Bima, the biggest Tel Aviv theater company. But the Cameri picked a theme in *Fleischer* that almost no Israeli can discuss without exposing the polarization of society and their own personal animus. To me, in the foyer of the Brooklyn Academy of Music, with my knowledge of Israel limited like most Westerners to news reports of the conflict with the Palestinians, it seemed an emotive yet marginal issue that must surely rank lower than the country's battle with the Arabs. Yet in Israel, the story of the butcher and his wife raised even more anger than a Cameri production staged the following year in which three Israeli soldiers tortured a Palestinian youth to death.

Over the years, I frequently saw Israelis, religious and secular, with the grim look of the audience that night in Brooklyn. I met them among 10,000 men, each wearing a black homburg, at a religious demonstration against Supreme Court rulings deemed anti-religious and therefore "anti-Semitic." I watched secular campaigners defending a shop against the government's "Sabbath inspectors," who had come to hand out fines for breaking the prohibition against operating places of business on the day of rest. In all of them, there was a deep anger. Still, I always felt that Shlomeleh's matches represented a little too much artistic license, a step beyond what was reasonable by a playwright who wanted to shock his audience with something that, in reality, would never happen.

That was what I thought. Until I met Elhanan Ben-Hakoun.

IN HIS DAUGHTER'S small garden, Elhanan Ben-Hakoun balanced a thick folder on the lawn table. Photos and CD-ROMs spilled out when he let go of the file to shake my hand for the first time. Photography was his business, and the disks—which carried Hollywood movies like *Free Willy,* the story of a killer whale rescued from miserable captivity by a young boy, and *Not Without My Daughter,* in which Sally Field struggles to escape the religious oppression of her Iranian husband—were a small sideline for him in his film-development store, Foto Elen, in the Bukharan Quarter of Jerusalem. The ultrareligious, the Haredi Jews who lived there, did not allow televisions in their homes. Certainly they never went to the cinema. But some would break the rules of their community and rent the disks for use on their home computers. When the Haredis began to take over the neighborhood in the mid-1980s, when they closed roads to cars on the Sabbath or when a noisy yeshiva hall took over the apartment next door, Ben-Hakoun's old friends moved out. Elhanan Ben-Hakoun stayed, and he thought he managed to work well with the religious. He photographed their weddings and bar mitzvah celebrations; he had dealings with some local religious politicians. Their rabbis complained about his CD-ROMs, because, to them, a Hollywood movie with men and women kissing or wearing skimpy clothing was tantamount to pornography. So from time to time, Ben-Hakoun stopped renting the CD-ROMs to placate them, but he soon began again. Back then, he couldn't see any harm in the movies. Later the snapshots of his life over the previous two years and the CD-ROMs that sprayed across the garden furniture when Ben-Hakoun greeted me would tell a story as dramatic and harrowing as anything in the films he used to rent.

Ben-Hakoun was born in 1940 in Salé, a town separated from the Moroccan capital of Rabat by a narrow river. His father, Rafael, worked as a barber in the French military base six miles from Salé. After the war, the Americans came to the camp and Rafael cut their hair too. Ben-Hakoun and his eight brothers and sisters spoke French at school and, for two hours a day, Hebrew. He remembered that, although the family followed the religious traditions of Moroccan Jewry, his father wore no yarmulke.

When the French left Morocco, the Jews believed the new Muslim government would attack them for the close connections many had formed with the occupying Europeans. Indeed there were anti-Semitic riots, including some in Rabat. Jewish Agency people stoked the fears and were rewarded with the mass immigration to Israel that they wanted. Within a few years, 250,000 Moroccan Jews fled to Israel. The Ben-Hakoun family went too. First, Elhanan and his younger brother Danny went on *aliyat ha-noar,* a youth immigration program. Three months later the rest of the family boarded a boat at Casablanca and came to Israel.

The Bukharan Quarter, where the Ben-Hakouns lived, was poor, but decent. There were Iranians, Poles, Moroccans. They were either totally secular or, more likely, only as mildly religious as the Ben-Hakouns had been back in Salé. After Elhanan finished his army service in 1962, he studied photography in night school and opened his photo store at 26 Yehezkel Street. He worked hard and, though he saw how the religious encroached on the neighborhood year by year, his earnings were good. By 2000, he could afford his own van and help two of his children buy cars. He had paid for four expensive vacations to the United States and had returned to visit Morocco seven times. "I'm not Rothschild, but I'm okay," he told a friend.

That ended in October 2000. By then, Ben-Hakoun was the only secular store owner on the street. It was during the eight days of a holiday called Sukkot. Outside Foto Elen, Yehezkel Street was busy with Haredi men. They rushed along with their eyes to the pavement and a skittling walk, as they always did, because the rabbis say walking fast leaves more time for Torah study and walking slowly allows the mind to wander into sin. Ben-Hakoun could see the diversity of these religious types through the glass of his storefront. There were men from Chabad, Lubavitchers with double-breasted Chicago gangster suits and open-necked white shirts and black hats; skinny Hasids with long, softly curling *peyis* growing from beside their ears; swarthy Moroccan devotees of the Shas Party who had never worn these kinds of clothes back home but had taken to the black suit to conform with the European religious sects; and the most fundamentalist of all, the Neturei Karta, who wore broad-brimmed hats like the Pennsylvania Amish, and gold-and-black-striped caftans and knickerbockers. They blurred past the store window, carrying the symbol of the holiday: the frond of a date palm, two branches of willow, and three sprigs of myrtle bound into a bundle called the *lulav.* On that day, however, some Haredi men did not rush by. They came to the window of Foto Elen, stopped, and began to gather.

Elhanan Ben-Hakoun stepped onto the sidewalk. There were five Haredis there, with their cream-colored prayer shawls draped over their shoulders and gathered at their necks. They turned to Ben-Hakoun, and one of them said, "Don't open the shop."

Ben-Hakoun stared at him. "What are you talking about? Today's not a holiday."

"It's Sukkot," the Haredi said, involuntarily shaking his *lulav* at Ben-Hakoun.

Ben-Hakoun knew that on the intermediate days of Sukkot, a period known as *Hol Hamoed*, work is permitted. He could have explained that fact, but these Haredis knew more about religion than he did. They spent all day studying the weird intricacies of Talmud and, he was sure, they could wrap him up in debate. "You don't know what you're talking about," he said.

"We're staying here until you close your evil shop," the Haredi said.

Ben-Hakoun didn't ask why his shop was evil. It was impossible for him to think in the strange, narrow, contorted logic of the Haredis—so much so that, though he believed in God and tried to observe some of what God commanded, he couldn't predict what would upset these men. A few months before, he set up a video screen in his store and ran some film he shot at the wedding of a couple of secular Israelis. It was intended to advertise his services as a wedding cameraman to people who stopped by the store. Haredi kids gathered around the screen, gawking at the men and women dancing together on the tape. Ben-Hakoun watched them. It made no sense to him that men and women should be separated at joyful moments, as they were at ultra-Orthodox celebrations. Look how fascinating it is to the young boys, he thought. That's surely a sign that it's not a bad thing. So what was evil about his store? It could have been the video screen with the wedding footage or the Hollywood CD-ROMs that upset the Haredis. Or maybe it was that his beautiful young daughter Karine, with her long legs and high heels and coy smile, used to work in the shop sometimes. Perhaps that violated their codes of modesty and sexual propriety.

The Haredis gathered around him. Though he was almost six feet tall and the Haredis were twiggy men who spent their days bent over their books, Ben-Hakoun was thirty years older than them and retreated into the store rather than risk a fight. He felt his anger rising. He was a highly emotional man. Beneath his own anger, he sensed a touch of desperation, because he understood how incidents like this could gather a destructive momentum within the Haredi community. Two years before, he had been forced to close the bridal salon his wife, Talia, ran next door to Foto Elen. Haredis used to spit at secular girls when they came to fittings for their wedding dresses wearing "immodest" shorts or low-cut shirts, until in the end no one came anymore. Inside his store, he called the police.

The police dispersed the little crowd of Haredis quickly enough, but they also wanted to give the religious time to simmer down. Haredi means "one who trembles before God." But in Jerusalem it is the supposed tremblers who make others quake with fear. A policeman came into Foto Elen. "We don't want any more trouble," he said. "Can you close the shop now? Open again tomorrow, when they've calmed down." Ben-Hakoun pulled the blue metal shutters across the front of the store, clipped in the padlocks, and went home.

It was not the end. The next day, there were flyers posted on notice boards all over the Bukharan Quarter and into neighboring Mea Shearim, Jerusalem's main ultra-Orthodox area. Such flyers, which the Haredis call *paschkevilles,* are the best way for religious and political authorities to communicate with their people, who don't watch television. The new *paschkevilles* were printed on red paper:

THESE SINNERS MAKE OTHERS SIN.

ELHANAN AND TALIA BEN-HAKOUN.

ENOUGH!!!

THOUSANDS OF SOULS OF THE SONS OF ISRAEL THEY
ALREADY SENT DOWN TO HELL.

HOW LONG!!!

YOUR SOULS WILL BE IN HELL AND SOON, IF YOU DON'T
DESIST AND CLOSE THE STORE IMMEDIATELY.

YOUR END WILL COME WITH AN AXE.

An axe? Hell? Your end? Ben-Hakoun couldn't believe it. He felt anger, because, after all, he came to this neighborhood before them. But he couldn't help feeling fear, for himself and for his livelihood.

He kept the flyer and placed it in a file next to some photos he had taken of the five men protesting outside his shop the day before. He began to gather a dossier of material about the Haredi protests. He put it in the back room of the store. Then he walked to his door and looked across the street. By the bus stop over the road, there was a single man in the gold-striped Sabbath robe of the Neturei Karta sect. He wore a *streimel,* a wide, round fur hat of the same dark brown as his chest-length beard. He held a placard in front of him that said Help. Don't Let This Corrupter Foto Elen Poison Us. With a look of the most intense concentration and hatred, he stared directly at Ben-Hakoun.

The hostile stare held. Every day, there was at least one Neturei Karta protester across the road from Ben-Hakoun's store. Sometimes there were three, which was the limit for a protest without a permit from the police. Every few weeks, usually on a Friday when yeshiva students were on the streets preparing for the Sabbath at sundown, the group would grow to 100, 200 people, and the police would come. All of the demonstrators would glare viciously across the street at Elhanan Ben-Hakoun, alone in his store, surrounded by photo frames filled with marketing pictures of smiling couples and kids hugging their pet dogs. A photo shop was supposed to be about love and happiness captured in an instant, and about memories of the good times displayed on a mantelpiece or bookshelf. But Ben-Hakoun's shop was invaded by the photographs of aggression and hatred usually reserved for the pages of Israeli newspapers.

Soon after the protests began, Ben-Hakoun received a call from an old client whose bat mitzvah he photographed eight years before. Now the woman was to be married and she wanted Ben-Hakoun to take the pictures. Elhanan noted the name of the wedding hall and agreed that he would be paid at the ceremony. When he arrived, the bride's sister stopped him at the door. "We're sorry, but you can't work here tonight," she said. "We'll pay you. Just don't come in." Though the bride and groom weren't religious, all Jerusalem's wedding halls needed to keep their kosher certificates if they were to have a piece of the lucrative religious market. In any case, under Israeli law, an Orthodox rabbi must conduct all weddings, so the halls have to abide by the rules of the state's Chief Rabbinate and submit to the de facto oversight of Haredi rabbis, whose word is law among their adherents. The owner of the hall found out that Ben-Hakoun was to photograph the wedding and, knowing about the growing protest against Foto Elen among the Haredis, ordered that a different photographer be found. Ben-Hakoun put his hand to his forehead as the sister carried on: "The owner told us that Foto Elen can't enter the hall. We don't want it to be this way. You know, fuck them. But what can we do?" She paid him $100 and went back into the wedding hall. Ben-Hakoun listened sadly to the echoes of the DJ's sound check inside the hall, and then went home.

Two weeks after the first protest, Ben-Hakoun left his son Rafi alone at the store. Rafi was twenty-one, just out of the army and training to be a photographer like his old man. A dozen Haredi men crossed the street and came into the store. They insulted Rafi, and punched him repeatedly in the head and body before they left. The young man was terribly traumatized by the assault. He went to the hospital and had stitches above his right eye. "I'm not going back there, Dad," he told Elhanan.

When the protests were almost a year old, the festival of Sukkot came around again. Ben-Hakoun went home early from the store to build a *sukkah,* the shelter in which Jews eat their meals during Sukkot as a reminder of the hardships faced by the Israelites in their forty-year desert wanderings. He left Karine to mind the store. His daughter was a confident, twenty-two-year-old blonde, but she sounded like a scared child when she called Ben-Hakoun from the shop. "They came in and attacked me," she sobbed. Twenty Haredis had entered the store. They slapped Karine and pushed her, called her filthy names, and trashed some of the shelves. Ben-Hakoun called the police and headed for Foto Elen, seething. He arrived at the same time as the police. He watched them take away a couple of Haredi youths who were hanging around outside the shop, but he knew it would be like all the other pointless arrests made in the year of protest. Whenever the police took someone away, Ben-Hakoun would see the troublemaker outside his shop again within a day or two. Elhanan tried to console his terrified daughter. He felt as though his entire life were under attack. Everyone he cared about was being hurt, and no one would help him.

Elhanan Ben-Hakoun struggled with himself. He would not break, he would not sell his store, would not leave. But he feared. The fear now was for himself alone, as his son and daughter no longer dared work at Foto Elen. There were constant annoyances and frequent dangers. He saw stickers in the phone booths of Mea Shearim that instructed the religious residents each to make three nuisance calls to Foto Elen: they tied up his phone constantly. Even if anyone was brave enough to want to hire him for a wedding, they would be unable to reach him. Haredi children leaned out the windows of their school buses and yelled at him to get out of their neighborhood. Every morning, the locks on his shutters were fouled; someone glued matches into the keyholes and then lit them, leaving a solid, gummed up mess of charcoal. Arriving at work with metal clippers, Ben-Hakoun broke into his own shop almost every day. Then, in the fall of 2001, Ben-Hakoun saw just how far this could go.

Elhanan Ben-Hakoun left Foto Elen at 6 p.m. It was dark as he climbed into his GMC van and drove away. At the Sanhedria junction, he looked up to see three ceramic floor tiles flashing from the back of a truck in front of him. The tiles smashed through his windshield. If Ben-Hakoun's van had been moving faster at the time, he would surely have been killed. Elhanan sat in his van in the middle of the intersection, shaking, unable to believe what had happened. There were two Haredi men on the back of the truck. *They* threw the tiles at him. They tried to kill him. No, it couldn't be. The traffic lights changed to red, and Ben-Hakoun still couldn't make sense of it. Was it an accident? No, it's too much of a coincidence. Yes, yes, they tried to kill me. To kill me.

When he reached his home, Elhanan Ben-Hakoun stared, shaken, at the photos of the protests and vandalism that he had shot over the previous year. There was a broken window from a stone someone had slung through the storefront. He held a snapshot of the police's Yasam unit, the highly trained riot squad, chasing Haredis past the bus stop outside the shop. There in the corner of the picture, behind the gray-blue uniforms of the beefy young officers, was Elhanan's dark red GMC van, the one he was driving when he almost lost his life.

Talia made him coffee and let her husband talk to calm himself. "They want to take me out of the store in a coffin," he said.

Ben-Hakoun picked up another photo. It was of a short man with a trim beard and a tall felt hat perched on the back of his head. The man stood outside the shop every afternoon for three hours, bobbing back and forth over his prayer book. When people stopped to ask him why he was praying there in the street, he would say only: "Against Foto Elen." Then he would go on with his *shockeling*.

It was a persecution that could only lead to one comparison for Elhanan Ben-Hakoun. "It has been fifty years and people forgot about the Nazis," Ben-Hakoun said. "Now the Nazis are back."

I ASKED BENJAMIN NETANYAHU about the battles between the ultra-Orthodox and secular Israelis. It was 1997 and Netanyahu was prime minister, struggling to force the Palestinians to stick to the Oslo Peace Accords and battling the competing religious, secular, and nationalist factions that ultimately destroyed his cabinet. "I think dealing with Arafat is easier," he answered. He wasn't kidding. In 2003, when Netanyahu was finance minister, he cut the government's financial allocations to Haredi families and yeshivas. At a Haredi rally near Tel Aviv, a leading rabbi compared Netanyahu to the pharaoh who ignored Moses and tried to keep the Israelites in bondage: "Bibi is worse than Pharaoh," the rabbi said.

If Jews and Arabs were, at least sometimes, negotiating a peace settlement, the ultra-Orthodox felt they already had their accord and that it was under constant threat from the bulk of Israeli society—which they deem to be "secular." In 1947 David Ben-Gurion, director of the Jewish Agency, sent a letter to the executive committee of Agudat Yisrael, the leading Haredi party. Ben-Gurion wanted to secure the support of as many sectors as possible within the Jewish *yishuv,* the community of settlers in Palestine. Agudat Yisrael had seceded in protest from the *yishuv* leadership twenty-two years previously after the secularists enfranchised women. The Ben-Gurion letter promised that religious scholars would be allowed to follow the study of Talmud—the compilation of biblical commentary and Jewish law from the first to the fifth century—free of the social and military obligations that fell on other Jews in Palestine. It was a promise enshrined as "the status quo" in 1948 and, in the new State of Israel, was made law in 1949. The chief rabbi at that time, Isaac Herzog, argued for the necessity that religious students should be encouraged to stay in yeshivas, to rebuild the learning destroyed in the Holocaust: "The very soul of the Jewish people is dependent on their existence."

The status quo, however, led to a distortion in Israeli society that helped to create an enormous political gulf between religious and secular people. Back in Ben-Gurion's day, there were few yeshiva students, so society was asked to make only a small sacrifice: to fund a tiny group of young men to tend the traditions of the people of Israel. By 2000, 10 percent of draft-age men held deferments for yeshiva study. In the United States, yeshiva students receive no state benefits and, on average, conclude their studies at twenty-five. In Israel, the average age of leaving yeshiva is forty-two, when a man is too old to be called up for military reserve duty for the first time. Yeshivas are subsidized with $170 million a year in government money and the estimated cost to the economy of all those men who do nothing but study is $1 billion a year.

Tommy Lapid, the leader of Israel's ardently secular Shinui Party, sat at a wicker table outside Café Basel in northern Tel Aviv, an area with almost no religious residents. When the wispy-haired, charismatic old fellow eventually finished flirting with the three middle-aged, peroxide blondes at the next table, he told me he opposed the influence of the ultra-Orthodox on Israeli politics, because they imposed "a tax on us." On *us*. Us and them, that's how almost every Israeli looks at this divide. On the Sabbath, the streets around Foto Elen were closed to traffic; anyone who drove there ran the risk of having his windshield smashed by a stone. At Kibbutz Shefayim, just north of Tel Aviv, the Sabbath was a time for shopping and profits. The kibbutz founded an enormous mall, and because its inhabitants were devoutly secular people whose founders claimed to follow the Zionist brand of socialist nationalism, Saturday was the big shopping day. During Netanyahu's government and under Prime Minister Ariel Sharon's first cabinet, the religious interior minister sent out "Sabbath inspectors" to fine businesses, like the Home Center at Shefayim, that operated on the day of rest.

The basic arena of ideologies in Israel is education. Essentially, parents must choose between a religious, secular, or ultra-Orthodox destiny for their children as soon as they enter kindergarten. Prime Minister Ehud Barak's education minister, a leading liberal named Yossi Sarid, told me the religious-secular divide was his most serious problem. "The ultra-Orthodox have to understand that the source of sovereignty is democracy," he said. That's a dangerous concept for the religious, who are outnumbered and feel a ghetto paranoia toward the democratic institutions of the Israeli state, which they view as essentially secular and hostile. As the ultra-Orthodox see it, the strictures imposed on life by God's edict in the Jewish holy books are not open to a vote. Neither are they interpretable by secular judges who lack religious training. At a demonstration against the rulings of Israel's Supreme Court, 10,000 Haredi men gathered on the edge of Romema, a religious neighborhood in Jerusalem. Some of the men told me they felt engaged in a "holy war" against a state that wanted Judaism to gradually die out. The sign above the dais, where the most prominent ultra-Orthodox rabbis in the country gazed out over the massed uniformity of black hats and bearded faces, read Torah Is Not a Judicial Matter.

The most extreme of the Haredi community created for themselves an existential Diaspora within Israel. Their loyalty was to the rules that guided the Jewish people since the days of the destruction of the Second Temple in Jerusalem by the Romans. One of the primary orders the rabbis imposed back then was not to preempt the redemption, not to attempt to rebuild the Temple or to hasten the coming of the Messiah, except through the living of a righteous life. Zionism seemed to the ultra-Orthodox to be just such a preemptive move and, therefore, something to be shunned. In the 1950s, the ultra-Orthodox sect Neturei Karta published a pamphlet:

> God is our king and we are his servants. It is our obligation and duty to preserve his teaching. Since we do not recognize the rule of the infidels, because they are rebels against the kingdom of our Creator-King, may he be blessed, it is forbidden to obey and work for a rebellious regime. Our Torah is our constitution and under no condition can we respect their [Zionist] laws.

This was the original declaration of war on people like Elhanan Ben-Hakoun, and a half-century later it was this same Neturei Karta that went into battle with him.

SHMUEL PAPPENHEIM gratefully took the mug of hot tea from Reb Yudel. The old man gave Pappenheim a blessing and poured another cup for the next sleepy fellow who had come for morning prayers at Toldot Aharon, the yeshiva of the Neturei Karta sect. Before he drank, Pappenheim recited a blessing over the tea: *Baruch ata Adonai, Eloheinu Melech ha-Olam, sheh ha-kol nihyeh be-davaro.* Blessed art Thou, Lord, King of the Universe, through whose word everything shall be. He leaned against the peeling mint-blue paint of the wall in the small synagogue and watched Reb Yudel. He knew all about him. Pappenheim knew everyone's details. The Toldot Aharon was a small group of 700 families worldwide whose members kept tightly together. Neturei Karta means "Guardians of the City" in Aramaic, but more precisely they were the guardians of each other, ensuring that they, at least, would not transgress the strict Halachic interpretations of their rabbis. For most Israelis, the Neturei Karta were invisible. Some Jerusalem residents might notice them because of their strange robes, so much more extravagant and outlandish than the black suits of most Haredis. But the Neturei Karta were fiercely aware of other Israelis, for they rejected Israel's right to exist as an independent national state. Pappenheim and his friends at the yeshiva operated outside the reach of the state. They didn't recognize the laws that the police tried to enforce outside Elhanan Ben-Hakoun's shop. The chief rabbi of their sect called for the UN to support Saddam Hussein in the hope that it would lead to the destruction of the sinful State of Israel.

Pappenheim had another more practical reason for knowing all the personal details of the men gathering in the synagogue for the 5 A.M. service: he wrote the weekly *Ha-Eda* newspaper of the Neturei Karta. As a journalist he had to keep up on the history of each member of the group. But Reb Yudel was special. Pappenheim looked at him now with fondness. The old man had been up since 3 A.M., as he was every day, preparing for this daily pre-prayer ritual in which he handed out tea to all the men of the community as they gathered for the day's devotions and studies. He was jolly and energetic for a man of seventy-three, laughing to keep up the spirits of younger men who, despite their love of God, would rather be sleeping. He was not an especially learned man—the usual measure of a Haredi Jew's worth and standing—but he commanded respect because of his long years of struggle for what the Neturei Karta believed was right in the eyes of God. That was why they called him "Reb," though he was not a rabbi: it was a mark of respect.

Pappenheim believed his journalism was a kind of activism for the Neturei Karta and for God, exhorting people to the right path and alerting them to the wickedness of the world outside their little universe. It was instructive to Pappenheim to consider the career of Reb Yudel, whose name was Yehuda Leib Shlomo Samet and who had always been one of the Neturei Karta's greatest fighters for that righteous path. Yudel was involved in protests against the breaking of Shabbat back in the first decade of the Israeli state, when the political power of the Haredis was negligible and the police were much harder on religious protesters. More than once, a Zionist policeman beat the young Reb Yudel quite severely. In the 1950s the police even killed a Shabbat protester named Rabbi Pinhas Saglov, though the Zionists said he died when he hit his head on the sidewalk assaulting their police officers. Reb Yudel's experience would be important now, because the Neturei Karta faced another long struggle against a persecutor of Jews and a violator of Shabbat: Ben-Hakoun, the owner of Foto Elen. Who could know what evil Ben-Hakoun would visit upon the Haredis and the excuses the Zionist police would make for the damage he would perpetrate?

The first thing of importance about Reb Yudel was that he was a conservative, which meant that he guarded the traditions of the Neturei Karta and of true Judaism. Pappenheim sipped his tea and enjoyed its heat in his throat. It was the end of October 2001, the time of year when Jerusalem becomes rainy and damp, and these early morning prayers would have been an uncomfortable test were it not for Reb Yudel's tea. Yudel's commitment to tradition was also there on the backs of every man in the room: he imported the cloth for their striped caftans. The caftan was a symbol of the Neturei Karta's deep roots in Jerusalem, which went back long before the State of Israel's founding and even before anyone calling himself a Zionist stepped onto a ship in Odessa bound for Haifa. When Israel arose in 1948, other Haredis fled Europe in their black suits. But the *Yerushaleime kaftan,* blue with thin white stripes during the week and gold with black on Shabbat, marked the Neturei Karta as the real guardians of tradition in the holy city. The cloth came from the Arab world, but Yudel managed to procure it even in the days before the Egyptian and Jordanian peace treaties, when Israel had no official relations with Arab countries. No one knew how he did it, but they were grateful that he kept alive the caftan in the same form that Neturei Karta believed Jews had worn in Jerusalem before the Romans exiled them. From Yudel, everyone bought the cloth, which cost about $160. Either they had his wife, Sara, sew it into a caftan or they took it to another seamstress who was, frankly, better at her job than the obstreperous Mrs. Samet. Pappenheim looked down at his own caftan, which he wore over thick black knickerbockers, a white shirt, and a *talit katan* that hung from his shoulders to his waist with tassels at each of its four corners. The caftan was stained here and there; a grubby brown undertone had worked into the blue and white. But it had lasted him fifteen years since he received it as a wedding gift. It demonstrated its adaptability as a garment in that Pappenheim had become quite a fat thirty-something during those years, but the caftan still tied comfortably over his belly.

Before the prayers began, Yudel cracked a joke and laughed. It woke up all the men, Yudel's tea and his sense of humor in the morning. Pappenheim thought Reb Yudel must be a happy man. He had a good family—eight children and many grandchildren in Montreal, Antwerp, and New York, where there were also Neturei Karta communities. He had been blessed to live long enough that some of his grandchildren had already married. The thought of children: that brought Pappenheim to the fight between Rabbi Kahn's sons and the role Yudel played there. It had been another mark of his zeal for tradition.

Seven years ago, Rabbi Avraham Yitzhak Kahn was near death. His two sons struggled to take over his role as head of the yeshiva of Toldot Aharon. The older, Shmuel Yaakov, was more liberal. People thought he might change things a bit. He wouldn't do anything dramatic, like recognizing the State of Israel, but he suggested he would loosen the sect's dress code and might at least have relations with Israel's governing institutions and take some of the state's money. David, the younger son, lived in Borough Park, Brooklyn, and he vowed not to change a thing. That was good enough for Yudel. Reb Yudel showed his support for David by traveling outside Israel for the first time ever to attend the wedding of David's son in Brooklyn. He organized a group of 100 people to go with him. Everyone saw it as a special sign, because Yudel never left Israel, even to visit his own grandchildren. He led the community toward David's candidacy, and the second son did, indeed, win the battle. David took control of Toldot Aharon, and the defeated Shmuel Yaakov set up his own new Hasidic community, Toldot Avraham Yitzhak, named after their father.

It was in the Neturei Karta's struggles against the outside world, however, that Reb Yudel truly had won his reputation. He had been close to Rabbi Amram Blau, a leader of the sect and instigator of the first Sabbath protests in the 1950s. Back then, Israel's political chiefs did not pretend to pay homage to religious leaders. Sure, they agreed to exempt the small number of Haredi yeshiva students from the army in 1948. But they didn't kiss the rabbis' hands or nuzzle their beards or fawn for a blessing from some senile kabbalist as do modern Israeli politicians, almost all of whom are just as secular as were the founders of the state. Rabbi Blau campaigned against violations of the Sabbath and practices that transgressed what Neturei Karta saw as true Jewish ethics. He protested mixed-sex swimming pools, because they promoted sinful, adulterous thoughts. He tried to stop autopsies, for fear that a Jewish body might not be buried whole, and he blocked archeological digs that he thought would disturb ancient Jewish graves. He called Israel's constabulary the "Zionist SS." When Blau was arrested in 1954, trying to protect the medieval grave of the great "Rambam"—Rabbi Moses Ben-Maimon, or Maimonides—in Tiberias, Reb Yudel went on trial with him. Pappenheim had a photo in his run-down office of Blau and Yudel in the dock of the Tiberias courtroom with Blau's son. The rabbi stared defiantly at the camera with his chin on his hand, while Yudel, whose hair and beard had not yet turned white, looked relaxed, if a little lost. Pappenheim kept the photo in a file out of sight, because Rabbi Blau ended his career a little strangely and out of favor with most of the community. He shook the entire Neturei Karta in the mid-1960s when he married a beautiful young French convert, Ruth Ben-David. Blau was ostracized and exiled to Bnei Brak, a Haredi town on the edge of Tel Aviv. He later claimed his testicles were damaged in 1948 and, therefore, he was forbidden from marrying anyone but a convert, according to the prohibition in Deuteronomy 23:1: "He that is wounded in the stones, or hath his privy member cut off, shall not enter into the congregation of Israel."

Reb Yudel suffered no Blau-like loss of reputation. He would never act outside the norms of the community, even if he did feel he could justify himself with some little-known snippet of Torah about his privy member. He was no expert in the minutiae of Jewish law, in any case. But he remained the man to whom the Neturei Karta turned for leadership on the street in their protests. And Foto Elen angered him.

Pappenheim and Yudel both knew how the conflict had developed with Ben-Hakoun. Foto Elen was the first photographic store in the neighborhood and relations were good for a time, when there were no competitors. As soon as other photo shops moved into the Bukharan Quarter, it seemed to the Neturei Karta that Ben-Hakoun started looking for other ways to augment his profits, and that was what caused the trouble. Gradually Ben-Hakoun started to stock more risqué movies that showed relations between men and women. The Haredi rabbinical court, the *Badatz,* summoned Ben-Hakoun before it. Badatz is the Hebrew acronym for Beit Din Tzedek, or Righteous Court; Ben-Hakoun could not completely ignore it, but he duped the rabbis by agreeing to halt his CD-ROM rentals, only to start again a few months later. He argued with the rabbis about what kind of films should be seen as pornography and which films simply constituted a document of modern life. The rabbis tried to explain that to them there was no difference: pornography was against Jewish law, and so was what people referred to as "modern life," including *Free Willy.* The Badatz handed down a judgment in September 2000, just before the first protesters arrived outside Foto Elen during Sukkot, barring the community from frequenting the shop. Most people followed the rulings, but Ben-Hakoun had his old regulars and so the rabbis sent yeshiva students to hand out leaflets and to dissuade the customers as they entered.

This was what Yudel and Pappenheim saw when they passed Foto Elen: Ben-Hakoun would lose his temper sometimes when he saw the protesters and would chase them along the street, knocking off their hats and yarmulkes when he grappled with them. Yudel and Pappenheim didn't think of the photo-shop owner as someone who suffered and felt under attack, someone afraid who lashed out from time to time. To them, he was an arrogant bully. They had seen things happen in front of their eyes: a young Haredi man stood almost blocking the door of Foto Elen, bobbing over his prayer book, and suddenly Ben-Hakoun sprang out of the door and sprayed Mace in the face of the retreating Haredi. Shortly before Sukkot 2001, when the protests were a year old, the Neturei Karta hired a video cameraman to sit on the balcony of a building across the street and document Ben-Hakoun's retaliations. Pappenheim stockpiled a lot of footage of Mace attacks from the videographer. When he watched the sequences, Pappenheim saw just the spray and the discomfort of the student, who had merely been praying, after all. He paid no attention to the way Ben-Hakoun would go back into his store, pacing, nervous and indecisive like a fearful animal that doesn't know whether to flee or take refuge deeper in its warren.

Pappenheim covered the depredations of Ben-Hakoun in *Ha-Eda*, which was written in Hebrew, and in an American Yiddish newspaper called *Der Blatt*. The Neturei Karta spoke Yiddish to each other, because Hebrew as a spoken language had been renewed by the Zionists, all of whose revivals the Neturei Karta reviled. Yet the Haredis learned to write through the Bible and, therefore, wrote mostly in Hebrew. When they did speak Hebrew, for example to an Israeli building contractor or someone else outside their community, they used the quaint locutions of a half-century ago, so secluded were their lives. The rejection of the Hebrew language, whose rebirth was seen by the Zionist leadership and by most Israelis as an achievement almost on a par with the establishment of the Israeli state, was deeply connected to the Haredis' perception of that state: once the Zionists took over your tongue, they would not stop until they expunged everything truly Jewish from your character. Pappenheim knew that his major task as the Neturei Karta's chief propagandist was to hammer this message into the 5,000 homes that subscribed to *Ha-Eda*. Foto Elen, he wrote, was part of the Zionist conspiracy: "The Zionist regime wants us to know that only they are the decision makers and only they have authority in this country. However, we know better." He cited an old Lithuanian rabbi to back his case:

> Just as the Gaon from Brisk said, "They are not building a state in order to have a state, but rather to excise faith and religion from the nation." They would be happy if the only place you could see children walking around with side curls and *tzitzit* was in a museum. This has been the chief goal of the state since its birth fifty-five years ago. Luckily the government has been occupied

with dealing with the Arabs. Otherwise they would turn their attention to us.

The conflict with the Arabs, which for most Israelis and certainly for foreigners observing the region seemed so central, existed for the Neturei Karta only as a screen, temporarily deflecting the attentions of the mass of Israelis from them. If that conflict did not exist, Pappenheim felt sure the secular establishment in Israel would descend on the Neturei Karta and other ultra-Orthodox sects and destroy them.

Each week, Pappenheim would develop some item of news until it became part of this conspiracy theory. No one but the Haredis read what he wrote; no secular Israeli would get beyond the first sentence before *Ha-Eda* would be consigned angrily to the trash. But Pappenheim's theory wasn't entirely untrue, neither as the Haredis saw it nor in fact. The Zionist establishment always hated the Haredis and, as they did with immigrants from Arab countries, tried to force them to change their lifestyles to something closer to Labor's socialist Zionism. Successive governments gave huge grants to yeshiva students to buy the political support of their rabbis, but there was so little interaction between the two communities that both viewed the other with paranoia, ignorance, and hate. Religion grew in political power in Israel for two reasons. First, that portion of the Haredi community that, unlike Neturei Karta, accepted the existence of the state had high birthrates, because their rabbis barred contraception. They, therefore, came to constitute a bloc of votes that couldn't be ignored, particularly when it was allied with the grassroots power of the ultra-Orthodox Shas Party among Mizrahi Jews. Second, Messianic religious Zionists drove Israel's West Bank settlement movement, forming a new alliance between Judaism and right-wing secular nationalists who simply wanted to keep as much land as they could. But the Neturei Karta weren't part of all that; they were outside and they always would be. In 1948 their leader tried to raise a white flag over Jerusalem and surrender to the Jordanians, so that the presumptuous Israeli state would have no dominion over Judaism's holy city. Rabbi Moshe Hirsch, the head of Neturei Karta, was Yasser Arafat's adviser on Jewish affairs, because Arafat was an enemy of the Israeli state. The conflict was simple for Pappenheim to elucidate: secularists simply wanted to destroy the way of life of the Neturei Karta, and Foto Elen was their Trojan horse. Pappenheim wrote:

> The story of Foto Elen is a mystery. The owner is not one of us. We have begged him to leave. He has no customers anymore, so he can't be making a living. Furthermore, he is selling pirated videos, but the police have done nothing to stop him. The only possible conclusion is that he is in the employ of an organization that seeks to brainwash Haredi youth.

Pappenheim crossed the synagogue floor to Reb Yudel and asked for a second cup of tea. Yudel smiled and ran another draft out of the urn for him. Even for a man as vivacious as he was, Yudel seemed full of adrenaline and action this morning.

"What's got you so excited, Reb Yudel?" Pappenheim said as he took back his mug of tea.

"I've been going every day to Foto Elen," Yudel said.

"To demonstrate?"

"No, I go to strengthen the demonstrators, and I draw strength from their protest. I was there yesterday. I stopped and said to the lads, 'What you're doing is right and just. *Kol ha-kavod* [well done].' "

"How did they reply?"

"Well, they said, 'Thanks, but you can't stay here or there'll be too many of us and the police will be able to come and disperse us.' So I just said, 'Well done to you, in any case,' and I went on my way," Yudel said. "But I worry about them there, because of the police and because of that man in the shop."

Pappenheim smiled fondly. He swallowed Yudel's tea and felt himself waking up.

THE NIGHTS IN THE VAN eroded Elhanan Ben-Hakoun's strength and resilience until he was ready to snap. For three months in the fall of 2001, he drove to Yehezkel Street at midnight and parked near Foto Elen. He wanted to catch the Haredi who glued matches into his locks every night during the few hours when the neighborhood slept. He punched the number of the police station into his cellular phone and put it on the dashboard, ready for him to press "Send" the moment he saw someone outside the store. Then he waited, slouched in the driver's seat like a movie detective on a stakeout. But in the movies the detectives never have to cool their heels with their Styrofoam cup of coffee for long, and in any case they wait quietly, self-contained: it's part of their job. Elhanan Ben-Hakoun fretted, alone in the dark, tormented, pulsing with rage and stress and fatigue. It was as though he were watching some part of himself withering away in the darkness outside the van, while he sat, passive, trapped.

Then he saw him. When the young Haredi man stopped and bent over the locks, Ben-Hakoun forced himself into action. His old body, stiff from the cramped seat and the tension with which he had held his muscles for hours, groaned out of the van and across the street. Ben-Hakoun forgot to dial the police, but he grabbed the youth anyway. In the shadows, he noticed that the kid had sprayed something on the shutters. He saw the youth's skin, pale and callow, his wisps of beard and his thick glasses. Ben-Hakoun knew the face. Every morning, this kid was across the street at the bus stop, waiting to watch him open the fouled locks on the store's shutter. One day, this very Haredi shouted over the road, "Get out of this neighborhood. This is *our* neighborhood." When that happened, Ben-Hakoun had called the police, but when they took him to the station, the youth gave them a false address. This time, a police car passed by even as Ben-Hakoun wrestled with the youth. The policemen took the youngster with little explanation; they knew the story of Ben-Hakoun. Elhanan said he would follow them to the Russian Compound, the police station in the center of Jerusalem, to file a complaint.

The police car pulled away and Ben-Hakoun stepped back. In the orange light of the street lamp, he could see what the Haredi youth had sprayed on the shutter in red paint: "Nazi." The strain of the nights alone in the car, of the days alone in the store with no customers, these things had damaged Elhanan Ben-Hakoun. But this one word shattered him completely. It forced an entire history, of his life and of the lives of millions of persecuted Jews, inside the little store where he had worked for forty years. In Morocco, the French and the Arabs taunted him as *un sale juif,* a dirty Jew. "In Israel," he said to himself, "I am a Nazi."

Ben-Hakoun drove to the police station, crying with anger and shame. In the station, the officers told him to go home and rest.

"We'll take care of the suspect," one of them said. Ben-Hakoun saw the youth, waiting to be charged. He must have been only seventeen years old, but he didn't look scared. He was lounging, relaxed on a narrow wooden bench under a fluorescent light outside the squad room. Elhanan knew then that the Haredis couldn't be beaten. He would have to give up.

The next day, Ben-Hakoun went to the neighborhood rabbi, whom he blamed for much of the incitement against him. "What exactly is your problem?" Elhanan asked.

"We want you to leave the area," the rabbi said. "You're not religious."

Ben-Hakoun looked at the little rabbi before him. He felt that it was more than religion that bothered the rabbi about Foto Elen. The rabbi's family came from Eastern Europe, like most Haredis. Ben-Hakoun felt decades of racism toward Jews from Morocco and other Arab countries eddying about him in the rabbi's cramped office. So anxiously did the man shift in his seat, Ben-Hakoun would have sworn with his hand on a mezuzah that the rabbi couldn't relax with a Mizrahi in the room. But perhaps it was only that the rabbi could not sit still because, filled with excitement, he felt he finally had Ben-Hakoun just where he wanted him.

"If you want me to leave, buy my shop," Ben-Hakoun said.

"You can donate it to the synagogue, and we'll make a study room out of it," the rabbi said.

Ben-Hakoun saw the weakness of his position. He hadn't considered it before, because all he now wanted was to give up and get out and put an end to his anguish. Nobody would buy the store, except the Haredis, because everyone else would be frightened of the same fate as Ben-Hakoun. But the Haredis didn't have to buy it; they had already beaten him. "Look, this is crazy," Elhanan said. "You can't expect me to give you the store."

"Well, if you donate to the yeshiva, we'll leave you alone," the rabbi said.

"I don't have the money for that. You ruined me already, financially."

The rabbi held the palms of his hands upward and shrugged. "I'm a busy man," he said dismissively.

Elhanan Ben-Hakoun walked back down the road to his store,

only 200 yards from the rabbi's office. Yehezkel Street was busy, as always. Buses raced down the hill past the old stone storefronts and the ramshackle new apartments opposite. Ultra-Orthodox men and women eyed Ben-Hakoun from across the narrow street as though they knew exactly who he was. Everywhere their endlessly multiplying, uniformly dressed children huddled as if plotting something from which Ben-Hakoun, the secular interloper, would always be excluded. He was so isolated here. The neighborhood was crawling with *them,* and they could do whatever they wanted with him. He imagined it was the sensation an Israeli might experience if he strayed into an Arab part of town, fearful of attack, knowing that no one would come to his aid. He tried to put the fear out of his mind and focus on his business. He would rent another shop somewhere else in Jerusalem and move all his equipment there. He would lose the value of the property here on Yehezkel Street, but he would at least be free of this little rabbi and his coercive demands. It was a good plan. But it didn't calm him. He kept thinking about this rabbi and all the other Ashkenazis, the European Jews, who hated him for his Mizrahi origin and for the laxness of his Sephardi religious traditions. To them, he may as well have been eating pork and shrimp, because he didn't count as a Jew. They hated him because he was secular, more than Israelis hated Palestinians, Ben-Hakoun was sure of it. He unlocked the door of Foto Elen and went inside. They didn't just stamp me down, he thought. They want to grind me into the dirt. He stood behind the counter. Two young Haredi men came to the door of the shop and resumed their protest prayers.

THOUGH THE HAREDIS broke Elhanan Ben-Hakoun, it was partly because *he* scared the life out of *them* with *Free Willy* and videotapes of mixed-sex dancing. Fear was at the root of Haredi violence, fear that modern life—in the form of its technology and its liberalism— would infiltrate young religious minds and draw them away from the study of Torah and into sin. The possibility of the loss of Torah knowledge was very real to the ultra-Orthodox. The learned Rabbi Ovadiah Yosef, founder of the Shas Party, gave a lecture one Saturday evening in 1997 at which he said that a man ought not to walk between two women, as it would cause him to forget the Torah. The secular Israeli press mocked Yosef, who looked somewhat ridiculous in his sunglasses and the bulbous ceremonial hat and braided robes he retained from his term as chief Sephardi rabbi. But the old sage was referring to a genuine Talmudic issue. When a man walked between two camels or two donkeys, ancient rabbis believed that he might imbibe their negative characteristics, precisely because they were not concerned with the study of Torah, according to the Talmud. Rabbi Ovadiah noted that the same was true of women, whose studies are limited in the ultra-Orthodox community. It was no use telling either side of the donkey debate, secular or religious, just how inexplicable their views seemed to their opponents. To the ultra-Orthodox, the mockery of one of their most respected men of learning merely confirmed the hostility to Talmud and Torah in mainstream Israel. In fact, the country was becoming more and more religious. But the ultra-Orthodox saw only the threat of modernity. Just as secular Israelis despised Rabbi Ovadiah for the power he wielded as dictator to a significant number of Shas Knesset members, the response of the Haredis to their own dread of modern life was to heap hate on a suitable scapegoat, like Elhanan Ben-Hakoun.

At the Haredi Center for Technological Studies, behind the narrow lanes of the nineteenth-century Mahane Yehuda market in Jerusalem, Rabbi Yehezkel Fogel tried to teach the benefits of the modern world without fear. When he opened the center in 1995, other rabbis accused him of luring people away from their yeshivas. The implication was that, once out of the yeshiva and trained in new technologies, Fogel's students would soon take a job among secular people and ultimately be lost entirely to the Haredi community. But Fogel got the backing of a few major rabbis who saw technological training courses under their control as a fine way to correct a weakness in their community: men were ignorant of physics and math and incapable of bringing in a substantial wage, while their women carried, as Fogel put it, "the yoke of living," teaching or working as secretaries, often among secular people.

Rabbi Fogel set boundaries for his students that kept the rabbis happy. In the men's class, many of his students studied at yeshiva during the day and came to Rabbi Fogel at night. The men could surf the Internet, but he barred the young women, whose classes were separate, from the temptations of the Web. Instead, he trained them to write programs for educational CD-ROMs. Some of the women in the class I visited were married already, although they were all in their teens or early twenties. The married ones wore wigs or frowzy hats. All covered their bodies with long skirts, long sleeves, and high, frilly collars. They were almost through an eighteen-month course in educational multimedia. I asked a seventeen-year-old, Esther Meir, if she would like to use her computer skills to poke around on the Internet. She told me, "It's not suitable, so it shouldn't be in the house. Somebody who's on the Net has access to the whole of the world. I'm not sure we need it."

The sheer success of the rabbis in cosseting their people within a world bounded by the Torah created a desperate need for the training Rabbi Fogel provided. Haredis were desperately poor. They received subsidies for their institutions, and each yeshiva student had some money from the government, unless they rejected the state like the Neturei Karta. The government cash was enough to make secular Israelis, who paid the taxes that funded the subsidies, hate the Haredis, but insufficient for ultra-Orthodox Israelis to live in anything but poverty. Rabbi Naftali Falk showed me around the Mir Yeshiva in Mea Shearim, one of the biggest and most prominent in Jerusalem. We crossed study halls bigger than football fields, packed with white-shirted students arguing at great volume with their study partners over the day's assigned page of Talmud. Most were youngsters, but plenty were middle-aged. Falk introduced me to one sixty-year-old who had studied all his life. As we walked along a narrow hallway past a coat rack hung with dozens of black homburgs, Falk admitted, "It's not easy to get by." At thirty-five, Falk had five children. His government grant was $200 a month. He came to Mir every morning at 6:45 and stayed until 6 P.M. In the evening, he would earn a little extra money tutoring or giving a lecture at another study hall. But there were plenty of other desperate men equally qualified to give such lectures, and the people shelling out for their lessons were Haredis, too, so they often lacked the cash to pay much. Falk just about managed to double his government allocation with this undeclared income.

A moderately religious government minister tried to correct the poverty of people like Naftali Falk. Finance Minister Yaakov Neeman tried to legalize yeshiva students' moonlighting during Netanyahu's government. But the rabbis saw this as a backdoor way into modern life. Although he was Orthodox, Neeman's yarmulke was not black; he wasn't from the ultra-Orthodox Haredi community, and he couldn't persuade them to believe in him any more than they would trust Elhanan Ben-Hakoun, even if Neeman did wish them *"Shabbat shalom"* at the end of each week. Menachem Porush, a leader of Agudat Yisrael who negotiated the original status quo between the religious and secular with Ben-Gurion, told me he wasn't concerned with compromises. The work and duty of the Haredis was to study Torah, not to edge their way into the same selfish, materialistic concerns as secular Israelis. "We are a holy nation. Every nation needs spiritual leadership, but ours in particular does so. When we sit and learn, it gives the Jewish people the spiritual power to exist. Even more than physical power this is important." Porush stroked his long white beard and smiled. "We are not interested in change."

THERE WERE TWO yeshiva students outside Foto Elen on the morning of November 14, 2001. Elhanan Ben-Hakoun leaned against the door frame in a light-blue shirt, khaki pants, and a matching vest. A stranger might have thought the tanned man in the doorway with the white comb-over was chatting amusedly to the two black-hatted religious men, because Ben-Hakoun seemed smiling and nonchalant. But one of the Haredi men put his fingers in his ears and the other raised his voice to pray louder. Ben-Hakoun tried to make his chatter and his smile seem mocking, but it was clearly a screen for his nervousness. Soon he waved his hand dismissively at the two and went back inside.

In the store, Ben-Hakoun watched as a crowd grew across the street. He called the police, but they didn't come. He wanted to close the store and go home. There were too many of them. It seemed like 500 people had gathered over by the bus stop, and that the street that he knew so well had been made part of another town—somewhere alien to him, like Iran, where the religious dominated public life, or prewar Poland, where everyone yelled in Yiddish. The panic of isolation came upon him once more, worse than ever. The demonstrators chanted and prayed. They were after him. He couldn't go out there. He couldn't get out of the shop. There were two men by the door.

They were right in the doorway. He couldn't get out. He called the police. Please come. The police didn't come. It was just him. And all of *them*. This was it. He would run out to his van. He wouldn't even stop to lock the door of the store. They could loot everything. They could ruin him, for all he cared. What was he talking about? He was ruined already. But he had parked across the street, where *they* were. He wouldn't be able to get to the van. If he got into it, there'd be too many people jammed around it for him to move away. Shit. There were so many of them. He couldn't make it. Call the police. You have to come, you must. It was 11:41 A.M.

A police van eventually pulled up outside Foto Elen at 1 P.M. Police officer Rimona Philosoph stepped out of the blue and white. She was short and slight with her hair pulled back in a slick, pomaded ponytail. Elhanan Ben-Hakoun hurried from his shop. "They shut me in the shop. I called you for two hours," he said. "But look, now you're here, I just want to leave."

"Who shut you in the shop?" the policewoman asked.

Ben-Hakoun looked about. There were more than two of the Haredis outside the shop now. In fact, there were six of them and a middle-aged woman. He spotted the first two protesters. "This one and this one," he said.

The policewoman addressed Ben-Hakoun and the two yeshiva students. "Let's step aside here. I want to talk about this." She reached out as if to guide one of the religious men to a spot where they could talk privately.

The yeshiva student, whose name was Aharon Heimlich, recoiled from the forbidden touch of a woman. "Leave me alone," he said. "Don't touch me." He retreated along the sidewalk.

Officer Philosoph asked Ben-Hakoun to bring Heimlich to the police van, so that she wouldn't offend the Haredi onlookers by touching the man. There was a male officer behind the wheel of the van who could have grabbed Heimlich, but he stayed in his seat and waited. Ben-Hakoun moved toward Heimlich.

Someone came between him and his target. Ben-Hakoun heard a scratchy, old man's voice telling him to leave Heimlich alone. He halted and tried to step around the old man. Ben-Hakoun focused on Heimlich, who dodged behind the old man and carried on shouting. The old one was Yudel Samet. On his aged, frail legs, he shuffled from side to side until Ben-Hakoun got around him. Heimlich doubled back and tried to weave past the two older men, but Ben-Hakoun clasped his arm. He got Heimlich with his right hand and pulled him toward the police van. Reb Yudel stepped in front of him. With the back of his left forearm, Ben-Hakoun pushed the old man out of his path. He thought he eased him away, but the force of the shove was too great for Yudel, who was off balance. Reb Yudel stumbled back a step, then another pace, faster, too fast, and fell backward. His head cracked against the metal footplate on the back of the police van. Ben-Hakoun turned around in the doorway of Foto Elen. He flapped his hands helplessly, like a small child who can't find the words to explain something that's driving him crazy. One of the Haredis on the sidewalk shouted at him, "Nazi."

Ben-Hakoun saw that a puddle of blood surrounded Yudel's head. He went inside to get a cloth to stanch the bleeding. When he returned to the sidewalk, Yudel was sitting, dazed but upright, with blood rolling down his blue-and-white *Yerushaleime kaftan*. His broad-brimmed hat was on the ground and a passerby was pressing a hand on the top of his bald head, where the wound was. Ben-Hakoun placed the cloth gingerly on Yudel's riven scalp.

A green Border Police jeep pulled up next to the first police van. Three Border Policemen got out. They were rougher than the blue-clad police; they were used to dealing with Palestinians at checkpoints on the edge of Jerusalem and were notorious for abuse and violence. They didn't wait in their vehicle for a policewoman to negotiate the situation. They grabbed Heimlich. As they shoved him into their jeep, they whacked him in the face a few times to shut him up.

Then an ambulance came to take Reb Yudel to Hadassah Hospital in Ein Kerem. A policeman brought Ben-Hakoun's car across to the store for him. He locked up and drove home, shaking.

Elhanan Ben-Hakoun went to the home of his married daughter Dana in Kiryat Yovel, not far from the hospital to which the ambulance had ferried Reb Yudel. As Ben-Hakoun sat in shock, unable to move, barely able to talk, it seemed as though he were the one whose head had been struck. In the evening, Dana called a police officer to say that she and her mother either wanted to close the shop permanently or to remove all the equipment from the store: they wanted to put an end to Elhanan's suffering. The policeman asked her to come and clear out Foto Elen at 6 A.M. "Don't worry. We'll protect you," he said. He asked her to call at 5 A.M. to coordinate the removal.

When Dana phoned in the morning, the officer was terse. "There's no need for you to come. There's nothing to take from there. It was all burned." Almost all—whoever torched the store in the night looted some of the equipment beforehand.

Dana came to her father in tears. "You've got nothing left," she cried. Elhanan Ben-Hakoun wept.

Ben-Hakoun couldn't bring himself to go to the store that day. He couldn't move. Dana went. She photographed the scene. On the limestone pillar next to the door, there was a red scrawl of graffiti: Jewish Blood Was Spilled Here. Firefighters had pulled the shutters off their hinges. The sign that had hung above the door lay against the wall, charred around the edges to make a black frame for the words "Foto Elen," like the obituary notices Israelis display around the neighborhood when a resident dies. Inside all was black, shapeless, and wet.

The fire truly did take everything from Elhanan Ben-Hakoun. He had been unable to get insurance on the store, because insurers knew to ask storekeepers about problems with the Haredi community in neighborhoods like the Bukharan Quarter. He sold his house to cover his expenses. He and Talia moved in with Elhanan's eighty-two-year-old mother, Simcha. The fire destroyed Ben-Hakoun's religion too. He had been moderately religious, following the traditions of his family without the fanaticism of the Neturei Karta, just as the Ben-Hakouns did back in Morocco, where Simcha's father was a prominent rabbi in Marrakesh. Ben-Hakoun had paid $1,000 for his own bench in his local synagogue. He wore a yarmulke, but only when he was in the synagogue. Yet on the day after the fire, he knew that he would always hate religion. He wouldn't return to the synagogue. He sat in Dana's apartment, paralyzed, running over the same dark thoughts.

The old man. He thought about the old man. Talia's sister worked at Hadassah Ein Kerem. Every day, Ben-Hakoun had his wife call her at the hospital to ask how Reb Yudel was doing. At first, he was under observation, weak but pulling through. Then doctors operated, and Reb Yudel went into a coma after the surgery. Ben-Hakoun couldn't believe it. He was not a violent man. How had this happened? After a few days, Talia's sister called. "You can uncork the champagne," she said, "because the old man went to the ward. He's not in the intensive care unit anymore."

Elhanan Ben-Hakoun went out and bought a memorial candle, a stubby tube designed to protect the flame inside from drafts. Fingering the candle, he thought of his brother Danny. Two days after the boy's bar mitzvah, thirty-five years ago, Ben-Hakoun's parents left Danny in Elhanan's care. The boy felt ill and Elhanan took him to Shaareh Tzedek Hospital on the back of his Vespa. Elhanan waited in the corridor, worried but certain that things would be all right. Three hours later, Danny died of respiratory failure. Ben-Hakoun recalled that he felt completely abandoned at the hospital when his brother departed. Over the years, he tried to keep Danny's spirit with him, so that he might never be so alone again. He felt that somehow Danny had helped the old Haredi man to get better.

When he heard that Reb Yudel had recovered, Elhanan Ben-Hakoun took the memorial candle to his brother's grave in the Givat Shaul cemetery, on the steep hill overlooking the road to Tel Aviv. The candle was to be lit in thanks for the old man's regaining consciousness and as a symbol of his full return to health. Danny's grave seemed the right place to put it. Talia waited in the van, because the cold wind was strong across the narrow terrace of tombstones. But the wind took the flame, each time Ben-Hakoun tried to light the candle. He put the candle under his jacket to shield it from the gusts, but it would not catch fire. He tried for almost an hour, with tears in his eyes. He should have grown cold, but he felt hot with a disturbing kind of desperation. After he gave up, he was utterly bereft. His livelihood had burned down, but when he wanted fire, there was none.

Three days later, a week after Reb Yudel's injury outside Foto Elen, Talia's sister called again. She had mixed up Yudel with another Yehuda Samet in the hospital. It was the other man who recovered. Yudel never came out of his coma. Now he was dead.

ON THE NARROW STREET outside Shmuel Pappenheim's office, the traffic through Mea Shearim was always jammed. Haredi men hastened between the slow-moving cars in the November rain, their black hats covered with plastic shopping bags to keep the felt dry.

Pasted to a notice board on the old stone wall by the entrance to the courtyard, a black-edged sheet that was already out of date:

> Pleas and supplications for the full recovery of the brave and dear Yehuda Leib Shlomo Ben-Gittel Zelda Samet, who is in serious condition and requires God's mercy. He was badly beaten by the reprobate while the Jerusalem police happily looked on and sent a brazen policewoman to hit the men who protested against the abominable store. Therefore, we must pray to God speedily to burn the abominable devil and his minions. May God send us a pure spirit and may we be honored to educate our children with holiness and pureness without any pitfalls. Amen.

Up the worn steps with the rusting balustrade at the back of the courtyard, Shmuel Pappenheim composed his articles for *Ha-Eda*. The newspaper's office was damp at this time of year, with streaks of bubbling paintwork on the walls and brown-stained dips in the ceiling. The filing cabinets along the back wall were a government-issue blue-gray. Seated before an incongruously modern desktop computer, Shmuel Pappenheim warmed his hands over a kerosene heater and typed out a paragraph for his next issue:

> The Zionists complain about the anti-Semitism that's rampant in the Arab press. However, do they not notice how they condemn the Haredis in their own newspapers? In Europe, during the time of the pogroms, the police would inevitably appear only after the pogrom was over and they would only arrest the victims. The same thing is happening here today. We must face the fact that we are engaged in a war for the purity of our neighborhood. We must not shirk our duty to fight this war. God is with us and, if we fight as we should, victory is assured.

Pappenheim saved the story to his hard disk and rubbed his reddish beard. He called up the layout for the front page of his November 27 issue. His headlines were usually long and replete with acronyms that were hard for a secular Israeli to decipher. This time, he wanted something simpler, with the punch of a banner front page in Israel's biggest newspaper, *Yediot Aharonoth*, published in Tel Aviv.

With four keystrokes, the Hebrew letters *reysh, tzaddi, khet,* and an exclamation point, he typed in 48-point white letters on a black background: "MURDER!" He had never written a headline like that. Then he wrote about the funeral.

Reb Yudel's cortege closed all the religious neighborhoods of Jerusalem. It began outside the Toldot Aharon Yeshiva in Mea Shearim, where Yudel had made the tea each morning. The crowd, forming a carpet of wide felt hats, pushed shoulder to shoulder around the blue van that would carry Yudel to Givat Shaul cemetery. There were thousands of young yeshiva students present, and every member of Neturei Karta in Jerusalem. They flowed along the narrow streets to Sabbath Square, the traffic junction at the heart of Mea Shearim. A series of ultra-Orthodox rabbis addressed them. Rabbi David Kahn, who owed his position as leader of Toldot Aharon to Yudel's conservative support against his elder brother, spoke to the crowd from the United States by a telephone link through the loudspeakers. Then the crowd moved the two miles to Givat Shaul. Some young students stayed behind at Sabbath Square and blocked traffic. They had a shoving match with the police.

At Givat Shaul, not far from where Elhanan Ben-Hakoun struggled to light the candle for him, Reb Yudel's body was lifted from the van, wound in a white prayer shawl. Each Haredi man tipped back his head to see over the brim of the hat on the man in front of him, even as they pushed forward to be close to Yudel. He had been a simple man, but Pappenheim had begun to transform him into a saint in the week he lay in hospital. Now that he was dead, the journalist aimed to finish the job. At the funeral, Pappenheim conceived of the subhead on the front page that would run beneath his "MURDER!" headline. It would be his epitaph for Reb Yudel: "The saint who was killed for the name of Israel and of God, the Hasidic Rabbi Yehuda Samet, blessed be his sacred memory, who fell in the battle for the holiness and purity of Jerusalem."

Ben-Hakoun was at home under police protection the night of the funeral. But it was not he who faced a new insult. Rather, it was his store. A leaflet went up around Mea Shearim and the Bukharan Quarter, asking the residents to deposit their trash in the burned-out ruins of Foto Elen. It was intended to make it even less likely that Ben-Hakoun would try to return and, at the same time, to show that

Haredi people considered Foto Elen to have been a place filled with the garbage of modern life.

ONE OF THE FIRST TIMES I went to see Elhanan Ben-Hakoun, he was preparing for another of Israel's frequent general elections. He volunteered as an observer at one of the polling stations and was eager to get to his job. He had joined the Meretz Party, the most left-wing of those Israeli political groups that still consider themselves Zionist. Meretz wasn't typically popular with people like Ben-Hakoun. Tradesmen with their origins in the Arab countries tended to vote for the Likud Party, because it took a hard line against the Palestinians and professed to stick up for the little Mizrahi guy against the privileged Ashkenazi Jews of Tel Aviv. In fact, beyond its anti-Palestinian positions, the Likud is little more than a tribal gang doling out patronage. Still, that Elhanan Ben-Hakoun turned from a longtime Likud voter to active support for the party that most represents the liberal Tel Aviv elite showed just how hard the confrontation with the ultra-Orthodox had hit his conception of the state in which he lived.

Ben-Hakoun was wrecked. At that point, in early 2003, he had been awaiting trial a year for causing death by negligence. There was no sign that the trial would be held soon. He would wait a long time in trepidation before he would find out the price of that shove with the outside of his left forearm against Yudel's chest. He was eventually acquitted in April 2004. But the daily cost was evident on his face. His eyes teared up the moment he began to talk about his shop. When he closed the Foto Elen file at the Tax Authority, he burst into tears on the clerk's desk. As we talked, he stopped and apologized each time the weeping came. Sometimes, after the sobs, he forgot himself and started up again in the French of his Moroccan youth, until he remembered that he had been speaking Hebrew. He wanted to tell his story because he needed to spread the message of disgust with the ultra-Orthodox and what they had done to him. He wanted to tell his story, because he thought someone would read it and send him help, give him money. I wondered if there was anyone who would want to give to a man who had gone through something like this. Wealthy American Jews seemed so much more likely to fund a religious institution than a man victimized by one.

I recalled a scene from the Brooklyn performance of *Fleischer*. The ultra-Orthodox real-estate broker returns to the butcher, whose financial woes are growing. The broker says he can still get Fleischer a good price from the religious people who want him to leave the neighborhood. "How come I work fifty years and I don't have a penny, yet you guys study all day in the yeshiva and you have money to buy apartments?" Fleischer asks.

Elhanan Ben-Hakoun wiped his eyes again. When he said goodbye and shook my hand, I felt his index finger still wet with tears against my palm. I walked out past the pine trees behind his daughter's apartment. I was silent, my jaw was tight, my face set like the furious Israelis I had watched striding out of the theater back in Brooklyn.

CHAPTER SEVEN

Adamah

Settlers and the Israeli Left

Kol dmey akhikha tza'akim alai min-ha-adamah.
(The voice of your brother's blood cries to me from the earth.)

—GENESIS 4:10

THE SUN SHONE, but it gave no light. He arose in the morning and the world was irremediably different. There could be nothing worse, yet his heart knew that forever he would feel no sensation that would alleviate this emptiness. It would be within him, a vacuum so vast that he understood it would leave no space for anything else. He gazed from his window at the Judean Desert, the ancient barrenness where the Israelite prophets divined their parched visions of blood and destruction, where David fled Saul, where the Romans hunted Zealots and the Zealots resolved to die rather than surrender. Then Dubak Weinstock, who loved the khaki bluffs and crumbling wadis of this wilderness, walked out into the land beneath which he buried his young son.

Weinstock ran it all back through his head that day. He had heard it happening on the walkie-talkie he carried as a ranger. The handset connected him to the network of Magen David Adom, the Israeli emergency medical service. The last moments of another victim of terrorism crackled through the feedback before 8 A.M. on December 1, 1993. The ambulance reached a car on the road near the settlement of Psagot, on the road to Shiloh, where Palestinians had shot at a few Israelis as they fixed a broken tailpipe. "There's one in very serious condition," the medic said. "We're administering CPR." Grave but composed, for he had heard such fatal messages before, Weinstock lis-

214

tened as the medic came back across the network: "It's not helping. I'll bring him in quickly."

Though it was early, Weinstock went to the head of the Gush Etzion Regional Council to tell him about the attack, which occurred in the Binyamin Regional Council's territory but could easily have involved someone from his own area. In 1993 there were not so many shootings on the roads near the West Bank settlements as there would be in later years, and Weinstock knew the council head would wish to be kept informed. Weinstock entered the council building and strode up the stairs to the chief's office. "You know there's been an attack up by Psagot," he said.

The council head, Shiloh Gal, was on the phone. He held up his hand as Weinstock entered and mouthed the words "Stay here." Putting down the receiver, Gal looked at the man before him, at Weinstock's broad belly straining his dirty blue shirt, his thick arms and ruddy face. Weinstock was the sergeant of Gal's platoon when the council chief served as an enlisted soldier twenty-five years before. Even then, Weinstock had carried a Falstaffian force that injected life and energy and laughter into every room he entered. Except this one. "Dubak, it's your son," Shiloh Gal said. "I just got off the phone with the head of the Binyamin Council."

"Which son?" Weinstock said.

"I think it's Yitzhak. He's been shot. Come with me to Hadassah Hospital."

The two men went to the hospital, which had Israel's best trauma unit, overlooking the old churches and convents in the village of Ein Kerem on the wooded western slopes of Jerusalem. They arrived just as the doctors rushed Yitzhak Weinstock's gurney from the emergency room to the operating theater. It was supposed to be his first day in the army, his first day in a rite of Israeli manhood that had been so important to his father. But it would be his last day alive, his last day above the earth. Dubak Weinstock saw his bloodied son wheeled quickly past him under the fluorescent light of the emergency room, amid the animated babble of the doctors and the nurses. There came upon him a flood of feelings. Then he never felt anything again. No joy, no sorrow. He was a corpse, like the cadaver of his son, wounded as destructively and as seriously as if it had been his own body that received the bullets of the gunmen.

When Dubak Weinstock marched to the grave of his son, there were crowds of mourners, 3,000 in all, and a clutch of journalists beneath the pines on the terraced hillside of the Gush Etzion cemetery. A few minutes before the burial service, an Israel Radio reporter pushed his microphone in front of Weinstock: "Maybe you have second thoughts about your ideology now? Tell me, what does a father who lost his child think now about the price of his politics?" Weinstock paused. He knew the dogma to which this reporter referred: many settlers believed with a fanatical fervor that the land on which Weinstock built his home, conquered in 1967 and renamed Judea, should remain in the possession of Israel, because it once was David's kingdom of Judah and would be the vehicle for the foretold redemption of the people of Israel. The same creed condemned the new Oslo Accords, signed by the Labor government of Prime Minister Yitzhak Rabin, which settlers feared would mean that one day Israeli soldiers might come to evict them from their communities and hand over the land to Yasser Arafat's Palestinian Authority. What Weinstock wanted the reporter to understand was that he did not deal in ideology. He didn't write op-eds or deliver messianic sermons in the synagogue. He believed in the earth, the land that you could feel with your hands, rough when you touched it, or gritty in your eyes when the hot wind gusted toward you, or cool over your head when your father buried you within it. He believed, because the land gave you the knowledge that this place on earth was yours. "I'm burying my son," Weinstock said. He looked at the reporter very intensely. "I'm burying him here in Gush Etzion. Everybody should know that if they want to evict us from here, first they must deal with me. Then they'll have to dig into the earth and take my son's body out of here. I have roots in this land now."

It was not Dubak Weinstock who reconsidered his ideology, even when people told him it was bought at the price of his son's life. As he saw it, it was Israel that had changed. The nation built on the ideal of settlement and driven by the sacrifices of socialist Zionists on spartan collective farms now wanted to stop all that, to take a new direction. Those leftists, whose settlement ideology inspired more traditional Jews like Weinstock to follow them and to found West Bank outposts in the years after the 1967 war, now behaved as though the settlers' actions were an inconceivable affront to democ-

racy. During the shiva for his son, Dubak sat with his old army buddies from the Suez campaign of the 1973 Yom Kippur War. Most were
leftists who lived in the populous central region of Israel near Tel
Aviv; they followed the mainstream of Israeli political thought that,
while suspicious of Arafat, was profoundly enthused by the prospect
of real peace with the Palestinians and a "normal" Israeli society that
would be as boring and devoid of headline-grabbing catastrophe as
Denmark or Switzerland, even if the West Bank settlements had to be
sacrificed in return. *They* changed, Weinstock thought, not me. "If it
weren't for the death of my son," Weinstock said, looking around the
room at the comrades with whom he had fought right across the Suez
Canal, "this would be the happiest day of my life, to see all of you
together. What happened to us?"

A couple of months after the end of the seven mourning days of
the shiva, another reporter came to Weinstock. The army had captured one of his son's murderers. Israeli television wanted Weinstock's
reaction. "What do you think about the murderers?" the reporter
asked.

"I don't condemn them," Weinstock said. He could see it was a
shock to the Israeli journalist, who no doubt was expecting a
response more typical of relatives when they lost loved ones in terrorist attacks. Usually the sententious baritone of the television reporter
would frame those emotions as they flickered between wistful recol-
lections of the victim's outstanding qualities and a despairing, vengeful yet impotent rage. "No, I don't even condemn them," Weinstock
said. "It's a war. In a war, you kill. You have to fight, not condemn.
I'm telling you, one day there will come a Jew who will kill Arabs, just
like they kill us. When he does it, I won't condemn him either."

The next day, February 25, 1994, Baruch Goldstein left his home
in Kiryat Arba, a settlement on the edge of the Palestinian town of
Hebron. A leading member of the right-wing Kach Party and a medical officer in the Israeli army, Goldstein took his Glilon rifle to the
Cave of the Patriarchs, the traditional location for the graves of the
biblical Abraham, Isaac, and Jacob, and three of their wives, Sarah,
Leah, and Rebecca. Muslims knew the site as the Ibrahimi Mosque,
and as they prayed there, Goldstein gunned down twenty-nine Palestinians before onlookers overwhelmed him and beat him to death.

The Shin Bet kept its eyes closely on Dubak Weinstock. In his grief,

they figured he might follow Goldstein's lead. There was something
of the cowboy about Dubak, unpredictable and wild. He fell into neither of the categories of settler that usually make it into news articles
and broadcasts. He was not a religious zealot incapable of acknowl-
edging the right of the Palestinians to struggle against the confisca-
tion of their land for the expansion of the settlements; nor was he an
apologetic suburbanite, pushed out of Jerusalem or Tel Aviv by high
housing prices and into the nearest settlements, where there were
government subsidies and relatively large apartments. The Shin Bet
reckoned it knew those types pretty well. But Dubak made the secret
police nervous. At first, it was easy to see why. Dubak showed the
strain of his son's loss. Two months after Yitzhak's murder, peace
campaigners blocked the main road through Gush Etzion. Dubak
drove up and got out of his jeep. As he approached the demonstrators, a policeman reached out and held him. "If I was demonstrating,
you could grab me," Dubak yelled. "But now *they're* demonstrating
and you still grab *me.*"

"Shut up, okay," the policeman said. So Dubak head-butted the
policeman and, for a few hours, was held under arrest.

The moments of uncontrollable rage, the head-butting anger, were
few. Mostly it was the emptiness of that day when he buried his son
that engulfed Dubak. In a confusion that, he later felt, carried him
into a kind of madness, he entered the only place that could match
the infinite void of his emotions: he went to the desert. Day and night
he rode his battered white Land Rover through the rolling plateau
between the Gush Etzion settlements and the head of the cliffs above
the Dead Sea. For three years, he sought the vacancy of the empty
slopes. From the Bedouin shepherds he befriended there, he learned
the secrets of their cisterns and fruit trees and the way they tracked
their animals in the desert and cooked chicken by burying it in the
ground with hot coals. There was a tall plane tree at the gate of an
abandoned army training camp, rising unexpectedly out of an otherwise stark expanse of dry earth. Every day, Dubak pulled his jeep to the
side of the dirt track and urinated on the tree's smooth gray bark. It
didn't seem to have any other source of moisture and he pissed on it
with grim amusement and watched its branches fill with leaves.

Eventually Dubak Weinstock realized that he had found a whole
world out in the desert, where others would see nothing at all. This

was the harsh environment that bred the values at the original core of Judaism, a world where logic was not modern and humanistic, but ancient and cruel. The politicians in Tel Aviv, negotiating away this land, operated on a set of beliefs that Dubak saw were alien to it, that belonged to another place, a completely different expanse of territory in Europe or North America. That was precisely why those same values seemed so logical and appealing to President Bill Clinton and the Western reporters who clung to the clichés of the disintegrating "peace process" more resolutely than a Bedouin would defend his precious well from an intruder illicitly drawing water. Dubak recalled the Book of Judges as he stood in the awesome quietude of the desert. He remembered that each judge was more a general than a jurist, marching out to fight the enemies of Israel, and that the Bible measured their success by noting the period in which "there was silence on the land." Dubak chuckled to himself: that was the unusual thing, the silence of peacetime, not the continuous battles; that was the man-bites-dog scoop worth recording in the holy book. With this insight, Dubak understood the land. The politicians argued that a withdrawal from the settlements would bring peace. What would the peace be worth if you didn't have the land, if you abandoned the core of your people's being, if you lived like an ersatz New Yorker among Tel Aviv's cafés and bars, its stock exchange and think tanks? From the hilltops where Roman soldiers built guardhouses to protect the ancient Jerusalem-Ein Gedi road, Dubak watched the settlements of Gush Etzion grow. They expanded despite the dangers, and Dubak saw it was good. If they kill one of us, he thought, there will be a tomb and all the efforts of the Palestinians will have gone into putting another Jew into another grave. But a grave is nothing. All *our* efforts will be toward building and planting, so that when they can boast of nothing but the graves they made us dig, the land will be covered with our homes and our orchards. The land was living and his son was alive within it, like the ancestors who fought on it and were buried beneath it and had decayed to the dust that flew thick in the air with every breeze. The centuries had made their reduced corpses indistinguishable from the very sands of the desert they battled to defend.

The Bible identified the harshness of the violence in this land. In Dubak's reading, when Joshua or the kings of Israel made war, they knew that to win was insufficient: they had to kill every man among their opponents. Later the memory of the Bible brought new wars to the land. The Crusaders, Napoleon Bonaparte, General Edmund Allenby—each fought in Palestine for the spoils of battle or through duty and geopolitics, just as when they made war in Constantinople, Borodino, or the South African veldt, but they also girded themselves with the ancient inspiration of Scripture and all the distortion and ruthlessness that was within it. Elsewhere war flared and ended, but in the land of the Bible, Dubak believed it was constant, as though on the same endless cycle as the Jews' weekly readings from their holy scroll, returning to the beginning each year on Simchat Torah. To keep itself alive, the land required constant sacrifices.

Dubak's idea of war began to take shape before he can remember, at his birth in 1946, when his mother went into labor during the mourning period for his grandfather, shot by jumpy British soldiers policing the incipient fighting between Arabs and Jews in Jerusalem. There were terrorist deaths in the family soon after, and they became a mantra to Dubak: his grandfather's sister-in-law in 1948, and his father's two cousins in the same year. The family lived in Jerusalem's Old City since arriving from Poland in 1848. Like the other Jews there, the Weinstocks were poor Hasids. But the arrival of secular Zionists from Eastern Europe in the decades before Dubak's birth changed the simple needs of the Weinstock family. Dubak's great-great-grandfather left Jerusalem to found a new community, Kfar Saba, which became a fairly prosperous satellite town of Tel Aviv. Dubak's father changed the family tradition by sending him to a regular school, not to an ultra-Orthodox yeshiva. Learning Hebrew there, Dubak found he could no longer talk to his Hasidic cousins, who conversed in Yiddish. At the school, he joined a youth movement that began to inculcate a love of the land. They taught him about the oak of Kfar Etzion, the only reminder of the Jewish settlement overrun by the Jordanian Arab Legion in 1948 with the loss of 250 defenders. The low, puffy spray of branches on the oak was visible over the hilltops inside Jordan from the Israeli border. Survivors of the battle would gather each year on the anniversary of their comrades' deaths to gaze across at the tree. The kibbutzniks and leftists who taught at the state schools gave little Dov Weinstock the nickname Dubak. On the side of the cheap Time cigarettes manufactured in Israel was the name of the company that made them, Dubek Ltd. They took the sound of that corporate title, which in Hebrew characters is similar to Dov, and the boy was renamed, although they altered the spelling. These teachers bestowed a name upon Dubak, but they also gave him a mission: to fight to reclaim that Kfar Etzion oak and the earth that succored its roots.

In 1967 Israel's army conquered the land of the West Bank and East Jerusalem. On the day after the war ended, Dubak went to the Old City of Jerusalem with his father and walked the narrow streets of the Jewish and Muslim Quarters. His father pointed out the weathered sandstone buildings where the family and its friends lived before 1948. Dubak loved to hear his father's memories and went every Sabbath to the Old City. He could visualize the generations who had lived there, as surely as if they wandered the alleys with him. Other Jews returned to live in the Old City, but Dubak wanted something fresh and clean and challenging. With his new wife, Sharon, who was born in Beverly Hills and came to Israel in 1964, Dubak became one of the first settlers in Gush Etzion, the Etzion bloc, built around the original Kfar Etzion kibbutz that fell in 1948. In 1972 Dubak and Sharon Weinstock joined a small number of other young couples on a remote hilltop, where they lived without water and electricity for their first year. At the edge of their settlement stood the old oak of Kfar Etzion, its trunk idiosyncratically split in two near the ground. Dubak remembered the stories he had been told in school about the oak and its distant symbolism of loss, and now here he stood close enough to touch it. They named their settlement Alon Shvut, the Oak of Return.

Dubak and Sharon lived in a small house with no amenities. He brought his grandmother to visit from Jerusalem. She looked about in disgust at the roughness of the place. "What are you looking for here?" she said. "You could live in Jerusalem. Such a nice place, Jerusalem."

"Wait and see what will happen here," Dubak said. "Your grandfather established Kfar Saba. You remember when that was only one house. Look at it today. That's what will happen here too."

"Are you crazy?" she said.

"Yes, I'm crazy, but crazy people are the engine of the Middle East."

There were 20 families in Alon Shvut then. By 2003, there were 600.

Those first families had little time to build before the men were called away. In 1973, when Dubak's eldest son was a year old, the Yom Kippur War began. Dubak joined his mechanized infantry unit, Brigade 204 of the Fifth Infantry. They headed south to the Sinai, where they were attached to the tank units commanded by Ehud Barak, who later as prime minister came closer than any other Israeli leader to giving up the West Bank. As their columns passed on a narrow desert road, Dubak saw his brother Yehuda traveling with another unit. That night, Yehuda took a bullet in the head and was permanently disabled—another addition to the sacrifices of the Weinstocks for the land. Dubak went on to Suez, crossing the canal and entering the town. There were two battalions of Egyptian commandos there whose presence had escaped Israeli intelligence. Dubak's unit went in before the armor and straight into a dreadful ambush. Dubak killed at close quarters. He felt like a butcher.

Though there were horrors in the war fought by Dubak and his comrades, it colored their view of Israel and its conquests in a positive light, just as the dismal Lebanon War of 1982–85 disenchanted the next generation. After the war, Dubak felt he belonged. He was a soldier who fought to defend Zionism, and a settler who acted out Zionism's highest ideal each day simply by being on the land.

Yet that time of belonging and togetherness was short-lived. Indeed, it was probably an absolute illusion. Behind the appearance of unity and purpose, Israeli society was built on internal struggle. After the murder of his son, Dubak felt this division very strongly. Though later it would be his own community from which he was alienated, in the strange days after Palestinians shot Yitzhak, Dubak listened to the politicians as they spewed judgment upon him and the settlers with a heedlessness for the feelings of others so typical of Israeli discourse. First the leftist education minister, Shulamit Aloni, commented that the settlers seemed prepared to sacrifice their children for the sake of their ideology. Then, a few months later, Prime Minister Yitzhak Rabin said the settlers were "dancing on the blood of the victims of the radical Islamic murderers, trying to turn these victims into a lever against the peace agreement." At other times, Rabin insulted the settlers, calling them "propellers," which in Hebrew signified people who generate a lot of noise and hot air, and also referring to them by a Yiddish word for a part of an engine that squeaks.

His intention was to let the settlers know that he would continue with the peace process no matter how they squealed and whirred and puffed in the background. The bond Dubak felt with all Israel in 1973, when he entered the long covenant of military sacrifice that Zionists traced from biblical times to the fallen of his own family in 1948, shattered against Rabin's thoughtless rhetoric. When Dubak went to the desert, he felt cast out by his prime minister, by his government: his beliefs were outlawed.

The style of speech Rabin displayed struck at Dubak Weinstock because it was aimed directly at him. But in Israel, this fissiparous mode of dialogue was the norm. It appeared in the often hateful and impatiently explosive way Israelis have of talking to each other about apparently quotidian issues. In the matter of Rabin and the peace process and the future of the land, these daily intolerances were magnified to supernatural proportions. Rabbis began to debate a judgment against Rabin that would declare him a persecutor of Jews. Some pronounced an arcane curse from the ancient books of rabbinic teachings. Ariel Sharon—the general who led Dubak across the Suez Canal and who later became the biggest government backer of the settlements and eventually prime minister—was one of several leading rightist politicians who slurred Rabin as a "quisling." The name of the collaborator who led the wartime Nazi government of Norway tarred Rabin with the taint of the Holocaust. When I first came to Jerusalem, I found the city's mailboxes and billboards dotted with caricatures of the prime minister wearing an SS uniform.

Just as Dubak saw the Book of Judges as evidence that there would always be war on the land, so the settlers who hated Rabin found their justifications in the Bible. Yigal Amir, who shot Rabin dead late on the night of Saturday, November 4, 1995, told investigators he acted after studying the section of the Bible known in the weekly schedule of readings as Balak. It includes the story of Zimri, an Israelite who took a Midianite woman as a lover. God had barred the Israelites from congress with the Midianites, so another Israelite named Pinhas ran a spear through Zimri and the woman, killing them. In Numbers, God forgave Pinhas, "for he was zealous for my sake," and made his offspring priests of Israel. To Western observers and most leftist Israelis, Amir appeared to have done something unthinkable. For a Jew to have killed a Jewish leader was an act of lunatic fanaticism that threatened to tear Israel apart. After the murder, when the country needed so much to find common ground, Israel's left refused to acknowledge any part in the creation of such a deadly division. On a television discussion program aired by a U.S. network, one of the leaders of Rabin's Labor Party, Haim Ramon, jabbed his finger at the Israeli right-wingers with him on the panel and yelled what professed to be the response of decent, Westernized Israelis to the assassination, but in fact carried all the accusatory, divisive, power-crazed violence that engulfed both sides and drove them apart. "The majority will decide," Ramon bellowed. "Those that are not going to respect it, from now on, will be crushed. We are talking about crushing, crushing unjust forces." But to Amir and those who thought with the Middle Eastern logic that Dubak identified, it was Rabin who split Israel by marginalizing the settlers and disregarding them. To divide a society generated the same sudden, massive, destructive force as the splitting of an atom.

Dubak Weinstock found it hard to mourn for Rabin. Police investigators combed the settler community for people who knew what the assassin had been planning. They called Weinstock in for questioning, though they soon saw that he knew nothing. But Weinstock slowly realized the profound lesson that the prime minister's murder taught him. Weinstock had never wanted revenge on Rabin for the callous way he spoke about the settlers after the death of Yitzhak Weinstock. He desired only that the prime minister should have shown understanding for the suffering of a fellow Jew, no matter their political differences. It stunned Dubak that he should experience with numbness the death of another Jew, leader of the land of which he was so proud. That shock began to bring him out of the years of wandering in the desert. The naked expanse where the Bedouin lived had kept Dubak alive somehow. He had grown to understand his connection with this land. Perhaps he would be able to bring the same understanding to the leftists who lived in high-rises in Tel Aviv and never saw the desert except on dope-addled weekend breaks in the Egyptian Sinai. Weinstock had to cross the lines if he was to re-create the singular purpose he had sensed throughout the Israeli nation after 1967.

Weinstock went to Shiloh Gal, in his office at the Gush Etzion Regional Council, and explained that he wanted to take secular, left-wing Israelis on tours into the desert. "I don't care if they still oppose the idea of the settlements afterward," he said. "I just want them to hear the song of the land."

Gal said he didn't have the money to finance Dubak's project. Weinstock brushed that aside and said he would find the funds somehow. "Listen, we want all the land," he said. "But if we don't have all the people, we'll never have the land too."

AVRAHAM PESSO caught the sirens outside his window late at night in November 1995. For Israelis, the overheard klaxon was always the first alert, the notice to turn on the television to uncover details of the latest outrage. "Something happened," Pesso said to his wife. "It's a terrorist attack." It was worse. Pesso stared at the television until 2 A.M., transfixed by the awful news that a Jew had assassinated the Israeli prime minister. He knew he would not sleep, so he took his mountain bike and rode to Kings of Israel Square, where Rabin took the bullets in his back. Somber crowds gathered there with candles, holding their heads with their hands in an instinctive posture of despair and incomprehension. Pesso wheeled his bicycle across the broad plaza. His body felt weak, as though his muscles were utterly exhausted by the shock and the anger he experienced.

Pesso's fatigue grew still stronger as frustration and desolation took control of him, and he fed it by refusing to sleep for three days. He sat at home or at his studio, watching television and reading every newspaper for the details of the killing and of the investigation of the man who pulled the trigger. Like Dubak Weinstock, wandering in the desert after his son's death, Avraham Pesso isolated himself in a daze born of grief. In his studio, his art surrounded him—vividly impressionistic renderings of the countryside through which he took his mountain bike on long rides each week. But, unable to work, he stayed inside, in the studio near Tel Aviv's old bus station, a run-down neighborhood that was home mostly to Nigerian, Thai, and Romanian laborers.

The paintings, which he priced according to size—up to $10,000 for a canvas taller than he and twice as wide—rested unfinished on his easel or leaning against the bare concrete walls. He slit open his cigarettes with a razor and mixed in a little hash to calm himself. Yet he was not soothed. His short, stocky body was as frenetically active as the brain inside his bald, broad-browed head. He cast his doleful blue eyes around the studio, at the rack of canvases ready for sale to the prosperous Tel Aviv lawyers and publishers who were his regular clients, at the shabby black curtain that screened the toilet bowl in a corner alcove, at the rows of Scheveningen oil paints he ordered in tubes from Holland. He came to the studio for the isolation that allowed him to work, to create. When he emerged from this room, he knew, he would begin to *do* something, something new, to protest the disaster that befell the nation in Kings of Israel Square. What form would it take?

After three days, Pesso had his answer. On the television, he watched a report about an extreme group of settlers. They went at night to the grave of Baruch Goldstein, who slew twenty-nine Arabs, and they danced and raised a glass to toast Yigal Amir, who murdered a single Jew. Pesso couldn't believe it. Surely, even in the basest country in the world, these people, who publicly rejoiced at the murder of the head of government, would be sent immediately to jail, he thought. Yet in Israel the government feared them and let them continue their campaign against everything decent. The emotions that gripped him now reminded him of his reaction back in February 1994, when he heard that Goldstein had opened fire on the crowd in the Ibrahimi Mosque. There ought to have been a wave of arrests after that awful slaughter, but the government was too scared of the settlers. There ought to be one law for everyone, but in Israel, it seemed, laws didn't apply to the settlers. When Goldstein struck, Pesso started to feel that the Oslo peace process, which he had supported with such optimism in the beginning, would eventually fail. No accord could survive mass murder and terrorist attacks from both sides. Now that Rabin, the political backbone of the peace agreements, was dead, Pesso watched the footage of the settlers at Goldstein's grave and decided that this time, the reaction of the left must be different from the timorousness that followed the shooting at the Hebron mosque. For years, Israel's left had protested in the squares and complained in their cafés about the right wing, while the rightists simply went out and took what they wanted. One group talked, and their opponents acted, so that in the end one side accumulated a thick portfolio of op-eds and a feeling of intellectual superiority, while the other side brought 200,000 people to live in the ever-expanding settlements. I could go to the square for another stupid protest, Pesso told himself, but that won't influence anyone, not those who are really in power. The left behaves as though it were frightened, while the right doesn't fuck around. Pesso, you come from an old family that has been many generations in this land. Show yourself that you aren't afraid of them.

Pesso was an artist. He made his living from the application of color. So he decided to protest with color too. For two days, he steeled himself. He knew that the settlers were dangerous people, that the government was afraid to sanction them and might not protect him from them. He thought of calling friends to tell them what he was about to do, but he knew they would dissuade him, so he kept it to himself. He anticipated what his best friend, a prominent lawyer named Rami Ben-Natan, would say: "What are you, crazy? You want to get killed?" Before he died, Pesso's father told his son never to worry about the opinions of others, just to push ahead with what he believed in. That was why Pesso became a painter, because in spite of the difficulty of earning a living from art, he knew what he wanted from life and his father lovingly supported that decision. In the quiet of his studio, Pesso felt his father's spirit fly up from the grave to him. "Father, am I doing right?" he asked. "Show me a sign." There was no sign. He prepared alone for his operation.

The color of the protest would be black. Pesso recalled how Rembrandt used peripheral darkness to highlight the bright center of his canvases. Pesso would make the settlements disappear with his black paint and, metaphorically, light up the core truth and decency obscured by the assassin and by the celebrants at the graveside. Four days after Rabin's death, Pesso took a large tube of his expensive Dutch oil paint and squeezed it into a one-liter glass bottle. He added natural turpentine to thin the black paste and mixed them. He put the bottle in a paper bag, tucked it beneath his arm, and went outside. The sky was cloudy as he walked to the bus station. He rode the escalators to the top floor and boarded the Egged company's number 405 bound for Jerusalem.

On the bus, Pesso clutched the bottle in his lap. He thought through what he would do when he reached his final destination: You'll sit and cover your head. You were in a special commando unit in the army, Pesso, but don't defend yourself. Let them hit you, kill you. Let them finish you off. Sit like a kamikaze. He arrived in Jerusalem and went to the disorganized taxi stand outside the bus station. He asked for a private taxi and was surrounded by drivers calling loudly to find where he wanted to go. "Kiryat Arba," he told them. Even in his agitation, Pesso saw the funny side of the drivers' reaction. They melted away in a matter of seconds at the sound of the name of the settlement where Baruch Goldstein had lived. It was known to be among the most extreme of the settlements, and the road there passed by a series of potentially dangerous Palestinian villages and along the edge of Hebron. Pesso pursued one of the drivers. "Listen, I'm a journalist," he told him. "I want to take a couple of photos, and then we'll come straight back."

"Okay, but you promise me we'll return right away?" the driver said. "There are refugee camps along that road. It's scary, you know."

Pesso sealed the deal with the driver. He had a good feeling about the man, but the nervousness that gripped him on the bus took hold of him again. He knew there was one thing he must do before he could go on his mission calmly. He slipped some coins into a public telephone outside the bus station and dialed his home. His wife answered. "I'm going to do something, Ronli," Pesso said. "Kisses to you and the children."

Pesso hung up the phone. As he did so, he heard Ronli nervously calling him down the line: "Pesso? Pesso . . ." She must have detected something unusual in the way he spoke to her, and now he had her worried. But it might be his last opportunity to hear her voice, so he couldn't help that it had disturbed her. His stomach turned upside down, and he felt a charge of adrenaline—enough, it seemed, to fill the liter bottle he held in his hands. He wondered if Ronli would understand: she was always quieter, harder to figure out than he. Pesso used to watch her on the beach in Haifa when they were teenagers, before they dated, sitting with her friends as he jogged by along the sand. She was so beautiful that Pesso was too ashamed to turn his head and look at her directly, but he saw her with a thrill every time he ran, from the corner of his eye. He met her again when they were both working in the art department at Ha-Bima Theater in Tel Aviv years later and they came together easily, as though renewing a friendship from the beach in their hometown. They married and had two children. They were good together, two lazy artists with poky studios and a modest living. But Ronli was more peaceful than Pesso. She never argued with people or shouted the way he did. Pesso knew she might disapprove of what he was about to do, but it had hold of him already.

The driver was tense on the road south to Hebron from Jerusalem, and so was Pesso. After the Gush Etzion junction, the road narrowed and curved down through a rich valley of Palestinian grapevines past al-Arub refugee camp. The bend was so sharp that the army had erected a tall chain-link fence along the boundary of the camp to block stones thrown at vehicles slowing to make the turn. Pesso looked at the muddle of cinder-block beyond the barrier. He had never been to the West Bank before, so this was the first camp he had seen and it looked to him like a place for dogs to live, not human beings. The driver pointed at Palestinians by the roadside, wondering if they might be dangerous, but Pesso paid no attention.

The Pessos had been nineteen generations on this land, according to family tradition. His grandfather, after whom Avraham Pesso was named, was a leading musician in Tiberias, on the shore of the Sea of Galilee, before the foundation of the Israeli state. On his oud, an Arab lute, he had sometimes accompanied Um Kulthoum, the famous Egyptian singer, and would travel to Beirut and Damascus for work. Arab musicians called him Biro, a nickname for Ibrahim, which in turn was the Arabic version of his Hebrew name, Avraham. That generation knew how to live with Arabs, Pesso thought, not like the settlers who took their land and scorned their humanity. Pesso had known the way of his grandfather's generation, too, as a small boy. He was born in Wadi Nisnas, a neighborhood at the foot of Mount Carmel in Haifa, where Jews and Arabs lived in the same shabby streets. His parents moved up the slopes to the Stella Maris area of town, and eight-year-old Avraham, enamored of the beautiful colors of the hillside, wandered there to stop people illegally picking the bright wildflowers. The boy threw stones at those who damaged the plants. Still, he recalled that his family raised him without animosity toward the Arabs.

Before noon, Pesso's cab arrived at the steel, barred gate of Kiryat Arba. On the left, there was a small row of shops. As the hill rose gently on the right, there were ugly square apartment blocks. Two Border Police soldiers came to the window to check the taxi. They saw that

Pesso was Israeli and let the cab pass, but first Pesso asked, "Where's the grave of Baruch Goldstein?" The soldier directed Pesso to a path next to the shops. Pesso told the driver to pull over nearby and wait for him.

It shocked Pesso that Kiryat Arba seemed so unlike the pioneering image of the West Bank that the settlers promulgated among the bulk of Israelis, who, like him, never came to see for themselves. The place was better tended than most towns inside Israel. The path the soldier pointed out was paved with stone and fringed by purple bougainvillea and the half-hidden black plastic pipes of a drip-irrigation system for the flowers and bushes. At the end of the path, Pesso came to a stone floor laid out in an octagon. In the octagon's center, surrounded by small lamps, there was a long rectangle of sandstone. It was the grave of Goldstein. After his death, Goldstein's family wanted him buried in the old Jewish cemetery in Hebron, next to the tiny Israeli settlement at Beit Hadassah, in the center of the city. The army feared that would bring fanatical pilgrims to the grave, increasing the friction with the Palestinians in the town. Instead, senior officers prevailed on the family to bury Goldstein in the settlement where he had lived, still close to Hebron. As Pesso now saw, that grave was no simple tomb. It stood alone, not in a general cemetery. He overheard a settler, who stood at the side of the grave, explaining the story of Goldstein to a British news camera crew. Pesso circled the tomb three times, listening to the settler describe the dead man as a holy martyr whose act of murder had been a righteous act, a preemptive attack based on Goldstein's belief that the Palestinians were planning a pogrom of Hebron's Jews. Pesso wanted the settlers and the crew to leave before he began his protest, but he couldn't stand to listen to those words anymore. The time is now, he thought. Swiftly he pushed between the settler and the camera crew. He lifted his bottle and smashed it down on top of the tomb, where Goldstein's name was inscribed. He moved so fast that the settler and the camera crew ran to the edge of the stone circle in fear. Pesso heard one of them tell the cameraman to shoot the scene. In an instant, Pesso kicked out the bulbs in the lamps at each corner of the grave, screaming with every strike. "Shame! Enough of this disgrace!" he shouted as he kicked. Then he sat at the side of the grave and called out to the people of Kiryat Arba, "You are invited to do whatever you want to me. I'm waiting for you here. If you're so brave, come here and face me." He wept, tears of stress released. He sat for over a minute rocking back and forth as the tension ebbed away. Then he stood. A group of about thirty settlers had left their shopping and come to the corner of the mini-mall to see what had happened. They stood before Pesso with Uzis hanging from their shoulders and handguns in their holsters. Pesso walked toward them. He felt something powerful in him now, and the settlers felt it too. They parted before him and it reminded Pesso of the Red Sea before Moses. His eyes cut through the crowd of settlers as though they were knives, so determined was his gaze, so strong was the feeling that supplanted all his nervousness and his days of fretting and frustration since the assassination. Pesso passed through the silent settlers to his taxi. The driver turned to him: "What did you do? What's the crowd all about?"

"Do me a favor," Pesso said in a quiet monotone. "Just drive."

"To Jerusalem?"

"Take me to Tel Aviv."

The taxi took Pesso north to the Gush Etzion junction. There the driver turned west and skirted the red-roofed villas of Alon Shvut to descend along the winding hillside road toward Emek Ha-Ela, the Valley of Ela, where the West Bank comes down to the broad Israeli plain. The car radio played a popular Israeli song by Boaz Sharabi called "To Give Your Heart and Soul." It was a sad song. It started to rain.

"What happened back there?" the driver asked. "You look bizarre."

Pesso told him what he had done. "I'm sorry I involved you," he said.

The driver raised his voice. "You threw paint on Baruch Goldstein. Oh, my God!" He held his hands to his head.

Quietly Pesso spoke to him. "Keep your eyes on the road and take me to Tel Aviv."

But the driver needed to tell someone. "I can't calm down until I talk about this." He spoke over the radio to his dispatcher. "Five to two, this is five calling two. You won't believe what happened. I've got a guy here who changed the whole country. You're going to see it on television." Excitedly he turned to Pesso: "I'm going to take you to Tel Aviv free of charge. You made my day. I always voted Likud. I'm a rightist, but I hate those fucking settlers."

Pesso gazed from the car window across the valley as the road descended. The steep hillside was scored with green and white in the parallel horizontal striations of olive trees, where they clung to their terraces, and rock, eroded clean of earth over the centuries. In the afternoon rain, the sunlight came purple through a gap in the heavy clouds and laid a finger across a small strip of the mountain. Pesso remembered his idea of blotting out the wickedness with the black paint and saw evidence of his accomplishment in the view before him. Now he understood that he could see the land once more, illuminated, no longer all dark and threatening and in the exclusive possession of the settlers. He made it part of himself again, like the little boy who protected the wildflowers.

The taxi dropped Pesso at his studio on Y. L. Peretz Street. He climbed the unlit staircase and called his friend, the lawyer Rami Ben-Natan. He told his story. He knew that he would sound like he was insane, but he still thought what he did was the only way to show the fanatics on the other side that they didn't scare him. It was something he would do only once in his lifetime, and he believed his friends would see that. After their initial shock, they would comprehend that he had done something that displayed all the things about himself that made them want to be his friend in the first place: the depth of emotion and genuine humanity and outrage at injustice. "What shall I do now?" he asked Ben-Natan. "Shall I go to the police? I'm not a criminal. I stand by what I did. I won't deny anything. But I'm willing to accept the consequences."

Ben-Natan put together a conference call with three other lawyers. Afterward he called Pesso again. He told him to wait for the police to come to him. Pesso understood that Ben-Natan accepted what he had done. Ben-Natan, by his own admission, was more of a regular Israeli leftist; he would never have done anything with the force that Pesso employed in his attack on Goldstein's grave. Pesso was different, and he had done something brave that might just give Israelis an alternative idea of how to handle the settlers, in contrast to the timidity of successive governments. Pesso had followed his feelings in a way that the mild, rational Israeli left never would have done.

"Why didn't you tell me what you intended to do?" Ben-Natan asked Pesso.

"You would have stopped me," Pesso said.

If Pesso had called him in advance of the trip to the grave, Ben-Natan conceded that he would have reminded his friend that his action might hurt the feelings of Goldstein's bereaved parents, and that would have been enough to dissuade Pesso. He had needed the clarity of his own emotions and not the qualification of how his demonstration would touch others. As he spoke to Ben-Natan, Pesso was once more on the verge of tears. To relate his story revived in him the stress of enacting it. Ben-Natan thought his friend might have a heart attack.

That evening the footage from the British camera crew appeared on Israeli television. Everyone began to call Pesso, including judges and lawyers offering help and support. His mother also phoned: "Oh, my God, what did you do? I'm afraid people will do you harm now. These settlers are murderers. They could kill you, Avi."

"Don't worry, Mother," Pesso said. "If they didn't kill me in Kiryat Arba, they won't do it at all. In any case, screw them. I'm through with being frightened by them."

Two agents from the Shin Bet came to Pesso's apartment late the following night. They told him they had intelligence information that settlers intended to attack him. They suggested he leave town for five days and that he remove his name from his mailbox and from the door of his studio. "Erase your name," one of them said. Pesso went to Klil, a small rural community in the Galilee, to stay with friends. Ronli insisted she stay behind with the children and keep up their daily routine. A Border Police jeep parked outside their apartment building, its crew on watch around the clock.

After a week, Pesso came back. At 3 A.M. the Shin Bet men returned too. They asked Pesso for his testimony and told him to make it short. "Listen, short I will not make it," Pesso said. He recounted his story for one of the agents, who took notes while his colleague napped with his head on the kitchen table. Pesso finished at 7 A.M.

The next day, Pesso went to his studio. He felt he might be able to paint for the first time since the assassination of Rabin. He set up a canvas about a yard square and prepared his palette. He sketched the rocky hillside and the olive groves on the road down to the Valley of Ela, filling in with his oils their green and white. He painted the purple shaft of light that descended through the stormy stratocumulus, to a single patch of land in the upper-right corner of the canvas. As he painted, he hummed "To Give Your Heart and Soul."

THERE WERE STONE, glass-fronted bookshelves around the grave of Baruch Goldstein, where people who came to venerate the dead man could take up a prayer book. Each of the half-dozen times I went to the site, there was at least one person next to the tomb at the center of the stone octagon, bobbing back and forth in devotion. Some of them talked to me happily about their martyred hero; others repelled my queries with a scowl, not even breaking the rhythm of their *davening*. Hidden inside the stone tomb, Goldstein lay, around the corner from the settlement's tiny shopping mall and overlooked by a hillside jumble of Palestinian homes on the edge of Hebron, in the incongruously sylvan setting of Meir Kahane Park.

Goldstein was a close adherent of Kahane, who headed the Kach Party and advocated the "transfer" of the Palestinians out of the West Bank, until his assassination. Kahane put Goldstein third on his slate for the 1983 Knesset election. In 1992 Goldstein was Kach's mayoral candidate in Kiryat Arba. When I arrived in Israel in 1996, Kach had been outlawed as a result of Goldstein's Ibrahimi Mosque rampage. It turned out that the group was not as far underground as I expected.

Hebron was the heart of Israeli settler extremism, largely because of its biblical connections. Abraham bought the Cave of Machpelah, at its center, from Ephron the Hittite for 400 silver shekels as a burial place for Sara, his wife. It was David's royal seat before Jerusalem and one of the four holiest places to Jews, along with Israel's capital, the ancient community of Tiberias, and the mystical Galilee town of Safed. The Oslo Accords divided Hebron between the Palestinian Authority, which took the bulk of the town, and a small Israeli-ruled area around the homes of 550 settlers. The Israeli sector, incidentally, also incorporated neighborhoods with hundreds of Arab residents. In 1996 I accompanied a group of American settlement supporters and a tour guide from Kiryat Arba named Moira Zeira. One of the Americans, a World War II veteran from Miami Beach, strapped on some bulletproof body armor he'd brought from Florida. The armor's white plastic cover was molded like a male model's torso to show heroically strong pectorals and chunky abdominal muscles, which made the wizened octogenarian look like a Star Wars Stormtrooper from his wattle to his waistband. When I explained to the bulletproof tourist what leftist Israelis said about the Hebron settlers, he told me twice that I was "a Nazi, making a Nazi argument." Moira Zeira fed on the fear of the Palestinians suggested by the old man's body armor. As the tour bus crept up the hill toward the Tel Romeida branch of the Israeli settlement, which was no more than three trailers in the center of a Palestinian neighborhood on a hill overlooking central Hebron, she whispered into her microphone, "I don't want to alarm you . . . but we are surrounded . . . by Arabs!" The Americans muttered to each other and blinked fearfully at the quiet Palestinian houses along the roadside.

Kach people viewed Hebron with less trepidation than the American tourists. At the annual Hebron Day celebration beneath the massive Herodian walls of the Tomb of the Patriarchs, Kach supporters danced giddily. Though there were Israeli police and soldiers in the West Bank who were meant to enforce order on the settlers, they allowed them to do more or less as they pleased. In Hebron the carte blanche was more profoundly obvious because, whereas most settlers lived in hilltop enclosures isolated from Arab villages, the Hebron Israelis were in constant violent contact with Palestinian neighbors. The views and aggressive actions of the Hebron Jews would not have been out of place in the bulk of West Bank settlements; it was only their proximity to local Palestinians that gave the Hebron settlers greater scope for mayhem. Many Israelis and almost all foreign reporters attributed the harshest, most violent ideology to the fringes of the settlement movement, but it was far more prevalent than anyone wanted to admit. When the Aqsa intifada began, every bus stop in the West Bank, and many in Jerusalem, was sprayed with the slogan Kahane Was Right.

The book *Baruch Ha-Gever*, which means "Baruch, the Man," but also, in a play on the Hebrew meaning of Goldstein's given name, implies "Blessed Is the Man," was a collection of memorial essays published in 1995 in honor of the killer of twenty-nine Palestinians. In that book, Meir Kahane's son, Binyamin, who formed a group called Kahane Hai (Kahane Lives) as a hard-line replacement for the supposedly banned Kach, wrote an essay comparing the quarrel between today's leftists and the settlers with the bloody battles of 2,000 years ago between the "Hellenized" Jewish upper crust, which had taken on many of the values and behaviors of the Greeks, and the Jewish fundamentalist Maccabees who fought it:

The problem is not the Arabs—the problem is the Jews. The truth, the way we look at it, is that there has never been an Arab problem. We could have solved that problem in forty-eight hours, if only we had wanted to. The real war is not with the Arabs, but with the Hellenized Jews. . . . The people really responsible for the bloodshed are Jews scared by the Gentiles and attached to distorted Western ideas.

The first settlement I ever visited was Alon Shvut. On the bus stop outside the main gate, someone had sprayed in yellow paint: *Kahane Hai.* But Alon Shvut wasn't one of the settlements Israelis and foreign correspondents habitually referred to as "crazy." That throwaway term was reserved for Hebron and Kiryat Arba or the remote outposts overlooking Nablus, not the Jerusalem commuterland of Gush Etzion. Soon after, I met Binyamin Kahane at a memorial service for his father in the Givat Shaul cemetery, in Jerusalem. One of his followers, a pirate-radio talk show host, described himself as "another Baruch Goldstein." Kahane was not about to moderate that man's politics. "It would be very good," he told me, "if the people who say they'll cause violence against the Arabs were to do it." After a terrorist bomb exploded in the Mahane Yehuda market in Jerusalem in November 1998, I noticed posters next to the fruit stalls for a Kach man running in the mayoral election. Binyamin Kahane's views became almost mainstream during the intifada, after Palestinian gunmen killed him and his wife as they drove through the West Bank. His supporters rioted in central Jerusalem. During all those years of the peace process, when diplomats and foreign correspondents and Israeli leftists wishfully wrote off the vicious Kach line of thought as that of a lunatic fringe, Kach activists were engaged in an underground war against the Hellenized Jews, a war they believed had to be won before they could deal firmly and finally with the Arabs. What these pro-peace process observers allowed themselves to see was only the irrelevant, comical side of the right wing, like the chubby Kach activist Baruch Marzel protesting outside the chief rabbi's office in 1999 because he didn't want the pope to visit Israel. Yet it was a Kach activist who publicly pronounced an ancient curse against Prime Minister Rabin, and the assassin Yigal Amir had read *Baruch Ha-Gever.* The work against the peace process of this supposedly irrelevant

extreme right had perhaps as great a hand in the destruction of the
Oslo Accords in the end as the suicide bombs of Hamas, and it
brought Israelis far enough around to the Kach way of thinking that
the slogan Kahane Was Right could pop up on walls all over the country during the intifada with barely anyone expressing discomfort
about it.

One night early in 2003, I sat with Dubak Weinstock in a cave
near Alon Shvut where he would go to instruct the children of the
settlement at the end of their nature hikes. In the darkness outside,
the eerie howling of the jackals in the valley echoed with an uncannily human timbre. By the light of the fire in the brazier, Dubak
recalled the end of his three unhinged years, his desert wanderings.
He recounted the story of Saul, who went to the desert looking for his
father's missing donkeys. Saul came upon the prophet Samuel, who
informed him that he would be made king of Israel. Dubak likened
Saul's surprise to his own revelation. "I fled to the desert because of
my loss, and I came back to inherit a kingdom of values," he said.

As the firelight glimmered, it highlighted the lines and curves of
Dubak's full, weathered face, the ripples in his long beard, and the
glistening enthusiasm of his eyes. There were cares engraved in the
face, too, like those that must have gathered around King Saul's
mouth and across his brow with each fluctuation of fortune in his
long wars against the Philistines over the same land Dubak now con-
tested with the Palestinians. For a long time, depressed and heedless
of his life, Dubak had not cared if his fate turned out as bloody as
Saul's. In 1006 B.C. the Philistines faced Saul at Mount Gilboa in the
Galilee. Realizing the massed chariots of the enemy would win the
day, Saul killed himself rather than be captured. In the aftermath of
the rout, the Israelites split for seven years into two states: David's
kingdom of Judah in Hebron and what is now the southern West
Bank, and Israel under Saul's son Eshbaal to the north.

I thought of Dubak's emotional deadness after his son's murder.
He patrolled the remotenesses of the desert, as suicidal as Saul, waiting, wishing for the violence that would be his end. Dubak never let
that sadness take him down the hateful path of the Kahanists. Whatever he did to the Arabs was for the sake of the land and never out of
pure racism. I wondered if it was possible for the land to reconcile
him to the loss of his son without the spilling of more blood. I was to

discover that this was only my hopeful but alien Western logic at work once more.

RAMI BEN-NATAN drove Avraham Pesso to his trial. Pesso's jawline rippled with tension. Just as he girded himself when he rode the bus to Jerusalem with his bottle of black paint, Pesso appeared to the others in the car to be preparing for a dangerous mission. He knew there would be protesters outside the Jerusalem District Court who would accuse him of things far more terrible than smashing a bottle of oil paint and turpentine on a gravestone. There had been many phone calls to his home threatening to murder him.

Pesso was glad to have Ben-Natan with him. They had known each other since their military service, when Pesso was in a special unit trained to free hostages captured by terrorists and Ben-Natan was a naval officer who offered Pesso a room in his apartment to use as a part-time art studio. Except for his friendship with Ben-Natan, the period of his army days was a dreadful time for Pesso. He entered the army with a firm belief in the unity of Israel. In 1977 he voted for Menachem Begin's Likud Party. As the descendant of a family of Middle Eastern rather than European origin, Pesso was a natural Likud voter. His father served time in a British jail before the foundation of the Israeli state for his role as an activist in the rightist Lehi militia, which often carried out operations with Begin's Irgun force. But Pesso had been particularly approving of the way Begin made his peace deal with Egypt, drawing opposition politicians into his cabinet so that the Camp David Accords wouldn't split the nation. Even Begin couldn't prevent the divisions from showing, however, when he took Israel into the Lebanon War, a conflict that left the soldier Pesso with a different feeling than the sense of belonging that came to Dubak Weinstock and others who fought in Israel's earlier victories. Pesso's unit saw one day of action. Eleven of his comrades died, and the survivors spent the rest of the war sitting around miserably behind the lines. The natural Likud voter became a confirmed leftist who hated the idea that Israeli soldiers could be dragged into an unnecessary conflict like the one in Lebanon by nationalist hard-liners. To Pesso, there was little difference between the West Bank and Beirut.

It was the state prosecutor who filed the charges Pesso would answer in court. Pesso was accused of damaging public property and desecrating a tomb. The state asked the court to jail Pesso for three years on each charge. Pesso had never been in a courtroom as the accused before, but here he was, facing criminal charges. On the road to Jerusalem, Ben-Natan told him a dozen times not to worry, but Pesso still couldn't believe that his government, the State of Israel, was against him so firmly. At the entrance to the court, police separated the two sets of demonstrators: a crowd of right-wingers, including Baruch Marzel of Kach, called out that Pesso was a murderer, while a group of leftists shouted their support for him. Pesso walked silently between these two fields of rage for two years as the hearings progressed. After the first day, one of Israel's biggest newspapers ran a headline: "Storm in the Court of the Painter Who Desecrated the Grave of Baruch Goldstein."

After the first painting of the hillside on the road to the Ela Valley, Pesso worked little during the trial. He couldn't concentrate. He needed to be clean, free in front of his canvas, so that he could explode onto it, just as he had brought his energy down on Goldstein's grave in a sudden torrent. He was too disturbed to paint. His wife came around to supporting what he had done eventually, though at first Ronli was a little frightened by the violent, screaming man she saw in the television footage of Pesso at the grave. Her family was of German origin, stiff-necked by the standards of Israelis, and such demonstrativeness was alien to them. She worried, too, about her children. They in turn were fearful for what might happen to their parents. After the Rabin assassination, it was clear even to youngsters that any Israeli could become the victim of political violence. Little Noga, barely more than a toddler, sought her mother's arms, wanting to be held more than she had before the trial. Uriah, who was ten, listened quietly and attentively to everything that passed between Pesso and Ronli.

Each time Pesso went to Jerusalem for another hearing, he stared at the judge, a religious man who wore a crocheted yarmulke. Pesso couldn't figure him out. It was a source of great tension for the painter, who felt secure about the justification for what he had done but feared the judge with the *kippah srugah*—the symbol of the nationalist religious movement—on his head might not be politically impartial. For much of the trial Baruch Goldstein's father watched the proceedings too. Ben-Natan didn't want the father to have a chance to discuss his feelings about his son's desecrated tomb when he took the stand, so he questioned him quickly and directly to ascertain that Pesso did no permanent damage to the grave: "You are aware that two hours after Pesso's action, the tomb was as good as new? He didn't spray acid or anything like that. He took some turpentine and black oil paint from his studio, and this is something which can be wiped off very easily." Goldstein's father answered quietly, not argumentatively. Ben-Natan had confirmed for the court that the grave hadn't been tarnished for more than a couple of hours, and he had avoided an emotional appeal from the father. When Pesso testified, he turned to Goldstein's father and apologized.

Even as Pesso's trial dragged on, the attention his action brought to Goldstein's grave had its effect in the Knesset. In 1998 a legislator from the left-wing Meretz Party, Ran Cohen, who had become a friend of Pesso's, secured passage of the Law Against Construction of Memorials in Memory of Perpetrators of Terror. The law mandated the removal of all the paraphernalia of a synagogue around Goldstein's tomb, so that it should stand as a plain grave. Pesso felt vindicated by the public's elected representatives, though not yet by the court. In his closing argument, Rami Ben-Natan told the judge it made no sense for the state to press for Pesso's imprisonment as a result of his rage against a symbol that the Knesset had subsequently outlawed. "This is not just a vandalism case. Pesso did not kick over a streetlight. He kicked over the light that illuminated the grave of a disgusting murderer." Ben-Natan went on, "The responsibility of this court is to proclaim to the world that the rule of law in the State of Israel does not protect a monument erected to a killer; that the State of Israel is not blind to the evil that the monument represents." Ben-Natan argued that the judge should accept Pesso's plea bargain, under which he would receive a symbolic sentence of one hour of community service, because "Pesso already has served the public" by drawing attention to Goldstein's shrine and setting in motion events that led to the Knesset's law. To Pesso's relief, the judge agreed to the plea deal. Pesso would have no criminal record, but he would donate one of his paintings to a joint Arab-Jewish community center in Jaffa as reparation to the government.

Cohen's new law seemed like a victory for Pesso. Once the trial was over, he could feel that his action had accomplished something concrete. Yet Goldstein's grave remained a place of pilgrimage for settlers and religious right-wingers in Israel. When Palestinians killed a settler at a remote outpost near Hebron in early 2003, an argument broke out between his relatives and friends. Some wanted him buried next to his hero, Goldstein, while others said the gunman's tomb was too sacred for anyone else to be laid to rest there. Meanwhile, the frustration among leftists after Rabin's death only grew more concentrated during the Aqsa intifada. Even Pesso began to believe that the Palestinians could never make peace with Israel.

Pesso's son Uriah came to him one day, after there had been another terrorist attack against Israelis. The boy, now a teenager, felt a hopelessness that afflicted many moderate Israelis during the worst of the intifada. "What's the point of continuing to live in a country like this?" he said. "There's no future."

Pesso found it hard to think of anything but banalities in response. At last, he said, "Everyone should leave the world a bit better than he found it. Be honest. Prove yourself. Listen to other people. It's difficult, but it's beautiful." Pesso recalled the time when he named Uriah. He chose the name from the Bible. Uriah the Hittite was the husband of Bathsheba and a loyal officer in King David's army. While Uriah was on campaign, David seduced Bathsheba, who became pregnant with his child. The king tried to persuade Uriah to go home and sleep with his wife, thus getting David off the hook for the pregnancy. But Uriah insisted on staying in the field with his troops. So David ordered his general to place Uriah in the front rank of his army, then to retreat so that Uriah would be isolated and killed. After Uriah's slaughter, David married Bathsheba. Pesso had an unusual interpretation of the biblical story. "I called you Uriah because the name represents loyalty," Pesso told his son. "In his situation, I would wish to be perfectly loyal to the man I admire. David sat before God, so Uriah told himself not to confront the king, even over his wife. I try to imagine the person you will grow up to be, Uriah. You're like your mother: you're quiet, smart; you read a lot; you stay away from confrontation. Me, you know, where there's confrontation I go to the middle of it. Like with the Goldstein thing, right?"

Uriah spoke up. "I wouldn't have done what you did to Goldstein's grave. But I understand why you did it."

That was all that Pesso wanted. "Yes, well, I'm not Uriah, am I?"
"No," the boy replied. "You're not Uriah."

IN THE VILLAGE of a-Twani, Ibrahim Abu Jundiyeh pulled some twigs of thorn brush from a bundle in the darkness to use as kindling. He lit the fire, bordered by four old stones set in a square, and placed his heavy black kettle in the flames. The small fire licked around the scorched metal and dancingly illuminated the stygian interior of Abu Jundiyeh's temporary home—a stable built in the time of Turkish rule over Palestine. His family, which included nine children, shared the muddy floor with their goats. For stools, we sat on the sacks of grain with which he fed his animals. His three-year-old son stood in the doorway urinating. The winter wind came sharp through the low entrance, from which the diffuse light of a rainy day reflected a headachy dullness into the blockhouse. One of the villagers allowed Abu Jundiyeh to move his family into this stable, because heavy rain washed down the steep hillside through the tiny village and flooded him out of the single canvas tent where they had been living. Abu Jundiyeh came to a-Twani from his own village, a-Toba, a few weeks before, when settlers from Maon sent Israeli soldiers to kick them out. The land had been declared a "closed military zone," which meant that effectively it was being annexed to Maon. In a-Toba, Abu Jundiyeh's home had been a cave carved out of the mountainside. Its doorway was elaborately etched in the rock to resemble the keystone and columns of a far more sumptuous dwelling. Within, it would have appeared little different from the rough stable where I found him, except that it was his: twenty-five yards square, with different levels cut into the earth to make a slight separation between the family's beds and the pen of its animals, and niches for candles in the cave walls. "In the cave, our life was happy and joyous," said Abu Jundiyeh. In the winter firelight, it was hard to imagine a life more primitive than Abu Jundiyeh's. But the fact that it was unchanged, unameliorated in the centuries since his cave was chiseled from the hillside must have instilled some comfort within its rough walls that was lacking in the chilly stable.

When I finished my tea with Abu Jundiyeh, I stepped out of the stable and took a breath of air that, though fuming with the scent of goat droppings from the animal pens all around, was not nearly as choking as the damp, fetid atmosphere inside. Down the hill to my left was the road to Hebron, a few miles away. To the right, around a bend in the rocky valley, was the forty acres of grazing land of which Ibrahim Abu Jundiyeh had been stripped. Above the cliffs on the other side of the wadi were the red, pitched roofs of Maon, bright through the cloudy dullness of the day. Here was the essence of Dubak Weinstock's Middle Eastern logic, and it was unashamed. All over the West Bank, those red roofs marked the Israeli contribution to the undermining of the Oslo peace process, a thwarting that the Palestinian violence of the intifada allowed Israelis to blame entirely on their opponents. The failure of the Israeli left to counter the settlers' logic was at the heart of the breakdown in progress to peace. In fact, it was why peace never truly came any nearer than it had been before the leaders signed the Oslo agreement.

There were some among Zionism's early leaders who foresaw the problems of attaching themselves to the concept of sovereignty or control over the land of Palestine. Theodor Herzl, the iconic Zionist campaigner, believed it was more important to unite Jews behind an idea of their nation, rather than that Jews materially should possess land that in turn would define those who lived upon it as part of a nation. Decades before Israel's foundation Ahad Ha'am, an early opponent of the mainstream Zionist leadership, identified among the new settlers in Palestine "a tendency to despotism, as always happens when a slave becomes a master." This tyranny was revealed in the way the Zionist establishment treated marginal subgroups of Jews and new Jewish immigrants, but it was most evident in the approach to Palestinians, whose rented land was bought out by the Jewish pioneers and who often ended up as poorly paid laborers on the Zionist farms. Those first socialist leaders of the Jewish yishuv in Palestine followed a settlement line that their leftist heirs finally abandoned during the Oslo years. By then it was too late to halt, for the right wing had learned those values, as Dubak Weinstock had in his youth movement, and refused to desist in obedience to the shift by the left.

Berl Katznelson, who's often called the leading ideologist of the prestate Zionists, described Zionism as "an enterprise of conquest. . . . It is not by chance we use revolutionary terms when speaking of settlement." Early Zionist propaganda movies of the 1930s, like *Land of*

Promise and *Adamah* (Land), employed the styles of Soviet art and cinema to bring that muscular, revolutionary feeling to the screen. When the Six-Day War brought Israel new territories, there were many among the political leadership who wanted to give the West Bank back to Jordan in return for a peace deal. But those still clinging tightest to their Zionist ideals insisted otherwise. A year after the war, Defense Minister Moshe Dayan argued that "the first step [in what to do about the West Bank] is the traditional one in the realm of action in the State of Israel: settlement."

The new era of settlement in the West Bank based itself around a profoundly messianic and religious vision of the land that supplanted the secularism of the earlier Zionists. Nationalism and possession of the earth, however, remained the common elements. Rabbi Avraham Kook, whose messianic reading of Jewish history was the essence of the settlement movement, believed the British government's declaration of support for a Jewish home in Palestine in 1917 marked the opening of an era of redemption for the Jews. The traditional Jewish concept of the Messiah is that he alone may be the redeemer and humans ought not to try to hasten his coming by their actions, except by performing the 613 mitzvahs, commandments laid out by ancient rabbis. Yet Kook and his son Zvi Yehuda, the spiritual leader of the settlers during the years after Israel conquered the West Bank, saw the secular Zionists as unwitting emissaries of the savior. Essentially, Kook eschewed traditional Jewish thought by making possession of the land of Israel the key to redemption. He founded the Merkaz Ha-Rav yeshiva, one of whose rabbis went to the hill of Kfar Etzion three months after the Six-Day War and established a new settlement there. The settlements emphasized the biblical and historical connections of their location: Beit El, where Jacob dreamed of the ladder to heaven; Shiloh, which first housed the tabernacle; Betar, where the second Jewish revolt against the Romans was finally crushed; and, of course, Kfar Etzion, where the Zionist defenders were slaughtered by Jordanian troops and a local Palestinian rabble in 1948.

As the settlers worked single-mindedly to possess the land, successive Israeli governments were divided in their approach to the new communities. Consequently, even during the times of the Oslo peace agreement, leftists protested against the settlements while their repre-

sentatives in the government continued to fund a doubling of the settler population. In the face of a much more powerful yet timid government, the settlers were united by a religio-political ideology that
was fearless and successful. That was why Israel's most famous author,
Amos Oz, compared the settlers to Hizballah, the fundamentalist Shia
militia whose tiny force of guerrillas compelled the mighty Israeli
army to end its long occupation of southern Lebanon. Oz called the
settlement ideology "Hizballah Judaism." A mainstream settler leader,
Yisrael Harel, responded that in Israel there were Jews, who lived by
the Bible and therefore supported the settlements, and mere Israelis,
who wanted to be a satellite of the West and, by implication, had forgotten their Jewishness. It was exactly what Binyamin Kahane wrote
in *Baruch Ha-Gever.*

Settler leaders understood that this was a battle over the values
that would underpin Israeli society into the future. In 2002 a forbid-
ding former general, Effi Eitam, took over as leader of the National
Religious Party, the main representative in the Knesset of the settlements, and became a cabinet minister. When I met him, he told me
he saw himself as a militant political leader who modeled himself on
King David, fighting for God's way. He argued that the Palestinians
ought to receive an independent state, but that it should be located in
the Egyptian Sinai Desert, "where there is space for them." Still,
Eitam's main concern was what he believed to be a cultural dilution
of Judaism in Israel by the destructive influence of Western television
and liberal values promoted by the Israeli left.

The left made its plays in that cultural war too. For decades, Israeli
schoolchildren had been taken to the old Herodian fortress at Masada
to see where 967 Zealots and their families killed themselves in A.D. 73
rather than face enslavement or death at the hands of the Romans
who besieged them. The Israeli army's tank corps swore in their cadets
in ceremonies at Masada, too, looking down the Roman siege ramp,
standing next to the ancient synagogue where the Zealots decided on
their suicidal course. In 1996 two Jerusalem high-school principals
decided to change the tours. Instead of hearing of the heroic sacrifice
on top of the orange rock and of the parallels to Israel's present, the
students would now receive a purely historical account of what happened and where. The principals argued that it was inappropriate to
present high-schoolers with the desperate, backs-to-the-wall national

myth of Masada in an age when Israel's struggle to defend itself against obliteration was over; the country was a nuclear power, after all. It was a direct challenge to rightists and settlers, whose ideology depended on the notion that the settlements provided a concrete military, defensive asset for Israel against a real, existential threat. The right insisted that the Zealots, who refused to subsume their national aspirations to a foreign, Roman resolution of their conflict, provided a model for the way Israel ought now to behave in the face of U.S. and European pressure to compromise over the land of the West Bank. A leader of the National Religious Party, Avner Shaki, told me the purely historical tours of Masada would miss the point: "Youth will know the facts about Masada, but what will they know about the values of the people who died there?"

Above the valley where Ibrahim Abu Jundiyeh had grazed his goats, I went to see this conflict between the left and right enacted at the settlement of Maon. It was the battle between those for whom nationalism was reserved for boring, pompous state ceremonies and those who felt it beneath their feet whenever they stepped across the land. A half-mile from Maon there was a trailer, erected illegally in just the way many settlements or their satellites began, on a hilltop of pitted rock so barren in the thin gray light between night and dawn that it seemed like a moonscape. The settlers called it Maon Farm. It happened that in late 1999, Prime Minister Ehud Barak wanted to prevent new outposts gaining irreversible footholds, though he continued to fund massive building within the boundaries of existing communities. As the sun rose pink, I walked up the hill to Maon Farm. Silhouetted against the roseate sky, unarmed soldiers of the Givati Brigade manhandled settlers away from the huts. The settlers rushed about, trying to get back to the huts and in turn being hauled away again. On a crest, I saw the bobbing outlines of a group of settlers shrouded in their white *talits,* making the dawn prayer. Eventually all the settlers were dragged away and the newspaper and television correspondents dispersed to report this tiny step in the peace process.

Maon Farm was more than a simple, daily story for me. Halfway down the hill, I talked with a group of young settlers who alerted me for the first time to the sense of abandonment by the original leftist proponents of Zionism that I would later hear so profoundly from Dubak Weinstock. They had learned how to settle the land from the left, but now that it was inconvenient for the weak, soft, Westernized people in Tel Aviv, it was deemed time to abandon Zionism, to drag Jews away from their land. David Lapid, a twenty-four-year-old with a black yarmulke, a thick beard, and side curls, had come in the middle of the night from Kiryat Arba to defend Maon Farm. Palestinians killed his father, Mordechai, and brother Shalom in Hebron in 1993: they were a sacrifice to the settlements. "Zionism is like a woman that is pregnant, and the leftists think they can abort the baby," Lapid said. "But I am the baby, and I am screaming that I want to live." He said he would come back as soon as the soldiers cleared out.

MERAV BROUGHT THE MAN who would become her second husband to Tel Aviv to visit her brother, Avraham Pesso. She came with her two children from her first marriage. Pesso liked the man, an immigrant from South America. Merav's first husband battered her, and Pesso was glad to see a gentleness and rationality about the way this new match treated her. The Aqsa intifada had just started and many Israelis were in a state of shock and depression at the pace with which violence appeared once more to have swamped them, but Merav was excited and voluble. She talked animatedly about the plans the couple had: "And we're going to live in Itamar, and we're—"

Pesso stopped her. "What? You're going to live where?"

"Itamar . . ." Merav's excitement ebbed as she realized that her brother was about to explode. Itamar was a settlement of religious Israelis, isolated east of Nablus, its tip reaching the slopes directly above the Palestinian village of Beit Furiq. Merav became religious when she first married, and although she wasn't ideological, she had always been more right-wing than her brother. Pesso had thought she was content to stay in Jerusalem. Itamar's reputation among Israelis was as part of the hard core of the settlements, though on my visits there I noted the large number of trailers housing new immigrants from the former Soviet states and Argentina who spoke stammering Hebrew and seemed to have little idea exactly where they were or why anyone should want them not to be there. The mayor of Itamar took me to a rock on the farthest hilltop inside the settlement fence and told me it was the burial place of Gideon, a leader of Israel's army in the Book of Judges.

"You're completely crazy," Pesso said. "I don't care if you want to go out there and die, but you're putting your kids at risk."

"We get a small apartment for a few hundred shekels a month," Merav said.

"Just to have a cheap place to live you'll risk your kids?" The news got under Pesso's skin. He stood and paced the room. "You're not responsible and rational if you take risks with your children."

"We won't be there very long," Merav said. She gestured to her future husband, who was an engineer. "He has to work somewhere and he can't drive every day to Tel Aviv on those roads. It's too risky with all the shootings. We won't be there for long, Avi."

"You shouldn't be there at all. *We* shouldn't be there. None of us Israelis." Pesso understood that, like many of the settlers, his sister's choice was based largely on economic factors. The political issues were remote and, in any case, easier to overcome when you were a religious Jew, as she was, who had been fed nationalist propaganda about the land. "Remember that someone could die on your account," he told her. "For me, if there were soldiers who might die because they had to protect me, I'd leave. Immediately. Not enough people died already? After one death, I would right away take my suitcase and leave. That's it. Never mind where I lived, in which country or whatever. Because the land doesn't belong to anybody and it's not worth a life."

After a silence, Merav's fiancé tried to lighten the mood. He invited Pesso to come and visit them in Itamar. Pesso cooled down. This was his sister, whom he loved, and her new partner was a good man. They weren't the cause of the violent situation in the settlements, and they shouldn't have to suffer all his anger about it. But anyway he was not a good visitor. Even when Merav lived in Tel Aviv, she used to have to come to him. Largely it was laziness, but also Pesso was limited because he didn't possess a driver's license. "No, no," he said. "The only time I went to the territories was when I did what I did at Goldstein's grave."

As the intifada continued, Pesso kept away from political pronouncements. Although the Israeli media came to him for comments from time to time, he always refused them. His concerns were more personal. He worried about his sister at home in Itamar and on the deadly roads past Nablus and its surrounding villages. He struggled to instill hope for the future in his son Uriah. He led a demonstration of local residents against a café that played loud music until the small hours. His friends joked that, typically, Pesso was the only one in the crowd of polite, middle-class protesters who managed to get so carried away, shouting and shoving, that the police arrested him.

Then, in the spring of 2003, Pesso detected something positive that he among Israeli leftists was almost uniquely able to understand. In February, Israel's left suffered a devastating defeat in the general election, and Labor's feuding panjandrums appeared indecently determined to strangle all remaining integrity from the party that backed the peace accords with the Palestinians. As usual, Pesso went for his regular Friday shopping trip to the Shuk Ha-Carmel, an open-air market in southern Tel Aviv. All the vendors were, like Pesso, of Middle Eastern, not European, origin. The place was so bellicosely right-wing that nationalist politicians on campaign photo ops were always greeted with the fervent atmosphere of a soccer stadium, while misguided leftist leaders who dared set foot there often found themselves pelted with eggs and soft fruit. Pesso got into conversations with the fishmongers and vegetable vendors whom he frequented each week. They knew who he was, and they knew his politics. At first, many of them refused to listen to his opinions, but over the years they had begun to debate him, always aggressively and at full volume. Anyone other than Pesso probably would have been tossed out of the market, but this time Pesso noticed something different.

"Fuck the settlers in Hebron," Pesso said.

"That's right, screw them," said one of the vendors.

It happened three times as Pesso passed through the market, making his purchases. He cursed the settlers, and these deeply nationalistic, chauvinistic traders joined in.

When he left the market, Pesso went to Rami Ben-Natan and told him what had happened. Ben-Natan, who would never have dared express such opinions among the roughnecks at the market, was amazed. "You see," Pesso said, "something really has changed."

WE SAT IN A CIRCLE at the top of the cliff. The red rock crumbled away to the Dead Sea, 1,200 feet below us. Grackles floated and dipped on the thermals from the bright water. It was the edge of the Judean Desert, and the center of the silence.

Rabbi Mike Comins brought us here, a group of American Jewish students and me, to understand the desert and to let it help us find something within ourselves. He began with a chant, the words taken from an old Eastern European Hasidic song and the melody drawn from a yoga meditation. "In the desert, your past and future don't matter," the rabbi said softly. "Here you are only one water bottle away from death. All that matters is now. Focus on the present, on yourself in the moment." We began to hike in silence, listening to our breathing and following the contact of our feet with the earth. After climbing 1,000 feet into the hills and wadis, we split up. The rabbi told us to take an hour and find a spot where we couldn't see anyone else. And sit there alone. "Most people come to the desert to conquer it. Let's let it soak us up instead."

I found a promontory of rock overlooking a deep canyon. At first my mind was full, observing that the distant hills were roughened by parallel goat tracks until they looked like the skin of a dusty elephant, or thinking about biblical times, when this place was a refuge for hermits and kings. Then the silence caught me. I listened, and as the hot wind dropped, I noticed that there was nothing: no distant city babble of car engines and horns, not even the crackling footfalls of animals and the warbling of birds, the noises one experiences as part of the quiet of a forest. I was at the center of a refuge that was simple and pure and empty. I wanted to stay there forever.

The desert gave an even stronger sense of cleansing to Dubak Weinstock. The land absorbed him and, in turn, he imbibed its values, and the traditions and philosophy of those who lived on it. With the help of the Jewish National Fund, Weinstock purchased a valley behind Kfar Etzion from a Palestinian who emigrated from Beit Jala to Chile. Weinstock used it as a base for his desert trips. After he took schoolchildren or soldiers or left-wingers into the sands, he would bring them to his cave in the valley. It was once the home of a shepherd-farmer from the wadi, like the one Ibrahim Abu Jundiyeh lost near Maon. One winter morning, I sat in the grotto with Weinstock as the rain fell on the long grass by the door. I asked him about the feeling of the land to which he often referred. What was it?

"What you're feeling now, in this cave," he said. "When you

return home to Jerusalem and try to remember it, what will you recall?"

"I would think of the smell of the stone, which is a little damp," I said.

"If you brought that smell home, your girlfriend would throw you out, but you enjoy it here."

"And I'd think of the rain outside, and the noise of the chickens on the other crest of the valley in their coops. Does all this nature speak to you?"

Dubak nodded. "It doesn't talk to me, but it tells me things."

Since 1998 when he began to take Israeli military cadets to the desert, Weinstock brought what he called "the song of the land" to 13,700 soldiers in five years. It was an unofficial arrangement that he tried to keep secret. If a left-wing Israeli politician heard about it, Weinstock feared the officers school would be forced to halt the trips. He funded his work, the food he gave the soldiers and the administrative arrangements, with donations from a retired New Jersey gas-company owner named Marcel Lindenbaum. Lindenbaum, who was no particular supporter of the settlements, backed Weinstock because he feared the mutual incomprehension and hatred of left and right in Israel could lead to even greater violence than the death of the prime minister. That Dubak found forgiveness for the left wing in the desert gave Lindenbaum hope that the leftists who went there with Dubak would find understanding for the right.

There was something in Lindenbaum's story that made him the fitting man to support Weinstock. Born in 1930, Lindenbaum fled Belgium in 1940. His father, a diamond merchant, took the family just across the border into France. The German army kept advancing, and the Lindenbaums ran south to Biarritz. From there, they soon had to flee to Spain, and then Portugal. The United States allowed them entry on a transit visa to Venezuela, but Lindenbaum's father secured permission to remain in New York. As I talked to Lindenbaum in his part-time home in the Rehavia neighborhood of Jerusalem, it struck me that this was the very history of Jews to which Dubak was reacting—when threatened, powerless, and landless Jews throughout history were inevitably forced to flee like the Lindenbaums. Dubak believed that if the land was yours, you could face down the attack in confidence. That adherence to the land might be more dangerous than flight, but it was preferable, nevertheless, and that was where the Western and Middle Eastern logics diverged.

With Dubak Weinstock and his friend Miro Cohen, a shepherd and security officer at the Tekoa settlement, a few miles deeper into the desert from Weinstock's home at Alon Shvut, I walked down a narrow path on the steep cliff of Wadi Tekoa. Cohen's big yellow Canaan dog, Shai, went ahead. The dog led us to the cave. Two days before, Cohen had discovered the bodies of two boys from Tekoa, bludgeoned to death with boulders. Around the doorway purple Syrian thistles climbed the rock. Inside the cave, Cohen showed me where he found the bodies. Kobi Mandell was on the right, Yossi Ezran on the left. Kobi was found in a sitting position, which led Cohen to believe that the boys knew their murderers. He surmised they were local Palestinian shepherds. Probably the boys sat with them for a drink of water. The heads of the two youngsters were smashed, their eyeballs hanging by single tendons somewhere behind their ears and all the bones of their cheeks and jaws crushed. Even two days later the sandy floor of the cave was crusted brown with dried blood. Spatterings of gore blotted the low roof of the cave and marked the heavy rocks that had been used to kill the boys.

Later that day, teenage friends of the two dead boys sang a song around their campfire at a spring on the path that led from their settlement to the fatal cave:

> When I die, something of you will die with me.
> When you die, something of me will die with you.
> All of us are one living tissue.

After the singing, Miro Cohen picked up the trash the kids had left behind and fed their leftover chicken barbecue to Shai. As I walked up the hill with Dubak, I watched Miro work, alone in the valley except for his fierce yellow dog. He used to tell the children of Tekoa, including the two dead boys, that it was possible to live with the local Palestinians, to befriend them as he had done. Now all he wanted was to kill the men who had crushed these two boys.

Dubak Weinstock felt an even deeper wound than Miro Cohen. The lingering pain of his son's death was a gash in his own living tissue. For years it moved him through the most dangerous places without fear, sure that his life would end on the mountains or in the valleys, butchered alone. He was not scared. At night, in the early days of the intifada, he drove his jeep around the sharp, slow corners of the road near Tsurif, a Palestinian village where Hamas was strong and weapons were plentiful. In the desert, he waited for the barrel of a gun to emerge from cars overtaking him. He would watch a beat-up Palestinian car coming in his rearview mirror—"Eh, what's this?"—and follow it into his sideview mirror—"Ah-ha"—then stare glumly at the vehicle innocently accelerating away, as though he were disappointed that this had not been the time of reckoning. If he died, it would be on the land. That would be a kind of revenge for Yitzhak's death, as if to prove what he said about the Palestinians exerting all their efforts toward Jewish graves, while the Jews won the territory around them. Beneath the oak at Alon Shvut, I once asked Dubak if there could be any solution, by Middle Eastern logic, to the conflict with the Palestinians. "Even among the Bedouin, who live by that Middle Eastern logic, if there's a murder, they meet to arrange a *sulha,* a reconciliation," I said.

"Blood is very cheap here," Dubak said. "If you kill, you can make a *sulha;* you'll bring me money or goods to compensate. But if you take my land, it's a different matter. This conflict is not about blood, it's about land, and for that there can be no reparation."

This was what lay beyond the reckoning of the Israeli left. In some ways, Dubak found, even the settlers didn't want to recognize the brutal logic on which they depended. The police investigated him nine times over the years. Sometimes he would go out at night to chop down Palestinian olive groves, after Arabs had destroyed trees in the orchards of Alon Shvut, or to plant spikes in the streets of Arab villages after Palestinians put nails on the settlers' roads, or to administer a mild beating to Palestinians stealing apples. It was risky to go about at night doing such things, and it put him in conflict with the police. There were disputes, too, with the new head of the Gush Etzion Regional Council, who replaced Dubak's old friend Shiloh Gal and gradually stripped the ranger of his responsibilities. The Shin Bet still watched him, assigning at least three informers from Alon Shvut to keep an eye on his nocturnal activities. One of the snitches had been a close friend of Dubak's, and a few years later, he still pointed out the man's house as "the home of Weiss, the *shtinker* who betrayed me." Colonel Noam Tibon, a respected battalion commander respon-

sible for Dubak's region of the West Bank, told him things were
changing. The settlements of Gush Etzion were becoming more
middle-class and less welcoming to a cowboy, no matter how grateful
they ought to have been for his sacrifices. "The days of the pioneers
are over here, Dubak," the colonel said.

Dubak believed that, while his community was happy for him to
do its dirty work, it would not stand by him if the police ever jailed
him. Only so long as he stayed in the darkness or in the wide emptiness of the desert would he be acceptable. His financial backer, Lindenbaum, urged him to find a compromise with the council head, but
Dubak couldn't bring himself to do it. Increasingly he felt he had no
place in his own society. Before the election of 2001, when the settlers'
old champion Ariel Sharon ran against the Labor prime minister Ehud
Barak, Dubak at first considered voting for the right-winger. Then he
looked one day at the photo on the wall of his living room. It was a
panorama of Yamit, the Sinai settlement Sharon evacuated and tore
down as part of Begin's peace deal with Egypt. No, thought Dubak, I
won't vote for him. I don't trust him not to do the same thing here.

The three years Dubak spent in the desert after Yitzhak died had
inured him to loneliness, he thought. He was a man of great warmth
and vivacity—when he had surgery under a local anesthetic, he made
the surgeon laugh so much the doctor had to put him under to preserve his concentration. Yet emotionally he was distant, even from
his four remaining children and his wife. In 2003 he retired from his
job with the regional council, though he decided to continue privately with his desert tours for the soldiers. His eldest son, Moshe,
saw the bitterness and alienation Dubak felt toward his own community and confronted him. "Listen, I don't understand," he said. "I
don't know anyone that people like so tremendously and yet who
hates people so much."

The blankness that Dubak felt on the day he buried his son
Yitzhak was only a screen for the real anger and hatred that lay
beneath. The police suspected what smoldered there. For almost a
decade, they refused to give him a gun license, despite the dangerous
places to which his job took him and the ease with which most settlers obtain their permits. In 2003 he applied again for the permit and
went for an interview at the Gush Etzion police station. "Don't worry,
I'm not just going to kill an Arab," he said. "I don't think that would

bring me any comfort. If I have a chance to kill the men who murdered my son, I will. I'm not afraid of what you would do to me. But you don't have to worry about anything else." Dubak left with a gun license and began to keep an Uzi on the front seat of his Land Rover. He thought of taking revenge on the killers, whose attack Dubak learned from Israeli authorities had been coordinated by the Hamas military wing leader Muhammed Deif. He believed he had an idea of where the murderers might be, but it was too complicated, too dense a Palestinian town for him to get through to them. In any case, another of his boys had already extracted a kind of vengeance.

Dubak's son Arieh spent his compulsory military service in the elite Egoz unit at the height of Operation Defensive Shield, when the Israeli army reconquered every city in the West Bank in spring 2002. Under the rules of the army, Arieh was exempted from combat duty because he had lost a brother in a terrorist attack. But Dubak signed a letter authorizing his son to waive the exemption, and Arieh went to a platoon on the edge of one of the largest Palestinian towns near the border of the West Bank close to Tel Aviv. There a gunfight broke out. Palestinians fired at an army checkpoint on the outskirts of the town. The soldiers returned fire, but couldn't take out the shooters. Arieh dashed into the Palestinian town and began to outflank the gunmen. Some of his comrades went with him, but he left them behind in his eagerness, so fast did he charge through the narrow, hostile lanes of the town. The nineteen-year-old ambushed the gunmen and killed two. Three others escaped, though Arieh saw that he had wounded them. He scooped up their guns and began to run back to his unit. While he was still running out of the Palestinian town, he pulled his cell phone from his pocket and dialed his father.

Dubak Weinstock answered his cellular and heard panting. Then came the excited, breathless voice of his son: "Father, Father, there is revenge. I killed two."

"When?" Dubak said.

"Two minutes ago. Father, there's revenge."

Dubak realized from the heavy breathing that his son wasn't finished with the operation yet. He didn't want to say too much while the boy was still in danger. It might make Arieh emotional, and in combat that could lead to a fatal mistake. "Great," Dubak said. "Thank you." He ended the call. Then he cried.

CHAPTER EIGHT

Matatya's Café

Arab Jews and the European Elite

It's as though we bear a stigma. A stigma of blood from the womb.
—RAMI DANON AND AMNON LEVI, *MIDNIGHT PRAYER*

THE FIRST VERSE in the song of Haim Uliel's life was the shouting and the chanting, and the Berber tabla rhythm and the clapping of the hands and the singer's fluttering eighth notes, and the money and the fights and the arak and the sweat, and the memory of Moroccan nights unknown and the forgetting of the suffering day, and his father's café. Matatya Uliel opened the first coffee shop in Sderot in 1960, six years after he emigrated from Morocco to Israel and asked to live in the heart of his people's longing, Jerusalem. The Jewish Agency officials who welcomed Matatya and the other Moroccans explained that Sderot was five minutes from Jerusalem and would be a good place for them. When they arrived in Sderot, they found themselves distant from the holy city, but five minutes from hostile Gaza, planted along the country's border to cement the lines on the UN maps into demographic facts on the ground. Dumped and forgotten, the Moroccans settled into the hard life of Sderot, mostly working at low wages for the kibbutz collectives that ringed their small town. Matatya Uliel's café gave them small solace at the end of the workday. Around 5 P.M., men in grimy undershirts with black-bronzed arms came to drink a beer at the café. The little boy who played there remembered the warmth of these men in their exhausted repose, eating their bowls of red or green *kubbeh* soup, chatting in the Arabic of the Maghreb, and dealing a hand of cards.

On Saturday nights, Matatya's café shed the workmen with their honest fatigue. It became the place of gangsters, whose response to the rough welcome of the Zionist establishment was to eschew the manual labor offered to North African immigrants. They turned to crime and made the kind of money that Matatya's late-afternoon clients could only imagine. They came to the Moroccan *hafleh,* the party, late on Saturday. The little boy Haim crept in to watch too. He noticed that the men seemed much too old to be married to the young women who accompanied them. They came from all over the northern Negev, from Netivot and Kiryat Malakhi and some from as far away as Beersheba, to see the best-known Moroccan musicians in Israel. The singers performed their Arabic songs all over the country at small public venues like the café: Raymond Abecassis, Suleiman, Sheikh Mouijoa. Competing to show their love of the music and appreciation of the singers, the gangsters showily handed over their *ghrammeh,* the almost devotional donation to the singer that would equal the monthly wage of one of Matatya's regular customers. They shimmied to the front of the café, arms out wide and hips bumping in stop-time, carving arabesques in the air with their hands, and plastered the banknotes onto the singer's forehead or breast, sticking them there with sweat or spit. From the dark corners, the little boy watched and listened and began to compose the song of his life.

Matatya Uliel brought his family to Israel from Fez, though his wife was born in a village nearby and the Uliels had lived for generations a little farther south in the small town of Sefrou. Jews had lived in Sefrou since the Romans exiled them from their province of Palaestina. The Jews of Fez had been prominent throughout Morocco's history as learned men and medical doctors. When Morocco's French colonial overlords pulled out, Jews feared Arab reprisals for the establishment of Israel, and immigration officials from the Jewish Agency gave the final push, so that within a few years 250,000 Jews left for Israel. Matatya brought two children and his wife with him to the immigrant camp at Sderot. Haim was the first child born in Israel, just after the family progressed from a tent to a tin shack. Until he opened his café, Matatya worked on the local kibbutz farms as a laborer.

In the camp and at Matatya's café, Haim Uliel began performing at the age of nine, singing the traditional songs of Morocco. As he grew up, it didn't occur to him that these songs could be his career. The music of Israel was not Moroccan. Israeli radio played the campfire songs of the kibbutzniks. Eastern European Ashkenazi Jews founded the collective farms and saw themselves as the pioneers on whom the responsibility for building the country rested. They therefore constituted the elite. Their music, dedicated to the "Land of Israel, beautiful and old," was colored by the tone and style of Russian folksongs. There was no place for the music of the immigrants from Arab countries, who were a majority in the new state within a decade. Their Sephardi lifestyle and culture, separated by centuries from their original kinship to the Ashkenazis, were denigrated or ignored by the elite, who called them "Mizrahis," or easterners. It mattered little that Poland and Russia were considerably to the east of Morocco, whence came most of the Mizrahis; to the Zionists, they were of the Arab world, little better than the Arabs themselves. To the Zionist elite, Mizrahi music was impenetrable. Certainly there is a complexity about it that's beyond the ear of most Westerners. In Western music, there are major and minor keys; Arabic music has two sub-keys within major and minor, each called a *makam*, and it's common to play in more than one key at the same time. Musical notes are divided by semitones in the West; Arabic notes can be separated by as little as a quarter tone. More than that, the rhythm of Moroccan music in particular was wild and nativistic to the ears of the European Jews who ran Israel's government radio station. So people like Haim Uliel faced a choice: limit themselves to singing before their family at home, or move into more acceptable, marketable Western-style sounds.

Moroccan families, like immigrants everywhere, recognized the need for their children to assimilate to the culture of the new country. Most spoke only Hebrew to their children, rather than the Arabic or French in which they conversed with each other. (It's reminiscent of the linguistic adjustments of Israel's Arab citizens, who often speak to each other in Hebrew when they're in Jewish towns, so as to fit in.) Haim Uliel grew up feeling ashamed of his Moroccan roots. Within the home, Moroccan music and culture was a source of warmth and togetherness; outside it was hushed up by his parents, while the Ashkenazi European Jews from the local kibbutz made it clear that he was not welcome there, neither to play his music nor to date their girls. In the narrow wadi that divides Sderot from Kibbutz Nir Am, Uliel and his friends used to collect apples. There were no apple trees in the valley: the collective farmers of Nir Am used to discard excess apples there, next to their fruit-packing plant. Before the apples were thrown away, the kibbutz farmers covered them in some kind of kerosene. The people of Sderot could never figure out why the apples should be smeared in fuel, except to discourage them from taking the apples to eat. Though the townspeople scrubbed the apples they collected from the wadi, Haim Uliel was fully grown before he ever tasted an apple that didn't also carry the scent of a gas stove.

Haim Uliel knew that taint, the taste of the apples and the constant reminder of inferiority, until he was twenty-seven. The late twenties is a time of decision in the lives of many men, when they must leave the wildness of youth and assess the kind of man they want to be, the stamp they want to make on the world around them. For Haim Uliel, there had to be a change. He played his guitar and sang at weddings and had a good time, but what pride in himself would he have accrued if he were to do that for the rest of his life? A little tango, a little paso doble, a touch of disco: these were not the performances that could support a man's faith in himself. If Uliel could have moved up from the small stages of Sderot and the Negev, taken his place as a performer in the Israeli mainstream, he would have done so. But there seemed to be no position for him. You aren't so young anymore, Uliel told himself. What do you have? You have your roots, and nothing else. He made a decision to build on those roots, without shame. So he formed a new band, Sfatayim, which means "lips." He included on keyboards Kobi Oz, a Sderot kid of fifteen who impressed Uliel at a local talent concert a year earlier singing a British pop song from the 1960s. Uliel wrote out a set list for the band's first gig, whose significance even he didn't foresee.

At a Moroccan wedding in Sderot in 1986, Sfatayim took to the stage in matching black suits. Uliel, Oz, and the four other band members went through the first couple of sections of the set. The guests had a good time, swinging through the ballroom dances. Then it happened. Uliel cued up the band for a set of classic Moroccan tunes, the songs people sang at home. Sfatayim began to play, there in public, in the wedding hall before several hundred Mizrahi guests. There was the slightest of pauses from the crowd. Later Uliel would realize that they couldn't quite grasp what they were hearing. Then he felt it: Boom! As though something exploded in the hall. It was the sound of a cheer of recognition and of joy, as all the guests got to their feet to dance. The crowd came to life. Haim Uliel had discovered the man he would be.

At twenty-seven, Haim Uliel understood that he had begun to write the second verse of the song of his life. He listened intensively to Moroccan music and wrote his new songs with Moroccan Arabic lyrics. He saw at the wedding that there was a demand for it, but more than that, he knew it was within him. He understood that he couldn't rely on his parents' generation for support in his new endeavor. They were too scarred by their hostile reception in Israel, by the need to conform and keep their heads down; the Moroccan culture they brought with them had already been shamed, and they figured the same thing would happen to Haim with his new project. His parents mocked Haim Uliel's Arabic accent for the tinge of Hebrew it carried. It hurt him to hear them laugh. How were they different from the European Jews who jested at his Hebrew, aspirated in the Mizrahi style where it should have been guttural? His mother's brother, Haim Alhayani, played Moroccan music in small cafés like the one Matatya Uliel owned. Haim Uliel asked him for the lyrics to some of the old songs so he could go into a studio and record an album of Moroccan music with Sfatayim. Alhayani laughed. "What chance do you have to make a record in Moroccan? Nobody'll listen to that. What a waste of time." Uliel hated the jokes and mockery, but it didn't make him hate his elders; in a way, the music he wanted to record was a way of repairing them, reviving the part of them that had been snuffed out by Israel's Zionist elite.

In 1988 Sfatayim recorded their first album, at their own expense and with Moroccan Arabic lyrics. It was made up of old Moroccan songs arranged in a modern style. No record company would take it on, and even small labels that dealt in Mizrahi music sung in Hebrew wouldn't listen. Executives told Uliel his music would never make it onto television or radio in Israel. But the album, available only on tape, sold well, mostly on the black market. Uliel officially sold 20,000 copies of the first two Sfatayim albums, but many more were copied illegally. In Israel, the market is so small that above-board sales of 20,000 earn a gold disk. The band gained a strange foothold in

Israeli radio stations too. Mainstream DJs ignored the cassettes Uliel sent out, but a few new shows started up at that time to showcase "world music," part of a trend toward appreciation of non-Western styles that was mirrored in the United States too. During those specialty radio shows, among the Malian guitarists and Cuban salsa bands, Army Radio and Israel Radio began to play songs in Moroccan Arabic by Sfatayim. Most of the first Sfatayim fans outside the Moroccan Jewish community were unaware that the Arabic hits "Lalla Isha" and "Ahlan wa-Sahlan" were recorded by five guys who grew up forty minutes south of Tel Aviv.

The new music confused television producers. They understood that this popular band ought to be on one of Israel Television's programs. But the two main music shows were *The End of the Citrus Season*, which showcased Hebrew-language songs, and *Sea of Tears*, named for the melancholy Mizrahi-Hebrew tunes of self-pity, loneliness, and longing that it featured. Uliel talked to the producers soon after Sfatayim took off, then reported to his bandmates: "On the one hand, the language is Moroccan, so the first show is out. On the other hand, we've never cried in our songs, so we can't supply their sea of tears." The energy and pride that grabbed the audience at the wedding when Sfatayim played its first gig were too much for the country's television.

The impact of Sfatayim began to spread. Uliel's former bandmate Kobi Oz founded a band he called Teapacks, which used humor and a somewhat more Western production sound to break into mainstream radio. One of Oz's first hits, "Betokh Neyar Iton" (In the Page of the Newspaper), was built around an insistent tabla beat Uliel resurrected from the traditions of the Berbers in the Atlas Mountains; it had become part of Moroccan Jewish music in the villages, where most Jews had lived. Haim Uliel understood that, though some Ashkenazi institutions continued to resist Sfatayim, Mizrahi music had one advantage: it was simply less threatening to Ashkenazi culture than other assertions of Mizrahi origin, particularly economic and social. There were no riots over Sfatayim's music, as there were over the decrepit housing conditions in towns like Sderot. He saw, too, that Moroccan traditions appealed to younger Israelis, who were less closeted than their parents, largely thanks to the music of Sfatayim and the bands that followed them. Even Ashkenazi brides began to have henna parties before their weddings, dyeing their hands and feet with blue and russet designs in the Moroccan tradition. There was a legitimacy to the decorative aspect of Mizrahi culture, at least—testament to that was the 150,000 copies of its albums Sfatayim officially sold by 1998, though the real amount in circulation was probably several multiples of that. Uliel recognized how much a part of the mainstream Kobi Oz's music had become. He heard the old Ashkenazi singers, like Shlomo Artzi, recording duets with Moroccans. Popular artists who made their mark singing Western pop began recording in the language of their parents: one of the country's biggest stars, Rita, recorded a song in Farsi, though most Israelis hadn't realized that she was of Persian descent. After thirteen years, the job of Sfatayim was done. Uliel began to feel burdened with his role as messenger of the Moroccan community. Haim Uliel folded Sfatayim. He began to think about the next verse in the song of his life.

SILVAN SHALOM arrived at the synagogue named for his father to the sounding of a shofar and a shower of candy that arched like confetti from the hands of old ladies and little children. The ram's horn laid its orotund tenor beneath the high ululation of the women in the lobby of the Shimon Shalom synagogue. They patted the local boy as he stepped from his black Volvo limousine through a few yards of thick Negev desert heat and into the cool of the hall. Israel's finance minister straightened his red tie and buttoned the jacket of his charcoal suit, conscious that he was the only man in the building wearing more than a short-sleeved shirt. He slouched forward to greet the women and to kiss his mother, who had walked fifty yards along the road from her home to this festive blessing for Shalom at the synagogue. He rubbed the dark stubble that showed through his pallid skin in the late afternoon. The screeching women and the rhythmic clapping men and the adulation for a political hero who will take the Mizrahis all the way to the prime minister's job, which one of their number has never held: this was the chorus of identification and political messianism, the refrain of the ethnic song to which Haim Uliel wrote his own distinctive verses.

Shalom was born in Tunis, shortly before his parents came to Israel. Like the Uliels, they didn't pick their place in the country—

Zionist functionaries chose it for them. Since the biblical patriarch Jacob labored here for his father-in-law to grant him the hand of Rachel, the most action Beersheba saw was when my great-great-uncles rode with the Imperial Camel Corps to outflank the Turks and pressed on to capture Gaza and Jerusalem in 1917. Though Israel's fourth-largest city, it was distant from the Tel Aviv–Haifa money-trade axis and from the center of political power in Jerusalem. It was dusty and neglected, home to 185,000, a third of whom were recent immigrants from the former Soviet Union dumped there just as the rest of the population had been deposited on their arrival from Arab countries in the first two decades of Israel's history. Shalom's father died when the boy was six, shot by robbers at the Bank Leumi he managed. Silvan struggled out of the town, working hard to earn an accounting degree from the local Ben-Gurion University of the Negev, then moving to Tel Aviv to study law. He became a journalist, ran the national electric company, married the irrepressibly vivacious and ambitious daughter of the country's biggest media magnate, and by the age of forty-three had been both finance minister and foreign minister, the two most powerful positions next to prime minister. In Beersheba, they saw him as a man who might force them onto the national agenda that for so long neglected them. Within one minute of shaking my hand, Beersheba's mayor, Yaakov Terner, told me three times that he was "a friend of Silvan."

Silvan Shalom sat on a platform at the front of the synagogue, facing the bima, which in the Sephardi tradition stood in the center of the hall. Beersheba's chief rabbi, Yehuda Deri, brother of the famous and disgraced Shas Party head Arieh, delivered an address pitched at the appropriate tone for the moment, a keening staccato as though he were a boxing emcee introducing the fighter in the blue-and-white trunks who emerged from the mean streets to become champion: "Moses wasn't a prince either. Silvan Shalom is the one. He's coming from down below, like Moses did. He feels the people's suffering. He'll be prime minister one day." He turned to the bashfully smirking finance minister beside him: "The peak of your life is coming, Silvan. You'll be prime minister." Shalom recited the mourner's Kaddish in his father's honor, then spoke briefly to the people gathered on the hot afternoon. He aimed his remarks across the men's heads to the women gathered outside the door, and in particular to his mother, who was there with her hair gathered beneath a cloth spangled with tiny mirrors: "You gave me the power. You did it, not me." Shalom's voice broke and he wept. His shoulders looked very small as he slumped into his chair and put his head in his hands.

Not even in the emotional melee that is Israeli politics could a leading Ashkenazi hack play on the sentiment of his constituency quite as Shalom did. Nor would an Ashkenazi make quite so much of his faith in God, if he were from one of the main, secular parties like the Likud, to which Shalom belongs. And not for nothing was Sfatayim's most popular hit a song called "Mama." Emotion, faith, and family: this was the chorus of an entire people, for whom no one else would sing in praise.

The Mizrahis did not register in the early Zionists' political calculations and never found a place in the collective memory of that movement. In 1895, when Zionism began to take hold, there were 10.5 million Jews in the world, and 90 percent were Ashkenazi. It was a ratio that would later be reduced by Hitler's depredations, but meantime it was European advancement that the Zionists saw themselves bringing to the Holy Land. "It is our intention to come to Palestine as representatives of culture and to take the moral boundaries of Europe to the Euphrates River," Theodor Herzl's aide, Max Nordau, told an early Zionist conference. Part of the Zionist sales pitch to the British government in 1917, which was rewarded with the Balfour Declaration in support of a Jewish home in Palestine, was the foundation of a European outpost. Europe was, thus, the basis for Zionism and its ideal "new Jew."

As with Holocaust survivors, Mizrahi newcomers to Israel found themselves largely cut out of the gravy train Zionism built for its apparatchiks in the Histadrut labor federation. In 1926, before most Mizrahis even considered heading for Palestine, Zionist leader Chaim Arlosoroff explained the division that was to define Israeli society for decades: "The Histadrut is a settlement aristocracy. If a proletariat . . . is to be found here, then it is among Middle Eastern and North African Jews." Histadrut officials got higher salaries than other workers, a fact about which Ben-Gurion was unapologetic. After an internal inquiry into these wage inequities in 1927, Ben-Gurion said he wanted to be not "more competent or honest, but . . . more Zionist than others." In the face of that kind of logic, who could be surprised that new immigrants to Israel turned to crime and, at the very least, rule-bending, as did the Saturday night customers at Matatya Uliel's café? Even among Ashkenazis, the Polish and Russian Histadrut leaders discriminated against Jews from Hungary and Romania, who were less involved in Zionism's early development. Essentially, the first Zionists set up an ideological system of socialist nationalism that drew deeply on the primacy of power, whether it were political, economic, or bureaucratic. Thus a tribal view of politics and of the world developed in Palestine, even before the foundation of the Israeli state. Newly arrived immigrants fell victim to this system, because of their dependence on the state: they arrived to a find a country where there were no rights, only patronage. Even within Ben-Gurion's Mapai Party, which formed the basis of the modern Labor Party, there were some who saw a need to break the hold of the apparatchiks. In the late 1920s, middle-class Eastern European Jews came to Palestine and, as the immigration known as the "Fourth Aliyah," were the first Zionists to bring substantial capital of their own. Most set up as tradespeople in Tel Aviv and remained outside the Labor system of control that ruled the bureaucracy, the construction and utility companies, and the collective farms. During World War II, the Tel Aviv branch of Mapai tried in vain to rid itself of the corrupt Ben-Gurion crony who ruled the city, but there was no fundamental change in the country's power structure until Menachem Begin won election as the Likud's first prime minister in 1977.

Meanwhile, Mizrahi Jews in immigrant camps that eventually became towns like Sderot were forced through a secularist resocialization. In the first camps, prayer shawls, yarmulkes, and even prayer itself were banned. In 1998 the Labor Party chairman Ehud Barak publicly apologized to the Mizrahis "for this pain, and the human suffering." A few of the more thoughtful Mizrahi activists welcomed the statement, but most were so discontented that they angrily dismissed these words, which they had clamored for decades to hear, as an attempt to curry favor for the forthcoming elections. Ben-Gurion's biographer, on the other hand, said, "What does this talk about 'harm' mean? What is Barak talking about?" The same year, a former general and a member of the Labor Party went on the radio to muse about the Moroccans, whom he called Israel's "most problematic ethnic group." By 2001, Labor had an Iraqi Jew as its leader, something the supposedly Mizrahi Likud never managed. Unfortunately, the Labor Party had been devastated by Barak's loss in a prime ministerial runoff with Ariel Sharon and the new leader garnered little Mizrahi support. Binyamin Ben-Eliezer only shepherded Labor further into oblivion with a brief reign that most party insiders thought appropriate for a political hack of few admirable qualities. When eventually Ben-Eliezer was ejected, he spoke darkly about racism and anti-Mizrahi currents at work against him within Labor. Barak may as well never have said he was sorry, for all the good it did.

The discrimination left Mizrahis with a sense of victimization at the very core of their being that deeply affected their entire political outlook. Mizrahis mostly espoused a right-wing nationalism that opposed the Oslo peace process and any other conciliatory moves toward the Palestinians. This was not a surface political factor. It was rooted way down in their insecurity about themselves in Israeli society. They were so tormented by Israel's first Ashkenazi elite that they could not countenance the possibility that Palestinians would cease to victimize them. They refused to forgive any element of what the Ashkenazis did to them, and so found it impossible to believe that some Palestinians might forgive them. The effect was truly destructive to the peace process. Once the intifada began, its violence only confirmed these beliefs and made the Mizrahi population angrier and more nationalistic.

Zionist leaders turned to the Mizrahis in the first place only as replacements for those Jews murdered in the Holocaust, as human capital that could be prevailed upon to immigrate to a new country short of manpower. But they did so with deep distaste. A decade after the Mizrahis began to arrive en masse, Ben-Gurion said, "The Moroccan Jew took a lot from the Moroccan Arabs. The culture of Morocco I would not like to have here." He didn't want the culture, just the bodies of a portion of the 900,000 Jews living in Arab countries in 1948 to populate the new state and defend its borders.

The Arabs played their part in giving Ben-Gurion his wish for new immigrants. An estimated 40 percent of Baghdad's population was Jewish on the foundation of Israel, but Iraq soon expelled its Jews. The Iraqi refugees came to impoverished camps in Israel. The trauma of those early years transmitted itself beyond the adults who fled and on to their children, those who came to Israel as infants and those born in the new state. For some, that translated to deep resentment of the Jewish state, which disinfected them with DDT on their arrival and looked upon them as born of a lower, Arabized culture. For others, there was a horror that never could be faced.

In 2000, I went to the central Israeli town of Ra'anana, shortly after President Clinton floated the idea of a peace deal between Israel and the Palestinians in which Jews who fled Arab countries would be paid compensation for the property they left behind, as would Palestinian refugees. In Ra'anana, I met Munira Mussafe, who fled Baghdad with her husband and young daughter in June 1951, bundled out in the middle of the night by government officials and police. She recalled the wealth the family left behind: the big house on the banks of the Tigris, the thirty-six handmade Persian carpets, the luxury cars bought used from the king of Iraq, $2 million in cash burned with sixty bales of cotton when her father's warehouse was attacked. In Israel, her husband, Salim, bought a small farm, trying to raise cows, goats, cinnamon, and sesame, without great success. In winter, their shack leaked and in summer it percolated with cockroaches and mice. Salim died in 1973, trampled by a horse on the farm. Munira was so severely depressed that she cried constantly. Her daughter Judith, six years old when they fled Iraq, watched her mother fall apart. The young woman worked hard on the farm, rising each day at 4 A.M. to milk the cows. But her mother's constant depression ate at her, and she, too, failed to come to terms with the harshness of Israel and the loss of the luxurious life she vaguely recalled as a little girl. "Why did you come here?" she used to ask Munira over and over. "This life is so hard." In 1988, when Munira was sixty-six, Judith hanged herself.

Munira Mussafe wept as we sat in her kitchen with her two surviving daughters, just as she had wept throughout her fifty years in Israel. "I don't sleep at night for thinking about my life in Iraq," she said. "In my dreams, I would be crying, and I would wake up and realize that I was, indeed, crying." As Munira cried, her daughters sobbed, tears like Silvan Shalom's for his mother, and tears for themselves and the burden of growing to adulthood with weeping, suffering parents who wanted only to be somewhere else but Israel, where the good life they loved in their youth was gone.

These tears were in the lachrymose Mizrahi-Hebrew songs that

Haim Uliel noted he never sang. There were also hard numbers behind the tears: a former Mossad agent who helped bring Jewish refugees out of Iraq told me the current value of the property they were forced to leave behind would be $15 billion. Jews all over the Arab world were compelled to flee without their wealth, right up to the expulsions from Libya in 1971 and Syria in the 1980s. In Haim Uliel, I sensed an anger beyond tears, the rage of people finally standing up that fueled the early Mizrahi social protests and movements. In 1959 Mizrahis rioted in the Wadi Salib neighborhood of Haifa for two weeks. The concept developed then of a "Second Israel"—the slums and immigrant camps of the Mizrahis, who had no part in the Israel of the ruling Zionists. By 1971 young Mizrahis from Jerusalem formed the Black Panthers, taking their name from the movement of U.S. blacks. The complaints of the Black Panthers were not so different in some ways from those of many Palestinians under the occupation of Israeli soldiers, a measure of how deep the animosity and division was. The group issued its first communiqué in March 1971: "Enough! We, a group of screwed-up youngsters, appeal to all those who have had it. Enough of unemployment! Enough of ten people sleeping in one bedroom! . . . Enough of being thrown in jail and hit every other day! . . . How long will they do it to us and we keep silent?"

There were changes after Begin took over in 1977. But Begin built his continued popularity on stoking that ethnic hatred. Just as later Shas would run its us-and-them campaigns, Begin won reelection in 1981 by stressing once more Labor's negative treatment of Mizrahis and that party's corruption. During Begin's first term, a Haifa University sociologist named Sami Smooha called Israel an "ethnic democracy." One ethnic group, the Ashkenazis, held institutional sway over the state, while allowing certain rights to minorities like Israel's Arab population or underprivileged groups like the Mizrahis. I believed that might have changed somewhat in the twenty-five years since Begin's election, when for all but five years the Likud sat in government. I noted that many of my Israeli friends had married across the Ashkenazi-Mizrahi divide. One-fifth of Israeli marriages are now matches between those two groups. But I also wondered if that might not lead almost perversely to a stronger association with one or the other group for the children of those unions. Politics remained highly divided along those ethnic lines, so without a truly new *Israeli* identity, it might be that children would be forced to choose the culture of one or the other of their parents, to take sides in the ethnic battle in an effort to define themselves.

For many, economics precluded any such cultural choice, in any case. Despite twenty-five years of rule largely by the Likud—where Mizrahi politicians like Silvan Shalom hold senior posts, though never yet the leadership—Jews from Arab countries continued to be at the bottom end of the social scale. Though only 17 percent of Israelis lived in "development towns" like Sderot, those places supplied 40 percent of the unemployed. Only one in ten Mizrahis was a college graduate, compared to a third of Ashkenazis. The average wage of a Mizrahi college graduate was 78 percent of an Ashkenazi graduate's salary. And new resentments were building. I felt them when I moved into a Mizrahi area of Jerusalem that was "gentrifying." Every piffling quarrel with neighbors clearly became charged with the residue of years of bitterness, blowing up suddenly and beyond all proportion to the matter at hand. Immigrants from the former Soviet Union experienced violent hatred when they were deposited in the same underprivileged locales as the Mizrahis, who believed the money spent on absorbing the Russians should have been paid to them instead. I went to Ashkelon to investigate the stabbing of a young Russian man near the beach by a group of Moroccans in 1999. At a café near the scene of the murder, a pretty young waitress from Kazakhstan brought me a Coke. When she came back to bring another, she told me a table of young Russians had just sat down and asked her quietly, nervously, "Is it okay if we speak Russian in here?" Marina Solodkin, a liberal legislator who emigrated from Moscow, saw the divide in terms of the intellectual game of the Russians and the Arab world's favorite game of chance and strategy: "We are playing chess; they are playing backgammon." We. They.

Silvan Shalom knew the rules of both games. Before the 1999 general election, Prime Minister Benjamin Netanyahu picked another Likud politician for the Finance Ministry. Silvan would have the job two years later, but meantime he wanted to make it clear that he wasn't to be snubbed. As the election approached, the Netanyahu posters that covered the rest of the country were absent from the Negev and, particularly, Shalom's domain, Beersheba. Party officials got the message: Shalom was ready to handicap the party, so long as it hammered home the lesson that he couldn't be treated like a second-rate Mizrahi who'd suck up ill-treatment from the Ashkenazi prime minister. In the spacious house where he lived with his wife and children in Ramat Gan, a suburb of Tel Aviv, Silvan Shalom recalled the thirty-two-square-yard apartment near the Shimon Shalom synagogue in Beersheba where he grew up with his mother and sister. His current home was beyond the dreams of most Israelis. It was the size of a suburban American house, but that ranks as a palace in Israel, where a one-hundred-square-yard apartment is a family's norm. "I always know where I came from," Shalom said, reclining in his den with his purple-haired wife, Judi. In the manner of politicians who build their power on a base of social and ethnic division, Shalom will make sure that everyone else knows where he came from too.

RACHEL OZAN introduced hundreds of people to Israel, as a manager of the Jewish Agency's immigrant-absorption center in Sderot during the 1960s. But Ozan, who emigrated from Tunisia in 1950, began to fear she would never bring her own child to the new town where she lived. The Moroccans and Iranians came through her office with their noisy swarms of children, five or six to a family. But Rachel tried eleven years with her husband, Yosef, and failed to become pregnant. In that town of immigrants, everyone knew Rachel personally, because at one time or another they needed her help in dealing with the unfamiliar bureaucracy of their new home, and everyone understood the pain she felt at her lack of a child. Each time the women returned with their broods to ask Rachel to organize something they needed, a government stamp or permit, she would admire their children and they would ask her, "Rachel, what about you?" It made Rachel Ozan sad when she replied, "Not yet. Nothing's on the way yet."

It was like that until not long before Rachel turned forty. Then she became pregnant. Even prior to his birth in 1969, Kobi Ozan was a celebrity, the miracle child of Rachel from the Jewish Agency. The wonder of his conception seemed to bestow upon him a positive outlook on life that was just as miraculous for a boy from Sderot. Only a little over five feet tall and narrow in the hips, Kobi grew up believing that he could overcome the prejudice of a society that denigrated him as the short-ass son of Mizrahi immigrants born in a worthless border town. He realized early in life that identity could be fluid in the new state. Kobi read William Golding's classic novel *Lord of the Flies*. In Sderot, where the Israeli state negated traditional cultures and time-honored social systems, Kobi saw similarities between the atavism of Golding's British schoolboys, marooned on their island, and the disintegrating lives of the Mizrahis around him. The early Zionists came largely as rebels, against the lifestyle of their Eastern European parents and their religious beliefs; they came as children without fathers and mothers, bullying their new world into the shape their ideology demanded. The Mizrahis came with entire family structures intact and a greater attachment to tradition than most European Jews, many of whom had modernized, assimilated, or developed progressive Conservative and Reform streams of Judaism. But the Mizrahis were driven to feelings of shame and resentment as the Zionists attempted to force them through the same parricidal political and social process they had undergone. Kobi saw the confusion that reigned around him and knew it to be a result of this Goldingesque degeneration. His insight was to understand that it afforded an opportunity to create a specifically Israeli identity in which a Mizrahi could build on the inevitably central Ashkenazi model for everything from art and music to food. The Zionists, who ran away from their homes and cultures like children, never grew up, in Kobi's assessment. The schoolyard harshness this brought to Israeli society, the deeply sectarian nature of life in the Jewish state, could be ameliorated by an artist who would form his own identity, drawing on his family's background in Tunisia, on his own warm upbringing among immigrants, and entering fearlessly into the heart of Ashkenazi culture. Kobi Ozan built himself a new identity as "Kobi Oz." Oz is a fairly common Hebrew name that means "strong." He began to mold the sparkling character who would sing the song Kobi Ozan might write.

It would be a song in the French of Tunisia, the Arabic of the Sderot streets, and the Hebrew of Israel. He took it from a tune of toleration that his parents seemed to hum absently as they went about their life. Each Friday night, the Ozan family would recite the Kiddush over the wine, but were otherwise unobservant of most of the Sabbath. When Kobi was fourteen, he grew angry at the Friday ritual, because he felt that his parents weren't truly religious. "Are you hyp-ocrites?" he shouted. "If you believe in God, why aren't you religious? Decide. Either you're secular or you're religious." Rachel and Yosef didn't understand what the boy meant; they didn't see that he had learned the sectarianism of Israel and couldn't handle the easygoing approach to Judaism they brought with them from Tunisia. The fam-ily ate their meal quietly after the youngster's blowup. Kobi used his pita to scoop up the Arab salads, the spicy *matbukha* and the *Turkiyyeh*. Then he came to a Waldorf salad. It struck him: This isn't a Mizrahi salad, but it's here on the table and it tastes good. Why am I telling them to decide? Why do I want them to be against something? I'm the one who's wrong here. He tried from then on to make toler-ance his watchword.

Kobi's father worked as a laborer in a storage warehouse in Sderot, where pool tables were stacked high, awaiting shipment to bars around the country. Yosef Ozan was the kind of worker who would stop by Matatya Uliel's café at the end of the day for a game of backgammon and a single drink. But he never saw the dangerous Sat-urday night side of Mizrahi life that Matatya Uliel and his son Haim experienced when the Moroccan musicians and the flashy gangsters came each week. Kobi sensed there was some deep sadness within his father. When Kobi was a teenager, he asked his father to tell him about the Yom Kippur War of 1973. First, Yosef asked what Kobi remembered about that time, when he was four years old. Kobi recalled that he had been in the synagogue in the late afternoon, watching the men of the community who were descended from the priestly caste bending beneath their *talits* for the Birkat Ha-Kohanim. The congregation was supposed to avert its eyes from this part of the service, but Kobi kept looking. There was a siren and the men rushed out, and soon there were convoys of military vehicles on the road heading south toward the Sinai. Yosef Ozan went south too, where he served in an artillery unit. Yosef, who was already in late middle age when he talked about this to his son, said that the whole time he had been away, his thoughts centered on his little boy. "It was so difficult for us to bring a child into the world," he said, "and then I thought perhaps I would lose my son; perhaps I wouldn't come home to him." In the Sinai, a shell took the head off one of Yosef Ozan's friends in his artillery battery. There were many horrors like this, but

Yosef didn't share them with Kobi. He told his son again and again that all the time, in the sand and the noise and the fear, he thought only about losing his son.

In most of Israel's development towns, negativity and resentment lay in the air, thick and discoloring, like the dirt of the Negev when a warm *sharav* wind lifts the desert grit and suspends it as an ochre cloud in the grip of the hot gusts. In the Ozan household, Rachel and Yosef saw to it that Kobi, who came to them as a miracle and a local celebrity, should understand the specialness of his existence. They did not complain of the world into which they brought him and its treatment of simple people like them, for they were grateful that he had come to them at all. Kobi found a similar ethos in the young mayor of Sderot in the 1980s, Amir Peretz. When Kobi went to Peretz's office in the evening to pick up the keys to a municipal hall for a band rehearsal, Peretz was always around, always accessible. He instilled a pride in Sderot that was missing in similar development towns nearby, like Netivot and Kiryat Gat. Before youngsters went to the army for their compulsory service at eighteen, Peretz came to the school and lectured them, shouting in his broad Moroccan accent from beneath a black, walrus mustache: "Don't be shy. Say, 'I'm from Sderot.' Be an ambassador for this town to the rest of the country and remember that the people of this town deserve proud ambassadors."

Peretz went on to be the leader of Israel's labor federation and described himself to me as "the last socialist in the world." He pointed at his mustache and said, "But I didn't grow this just so that I'd look like Stalin, no matter what you hear." As a left-winger, he created a bridge for Sderot's largely reactionary, right-wing population with the socialist kibbutzes that ringed the town. He was an activist mayor who worked for the good of the town, not for his own bunch of cronies. It made a strong impression on young Mizrahis, because few were as free of the resentful influence of their parents' generation as Kobi Oz. Most fell into the defining Israeli pattern of aligning themselves against something or other, rather than in favor of anything. No one wants to be a *freier*, or a sucker; no one can allow another to succeed or benefit without criticizing, spoiling, or undermining it somehow; compromise is to be eschewed entirely, for it might lead to your being taken for everything. It was a truth Kobi Ozan made into part of the character of Kobi Oz.

Early in my time in Israel I learned the same lesson from a Hebrew joke my language teacher Yaron Friedman told me: "A group of thugs goes to the bus station and they say, 'Who's Berkovitch?' A little guy steps up and says, 'Me, I'm Berkovitch.' The thugs grab him and beat him almost to death, but the little guy laughs and laughs. 'Are you crazy?' the thugs say. 'Why are you laughing?' The little man looks at them with amusement and says, 'I put one over on you. I'm not Berkovitch.' " Every Israeli knows the destructiveness of that attitude, but it's on display to anyone in Israel who makes his way from home to office to government department to highway during an average day. Moreover, it's unsupportive and negating. As a journalist, I never had a scoop or an unusual story idea that didn't draw an Israeli to signal somehow that he had thought of it first and knew some secret about the subject that I had missed. I often wondered how battering it must be to grow up in the face of such undermining, and how great the insecurity must be that forces people to express themselves that way.

Kobi Oz aimed to communicate exactly the opposite ethos. Just as he felt pride in his town, Kobi was proud of the Mizrahis when he played his first gig with Sfatayim at the age of fifteen. That was at the wedding when Haim Uliel, twelve years Kobi's senior, decided he must define the kind of man he would be and asserted his pride in his Moroccan background. It was a revelation for young Kobi, though he had to leave the band for his compulsory military service soon after. Back in civilian life after three years as a radio operator, Ozan made the full transformation to Kobi Oz. He knew the joyful character he wanted to portray in his music, but he needed to create the stage persona. He learned Elvis Presley's pelvic swivel, and the footwork of Greek bazouki singers, and the hand-pirouettes of Moroccan dancers. Then it dawned on him: he hadn't chosen anything that wouldn't have come naturally to a young man with his background. He had chosen himself. Okay, he preferred to attach himself to the rhythmic, vibrant Moroccan music rather than the melancholic Tunisian forms, but they weren't a million miles away from each other. In fact, they were all part of Sderot. I had to change my name to be myself, he thought. But at that stage, there was still something of a fantasy, something a little Ziggy Stardust about the formulation of an alter ego for the new artist. It seemed the opposite of what Haim Uliel did in returning to the music he might have played and the man he might have been in Morocco if Israel had never existed. Uliel wanted Israelis to listen to the sound of his Moroccan roots; Oz wanted to make a new sound that would define a culture specifically Israeli.

Yet unlike Uliel, there was no conscious manifesto to the band that Kobi Oz formed with three youths from the kibbutzes around Sderot. Instead, he and the kibbutzniks did what their society hadn't wanted them to do: they assimilated, one to the other. Oz wrote most of the music, so the bass player from Kibbutz Nahal Oz began to learn Mizrahi styles, but he also retained the pulse of the Western rock he grew up playing. The same was true of the drummer from Kibbutz Nir Am and the guitarist from Ruchama. Oz called the band Teapacks. In Hebrew it's pronounced "Tippex," like the British brand name for Wite-Out that was sold in Israel, because the band whited out their cultural differences. For reasons of playfulness, Kobi Oz spelled it differently in English. They followed a more traditional route than Sfatayim, playing without pay and sweeping the venues clean after their early gigs. They borrowed from Uliel the old black suits in which Sfatayim first performed and put together songs that were a mélange of Moroccan, rock'n'roll, electro, and cheesy wedding music. Then Teapacks recorded a demo that attracted the attention of managers at the Beit Lessin Theater in Tel Aviv and they began playing there regularly, soon signing to a small label. Four years later, they joined a major Israeli record company. The band's first song on Israeli radio was "Rabbi Joe Kappara," which told a story about a Mizrahi holy man who performed miracles. Oz noted that people seemed confused that a new band would release a song that didn't include the words "I love you." Though Teapacks's songs were invariably funny, they were about reality, not the idealized love songs that most Ashkenazi groups sang. Oz never ignored the rotten side of the development towns, with their boxy tenements and dirt lots, but his humor neutralized the threatening anger of many Mizrahis. His hilarious song "Disco Maniac" told the story of a development town where the nearest thing to the excitement of a nightclub was the flashing light and wailing siren of a police squad car.

Before long, music critics in the Tel Aviv newspapers began to link Sfatayim, which was by that time an underground success, and Teapacks, with its radio-friendly hits. As other new bands came out of

Sderot, the critic for *Yediot Aharonoth,* the country's biggest newspaper, said that the development town was like Liverpool in the '60s. Teapacks's eight albums eventually sold 300,000 copies, though several times that amount circulated on Israel's prolific black market for CDs.

Kobi Oz needed a different outlet for his beliefs, for the tolerance he wanted to teach. Unlike Haim Uliel, he didn't have to break up the band to do it. In 1999 he took a year off from music and toured schools in development towns like Sderot. He preached a message of hope, that the discrimination against Mizrahis was not a real barrier, not unless the students who sat before him allowed it to become one. His words posed the challenge of belief to reality, and they found a parallel in his writing. In 2003 Oz published *Petty Hoodlum,* a novel about low-life mafiosi, mystical rabbis, and Holocaust survivors living in the "Second Israel" identified by Mizrahi social campaigners three decades earlier.

Kobi Oz sketched out the storyline of *Petty Hoodlum* in white chalk on the green-painted walls of his study, until the whole room was covered in plot and character and jokes and snatches of dialogue. Oz looked from the window, across the square, concrete rooftops of Tel Aviv's apartment buildings. There, between the cylindrical white tanks and angular thermal sensors that warmed the water supply in the heat of the sun, he could see a shimmering divot of blue. It was the Mediterranean, and it had always been something that moved him strongly. Even this little piece of it gave him a moment of warmth, as though he were floating in it. Then he realized the beautiful geography of this expanse of water. This sea touched the shores of the land where his parents were born, and on its other edge, it lapped on the sands of Europe, the home of the Ashkenazis. The Israel that was home to "Kobi Oz," the character built by Kobi Ozan fifteen years before, was a mixture of both these places, a straddler of the Mediterranean that was distinctively Levantine. Oz thought about the blue shades of the sea, and he sketched out another plot line on the green walls of his study.

Oz wrote of a character named Eliyahu Ha-Navi, a tzaddik, or holy man. Eliyahu was bemused by his Israeli grandchildren, kids from the projects constantly in trouble with the worthless local cops. Eliyahu, who worked as a janitor, immigrated to Israel from Morocco. But he dreamed about Europe under Nazi occupation. As his strange dreams of an alien continent became more frequent, he noticed a blue smudge on his forearm. Every day he dreamed about his life as a child in a European ghetto. He met an Ashkenazi woman his own age, a judge. She lived through the Holocaust, though her husband died in Hitler's concentration camps. She noticed the blue smudge and looked closer. It was a series of digits, tattooed like the identification numbers given to camp inmates. It was the number of her dead husband. Eliyahu and the judge became husband and wife.

Oz looked at the chalk across his wall. He had made the blue of the Mediterranean into something that brought together the two tragedies, the Holocaust of the Ashkenazis and the traumatic immigration of the Mizrahis, and he had married them. He had brought them together, fantastically and artistically, gluing them and making them one. It was, he knew, the key to the tolerance and wholeness he wanted his Levantine Israel to epitomize. The Holocaust identity number on the arm of the Mizrahi would be offensive to many Israelis. It would imply that what happened to the Mizrahis at the hands of the Ashkenazis was somehow as bad as what Hitler did to the European Jews. But that was the heart of what Oz meant: let go of your sufferings, and acknowledge that every Israeli is the product of a history of oppression and disaster, and that yours does not have to be certified as the worst of torments. Only then, he decided, would Israelis be able to understand that, beneath all their neuroses of suffering, they had founded their own country and they ought to enjoy it. Meantime, Oz saw Israel as a big ghetto. Jews had outdone the anti-Semites, from the doge of Venice, who decreed the first ghetto, to the Nazis in Warsaw, who encircled the worst, for they had cloistered themselves behind walls of paranoia. For each of their different groups within Israeli society they had built sub-ghettoes. But perhaps to let go of the memories of suffering was to cease to be Jewish somehow. After all, the Book of Deuteronomy tells the Israelites to remember what God has done for them and to remember, too, what their enemies have inflicted upon them. Each year at the Passover seder, Jews are called upon to "Remember that you were a slave in Egypt." Kobi Oz considered this, but he had one thing in common with the first Zionists and that was the desire to make a new Jew. His creation would be a Levantine freed of the obligation to be smaller than God and crushed beneath the weight of his suffering. He would be free to forget.

RABBI YAAKOV IFARGAN lit a candle. His soft hands hovered about it, as though he were molding the flame. The young rabbi's fleshy lips quivered, bright in the center of his black beard. Stare at the flame, he told me, look within it and you will see inside yourself. "The candle of God is the soul of man," the medieval Jewish mystics said. Ifargan's followers called him "the X-ray," for he would read your flame and through it he would see your inner self. He would read the energy of a crowd, too, and channel it for the good of *Am Yisrael,* the People of Israel. In his newly renovated, split-level salon, the small, chubby Ifargan told me about the *tikkun,* the restorative, mystical performance prayer he would give later that night. "I will cleanse the people," he said, rocking back and forth with his eyes closed tight in concentration. "And when all the people are clean, all their energy will heal the sick people who come there."

Though Ifargan wore the black suit and tall black fedora of the ultra-Orthodox Ashkenazi Jew, he was descended from a 500-year line of Baghdad rabbis. Their portraits, wearing simple white robes and tarbooshes rather than double-breasted suits like his, decorated the walls. His father came to Netivot, another "development town" of Mizrahis on the desert plain near Sderot, and set up his ministry alongside a crowd of similar hereditary religious figures who were more than just rabbis: they were tzaddiks, righteous ones, saints.

The tzaddiks are some of the most revered and controversial characters in Israel. They constitute one of the most contentious elements of the divide between Ashkenazi and Sephardi Jews. Ashkenazi Jewry has its wizardly *rebbes,* but only the Ashkenazi ultra-Orthodox pay them obeisance. Secular Ashkenazis and even many Orthodox religious Israelis of European descent credit them with considerable learning but feel little respect for them, and certainly nothing approaching awe. Among Mizrahis, the growing prestige of the holy men represents a link to, and a revival of, the traditional cultures of their centuries in the Arab lands—an era that the Zionist establishment and the Ashkenazi religious world attempted to crush. When I first came to Israel, I noticed that in every corner shop or kiosk there were portraits of gray-bearded, wizened men in white cowls, whose fingers were raised in signs of benediction. The images decorated the stores like charms. The people who displayed them were always Mizrahis who spoke of their magical rabbis and the miracles they performed with pride and wonder. The Ashkenazis with whom I discussed the phenomenon were, I detected, more filled with contempt and hate for these human amulets than they felt for all but the most vicious of Palestinian terrorists. Before I came to Israel, I thought of Judaism as a religion without saints, a creed condemning as idolatry the worship of anything other than the One God of the Shema, the Jewish declaration of faith. Yet in Israel I found that these curious-looking figures seemed imbued with the divine qualities that Judaism in its Western manifestation abhorred to ascribe to any human. To Mizrahis, these were holy men with godly powers, closer to God than ordinary mortals, able to impart knowledge that can, in itself, influence a man's destiny, capable of seeing the future and reading the diseases and fears that dwell in a man's guts: the tzaddiks can see what God has written in the book of life and ask—maybe tell—him to change it. As Haim Uliel turned to the songs of his forefathers so that he might know what kind of a man he was, so almost all of Israel's Mizrahis feel some kind of traditional bond to the tzaddiks and many allow the power of these Jewish saints to rule their lives—socially, economically, medically, politically.

To capitalize upon the feelings of marginality of their Mizrahi followers in Israeli society, the deified rabbis relocate their people at the heart of God's struggle for the sake of the universe. When Ifargan explained the importance of this piece of land called Israel and of this state where the Mizrahis toiled to make ends meet, it seemed to me that he elevated the hard labors of life here to the level of the angels, exerting themselves on God's behalf. "Israel will always have problems," he said. "It is the center of the world and it is the most important place. Everything that happens in the world travels through Israel and this makes it turbulent. If it weren't tumultuous, it would mean that it had stopped being the center of the world, that it had been closed up as a conduit for the world's energy, and then the world would end."

One of the most powerful of the tzaddiks was Rabbi Yitzhak Kaddouri. A small group of people gathered outside his house in the

Bukharan Quarter on the edge of Mea Shearim, Jerusalem's most run-
down ultra-Orthodox neighborhood, when I came to see him at the
end of 2000. A woman leaned on a pile of freight pallets to write a
note to the rabbi, kissed it, and handed it to Kaddouri's son. The
building was a typical Israeli construction of the 1950s, boxy sandstone with ugly balconies that had been enclosed cheaply and without building permits to make extra rooms for the small apartments. I
entered beneath a sign that read The Yeshiva of the Oldest Kabbalist.
Kaddouri and his home bore little resemblance to the trendy kabbala
centers funded by Madonna and frequented by various Hollywood
celebs on the hunt for the latest spiritual shtick. Certainly this deaf,
hunchbacked, chain-smoking centenarian was unlikely to become
guru to the stars, though he had acquired a wife forty years his junior,
in the style of a Los Angeles movie mogul. But in Israeli politics and,
more broadly, in society, Kaddouri's knowledge of Jewish mysticism
and his origins in Iraq made him an attractive figure. Visitors to the
old rabbi, who came to Israel from Iraq in 1920 and could only say
that he believed he was about 100 years old, asked him to intercede
on their behalf with the angels. He would write an amulet for them, a
charm based on arcane kabbalistic theory. Sometimes, if the request
was very special, he would inscribe the strip of parchment in ink colored with gold dust.

On the knubby olive fabric of the 1970s couch in Kaddouri's waiting room, I sat beside Elazar Bar-Yochai, a forty-two-year-old man
from Tiberias, who worked as a kosher inspector in the kitchens of
the city's hotels. He had been born Elazar Elul, but he changed his
name to honor Rabbi Shimon Bar-Yochai, the second-century Talmudic scholar who hid from the Romans for thirteen years in a cave and
was credited for centuries as author of the kabbalistic work The Zohar.
(In fact, Moses de Leon, a thirteenth-century Spanish rabbi, constructed the book and pretended Bar-Yochai wrote it, because he figured people would pay it more attention that way.) Like everyone I
met in the anterooms and courtyards of tzaddiks, Elazar had a miraculous story of his favorite rabbi's impact on his life. Elazar had been
diagnosed with a liver infection at Rambam Hospital in Haifa. His
doctors wanted to operate. Elazar came to consult Kaddouri. "The
rabbi told me, 'It's bullshit. Don't let them do it,' " Elazar said. "He
sent me to a different doctor and wrote me an amulet." Elazar held up

the amulet, a small tube of parchment rolled tight like a cigarette, preserved incongruously in Saran Wrap. The new medical treatment had been painful, but Kaddouri reassured an almost suicidal Elazar that he would have good news soon. Two weeks before I met him, Elazar's doctors told him the infection was gone, months before they had expected him to be cured. There was no doubt in Elazar's mind how his liver was saved: "I'm better because of the rabbi. He controls everything. When he rules that a man should be healthy, God obeys. With his power, the rabbi can command God. Because God yearns for the prayers of a tzaddik."

The tzaddik Yitzhak Kaddouri arose from his bed daily at 5 A.M. and, slowly with shaking hands, wrapped the leather straps of two tefillin around his skinny arm and two more about his forehead, each bearing parchments inscribed with two passages from the Torah. For the ordinary Jew, one tefillin on the forearm and another above the eyes was enough, but Kaddouri followed the practice of some extremely observant Jews who argued that it was unknown which of the biblical passages should take precedence and so wore two sets of tefillin, each with a different parchment placed first, to be sure that one of their tefillin should be correct. In any case, Kaddouri's followers said, the kabbalist must make his representations to God doubly deeply. He prayed and studied until 10:30 A.M., when his fifty-eight-year-old wife brought him toast and tea. From eleven to two, the rabbi held audiences in the tiny room where he worked, the shutters lowered, a single light bulb illuminating the walls with their brown stains from the damp in the bricks and from the nicotine in Kaddouri's cigarettes. He gave few of the lectures that other rabbis made so much of; his work was practical, hearing the requests of only so many individuals as could fit into this single room to bend close to his ear and bellow their spiritual needs through his deafness. The money paid for each amulet went to Kaddouri's grandson Yossi, the old rabbi's impresario in effect, who claimed that after paying for the keep of the forty advanced students at Kaddouri's yeshiva, there was only $300,000 left each year. Others involved with the community of tzaddiks told me rabbis like Kaddouri cleared closer to $1 million per year, particularly in the last decade when the phenomenon of the tzaddiks became bigger and the fame of this old Iraqi kabbalist in particular spread.

The political power of Kaddouri was a significant factor in the electoral successes of Shas, the Mizrahi ultra-Orthodox party that mixed religion with ethnic politics and held the balance of power in several Israeli governments in the last decade. Until the late 1980s, Kaddouri was a largely unknown tzaddik. He had little money and his influence extended only to those people who came directly to consult him. He was transformed by a confluence of the financial interests of his son and grandson and the political concerns of the new Shas Party. On the day I visited him, Kaddouri's aides awaited the results of an appeal in the corruption trial of the former Shas leader Arieh Deri, sentenced to three years in jail for taking bribes while serving as director-general of the Interior Ministry and, later, as minister. Deri built Shas in the early 1990s by combining the great respect accorded to the learned former chief Sephardi rabbi Ovadiah Yosef with the simplistic belief in tzaddiks like Kaddouri that was felt by ordinary Mizrahis. It made the frail old man into a national power broker, or at least the tool of one. To secular Israelis and to Ashkenazis in particular, the sight of leading politicians like Benjamin Netanyahu wearing black yarmulkes and bending to Kaddouri's ear at his synagogue was a symbol of the descent of national politics to the level of insane superstition.

Kaddouri shuffled the tiny strips of parchment on the teak tray balanced before him across the arms of his old easy chair. With thin fingers ribbed by liver spots and turquoise veins, he aligned the papers, the pens in their sandalwood box, the inkwell, his long white cigarette holder, and the smokes that stained his beard yellow. Kaddouri's endorsement earlier in 2000 helped earn Moshe Katsav, an Iranian Jew by origin and mediocre politician by trade, victory in the Knesset election for the position of Israel's president against Nobel laureate Shimon Peres. Now Yossi Kaddouri, his grandson, wanted to ask if the rabbi thought Katsav would issue a pardon for Deri, before the Shas leader went to jail. Kaddouri hunched in his chair, small in his loose gray jerkin. "Is there going to be a miracle and Deri won't have to go to jail? Will the president give him an amnesty?" the grandson yelled into the less deaf of Kaddouri's ears. The rabbi wheezed a dismissive chuckle, adjusted his fez, and shakily lit another smoke. Yossi Kaddouri asked again, but got only a raspy snigger that seemed to say, Bring me a cripple or someone with a kidney disease to cure, but don't ask me to perform impossible miracles. His grandson sighed and, impatiently, beckoned to the corridor. A mother rolled in her teenage son in a wheelchair for Kaddouri's blessing.

The traditions of Iraqi Jews like Kaddouri go back to their exile by Nebuchadnezzar in 586 B.C. and to the formulation of the Babylonian Talmud, the richest, most important source of Jewish learning and law. During the centuries of Diaspora, Moroccan Jews lived a simpler life at the opposite end of the Arab world from Iraq, often in the mountain villages of the Atlas. They shared many of the same customs as their Arab neighbors, including the worship of holy men and the veneration of their tombs. The Israeli government suppressed those traditions after the bulk of the Moroccans arrived in the 1950s. Their revival gradually initiated a process of ethnic identification that had such appeal for Mizrahi Jews that Moroccan customs, when restored in Israel, soon became the traditions of all the country's Mizrahis.

In 1965 a group of Moroccan Jews from Fez revived their old custom of Mimouna, the celebratory feast on the day after Passover. Some believed the ancient festival was linked to Rabbi Maimon Ben-Yosef, father of the famous Rabbi Moses Ben-Maimon, or even to Ben-Maimon himself, known in the West as Maimonides and to Jews by the Hebrew acronym Rambam. The holiday's true origin was gradually lost, but the Mimouna became an event of great importance once it came to Israel, as Mizrahi Jews whose families emigrated from all over the Arab world indulged in huge festivals in city parks. I tested the knowledge of Israelis about the stories behind Mimouna in Jerusalem's Sacher Park, where the city's main celebration was held every year. Each group of barbecuing Israelis had a different opinion about the festival. As Sarit Hadad, a brassy young Mizrahi singer and a protégé of Kobi Oz, performed her latest hit on a stage set in the hollow below us, I wandered from one family to another. "Mimouna is about food, barbecue, family," one man said loudly and expansively.

"No, I mean, what does it signify?" I said.

"It's the day after Passover."

"That's right, but . . ."

"Ask my grandma. She'll know."

Grandma: "It's a Moroccan holiday. We're Tunisians. You have to ask a Moroccan. Ask him, by the barbecue over there. He's Moroccan."

The man at the barbecue: "Mimouna is about good food on the flames and your family in the park and everyone together."

"But what does it celebrate?"

"It's the Rambam's birthday, I think."

"His birthday?"

"Ah, I don't know. It's *our* day, in any case. You want to taste my hot dogs? Come on, they're excellent."

It's *our* day. And the biggest of all the Mimouna celebrations, the most prominent of these festivals of Mizrahiness, is the gathering at the tomb of Baba Sali. Rabbi Yisrael Abuhatseira, known as Baba (or father) Sali, came to Israel from Morocco in the early 1960s. He gained a reputation for deep learning before he died in 1984. I noticed the enduring nature of his power when, during the 1999 election, the ultra-Orthodox United Torah Judaism Party ran an election ad in which a woman who would barely have been out of diapers when Abuhatseira died proclaimed that she would support the party because "Baba Sali said to vote for them." Baba Sali's tomb, whitewashed and low-walled in a sandy field on the edge of Netivot, looked like a movie set for a remake of *The Alamo*. Like the movies, Baba Sali was a good show that was also big business for his son and successor Baruch Abuhatseira, the self-styled "Baba Baruch." Baruch spent the four years before his father's death in jail for fraud, forgery, and accepting bribes while serving as a local politician in Ashkelon. After his father died, Baruch became a tzaddik entrepreneur who stoked the glorious glow of his father's holiness so that it would keep his wallet warm. Where his lean father wore a white cowl, portly Baruch preferred slimming black. His father studied long hours; Baruch confessed to Shas's spiritual guide Rabbi Ovadiah Yosef that he didn't have time to study. But he turned his father's tomb into the most important place of pilgrimage in Israel for Mizrahi Jews.

The wide courtyard was filled with tour buses on each of the occasions I visited. The baking desert heat grew stronger near the entrance to the tomb, where visitors threw candles into a blazing black metal brazier. Kids played paddleball as if it were the beach. A long shelter abutting the courtyard wall was filled with families barbecuing strip steaks and hot dogs. Nissim Biton, a fifty-eight-year-old construction worker from Ramat Gan, a Tel Aviv suburb, flipped the chicken pieces and burgers on his grill in the parking lot. He wore a gray T-shirt and, because he was in the presence of the Baba Sali, a black felt yarmulke. As he tended the griddle, he told me he used to have fits of pain in his stomach. At Tel Hashomer Hospital, they explained that he had a tumor in his belly that would have to be cut out. Baba Sali came to him in a dream as he lazed on his living-room couch. "Don't be afraid, my son. You're going to be all right." Then Baba Sali punched him in the stomach. The next day Biton went to his doctors. "Where's the tumor?" the puzzled surgeons said, searching in vain. Biton knew where it had gone. A miracle! Like Elazar Bar-Yochai in Kaddouri's waiting room, Biton believed the holy men were other-worldly. "God and Baba Sali are on the same level. The tzaddiks are like angels who transfer our prayers to God," he said. But then he added, "It's a source of pride for us Moroccans that a man like this was one of us." The women in his group ululated and began to sing and clap as Biton's son fingered a rhythm on a bongo drum, the same beat as in one of Haim Uliel's songs. There was pride in Baba Sali, and pride gave them the joy to sing.

At the tomb of Baba Sali, you could be forgiven for thinking that Netivot was not a backwater, so busy and noisy was the scene. But a few quiet streets away was the home of Baba Baruch. Clean and lavish in an otherwise low-income town, its white walls and red roof were surrounded and shaded from the afternoon sun by weeping willows. On the sidewalk, an old gardener stopped me: "Why did you come now? The rabbi's sleeping." I went in anyway, past the rabbi's Chevrolet Suburban with its blacked-out windows. At the door, Baruch's secretary supplied an alternative reason why I would have to wait: "He's meeting with some important rabbis just now."

When Baba Baruch awoke from his important meeting, he greeted me in a black robe and a black felt fez with a thin black cape draped over it. His face was broad and fleshy with a trim gray beard. He sat at a table in his reception room, smoking a long, thin Capri. The cigarette pack lay on the table next to two cellular phones. His father had constantly questioned why anybody would come to see him. "Who am I? I am nothing," he used to say. Baba Baruch had no such doubts. "I felt my father's powers pass into me, when he touched me just moments before his death." But he also believed that it was more than superstition or simplicity that made the tzaddiks such a power in Mizrahi society; it was the great tradition of kabbalistic, mystical Judaism going back to Isaac Luria in the Galilee town of Safed during the medieval period. "Kabbala goes back hundreds and hundreds of years for the Sephardis," he said. "For the Ashkenazis, they only have it since the Baal Shem Tov two hundred and sixty years ago." Baba Baruch cashed in on this tradition. He admitted to making $1.2 million a year from his ministry, though he claimed his expenses were much greater than his earnings.

The competition between the holy men of Netivot is vicious. They compete for the rights to that long kabbalistic tradition, for political power in present-day Israel, and for the money that these things bring. The first time I went to Baba Sali's tomb, I met a man named Herzl Aharon, who claimed his favorite rabbi promised him that, after many years of trying, his wife would soon become pregnant. But Aharon came to Baba Sali's tomb largely because it provided the only nice shady spot for a picnic in Netivot. The rabbi who had been proved correct when Mrs. Aharon bore a child was Yaakov Ifargan, the X-ray. "He is for us a psychologist, a doctor, and a messenger of God," Aharon said. It would have driven Baba Baruch crazy to hear such praise for his big Netivot rival at his father's tomb.

Baba Baruch's concerns were clearly very much of this world. He was a political jockey switching his allegiance as prime ministers faltered, a businessman boasting of the CEOs who came for his advice on important deals, and a showman with a magician's jealousy that the X-ray had developed some flashier tricks than he. But the appeal of men like Baba Baruch was in the contrast they made with the modern Israel that so alienated many of the country's people, particularly poor Mizrahis. These people typically felt they gained little from the infusion of wealth and modernization that had transformed central Israel over the last two decades. Where there used to be simple little towns and moshav collective farms, now there was a continuous conurbation that at its best recalled modest suburbs of Miami and, in less affluent areas, was seedily redolent of South Central Los Angeles in the midst of a very prolonged heat wave. Modernity's consumerism and homogenization, which leaves so many Americans feeling bereft or searching for spiritual answers, had the same effect on Mizrahis in Israel. The key to the growth of the tzaddiks was that they didn't claim to be experts in Halacha, Jewish law. That rigid discipline was the field of the Ashkenazi ultra-Orthodox. Guided by the traditional religious tolerance that Kobi Oz found so important, Mizrahis took little solace in the restrictive life of the ultra-Orthodox. Instead, they looked for spiritual leaders, rabbis who could make sense of this tormented, meaningless life in towns that sprawled, ugly and alienating, expanding out of range of the close ties of the old days in small communities. Mysticism gave an answer to the identity issues of Mizrahis.

Many religious Israelis found that spirituality in the land of Israel itself, with its deep roots in the Torah and their own history. Mizrahis, who had such a difficult initiation into this land under the Zionists, seemed to need something more. God remained remote, in the clouds, and they could not imagine his presence in the hills of the West Bank or the stones of Jerusalem's Old City, as many Ashkenazis did. Many Mizrahis needed someone close, real, tangible, who could bring God to them with his presence. Sometimes that could be found in the form of a living person like Ifargan, or a man recently dead like Baba Sali, but it might also be through the ancient tombs of the tzaddiks. This process usually didn't involve historical fact, because, after all, it was a spiritual maneuver.

In 1993 a Tiberias kosher inspector, Rabbi Rafael Cohen, discovered a tomb he said Jews built 1,600 years previously on the hillside overlooking Tiberias and the Sea of Galilee. It was, he declared, the Tomb of Rachel, wife of the Talmudic rabbi Akiva Ben-Yosef. Cohen persuaded a wealthy London Jew to fund its renovation, after praying with him at the site for a match for his daughter. When I met Cohen at the tomb, he described how Akiva, a simple shepherd who lived from A.D. 45–135 , lacked the funds to study religion until he married his wife, twenty-two years his junior. She agreed to wed him only if he would dedicate his life to Torah, and later, when he was a famous sage, he told all his pupils that they, like him, owed everything to Rachel. The tomb, on the other hand, may have owed nothing to Rachel. Scholars identified it as a Muslim shrine to Lady Sakina, a relative of the prophet Muhammed who died in 745 in Medina and whose "body" made a transition to Tiberias no less miraculous than that of Rachel. In any case, thousands of people come to the tomb every year, almost all of them Mizrahis. "The Mizrahis are simple people," said Cohen, who was born in Morocco. "It's a tradition." As we talked in the courtyard, a young man came and stood before the souvenir booth next to us. He cleared his throat, and began to rock back and forth, tearfully lamenting the long-deceased wife of Akiva: "Oy, oy, oy." Cohen tapped him on the shoulder. "That's the gift kiosk," he said. "The tomb is in there, that way." The young man stopped his wailing immediately, thanked Cohen, and went inside.

The Mizrahi cult of holy men like Ifargan and Baba Baruch was doubly at odds with Ashkenazi Jews. Secular Jews of European descent saw it as primitive nonsense that nonetheless exerted political power over their own governments, through the courting of the mystical rabbis by secular politicians. Ultra-Orthodox Ashkenazi Israelis thought of it as superstition that was not grounded in the true learning of the Torah. Secular Israelis seized on the case of Arieh Deri, the convicted Shas leader, as evidence that there was nothing real in the Mizrahi tzaddik cult: it was all a vehicle for frauds like Deri to exert power over their people and, thus, to screw government subsidies out of the taxes paid by hardworking, middle-class Ashkenazis. In Sondra Silverston's 2001 stage play, *Rav Kameah* (Rabbi Amulet), the eponymous holy man is a covetous, rapacious trickster who plays on the Mizrahi superstition of Yaakov, a spiritually unsatisfied businessman, to rob him of his money. Yaakov returns to his family from a tour around the tombs of righteous men in the Galilee feeling good:

YAAKOV: Nothing makes you feel as light as a grave in the Galilee.
TIKVA: He came back light. They emptied his wallet again.

To secular Tel Aviv theatergoers, the condemnable superstition is matched to the old feelings of contempt for the Mizrahis as somehow more base and crude, thus creating a thoroughly repulsive creature. When Rabbi Kameah tries to seduce Yaakov's wife, he debases Shylock's old plaint: "Has not a tzaddik a soul? Doesn't he have eyes to see you, a heart to feel you? If you punch us, will we not scream? And if you suck us, will we not come?"

Similarly, ultra-Orthodox Israelis who spend their days immersed solely in the minutiae of their religion reject the easygoing spirituality of the living saints. Tzaddiks experience the advice they give to their followers, they *feel* it; they don't draw it from ancient texts as absolute, immutable rules. Ifargan, the X-ray rabbi, will often tell people, "Maybe you ought to go see a doctor. Do me a favor, go and ask for a checkup." (Of course, if he attempted to be more precise, Ifargan would be proved correct less frequently and his followers wouldn't have been able to tell me, as they consistently did, that he discovered their heart condition just in time, and so on.) But Ashkenazis would never revere living rabbis with the fervor they have for long-dead religious leaders. Talmudic scholars believe "the generations are declining," which is to say that rabbis are growing further and further from the absolute truth of the men who formulated the Talmud.

Yet some scholars find a truly redeeming quality in the veneration of the living rabbis that could be beneficial for all Israel, if only Ashkenazis would understand it and be more tolerant. Yoram Bilu, a Hebrew University anthropologist who studies the tzaddiks and their tombs, believes that the transmigration of burial places from the old country to Israel and the physical presence of holy men there suggests Mizrahis finally found a way to feel at home in a society that at first rejected their culture, rejected their selves. If the place is good enough for the Mizrahi holy men, it's good enough for ordinary Mizrahis. "It's a way of making peace," Bilu told me. It's this recovery of their traditions that signals Mizrahis reached something of an accommodation with their difficult past in Israel. The rabbis have immigrated to Israel, made aliyah like the Mizrahis. In Safed, a poor worker declared that the grave of Rabbi David U-Moshe, which actually lies in the western Atlas Mountains of Morocco, was now in his living room in a housing project called the Shikun Kanaan. To Ashkenazis, that was a ridiculous proposition. To the thousands of Mizrahis who visited the new tomb each year, it was a sign that maybe the Shikun Kanaan—like the similarly underprivileged places where they were condemned to live—wasn't so bad after all.

Far from seeing this positive side, Ashkenazi politicians in particular found it difficult to bear the intrusion into the Israeli discourse of a mode of thought their secular Zionist forebears believed they left behind with the simple-minded Hasidic peasants of Eastern Europe— not to mention that it created a new impetus for Mizrahi political power. The Likud Party took control in the 1970s on the back of Mizrahi voters, but has yet to have a leader who isn't a descendant of European Jews. When Shas came to the fore, it was born of Mizrahi

resentment and the adherence to traditional Judaism of most
Mizrahis. Rabbi Ovadiah Yosef gave the party spiritual standing. He
wanted to rebuild the lost learning of Mizrahi Judaism, stamped out
during the early years of their immigration by a combination of secular Zionist disapproval and ultra-Orthodox Ashkenazi rivalry. Yosef
studied at Porat Yosef, an Old City yeshiva that was the only major
seat of religious learning to follow the long traditions of Sephardi culture. As he saw it, other Mizrahis either drifted away from the study
of religion or, if they showed promise, were picked out of the immigrant camps by Ashkenazi rabbis and taken to their yeshivas, which
taught an entirely different tradition and made sure to discredit the
Sephardi heritage. The Ashkenazis destroyed Sephardi high culture in
the yeshivas and then condemned ordinary Mizrahis for seizing upon
the low culture and superstition that was all that had been left to
them.

It was the man Yosef backed to run the Shas apparatus who really
put the party on the map. Arieh Deri became the brightest young star
in Israeli politics. Unlike other religious politicians, there was even a
time in the early 1990s when secular Israelis didn't hate him. They
simply had to acknowledge that he ran the Interior Ministry—where
all Israelis must stand in line for mundane bureaucratic tasks, like
renewing their identity cards or registering births—better than anyone else ever did. Rather like Hamas, Shas formed a social network
that made it the most helpful of institutions for people in underde-
veloped "development towns" like Netivot and Sderot. It provided
longer school days for children in underprivileged, usually Mizrahi
neighborhoods, though of course it flooded the schoolrooms with
lessons that matched the party's ultra-Orthodox line. Deri did it with
backstairs political maneuvers that made him the equal of old political hands like Shimon Peres, Israel's master of shameless compromise.
But when Deri and his party chose to oppose the secular Ashkenazi
Labor Party, its hacks took a different view of Shas. In a series of elections, Shas campaigned by distributing amulets with blessings written
by Rabbi Kaddouri. Officially, the amulets merely offered good health
and prosperity. However, many party activists handed them out with
that promise only on condition that the recipient would vote Shas.
To a population that felt it never received a fair shake from the big
political parties and which had grown attached to the great kabbalis-

tic rabbis, it seemed like a good offer. Yossi Beilin, the best thinker of Labor's left wing, told me the amulets were "antidemocratic." One of Shas's leaders, Shlomo Ben-Izri, claimed he disapproved of the amulets. Still, when I met him in his Knesset office in 1999, he conceded that "the Jewish people is looking for another way. Therefore they go to the Baba Sali." Clearly the phenomenon of the tzaddiks was useful to Shas in its political campaigns, but some of its more learned leaders had their doubts. Rabbi Yosef, whose own understanding of Torah and Talmud was acknowledged as unparalleled, was said by those around him to despise the cult of Rabbi Kaddouri, the kabbalist, who Yosef believed did not ground his work in true Jewish texts.

The essence of the doubts Yosef held was even stronger among Ashkenazis. After all, Zvi Zohar, a fellow at the Shalom Hartman Institute in Jerusalem, explained to me that Judaism's underlying principle was that an ordinary man cannot manipulate God, even if he is a tzaddik, and that the Torah decreed the death penalty for those who perform magic. "The people who venerate these guys as saints are the people that'd be worshipping the golden calf back in the Sinai," he said. Ashkenazis tended to laugh at Rabbi Yosef, because he wore an eccentric hat, gold-braided robes, the dark glasses of a 1950s hipster, and spoke ungrammatical Hebrew. But no one laughed at Arieh Deri. When Deri went to Jerusalem District Court on Salah ed-Din Street in March 1999 to hear the verdict in his long corruption trial, it was as though the entire future of Israeli democracy rested on the outcome. To secular Ashkenazis, Deri represented the blackmail and religious coercion that surely would increase Shas's political power if he weren't put in his place now. Supporters of Deri outside the court believed he had been framed, or at least that he had done nothing secular Ashkenazi politicians hadn't been getting away with for decades: the establishment cut him down because he was Mizrahi and powerful, too threatening to the Ashkenazi elite. The enmity was great. A Shas activist held up a banner comparing Israel's European Jews with the anti-Semitic Christians who ejected the Jews from Spain in 1492: Spanish Expulsion, Ashkenazi Style. A small group of secular counterdemonstrators gathered across the street. A short, dark Shas man wagged his finger at them: "You should go and make some babies. You're all homosexuals and lesbians."

Shas was soon back in the cabinet of a left-wing prime minister, Ehud Barak. But these Israeli governments were bound by no real underpinning belief—except that when Arabs attack, Israelis should make a united front against them. Within the government, as within the society, the parties pulled in different directions and sometimes punched wildly at those closest to them. As soon as the violence of the intifada began in September 2000, Shas's leader in the cabinet, Eli Yishai, called for harsher military action against the Palestinians. Until then, Shas was always fairly mild in its advocacy of battle and in its approach to the peace process. It was more important that the party extract the funds from the government to support its educational institutions, rather than posture about security, as the many former generals in the cabinet liked to do. But now Yishai appeared on late-night news broadcasts after terrorist attacks, pushing Barak deeper into the violence as the prime minister tried to maintain his coalition.

By that time, Deri had returned to his studies as he awaited an appeal. To strengthen his knowledge, he turned to one of Jerusalem's most famous kabbalists. In the Mekor Baruch neighborhood of Mea Shearim, Rabbi David Batsri taught kabbala to Deri in a second-floor study room ripe with the odor of overheated men in black suits. Surrounded by cheap metal bookshelves, Deri sat before the scratchy-voiced rabbi, who wore his prayer shawl across his shoulders and his tefillin on his forehead and forearm whenever he had a book of religion open before him. As a young man, Batsri studied with Kaddouri. He became famous—or in the reading of the secular press, at once infamous and laughable—in 1998 when he exorcised a malign, wandering spirit called a dybbuk from a woman's body by commanding it to exit through its screaming victim's big toe. Like the other kabbalists, his word was political currency, even among secular politicians who wanted to snatch religious Mizrahi votes. The day before I visited Batsri, he had received Ariel Sharon. Deri, who was banned from political office for twelve years as part of his sentencing, wasn't looking for votes so much as he was concluding the process of his beatification. He became a saint devoted to the study of Judaism who patiently suffered his Ashkenazi persecution. During Shas's previous election campaign, Deri was the focus of its broadcasts, wearing a white shift and looking angelic. The slogan of the campaign was He Is Innocent.

Rabbi Yaakov Ifargan came to the *tikkun*—the ceremony of spiritual renewal and strength he described when I visited his house in the afternoon—wearing the same saintly expression Deri bore in the election broadcasts. It was the face of one transported: slightly wry, emanating love, pained by the foreknowledge of suffering and misunderstanding, and yet reconciled to it as a test of faith that would be overcome through fervent belief. It was reminiscent of the self-sacrificing Christ, scourged and abused and luminously overcoming on the climb to Golgotha, in countless Renaissance masterpieces. It was 11 P.M., at the grave of Ifargan's father, across an empty sand lot from the Baba Sali mausoleum. Below the tomb of the father, a pallet full of fist-size boxes of Sabbath candles lay below the floodlights inside a chain-link enclosure. I calculated 36,000 candles on the pallet. One of Ifargan's people confirmed my figure, telling me the old tradition was that there always are thirty-six true tzaddiks on earth and Ifargan, who was one of them, would burn 1,000 candles for each. By the end of the evening, the candles would be gone, hurled by Ifargan into the brazier built into the hillside. Fire, like the flame of the single candle Ifargan showed me in the afternoon, was central to kabbala in a way that, to many conventional rabbis, was little different to paganism. More than 100 women waited outside the enclosure on a sandbank, chanting and banging tambourines. A chubby man in a purple fez hovered at the door in the fence, obviously deranged. "The X-ray can make the blind men see," he shouted. "I've seen him do it."

The night was balmy, after the rough desert heat of the Sderot daytime. One of Ifargan's aides addressed the crowd through a loudspeaker. He told them that their singing would be their connection to the rabbi and the way for them to strengthen him as he prayed. He led them in Rabbi Nachman of Breslav's "Gesher Tsar Meod," chanting that life is a very narrow bridge and not to be afraid. The singing built as Ifargan's white BMW pulled across the parking lot. He came through the crowd with bowed head as the men bent to kiss his hand. Small, about five feet five, Ifargan let the crowd buffet him. It was as though his will was not within him. It deserted his body to power the spirit that he would send into the flames to emerge renewed and replenished with the force of God who made the fire. In the enclosure, he circled, kicking his feet a little, rolling his neck like a fighter awaiting the opening bell. At the head of each circle, he threw a box of candles, uncannily accurate, thump into the back of the brazier with a hiss of melting wax. The women sang the traditional songs "Ya'ase Shalom" and "Od Avinu Chai"—He Will Make Peace, and Again Our Father Lives. With his eyes screwed tight in concentration, Ifargan tossed the boxes into the flames from behind his back and over his shoulder, like a basketball star flicking trick passes. The flames were fifteen feet high, and wax ran in a thick rivulet down the slope past the rabbi. He began to intone Shaarei Ratzon, a Yom Kippur prayer, a pledge of atonement, and the crowd joined him. He threw the candles and prayed with the crowd and threw again and mumbled on until 12:30. "All Israel's people have problems. Ask God for purity. Unite. If everybody purifies as individuals, the whole crowd will be pure. Thanks to the tzaddiks and my father and Baba Sali. Pray from the bottom of your heart."

The men within the chain-link fence made a tight circle around the rabbi and danced, sweating from the flames and singing. They brought a blind boy to the center of the circle. Ifargan turned the boy's face to the towering flames and whispered in his ear. He closed the boy's eyes, touching them gently: "Sit with your eyes shut and feel the light inside them." The men took the boy to the side of the enclosure.

At 1 A.M., Ifargan began the *tikkun* prayer, the reparation of the damaged world about him, leading the crowd in his chant as he faced the flames. He implored God to send "Peace in this land. Peace in the universe. The Holy Spirit in our homes, the Holy Spirit in our homes. Help in our hospitals, that sickness shall be cured. Bring a good marital match. Good health. Bring children this year. Protect us against the evil eye." Ifargan called on the tzaddiks buried in the Galilee for aid. He grabbed a towel and wiped his face, but he didn't remove his black jacket and matching homburg. The men gathered tightly around him again, kissing his beard. They took Gabriel Rafael from his wheelchair and carried him to the rabbi. He suffered from multiple sclerosis. In the crush around Ifargan, Rafael was upright, though it was the press of bodies that supported him. "Are you a believer?" Ifargan said. "You will start walking. At the beginning it will be hard." In the center of the heat from the flames and the press of the bodies and the powerful belief that seemed to be given physical presence by them, I realized that I, too, wanted the kid to walk. I wanted a miracle. As the crowd jostled back and forth, I wondered if I desired the miracle because it would make a good story, or because I couldn't stand to see this poor twenty-two-year-old cripple's hopes raised pointlessly. Or had I entered the trance that the flames and the prayers and the singing and dancing aimed to induce? The youth was struggling to stand five minutes later when they put him in his wheelchair, kicking his legs back and forth. He came to his feet, almost fainting with the effort, smiling and grimacing, looking pale and nauseated, and sat again. Gasping, he told me, "I do feel much stronger. The truth is that at home I can walk a bit more than this with a frame. But it helped me tonight." Ifargan didn't end Rafael's four years in a wheelchair, but he had given him hope. At 2 A.M., Ifargan shuffled, exhausted, toward his BMW. The flames still burned high and flickered their orange and red light across the rabbi's devotees as though they themselves were on fire.

OUTSIDE HAIM ULIEL'S terraced house in Sderot, two neighbors watched me knocking on his door. With a smile, one of them said, "Knock louder. He's probably asleep." It was close to noon. The song Uliel composed for his life began as firmly traditional, but there was something unconventional about the choice of rhythm he construed for it that crescendoed in him as he moved beyond his old band, Sfatayim. He made his living from wedding performances and, for the last few years, as an organizer of municipal music projects with a modest salary from the Sderot town council. When he talked about that job, his rough, deep-brown face grimaced in pain and embarrassment, as a talented actor might wince when he told you he waited tables to make ends meet. After he put an end to Sfatayim, Uliel made a musical move that his fans—those who loved him for championing their traditional Moroccan style—disliked. But Uliel wanted to be different. He had asserted his Moroccan-ness; now he needed to produce an album that would be his alone. Just as the adherence to the tzaddiks and the transposition of their graves from Morocco to Israel suggested Mizrahis finally were ready to accept the combination of Israel and the Arab world that dwelt within them, so Uliel's new music was a unique mixture of the rhythms and chants of Morocco with a European pop and techno production. He called the album *Sanduk La'ajiv,* Maghrebi Arabic for "magic box." In Morocco, the Berber tribesmen referred to televisions as magic boxes when they first saw them, and the more sophisticated Jews laughed at the simple mountain men. When those same Jews came to Israel, they found themselves suddenly the primitive ones, the subject of derision. There was techno magic to songs like "Simanei Sa'ara" (Signs of a Storm) on the new album, but Uliel's irascible politics came through, too, as he warned of the discontent gathering like thunder in places that never made the newspapers, such as Sderot. Yet faced with this new music, his fans were as disapproving and disconcerted as Berbers before an incomprehensible television screen.

Few of Uliel's fans saw his musical development the way he did. In Sfatayim, he had supplied the sound track to their bar mitzvahs, their weddings, and they wanted to hear more of that style. Many of them told Uliel on the streets of Sderot that they thought his new songs with their European production sound suggested he had "become Ashkenazi." It was easy for them to say, after all, because it's an insult used frequently enough to have coined a new slang Hebrew verb: *mishtaknaz.*

HAIM ULIEL and Kobi Oz did not feed on their own paranoia. They were unusual in this, for the intifada brought upon Israelis both a broad illusion of solidarity and an underlying, unmentionable fear that their sector of society, whichever it might be, would find itself victimized by the rest, just as all Israeli society felt itself terrorized unjustly by the Palestinians. If the Palestinians can do it to all of us, then the Ashkenazis or the secular Jews or the religious or the settlers can do it to me and my kind too. It disappointed Kobi Oz, who thought that the years of the peace process had been a good time, where young Mizrahis and Ashkenazis came closer together than their parents ever could. Since Sfatayim recorded its first album in 1988, Israel signed peace treaties with the Palestinians and the Jordanians and there was a tremendous outing of Moroccan culture in Israel. The combination of the two tracks, peace with the enemy and peace within Israeli society, seemed a beautiful period to Kobi Oz. But the first signs of trouble in the intifada erased all that. Within days of the onset of the intifada's violence, Israelis closed up, ceased to acknowledge the suffering and humanity of the Palestinians. (Of course, there was dangerous two-way traffic, as Palestinians dehumanized the Israelis in their official media and political discourse, celebrating suicide bombers.) Maybe there had been other signs of trouble in Israeli society in the build-up to that time. In the election of 1999, the biggest successes were Tommy Lapid's Shinui Party, stridently opposed to the participation of religious parties in the government, and Shas, with its religio-Mizrahi message of resentment, victimization, and hate. The election results were a hint that, when things did explode in the occupied territories, Israelis talked a good togetherness game, seeming to unite behind nationalist symbols like the army, but in reality felt isolated and fearful. After the right wing scored a big victory in the 2003 election, Kobi Oz thought of Israel's internal conflicts as stored in a back room: "The back room is closed now because of the war. I can't wait to open this door and slide all the monsters out and try to create love for all kinds of Jews. But every time someone starts to shake the keys at the door to the back room, everyone says it's not the time now. I thought it was the right moment in the 1990s, but now the time is terrible for individuality." When a nation tries to assert its oneness, because its back is against the wall, everyone can stand together. But the act of doing so seems only to highlight the emptiness of the camaraderie. It also forces an individual to see himself passively as others perceive him, as a soldier or a potential victim of terrorism or a settler or simply an Israeli, whatever that is, instead of learning who he wants himself to be, as Haim Uliel did.

In 1999, before the intifada stunted Israelis' examination of themselves and also made it hard for them to travel, even in relatively friendly Arab countries, Kobi Oz and his parents visited the town of Bizerte, where Rachel and Yosef Ozan were born. Oz stood with the two old people in the central square. To him, it looked like the little Tel Aviv of the 1940s that he had seen in picture books. Yosef gestured to the storefronts: "That was the candy store, and that was the delicatessen." But the shops were shuttered and the town square seemed sad, as though the void of liveliness left by the Jews was never filled. Elderly Muslims recognized the Ozans and reminisced. Yosef pointed out where the café had been and told his son that the Muslim owners used to allow Jews to drink there on the Sabbath and pay later. To Kobi Oz, there was wonderful togetherness in that. Jews were forbidden to carry money on the Sabbath, so the Muslim owners made allowances; but the visit to the café on that day also showed that the Jews of the town were more flexible about their observance than a religious Ashkenazi Israeli, who would not even enter a place of business on the Sabbath. Oz realized the Mizrahis had learned the unyielding ways of the Haredi Ashkenazis.

The visit to the town of his forefathers was another addition to the collection of items in the identity of the artist known as Kobi Oz. Every Israeli instantly recognized his lively face, his goatee clipped carefully and thin, his hair shaved almost away, his eccentrically colorful spectacles. The image was no longer quite so important to Oz himself. He understood by now who he was, what kind of man he was. The teenage Ozan invented "Kobi Oz" so that he could enact an ideal persona. Though he was successful in that, there was a development to the guise of Kobi Oz that could not stop, just as Israeli society could never cease to change. He had taken up the melody of Haim Uliel's song of defiance and brought to it his own deeply loving, tolerant, hopeful spirit. When he looked ahead, this was the maturity that Kobi Oz wished for himself and for Israel, when he would write the coda of the song of his life:

Kobi Oz was a grandfather, with many grandchildren. He sat in a big study filled with gold-leafed volumes and claret leather armchairs, like the quiet, meditative library of a British country house. Outside, there was the sea, the beautiful, open Mediterranean. Kobi Oz looked through the window and sensed his own political and artistic freedom, as unencumbered by boundaries and borders as the whitecaps that rolled from Spain and Morocco to wash up by his home. He heard his grandchildren laughing out on the beach, barely audible above the crashing of the surf. He smiled. He rolled a sheet of paper into his manual typewriter and picked out the keys to write, "I am very happy. I am a normal grandfather. I view this as a privilege, because nothing has been normal. These are the most precious of times for me."

Afterword: "Every One That Findeth Me Shall Slay Me"

If I am not for myself, who will be for me?
If I am only for myself, what am I?

—RABBI HILLEL, IN *THE CHAPTERS OF THE FATHERS*

IN THE VICTORIA EMBANKMENT GARDENS, I scouted among tall, rain-dripping oaks and office workers huddled over their lunchtime sandwiches, seeking the monument to the men of the Imperial Camel Corps. At first, I felt sure it must be the ornate pavilion near the gate. Its explosive design seemed to correspond to the spark the Palestine campaign struck in the tinder of subsequent Middle Eastern history. But the rococo carvings at the park's entrance were, in fact, part of a massive baroque fountain. The Camel Corps memorial was farther along the path, and much smaller: a shoulder-high granite plinth carved with the names of the regiment's casualties and, atop it, a three-foot bronze of a trooper riding a camel. The beast reared its head, but the soldier, as much at home on his strange mount as an Arab would be, cradled his rifle in his lap and stared off in reverie from beneath his pith helmet across the choppy gray Thames toward the Royal Festival Hall. At one with the Orient, the bronze rider froze in that romantic moment, but the Camel Corps did not. As the British moved beyond the desert and up to the fertile plains before Damascus, the camels became less useful, and the troopers, including my great-great-uncles Dai and Dan Beynon, shipped out to France. Attached to the Welsh Regiment, they fought the last months of the war as infantry in the Flanders mud.

The bronze cast of this solitary rider was a fiction. The reality of the desert campaign was grittier. Dan Beynon lost his middle finger above the first knuckle, bitten off by a Turk; Dai was shot in the backside as the British secured Jerusalem and, my father remembers, used to get drunk at Christmas and drop his trousers to display the scar. Their campaign began in the desert heat of Sinai, but by the time they made Jerusalem, it was a sleeting November in 1917, and Dai and Dan were still clad in their light desert fatigues. Like most war memorials intended as a remembrance of what those troops went through, this one instead institutionalized a willful forgetting that lingers in current attitudes toward the Middle East. Many Westerners adhere to the picture-book simplicity and easy dualism of television news. Like the monument to the Camel Corps, the media's conceptions are inscribed immutably in stone. In trying to show both sides, they tell at best half the truth. The Middle East's regrettable reality grows not from war and the actions of "great men," but is born of the humiliations and grievances that pervade everyday life for Israelis and Palestinians within their own societies. These tribulations rift every seam of a society until they define it for those who live there.

To ordinary Palestinians, the battle against Israel is much like the Camel Corps monument: a national myth adorned with stirring imagery, yet eliding its cruel effects, in this case the destruction of family, bread, and individual fulfillment. In their true experience, the heroic freedom fighter of fable manifests himself rather as the Gaza gunman subverting the chances for peace to prolong his gangster dominion, or the Arafat henchman who opposes democracy for fear that responsible government would deprive him of his privileges. It is the tainted world of Gaza's General Intelligence deputy commander Zakaria Baloush, who saw from the inside how Arafat's people failed to make the transition from corrupt, terrorist cowboys to responsible government. Those who still believe in the struggle are driven to fratricidal violence, like Imad Akel, whose brother died at the Hamas demonstration in Gaza, because the actions of the men who hold power in Palestinian society constitute such an affront to the very ideals they purport to espouse.

Israelis project the same fiction to outsiders that the conflict with the Palestinians is all-consuming and unifying. In fact, their society is a skein of fraternal hostility. Many ultra-Orthodox Jews like the Neturei Karta refuse to acknowledge kinship with a majority they see as "anti-Semitic" and the "blasphemous" Israeli state, turning their fearful venom on those, like shop owner Elhanan Ben-Hakoun, whom they see as missionaries of their oppressor. West Bank settlers like Dubak Weinstock flout the laws of a society that they believe would hamper the Israeli people's holy task of colonization, until leftists, like artist Avraham Pesso, feel their only recourse is to protest in a way that also violates the rules of the state.

Just as my expectations of the Camel Corps memorial were that those fighters merited a more massive public space than the one accorded them, so my study of the internal divisions of the Palestinians and Israelis has given me an understanding of the centrality of something usually seen as peripheral to the true battle. It seems to me now that the conflict between the Israelis and Palestinians is like the spark that jumps between two electrodes. The electrical charge flashing between the two sides is real, but to focus entirely upon it, as interpreters of the Israeli-Palestinian struggle do, is to ignore the tangle of wires leading back from each electrode to the source of the current. I began to see those wires, the internal conflicts they represent, everywhere. In the medieval chapter house of Salisbury Cathedral, in the southwest of England, I stood before a famous frieze of sculptures representing scenes from Genesis and Exodus. The tableau depicts Cain kicking Abel to the ground and driving a hoe into the top of his skull, which is covered in curly hair. Cain wears a conical hat that reminded me of the "fool's hat" with which early Israeli kibbutz settlers shaded their heads from the sun. For a moment, I thought of the frieze as prefiguring the persecution of Mizrahi Abel with his tight coils of hair by Ashkenazi Cain from the elite of the agricultural kibbutz. In fact, Cain's headwear is a "Jew's hat," which Christians compelled Jews to wear throughout Medieval Europe. As is common in the art and literature of the Middle Ages, the carving depicts Abel as a Christ-like figure, unjustly done to death by a Jew. Cain's injury to his brother was re-created constantly throughout history and, as the hat suggested to me, mirrored in the way Israelis behaved toward each other.

The blood drawn by Cain's first blow stains the ground where it fell, still. In Damascus, the legend is that Cain disposed of his brother's corpse in a cave on Mount Kassioun, overlooking the valley where the Syrian capital now stands. The streaks of red in the rock of the mountainside are the bloodstains left by the world's original victim. Those bloodstains doomed Cain too. His fight against his brother made him a marked man. He paid for his wrong with the sacrifice of his sense of security and he lived all his years in fear. His torment personifies the troubles of Palestinian and Israeli society, where factions react collectively like a single traumatized psyche: striking out with disproportionate force, unable to concede the validity of another's suffering or its own responsibility for that anguish; constantly fearful of attack; and deeply defensive. Yet the traditional reading of the biblical story of Cain and Abel reflects the simplicity with which each side of the present Israeli-Palestinian conflict wishes to see itself. Each exists in a fantasy world of blamelessness, shifting guilt to a distant enemy and away from the consequences of the divisions within its own society, the pain Palestinians inflict on Palestinians and Israelis on Israelis. Each wishes to see himself as Abel, no matter how much he might in reality be Cain, lashing out resentfully at his own.

There are Israelis and Palestinians who show that it's possible to erase some of that ancient bloodstain. In artists like Kobi Oz and Nizar Hassan, I detected an ability to confront their own selves, to break down their histories through their art and thus to create music or films that reach past the blindness of politics and the gun. These are people who see Cain's field as a place in which crops may grow beside Abel's flock. There, the enmity within their societies can be rewritten for a contemporary morality, just as ancient teachers formulated the myth of the first murder to restrain men not yet civilized.

Despite those few who struggle to see beyond Cain's tale, the son of Adam seems still to stride, thunderous and paranoid, through his field, fearing that "every one that findeth me shall slay me," as he repined at God. In the end, Cain was, indeed, slain. The Midrash Agada, the homilies by which early rabbis sought to elucidate biblical narratives, detailed his demise. Cain was killed, not by the enemies he feared so much, but by an arrow from the bow of Lamech, his own great-great-great-grandson.

Acknowledgments

MY WARMEST THANKS are due my colleagues in the Jerusalem bureau of *Time:* Jamil Hamad, whose integrity makes him exceptional among both Palestinians and journalists, and Aharon Klein, whose sensitivity belies his expertise in military affairs. I owe a profound debt to other *Time* coworkers, particularly Jim Kelly, Lisa Beyer, Michael Elliott, and Norman Pearlstine. Thanks for their various roles in this book to: Larry Kaplow, Ilene Prusher, Ben Lynfield, Matt McAllester, Azmy Keshawi, Khadr Abu Sway, Matthew Kalman, David Blumenfeld, Yonit Farago, Alon Farago, Bob Slater, Janine Zacharia, Rachel Miskin, Atara Triestman, Nathan Englander, Danny Klaidman, Joe Lertola, David Rubinger, Jean Max, and Benny Morris; and especially my fabulous agents Deborah Harris and Joy Harris. At Free Press, the editorial deftness and thoughtfulness of Dominick Anfuso and Wylie O'Sullivan made the preparation of my first book much less painful than everyone told me it'd be. Finally, though she claims not to remember it this way, I remind my partner Devorah Blachor that all the best ideas in the book were hers.

About the Author

MATT REES is the Jerusalem bureau chief for *Time* magazine. He was born in Wales in 1967 and educated at Oxford University and the University of Maryland. He has worked as a correspondent in London, Washington, New York, and the Middle East. In the Middle East, he has been correspondent for *The Scotsman*, Scotland's national newspaper, Middle East correspondent for *Newsweek*, and since June 2000, *Time*'s Jerusalem bureau chief, writing award-winning stories about the violence of the Aqsa intifada. While on assignment for these publications, he has traveled extensively, particularly in Lebanon, Jordan, and Syria, where he was the only Western correspondent in Damascus on the day President Hafez Assad died. He has also written for *Men's Journal, The New York Daily News, The Johannesburg Star*, London's *Daily Mail, The Jerusalem Post*, and *Time*'s POV magazine. He has been a frequent commentator on CNN including *Late Edition With Wolf Blitzer*, BBC Radio, and numerous U.S. radio stations. Before moving to Israel, Rees worked in New York for *The Wall Street Journal, Forbes*, and Bloomberg News, for which he won a Society of Professional Journalists award. In 2003 he won a Henry Luce Award for Reporting for his coverage of the battle in Jenin during the current intifada. He has published short stories and nonfiction in *Nerve* and *Keltic Fringe*.